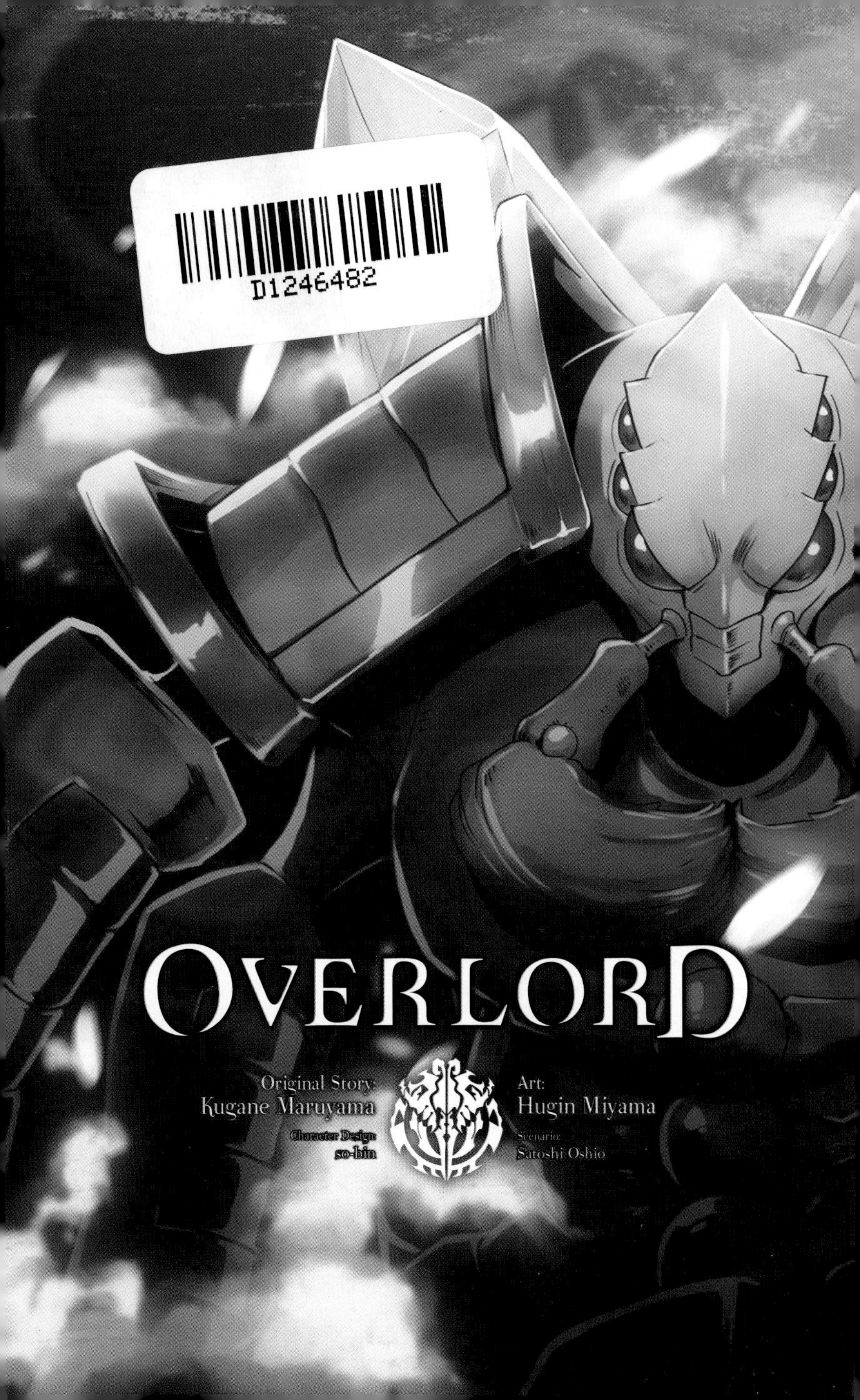
D1246482
OVERLORD
Original Story:
Kugane Maruyama
Character Design:
so-bin
Art:
Hugin Miyama
Scenario:
Satoshi Oshio

OVERLORD

Original Story:
Kugane Maruyama

8

Art:
Hugin Miyama

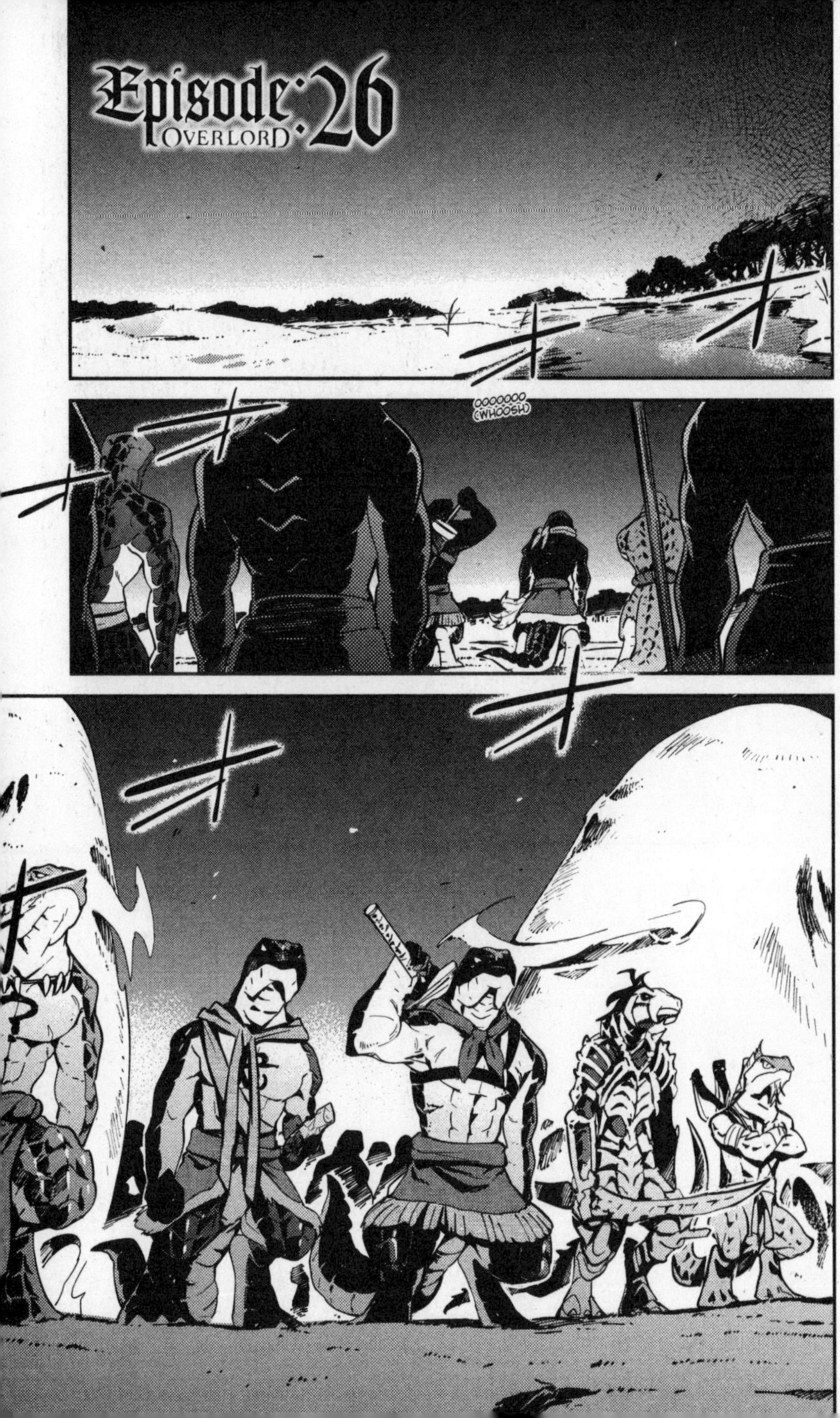
Episode: 26
OVERLORD
OOOOOOO
(WHOOSH)

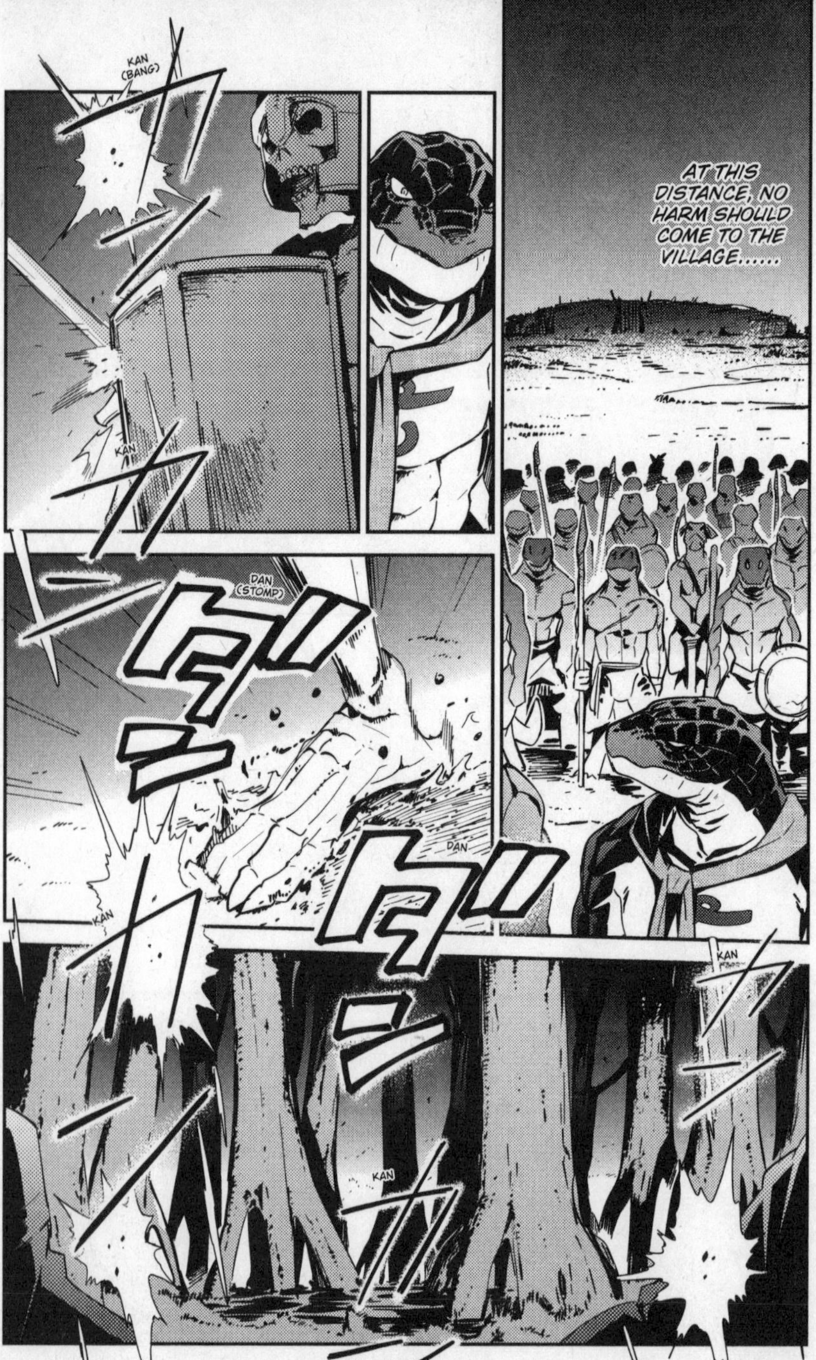
AT THIS DISTANCE, NO HARM SHOULD COME TO THE VILLAGE......
KAN (BANG)
KAN
DAN (STOMP)
DAN
KAN
KAN
KAN

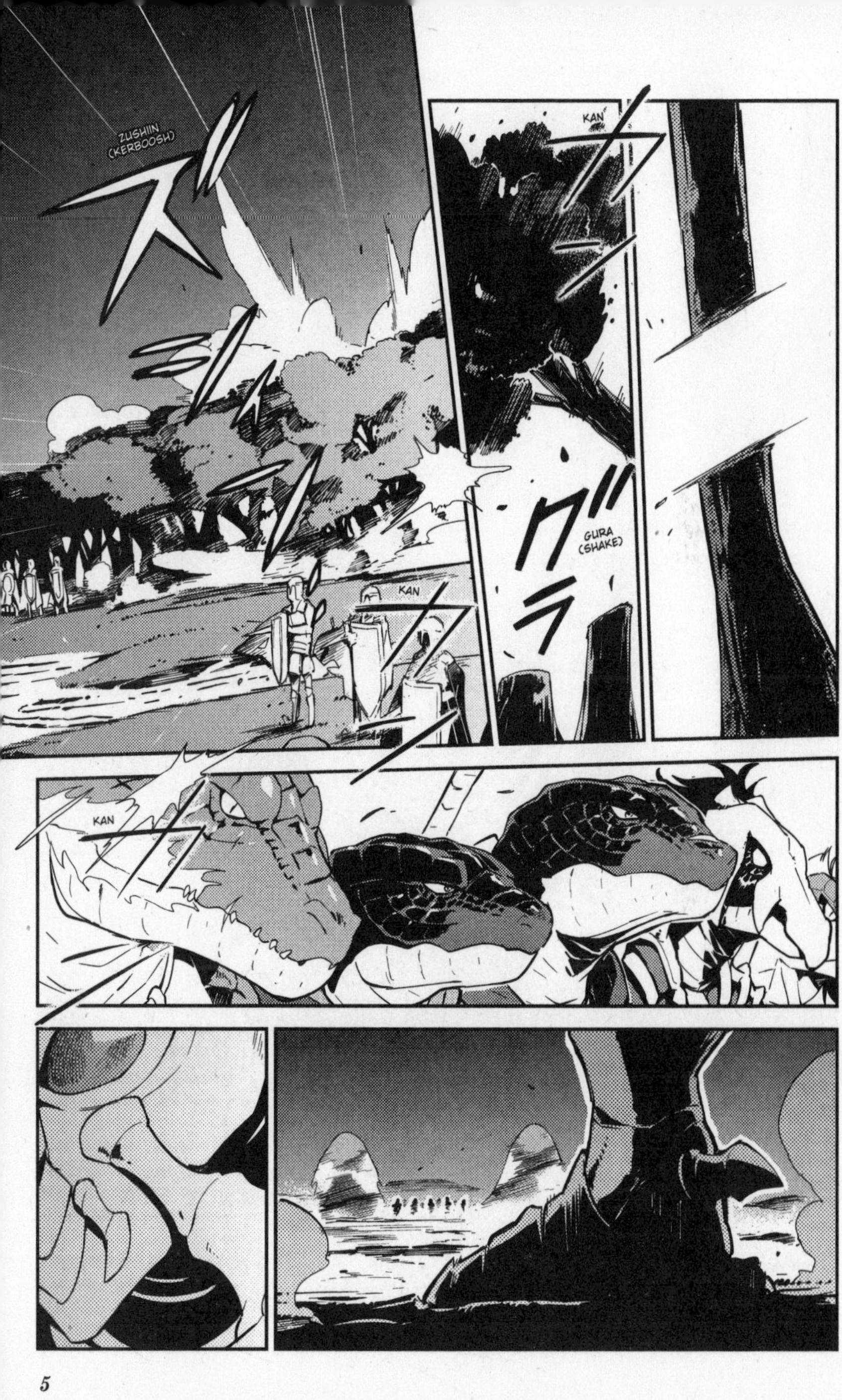
KAN
GURA (SHAKE)
ZUSHIIN (KERBOOSH)
KAN
KAN

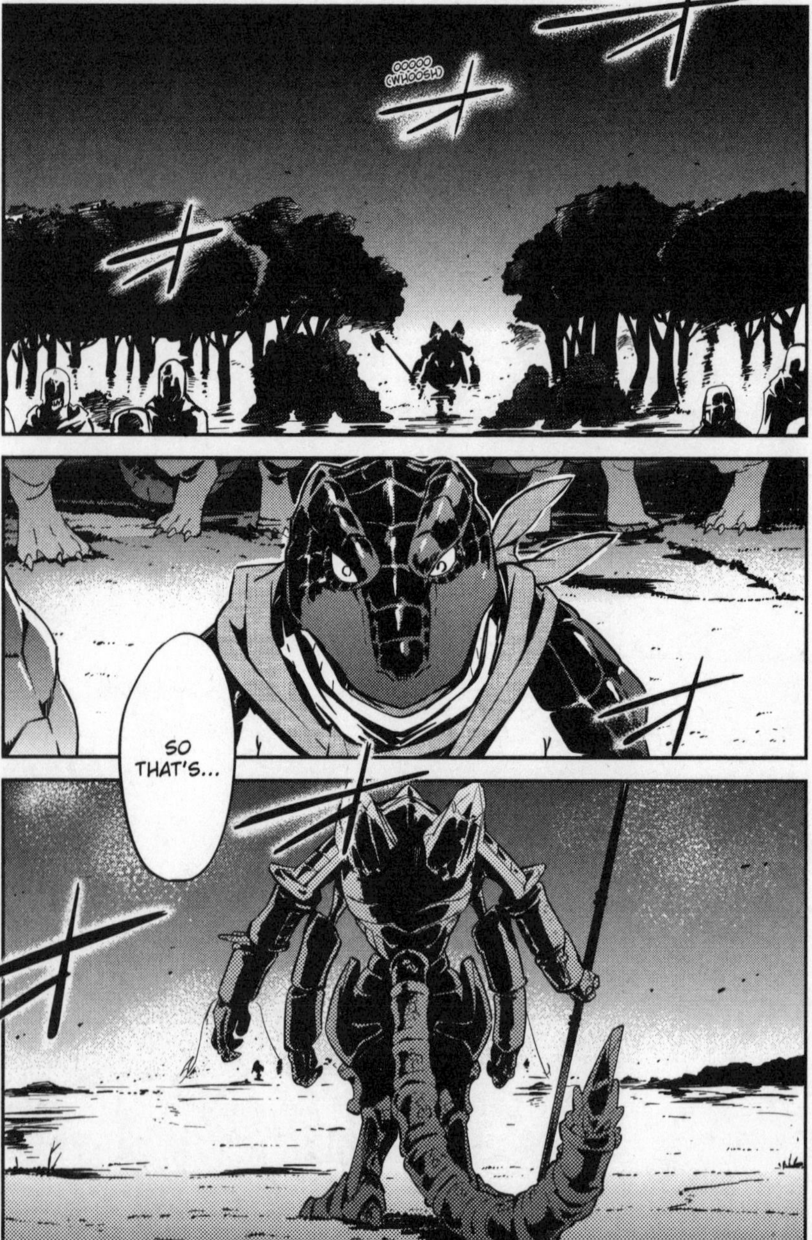
OOOOO (WHOOSH)
SO THAT'S...

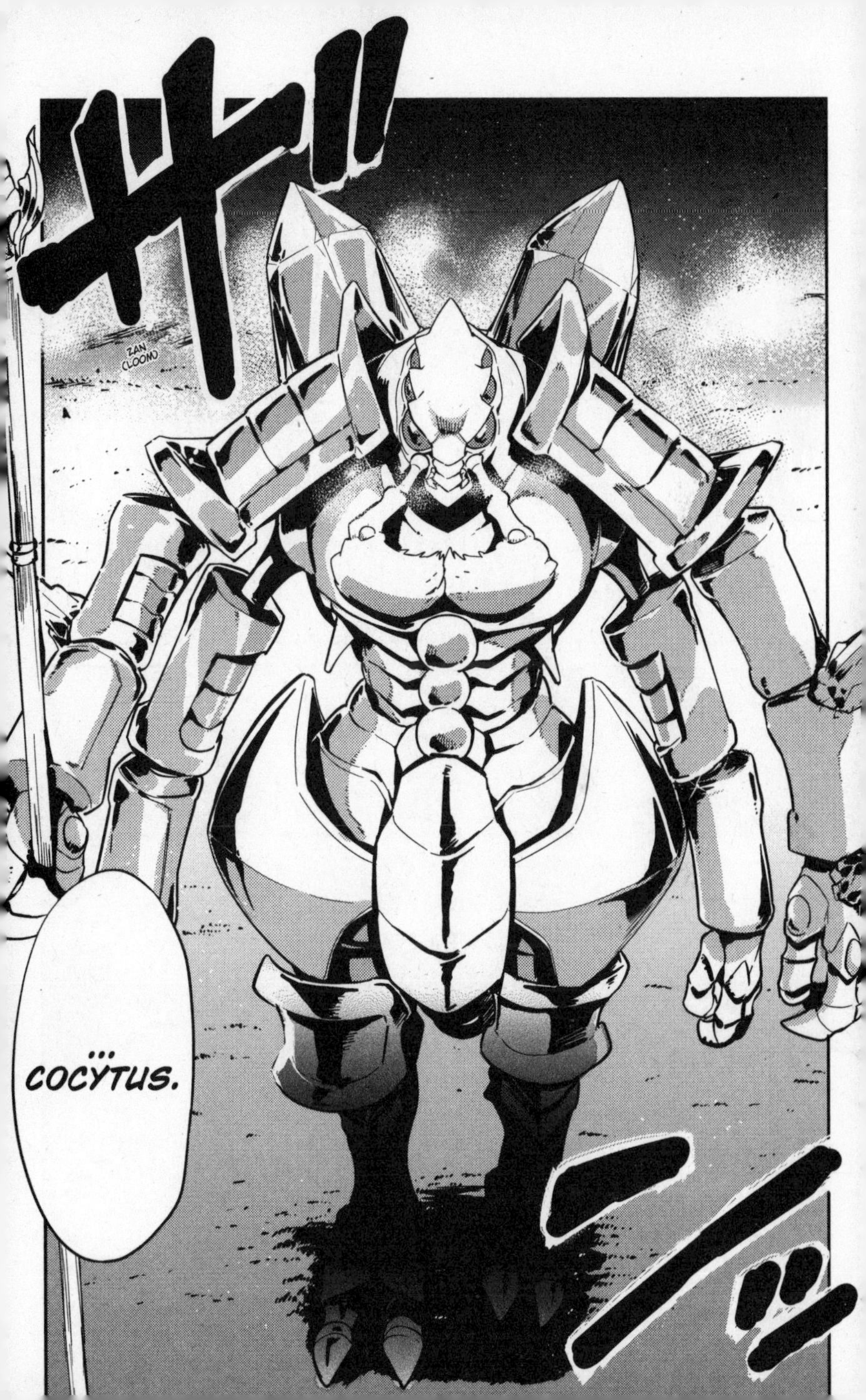
ZAN
(LOOM)
... COCYTUS.

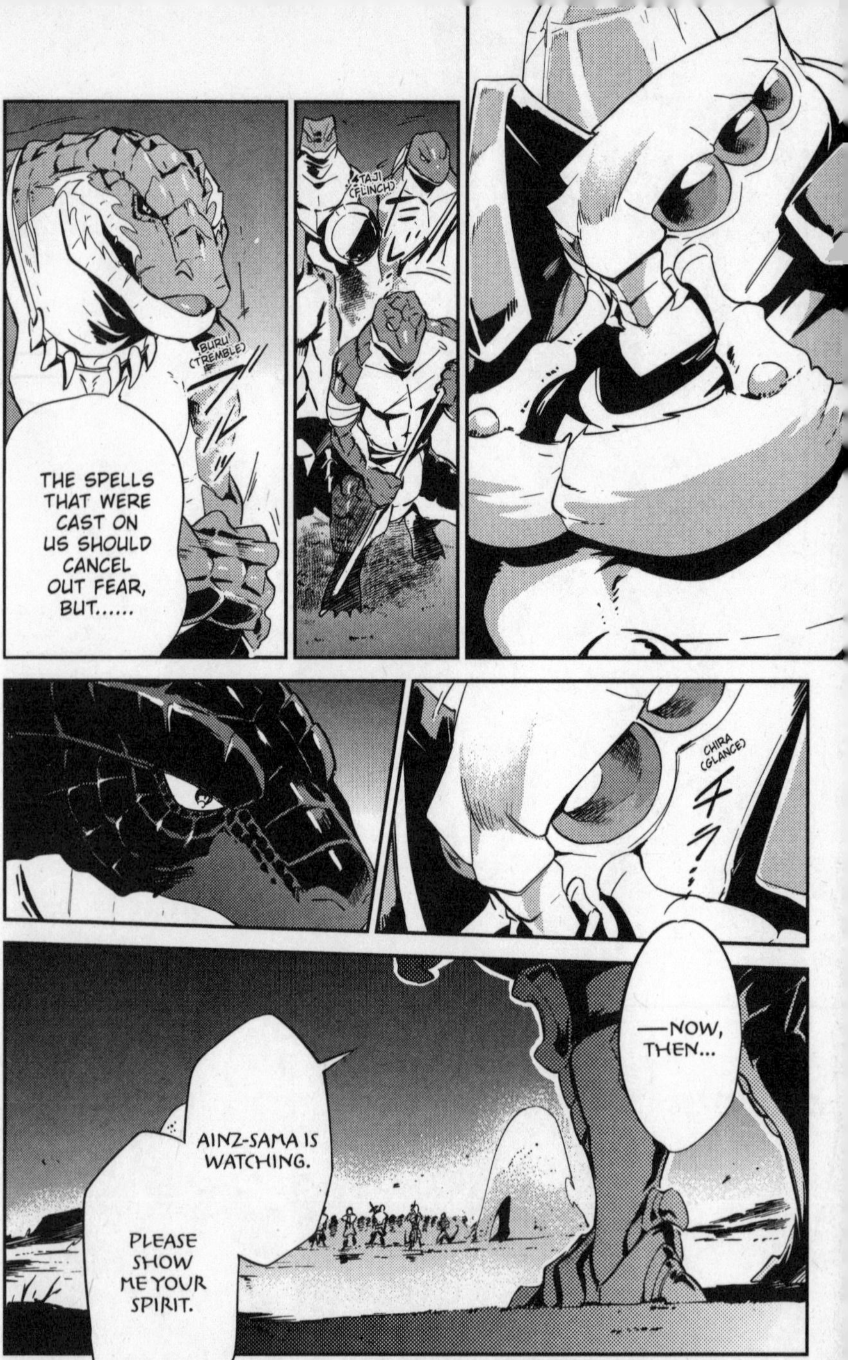
TAJI (FLINCH)
BURU (TREMBLE)
THE SPELLS THAT WERE CAST ON US SHOULD CANCEL OUT FEAR, BUT......
CHIRA (GLANCE)
—NOW, THEN...
AINZ-SAMA IS WATCHING.
PLEASE SHOW ME YOUR SPIRIT.

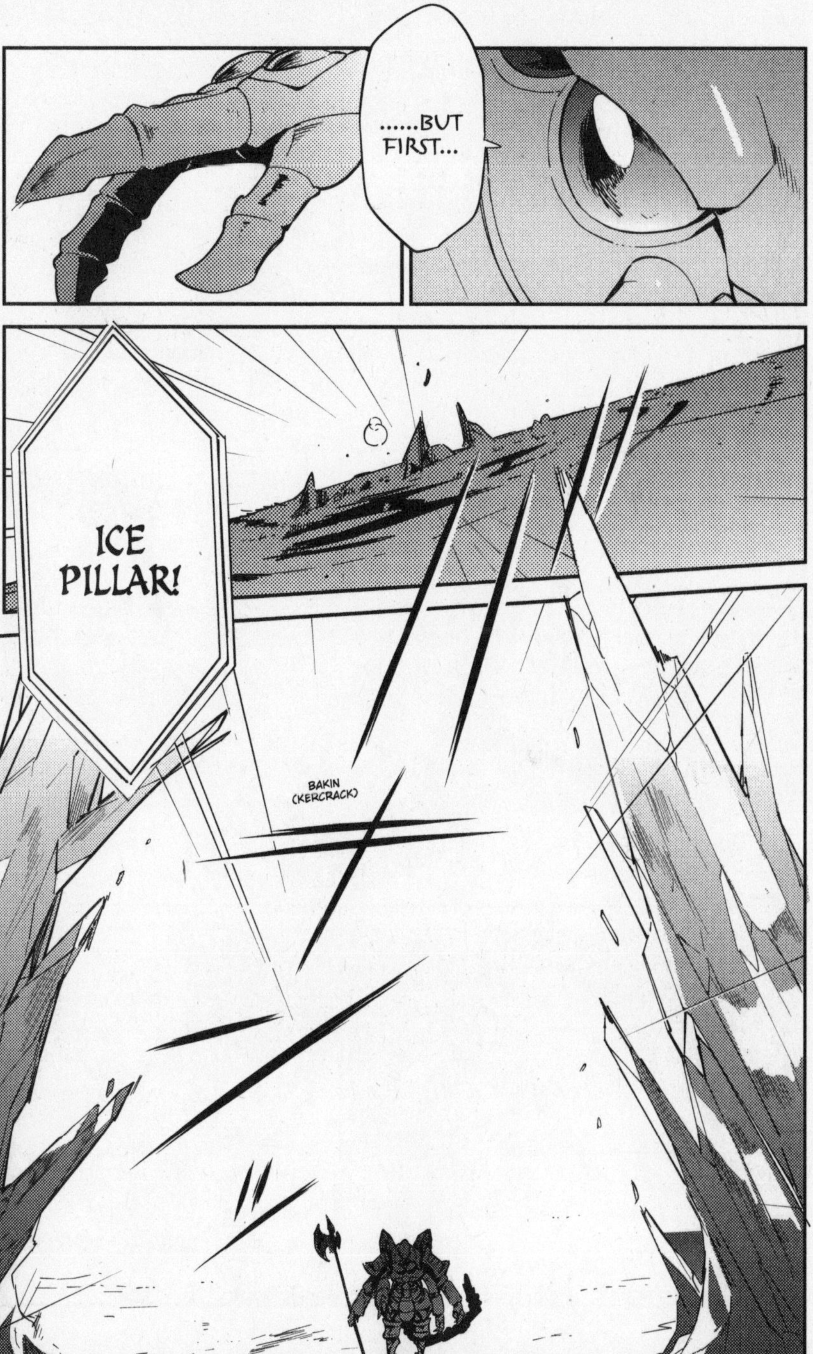
......BUT FIRST...
ICE PILLAR!
BAKIN (KERCRACK)

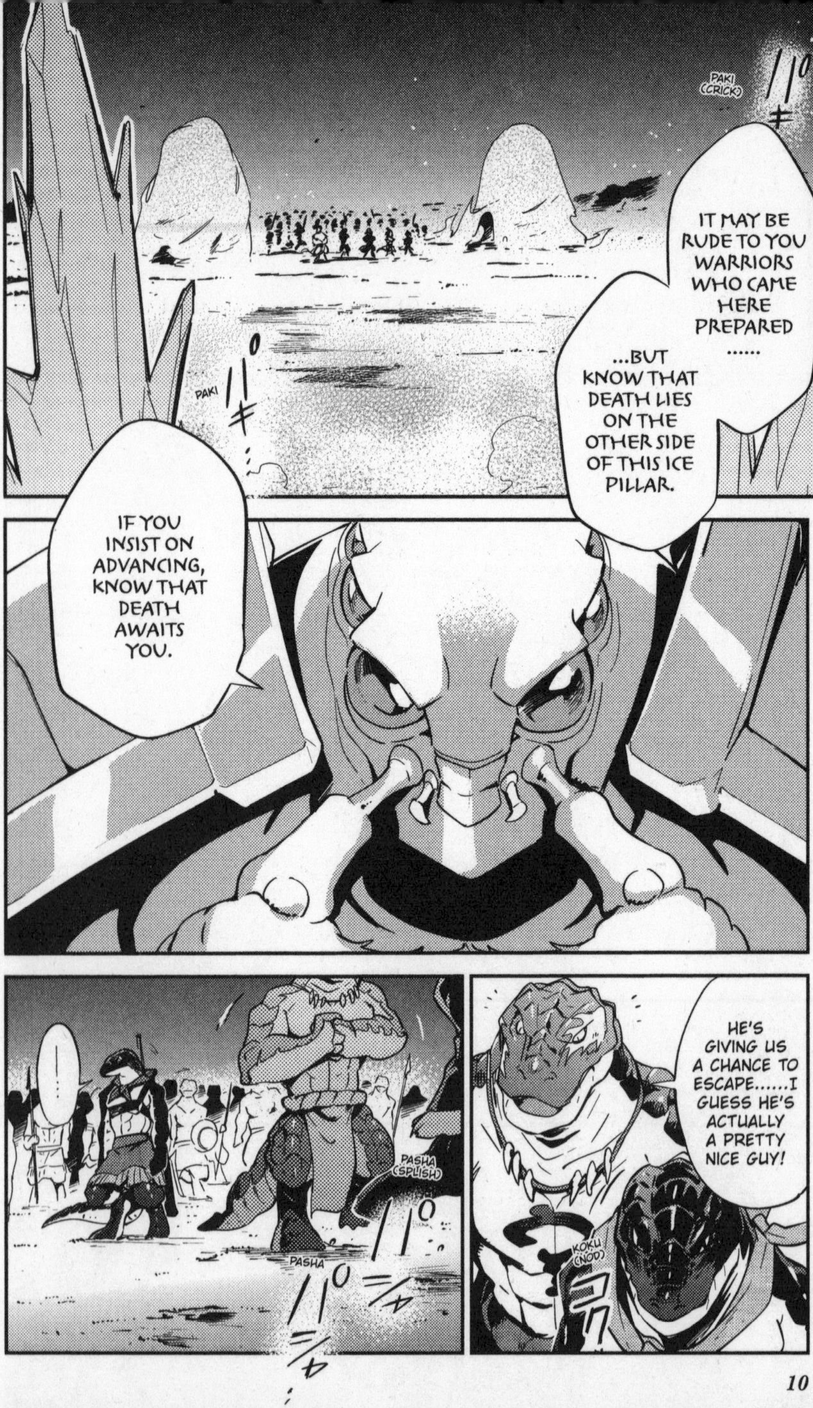
PAKI (CRICK)
IT MAY BE RUDE TO YOU WARRIORS WHO CAME HERE PREPARED ......
...BUT KNOW THAT DEATH LIES ON THE OTHER SIDE OF THIS ICE PILLAR.
PAKI
IF YOU INSIST ON ADVANCING, KNOW THAT DEATH AWAITS YOU.
HE'S GIVING US A CHANCE TO ESCAPE......I GUESS HE'S ACTUALLY A PRETTY NICE GUY!
KOKU (NOD)
!......
PASHA (SPLISH)
PASHA

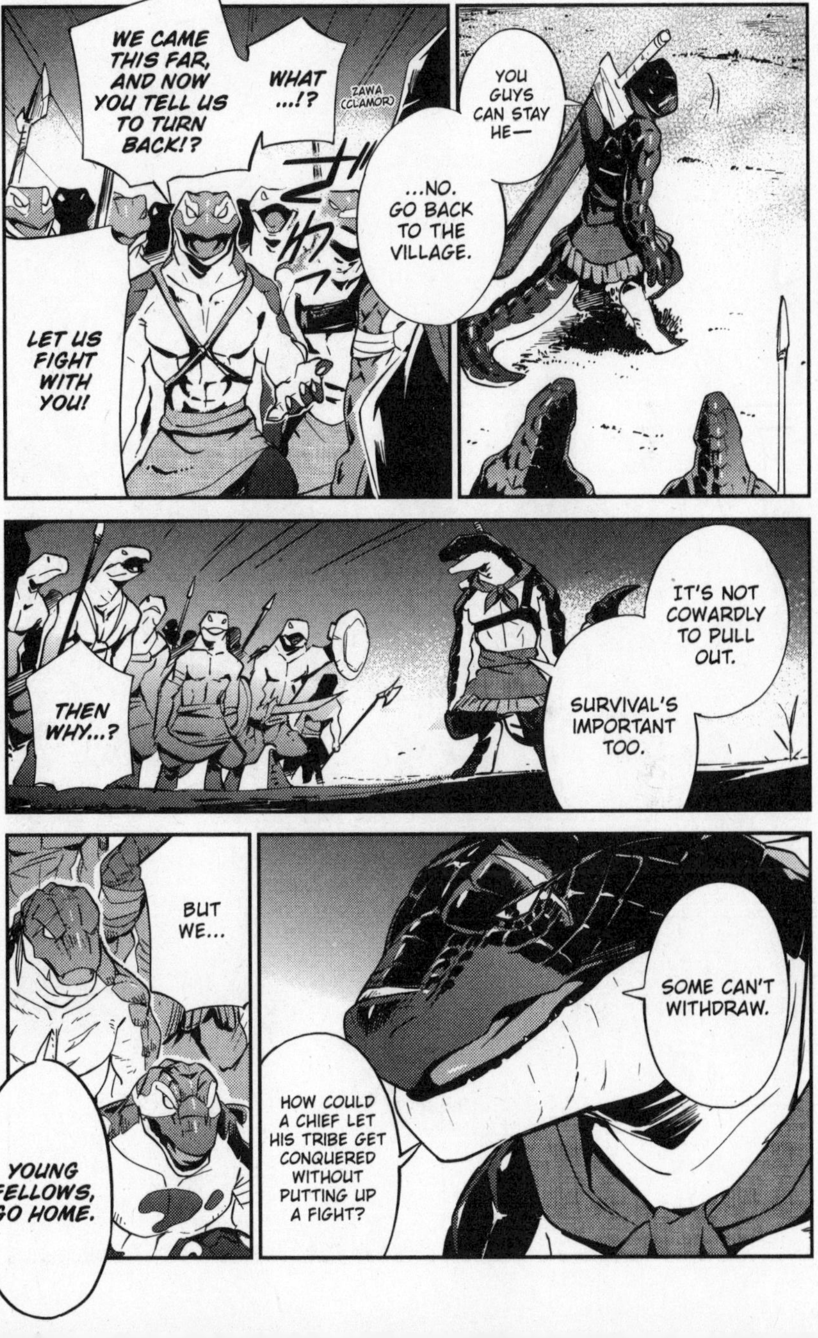
YOU GUYS CAN STAY HE—
...NO. GO BACK TO THE VILLAGE.
WHAT ...!?
ZAWA (CLAMOR)
WE CAME THIS FAR, AND NOW YOU TELL US TO TURN BACK!?
LET US FIGHT WITH YOU!
IT'S NOT COWARDLY TO PULL OUT.
SURVIVAL'S IMPORTANT TOO.
THEN WHY...?
SOME CAN'T WITHDRAW.
HOW COULD A CHIEF LET HIS TRIBE GET CONQUERED WITHOUT PUTTING UP A FIGHT?
BUT WE...
YOUNG FELLOWS, GO HOME.

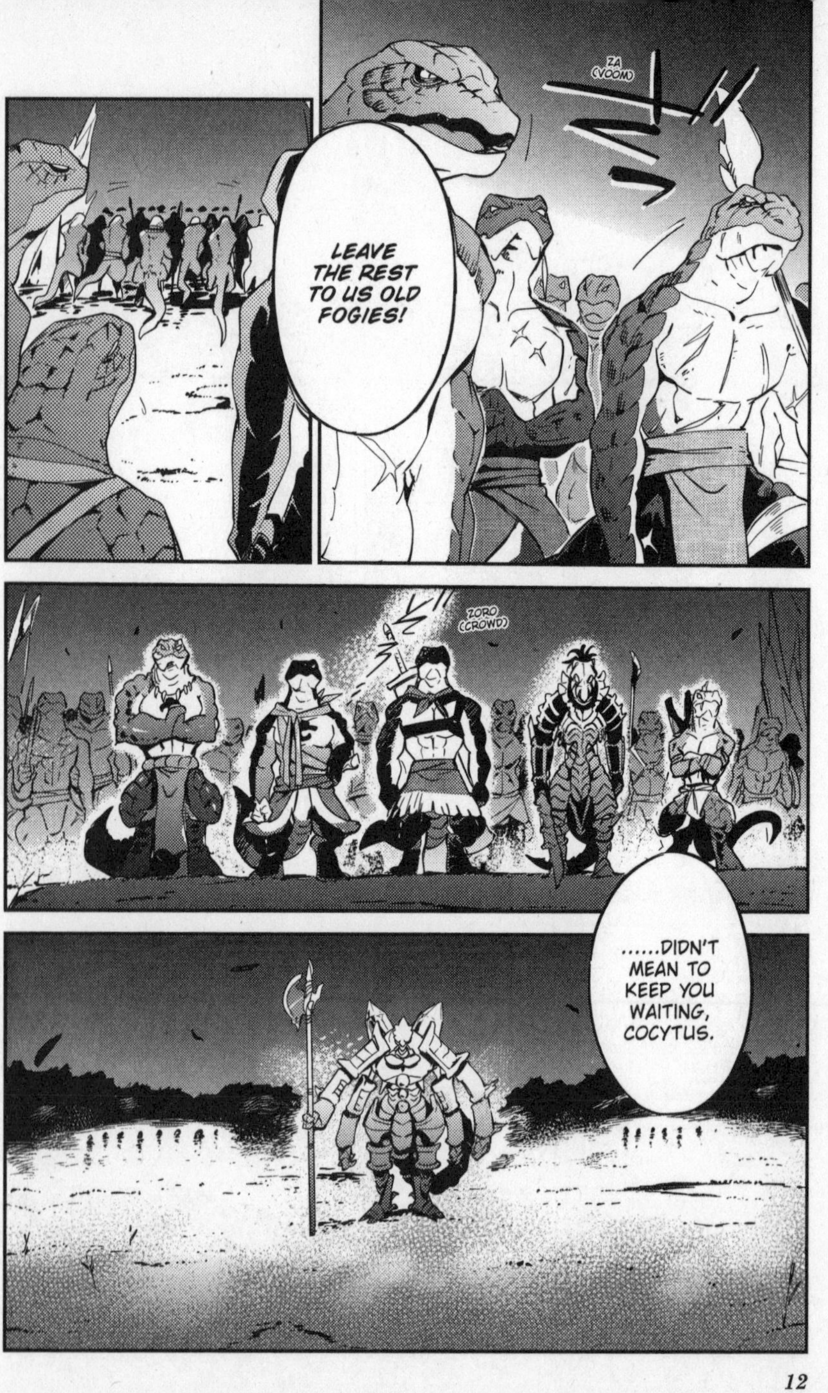
ZA (VOOM)
LEAVE THE REST TO US OLD FOGIES!
ZORO (CROWD)
......DIDN'T MEAN TO KEEP YOU WAITING, COCYTUS.

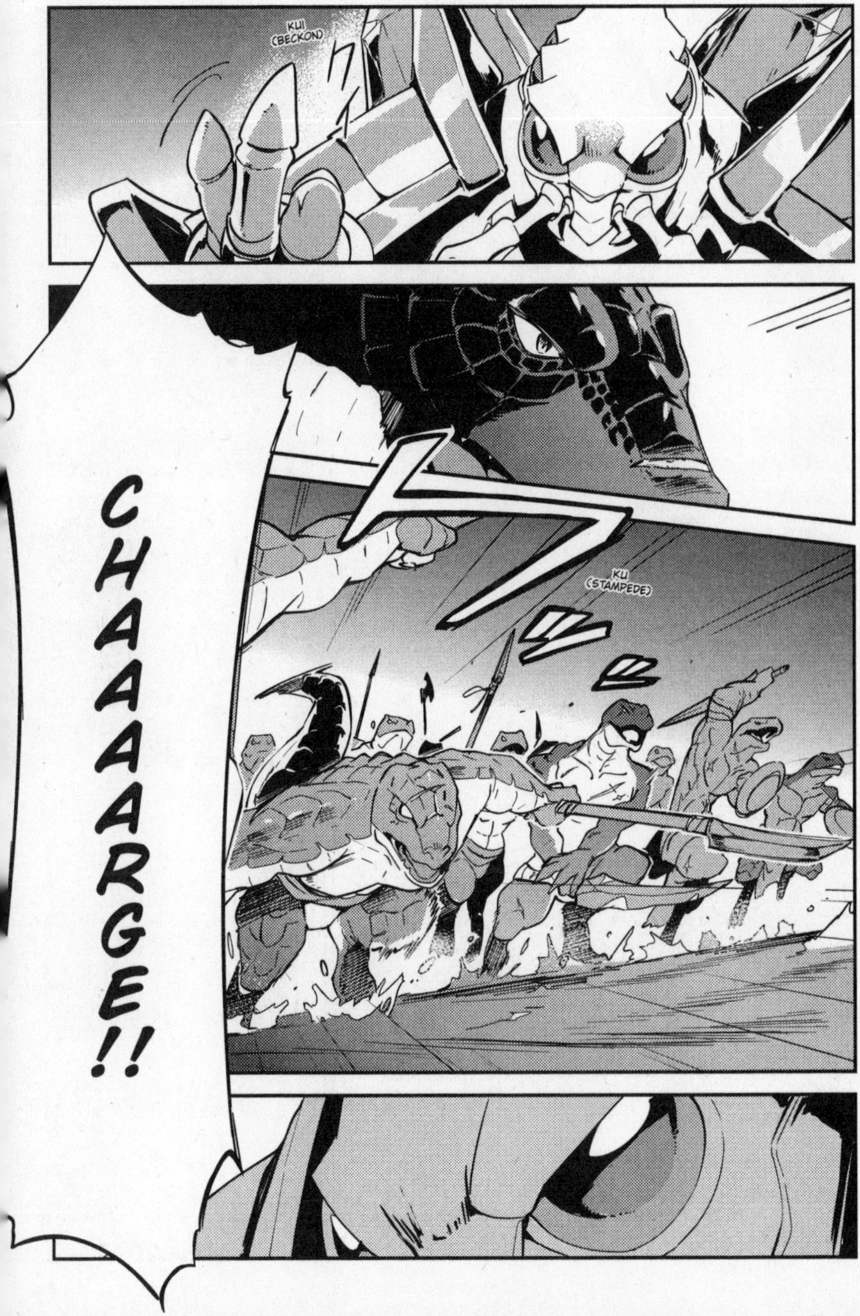
KUI
(BECKON)
KU
(STAMPEDE)
CHAAAARGE!!

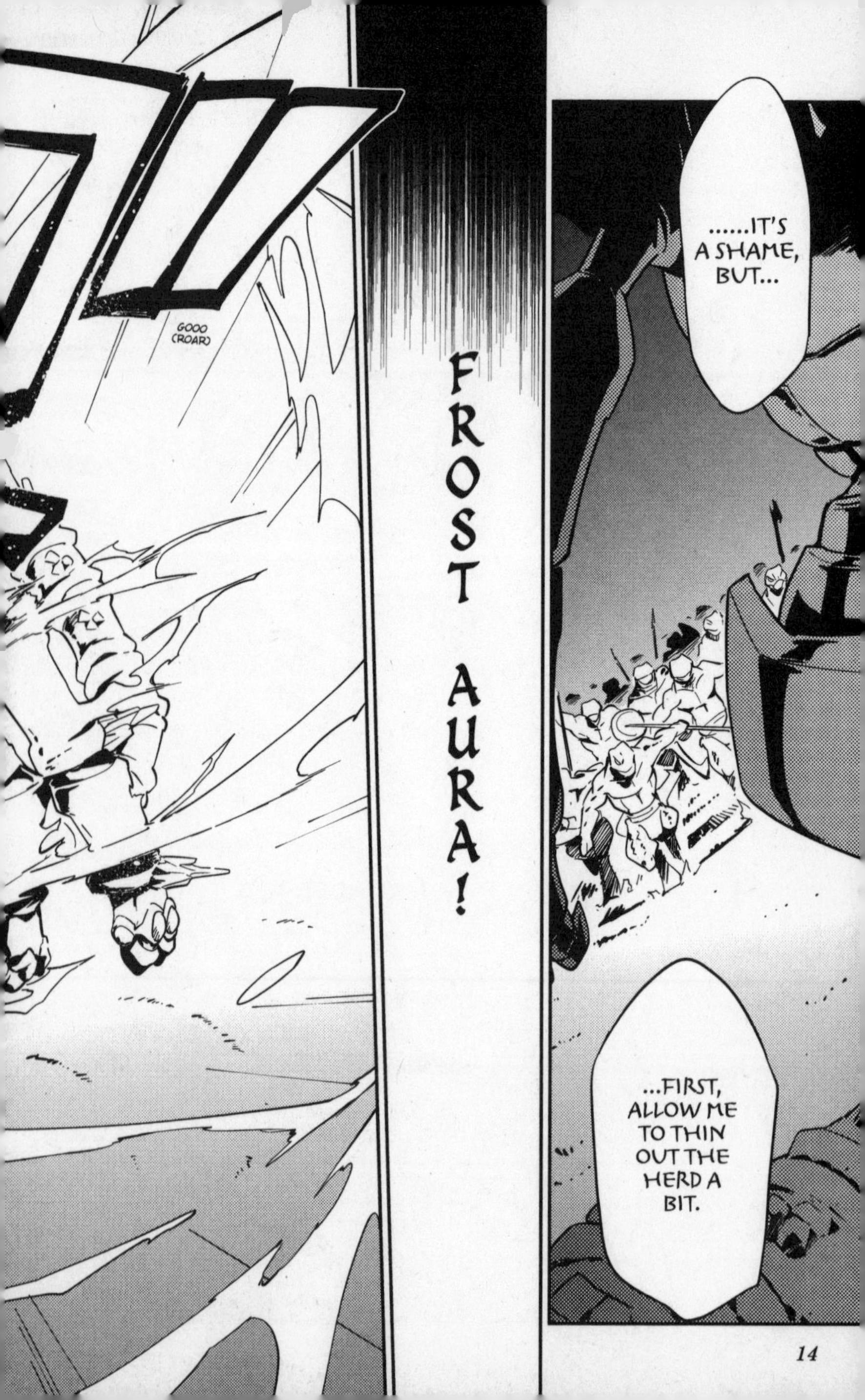
......IT'S A SHAME, BUT...
...FIRST, ALLOW ME TO THIN OUT THE HERD A BIT.
FROST AURA!
GOOO (ROAR)

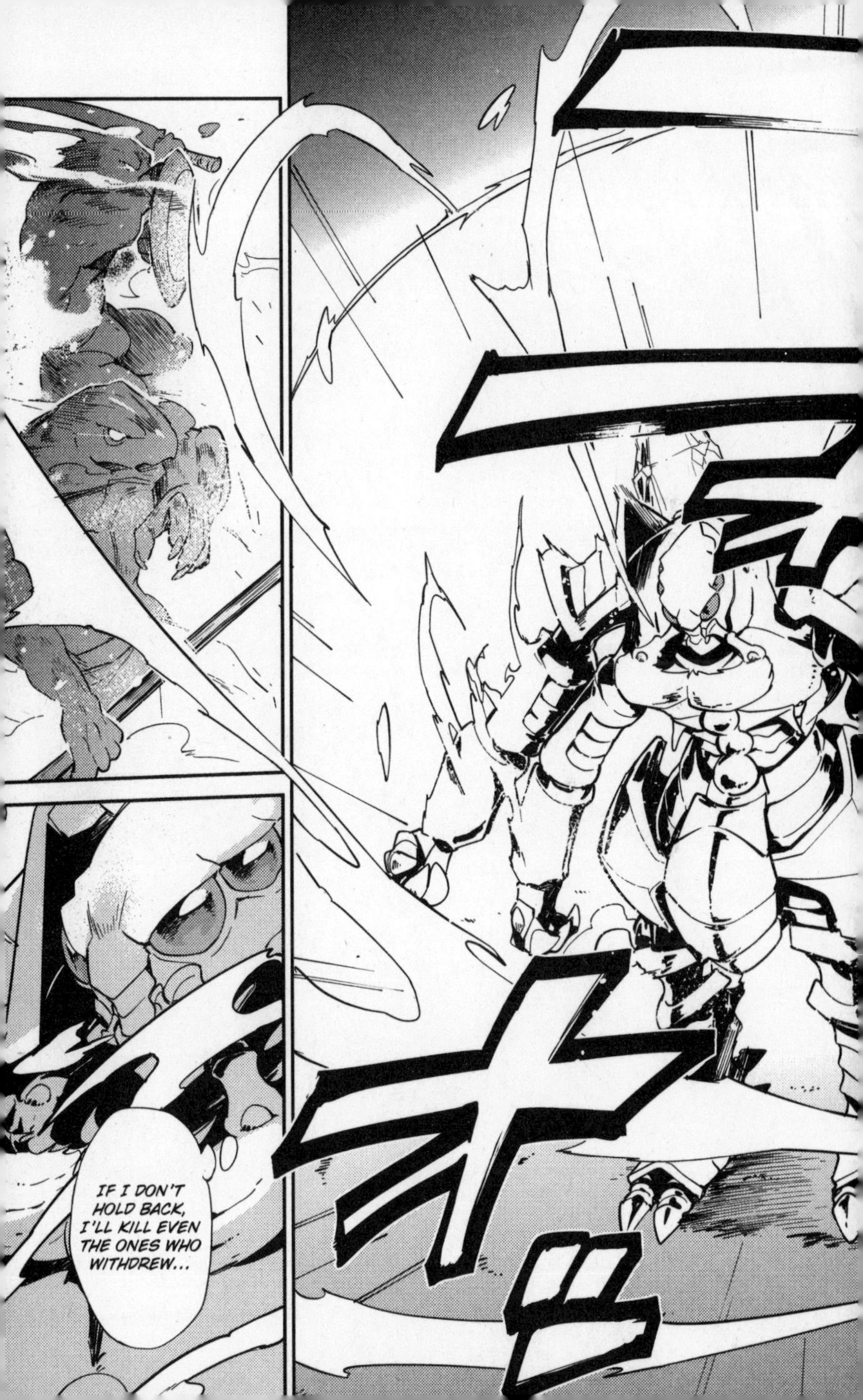
IF I DON'T HOLD BACK, I'LL KILL EVEN THE ONES WHO WITHDREW...

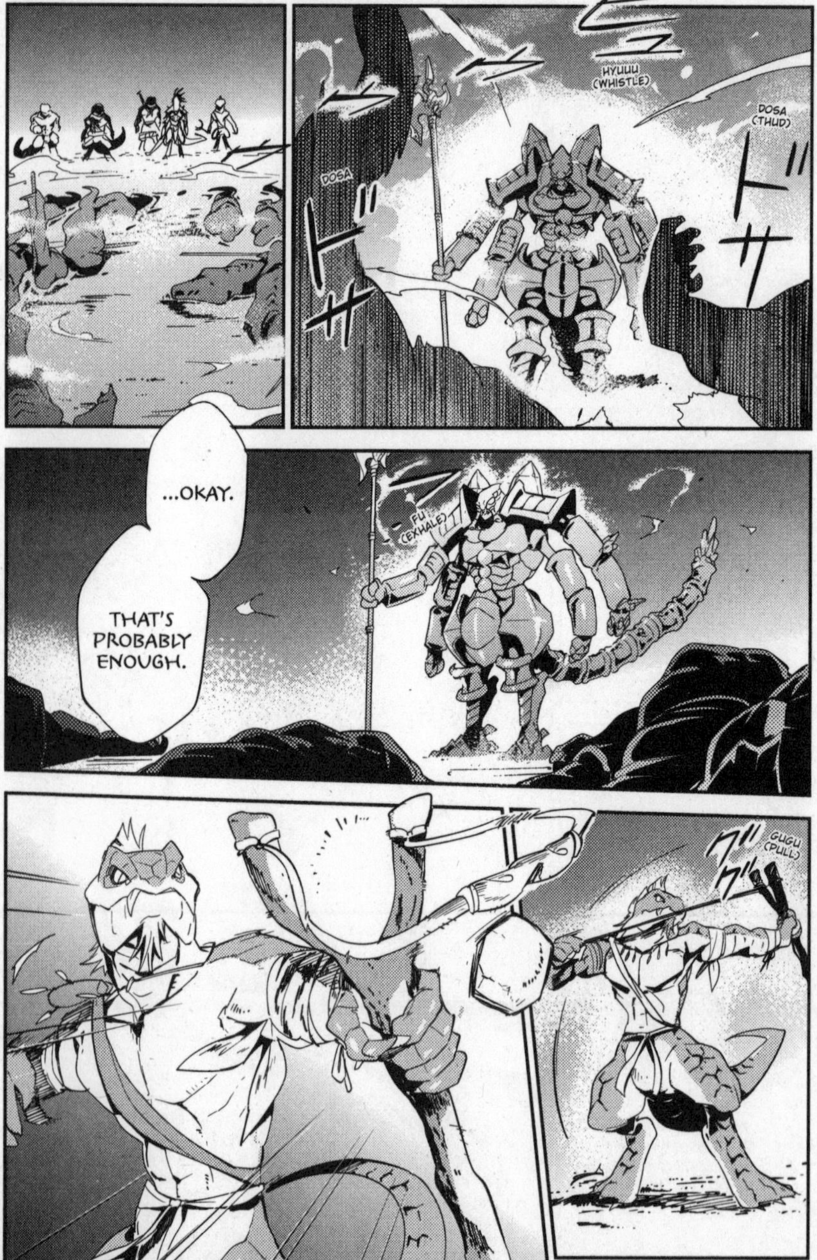
HYUUU (WHISTLE)
DOSA (THUD)
DOSA
FU (EXHALE)
...OKAY.
THAT'S PROBABLY ENOUGH.
GUGU (PULL)

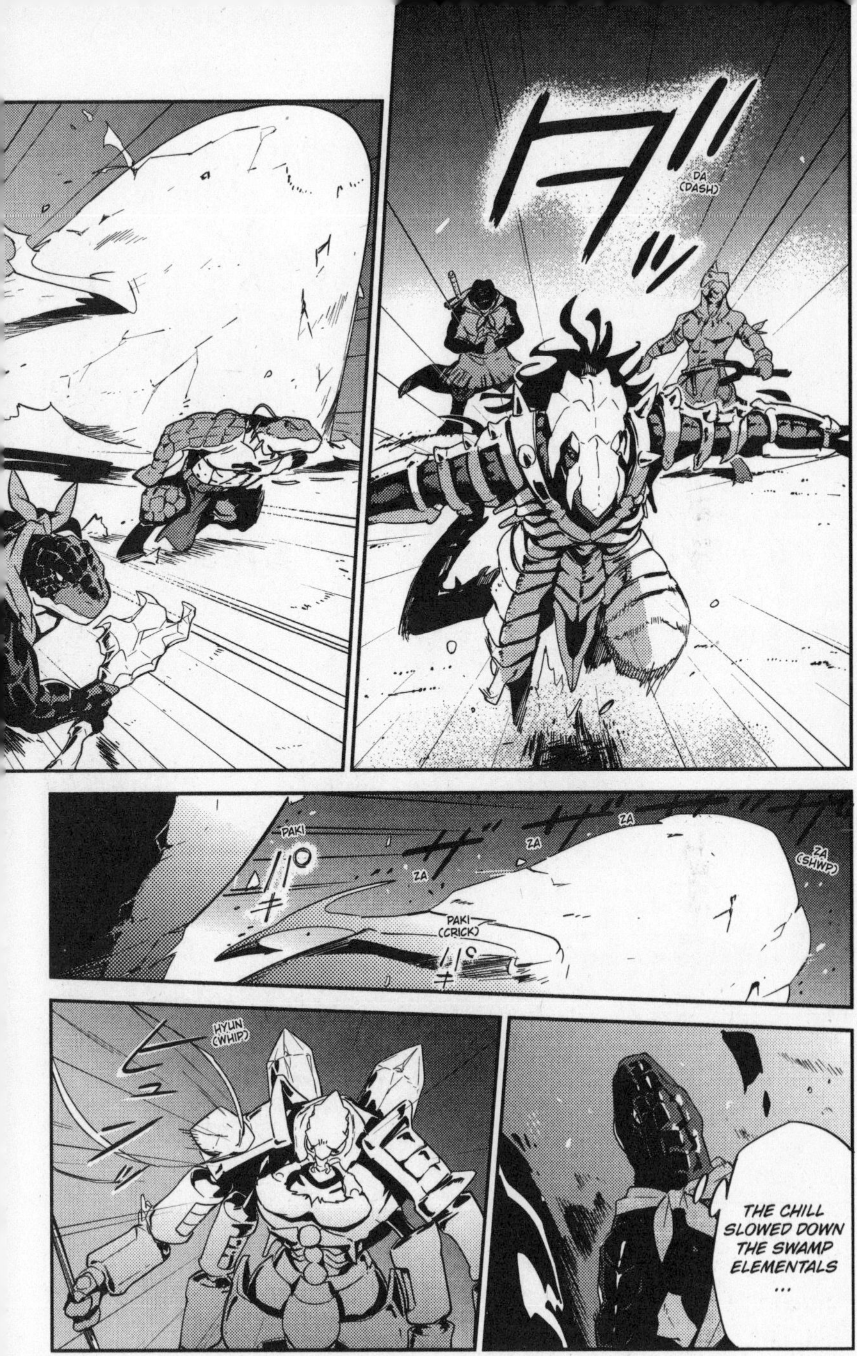
DA (DASH)
ZA (SHWP)
ZA
ZA
PAKI
ZA
PAKI (CRICK)
THE CHILL SLOWED DOWN THE SWAMP ELEMENTALS ...
HYUN (WHIP)

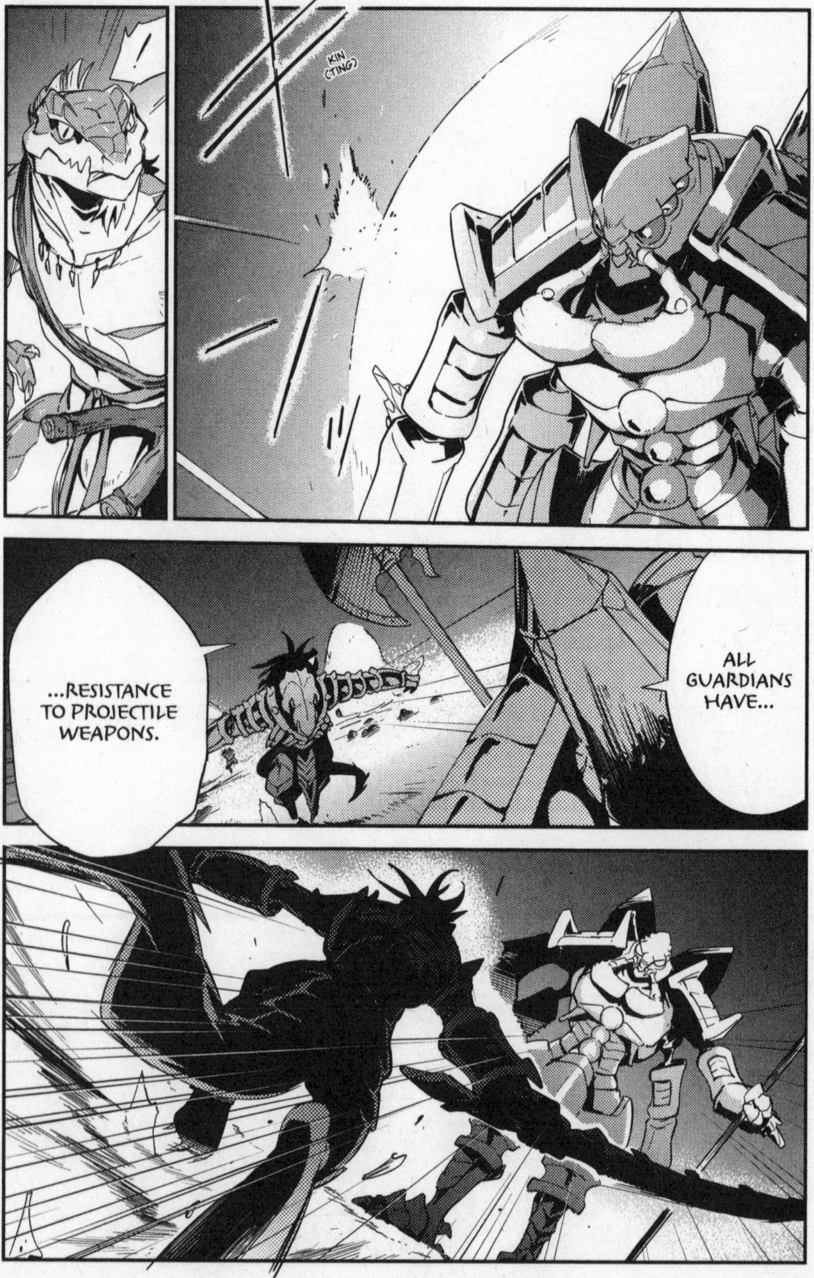
KIN (TING)
!
ALL GUARDIANS HAVE...
...RESISTANCE TO PROJECTILE WEAPONS.

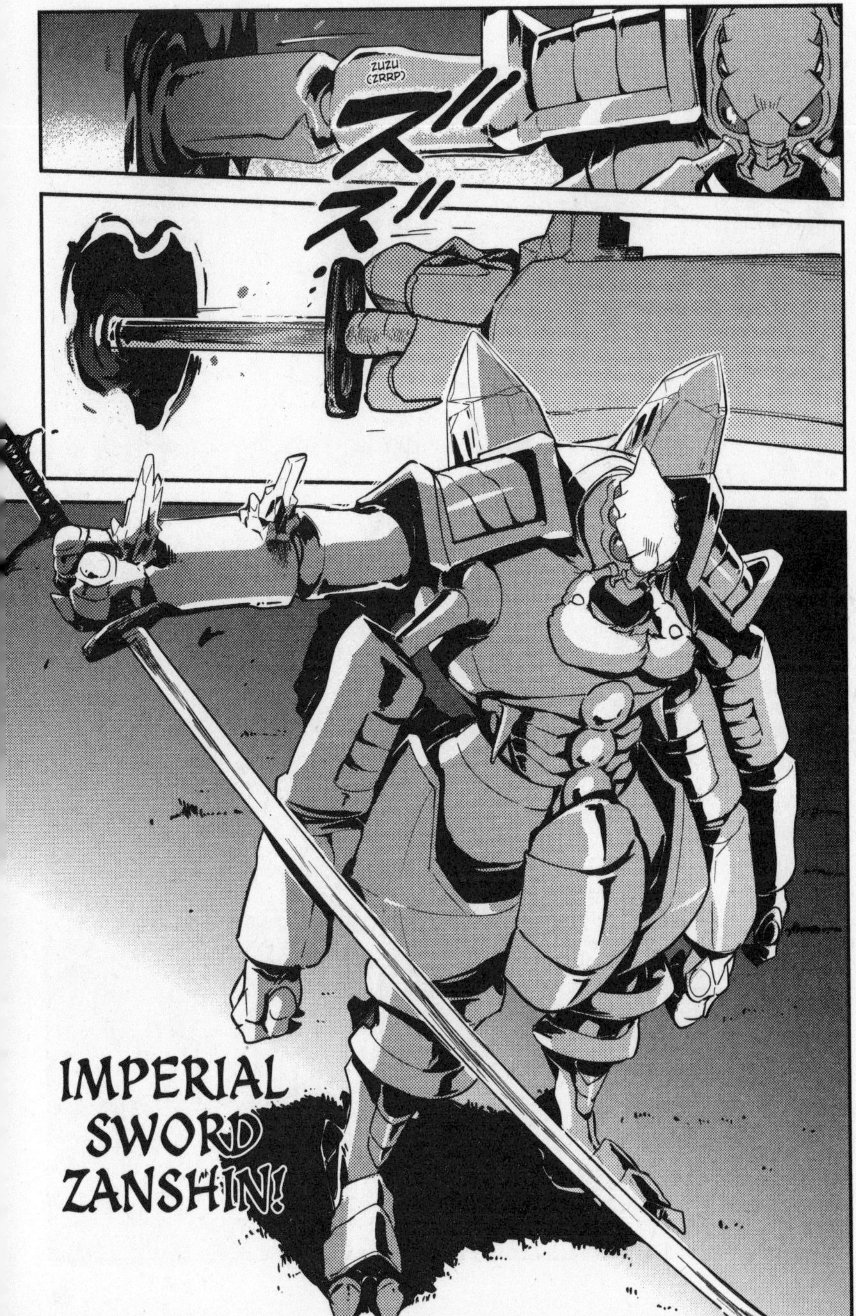
ZUZU (ZRRP)
ズズ
IMPERIAL SWORD ZANSHIN!

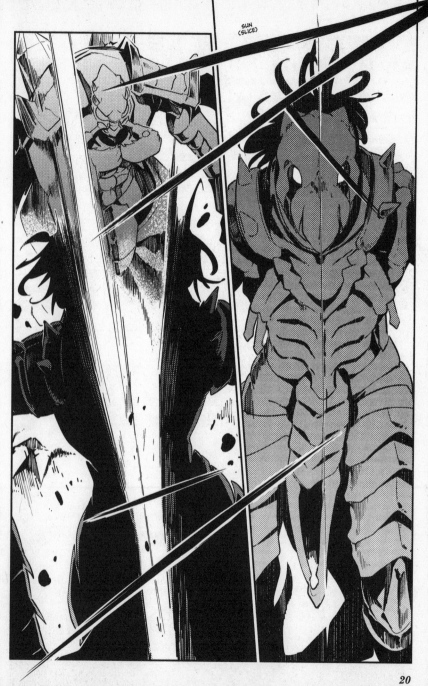

SUN
(SLICE)

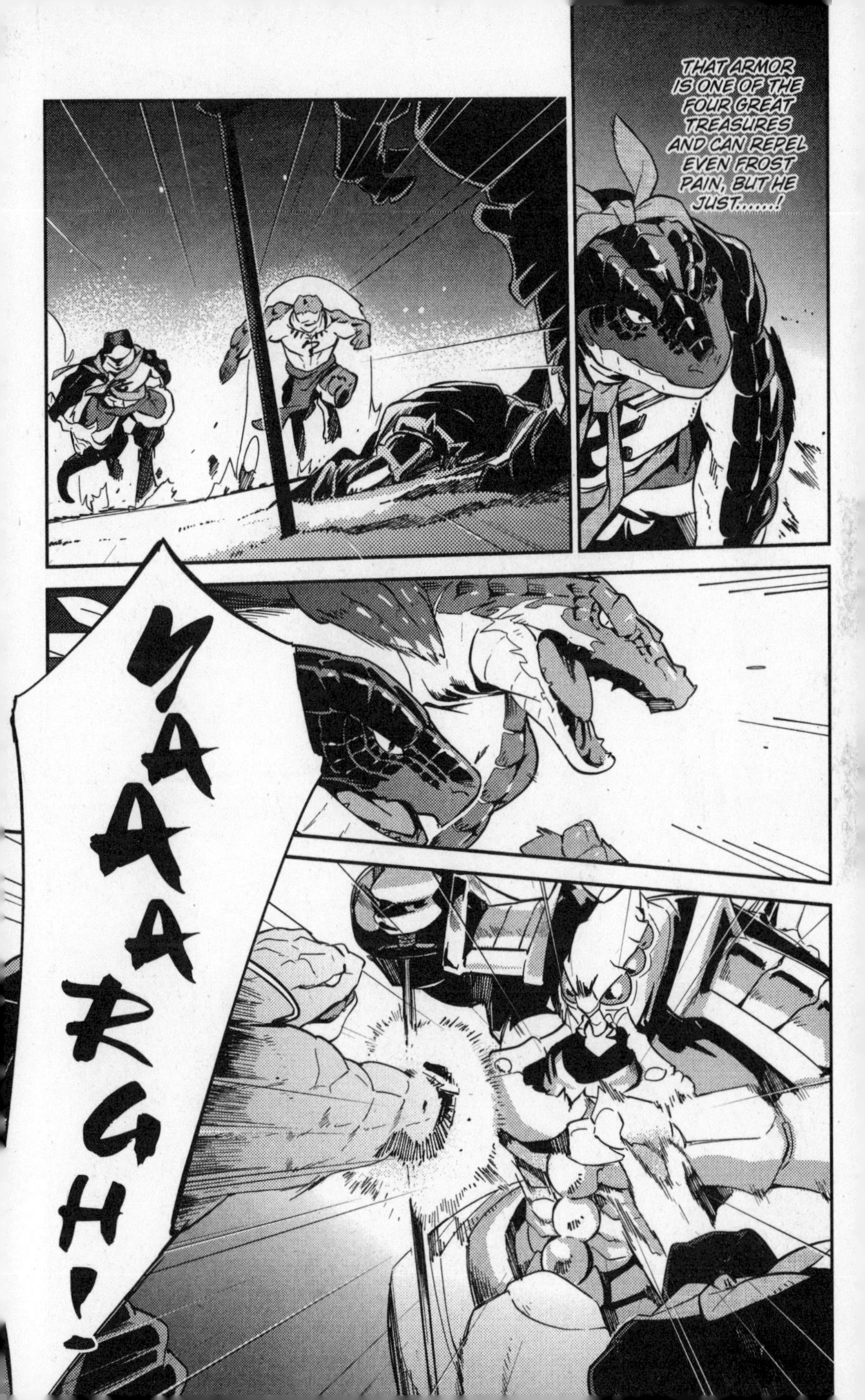
THAT ARMOR IS ONE OF THE FOUR GREAT TREASURES AND CAN REPEL EVEN FROST PAIN, BUT HE JUST......!
MAAARGH!!

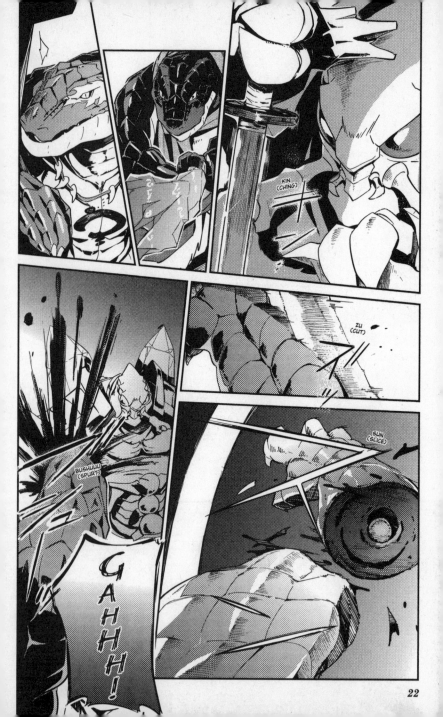

KIN
(CHING)

ZU
(CUT)

SUN
(SLICE)

BUSHUUU
(SPURT)

GAHHH!

22

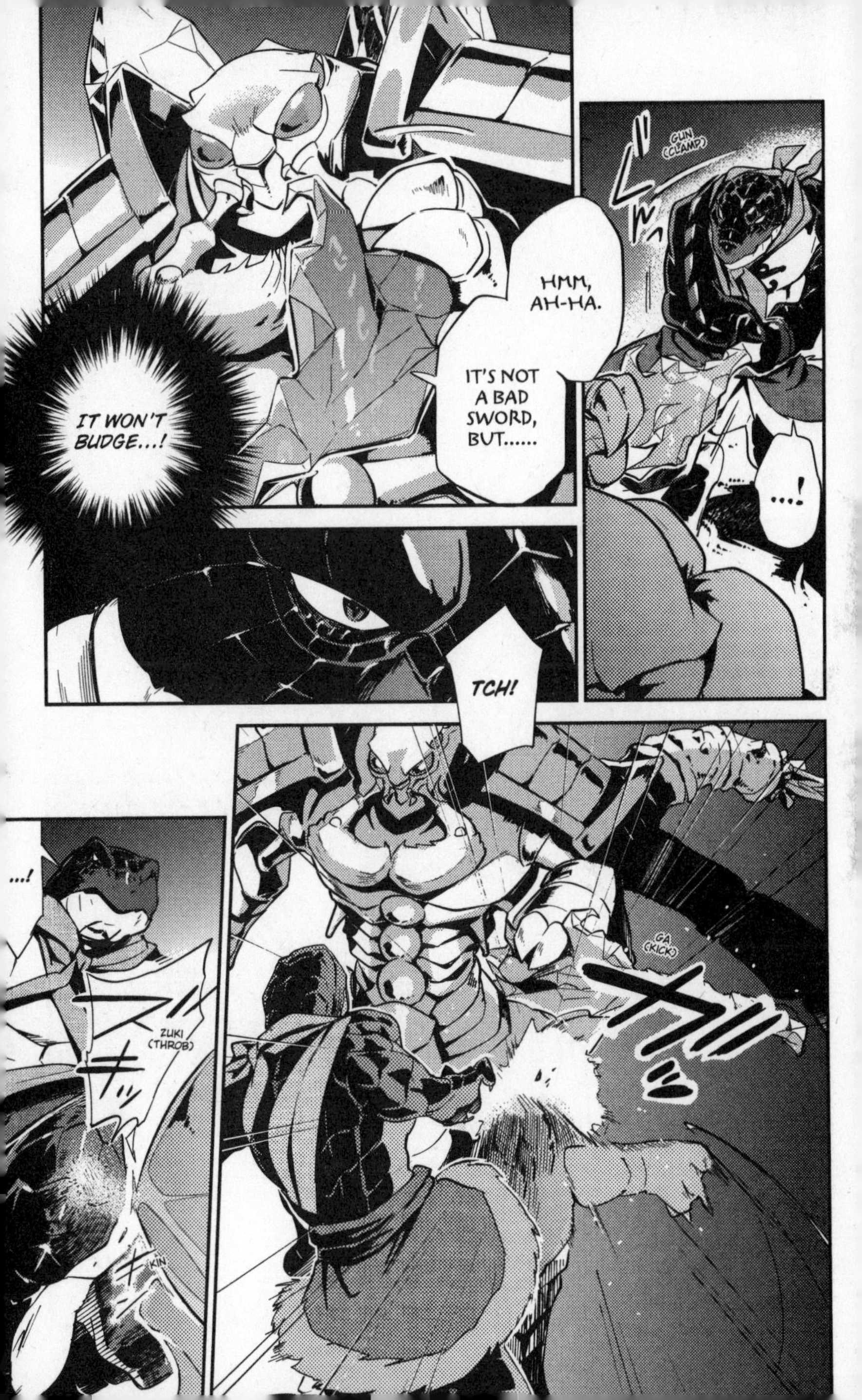
GUN (CLAMP)
...!
HMM, AH-HA.
IT'S NOT A BAD SWORD, BUT......
IT WON'T BUDGE...!
TCH!
GA (KICK)
...!
ZUKI (THROB)
KIN

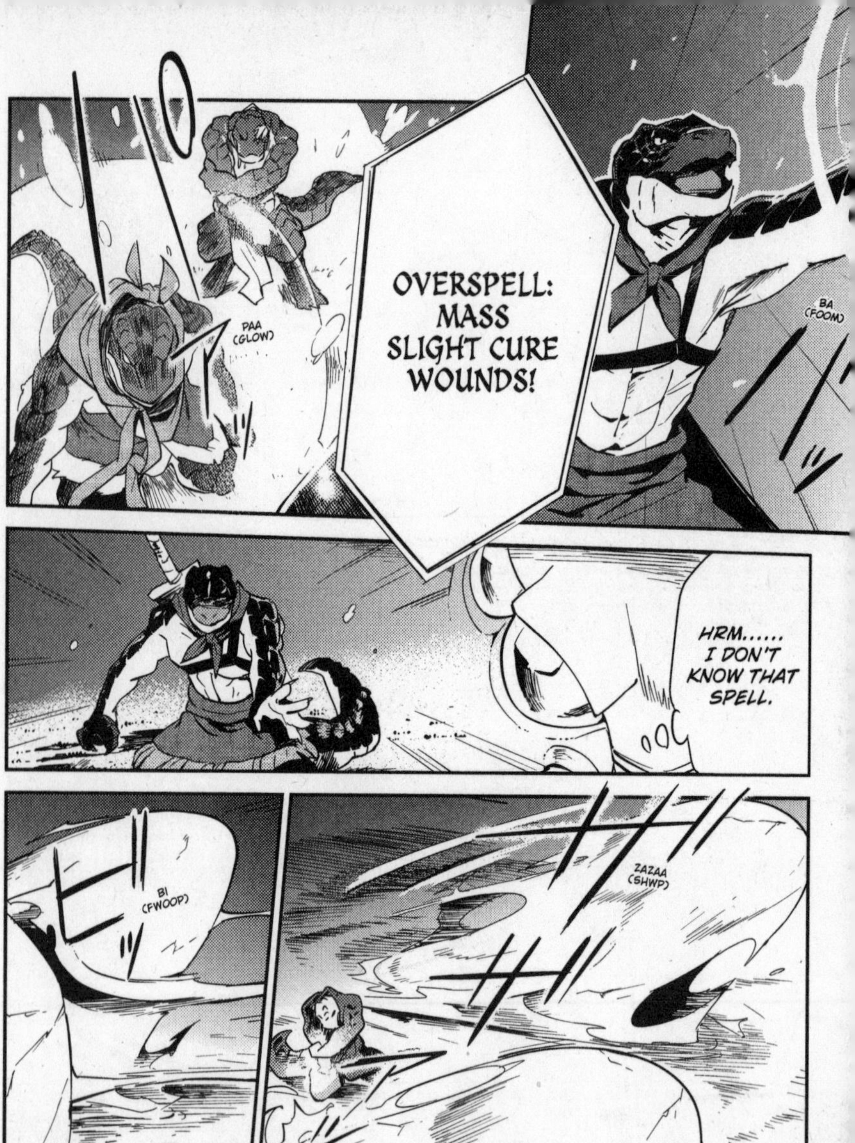
OVERSPELL: MASS SLIGHT CURE WOUNDS!
BA (FOOM)
PAA (GLOW)
HRM...... I DON'T KNOW THAT SPELL.
ZAZAA (SHWP)
BI (FWOOP)

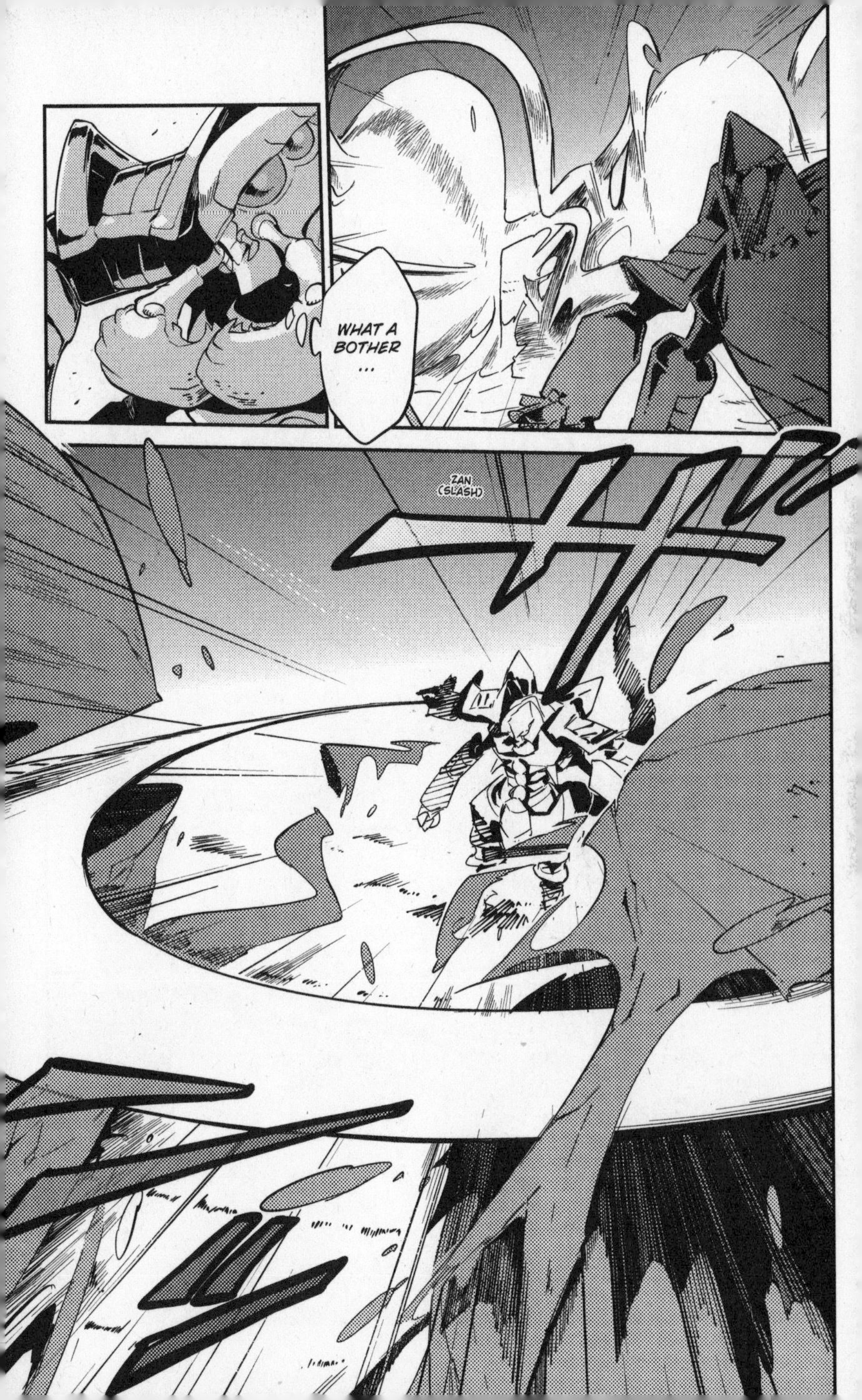
WHAT A BOTHER ...
ZAN (SLASH)

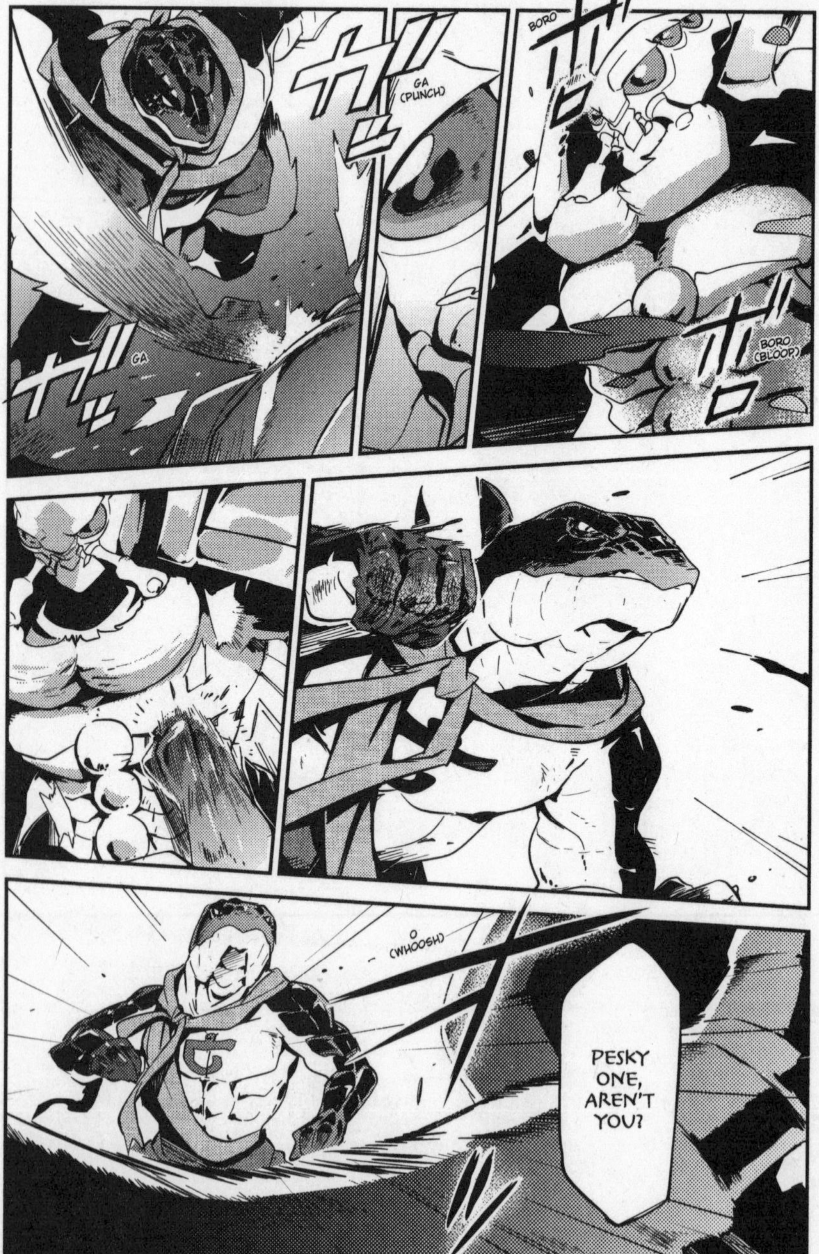
BORO
BORO (BLOOP)
GA (PUNCH)
GA
O (WHOOSH)
PESKY ONE, AREN'T YOU?

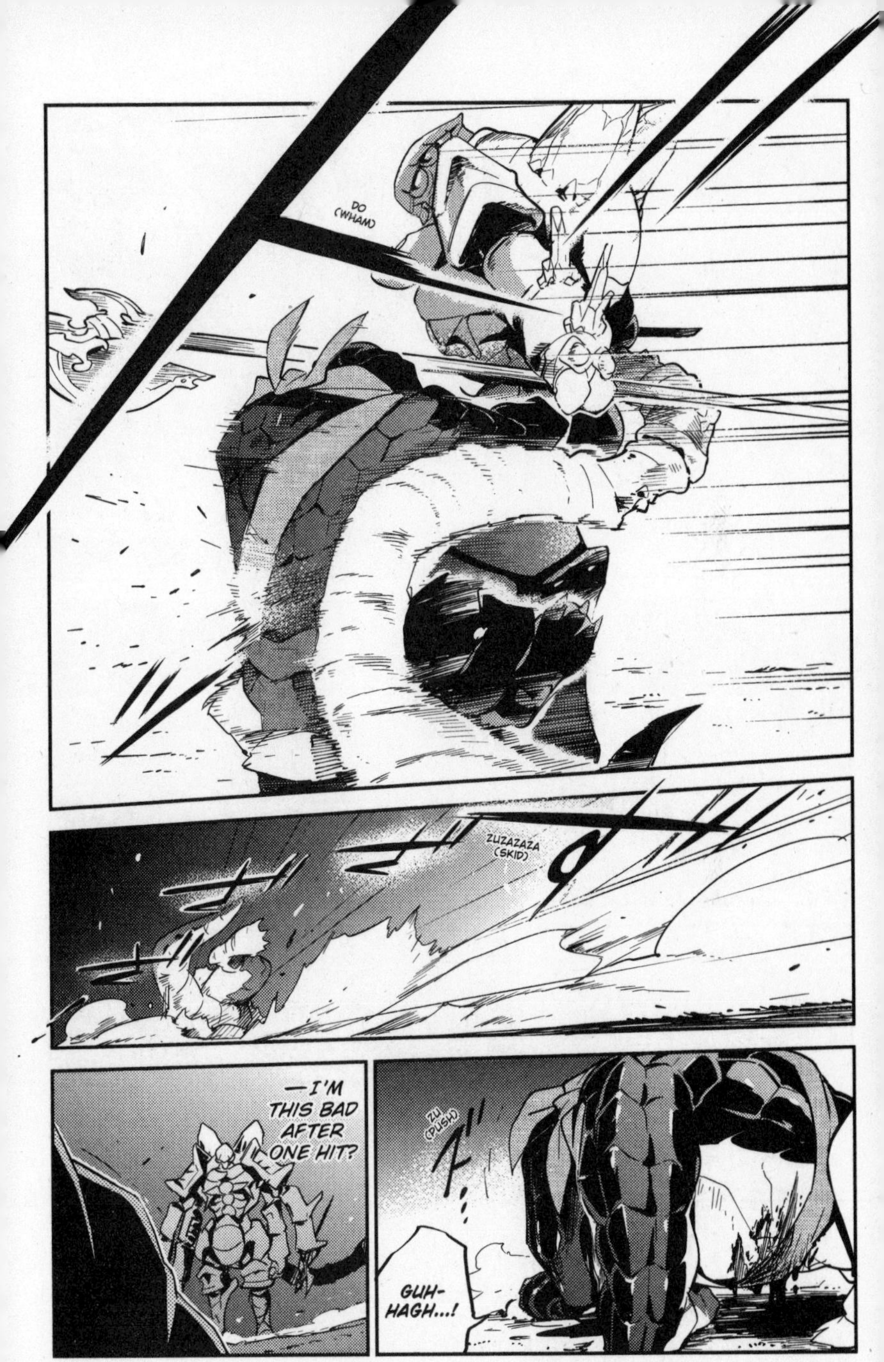
DO (WHAM)
ZUZAZAZA (SKID)
ZU (PUSH)
GUH-HAGH...!
—I'M THIS BAD AFTER ONE HIT?

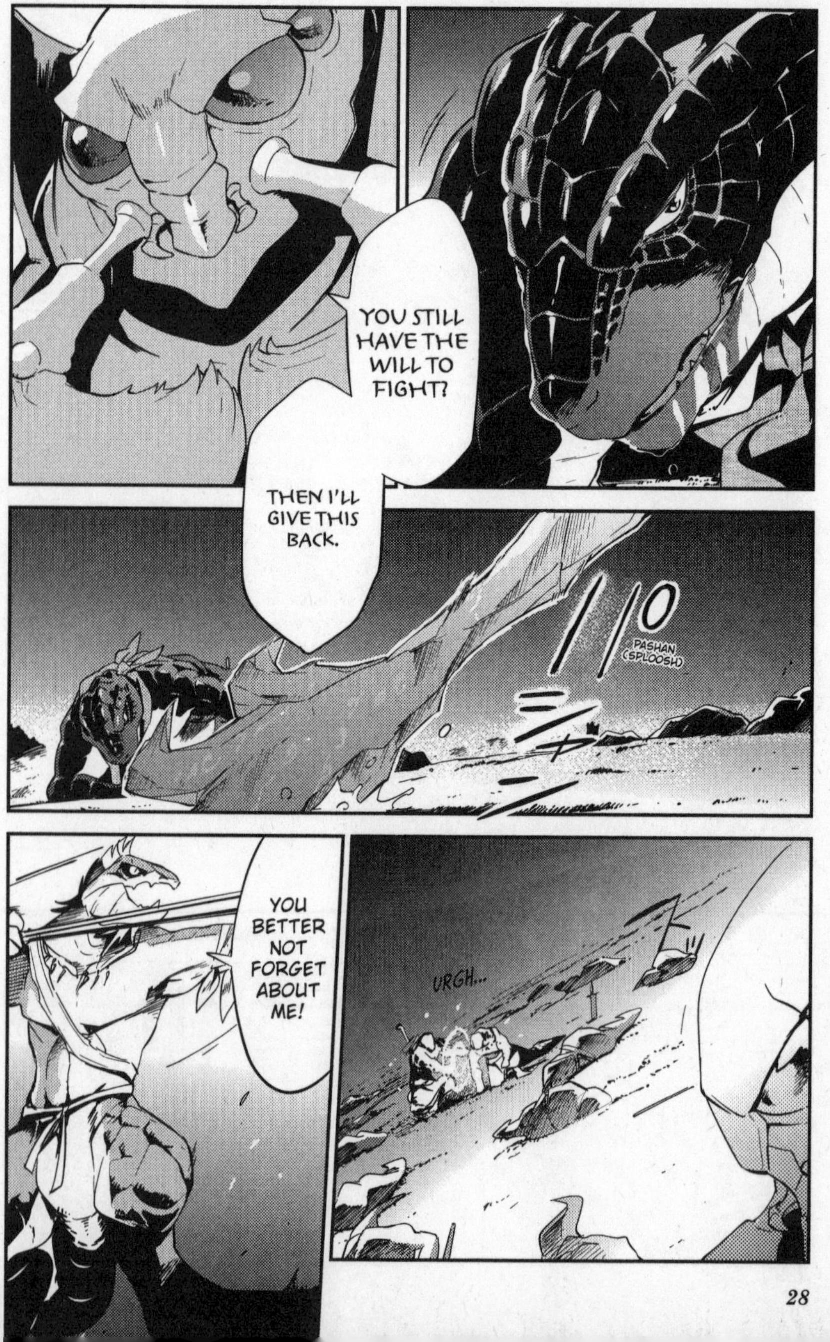
YOU STILL HAVE THE WILL TO FIGHT?
THEN I'LL GIVE THIS BACK.
PASHAN (SPLOOSH)
URGH...
YOU BETTER NOT FORGET ABOUT ME!

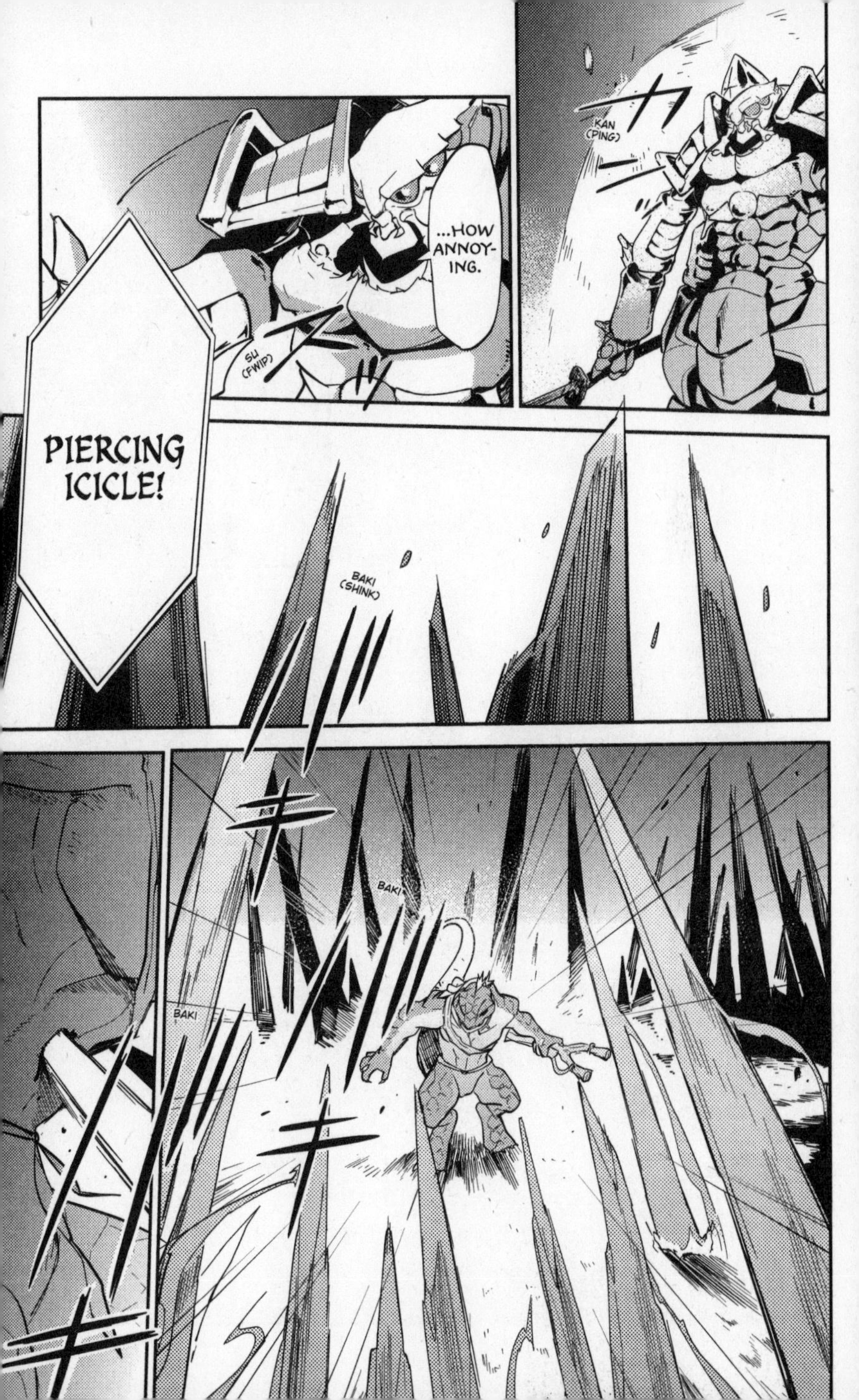
KAN (PING)
...HOW ANNOYING.
SU (FWIP)
PIERCING ICICLE!
BAKI (SHINK)
BAKI
BAKI

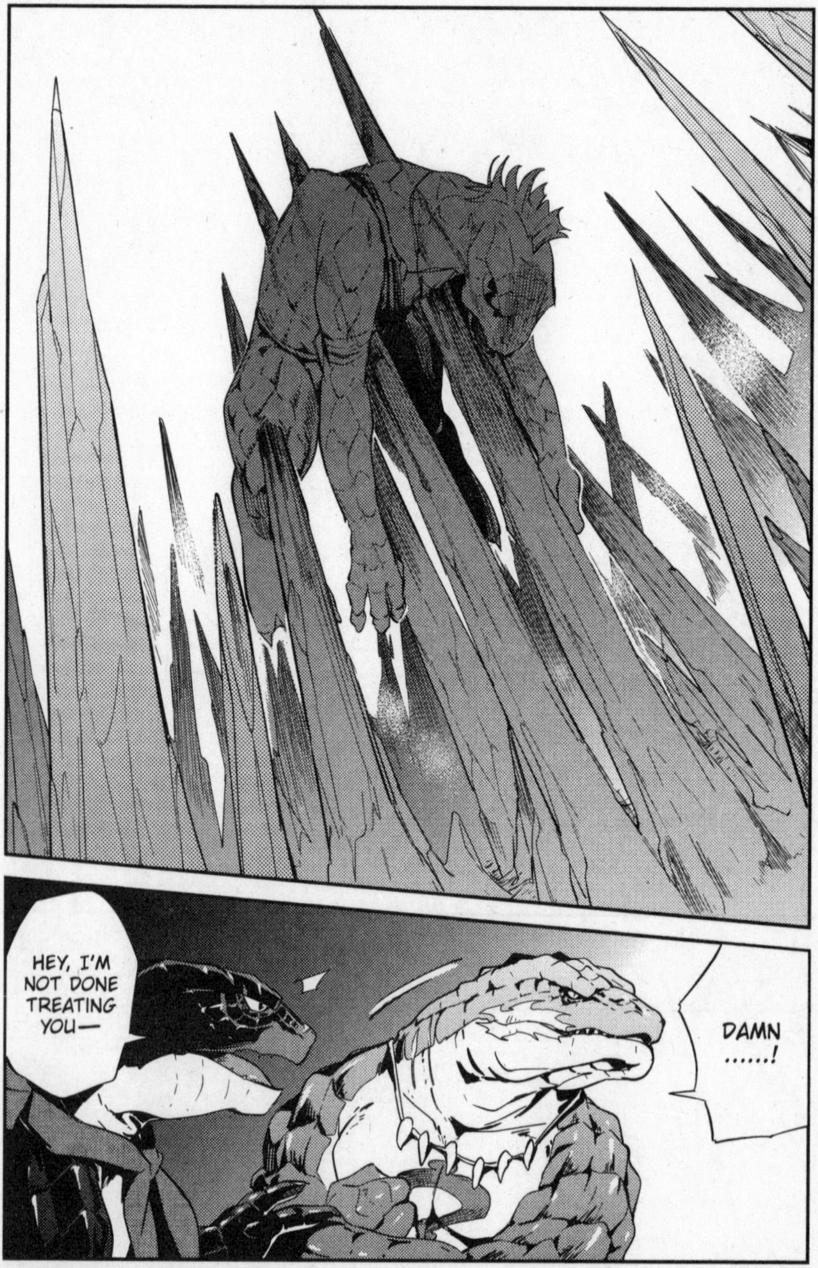
DAMN ......!
HEY, I'M NOT DONE TREATING YOU—

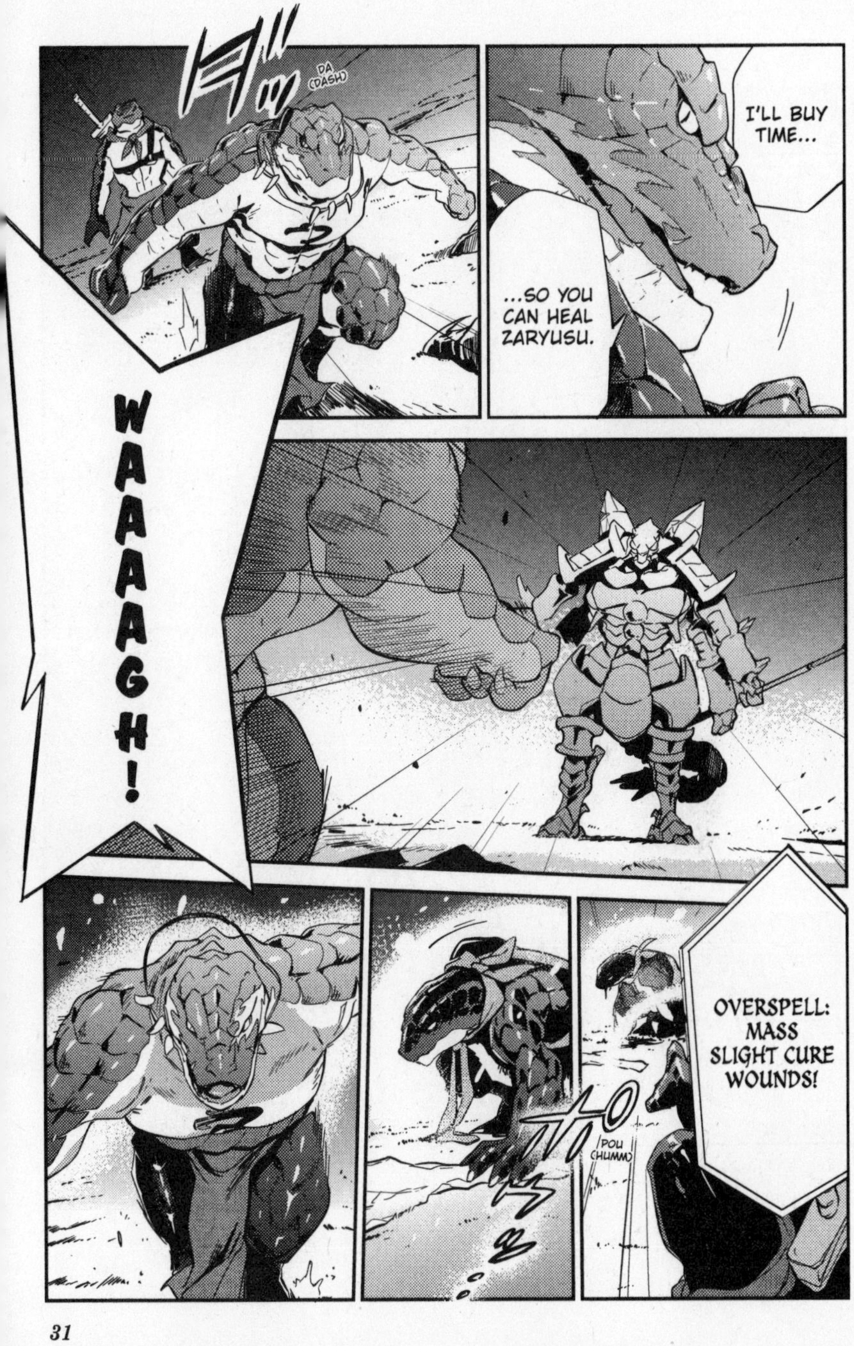
I'LL BUY TIME...
...SO YOU CAN HEAL ZARYUSU.
DA (DASH)
WAAAAAGH!
OVERSPELL: MASS SLIGHT CURE WOUNDS!
POU CHUMM

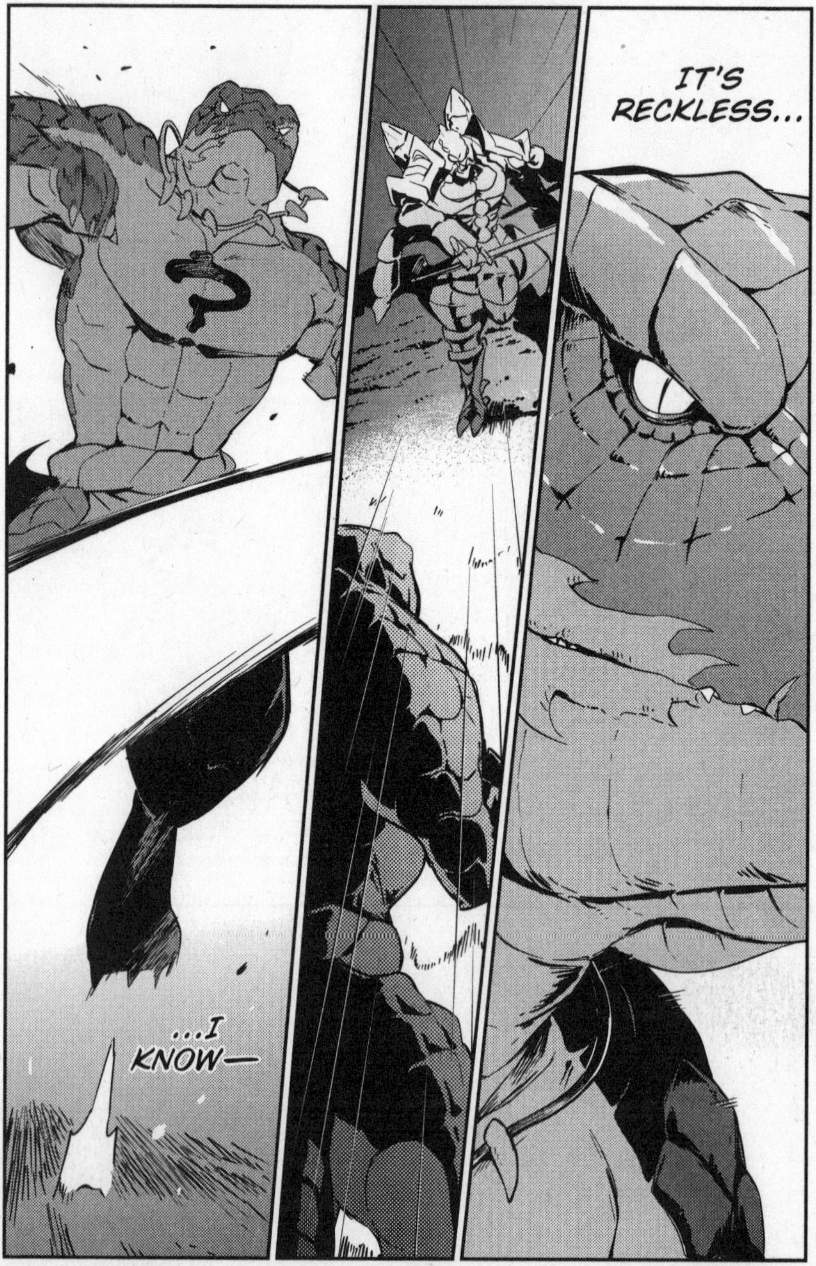
IT'S RECKLESS...
...I KNOW—

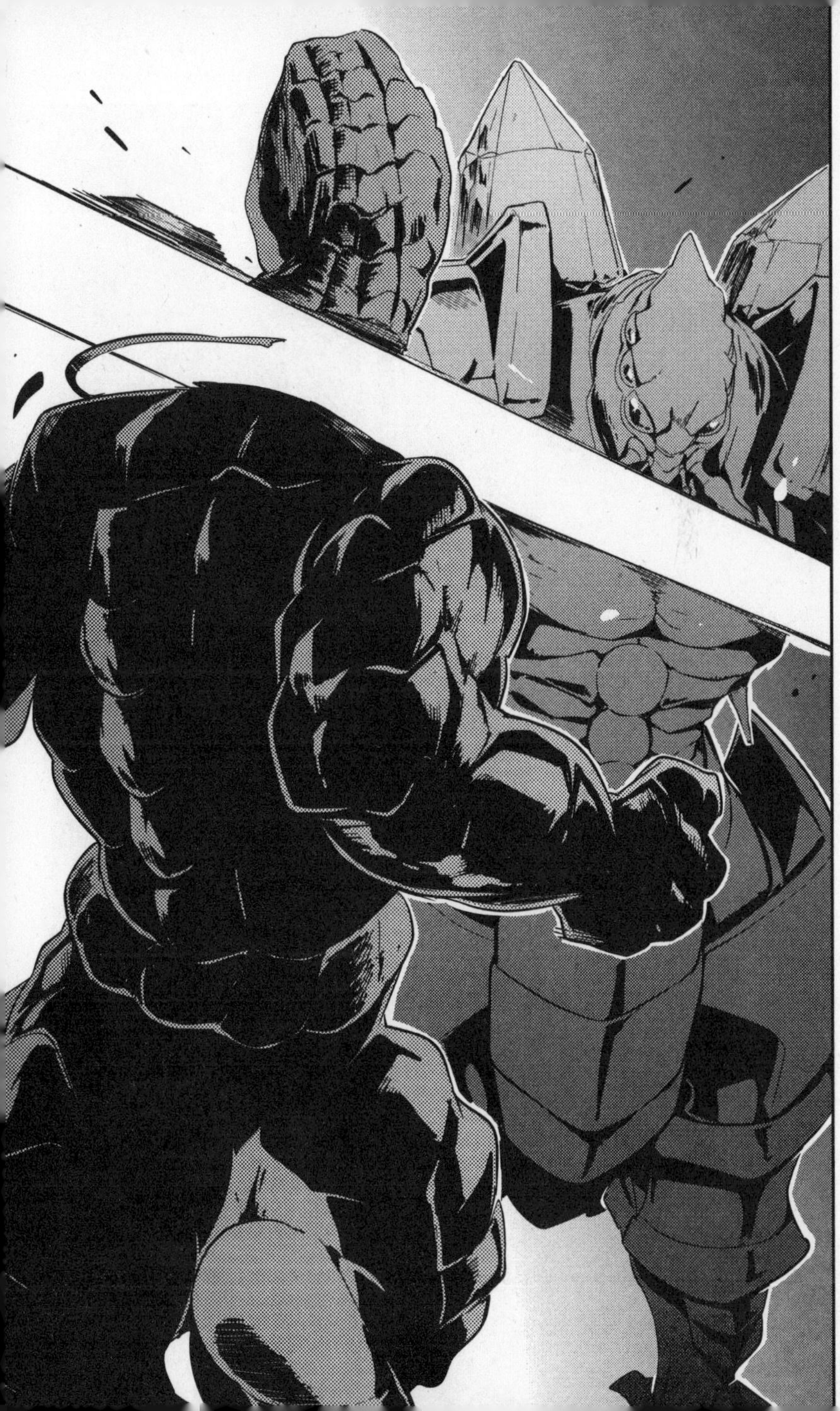

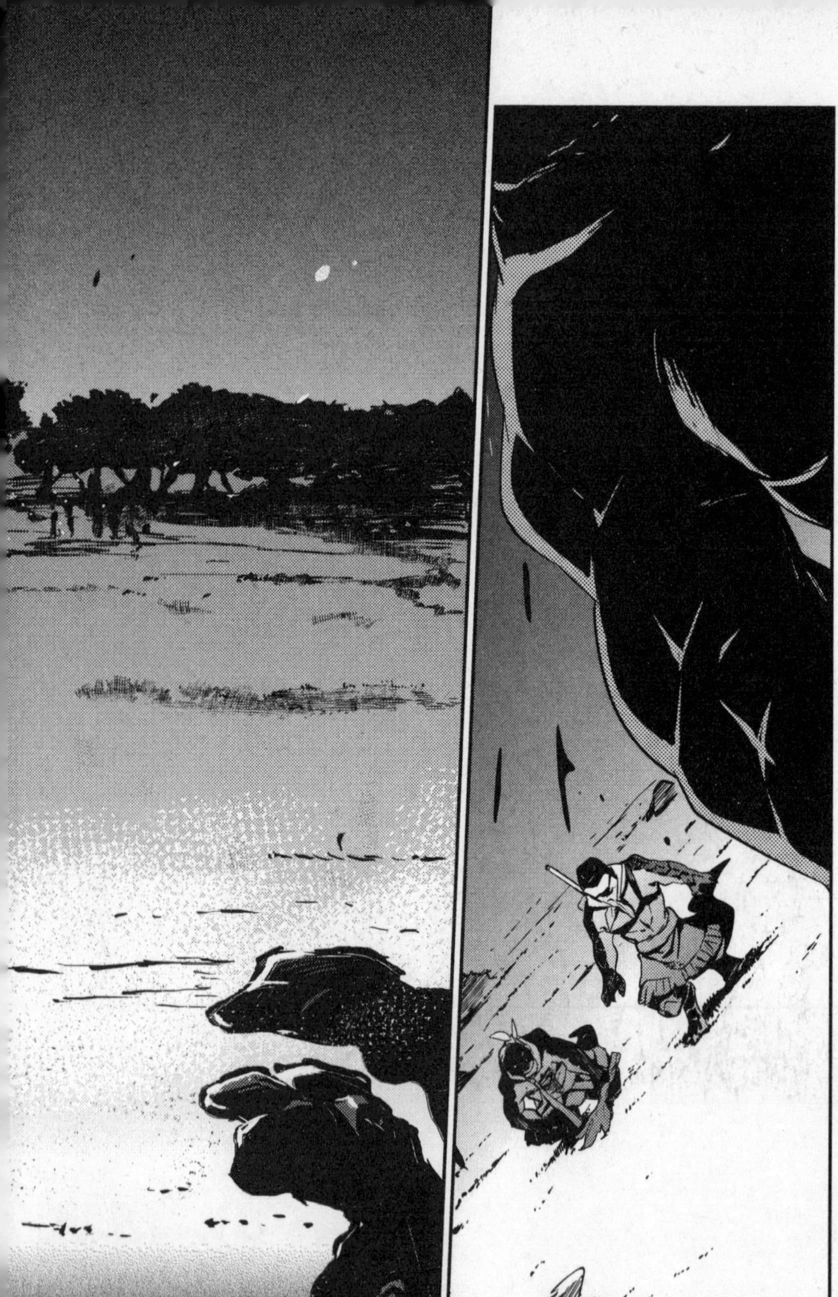

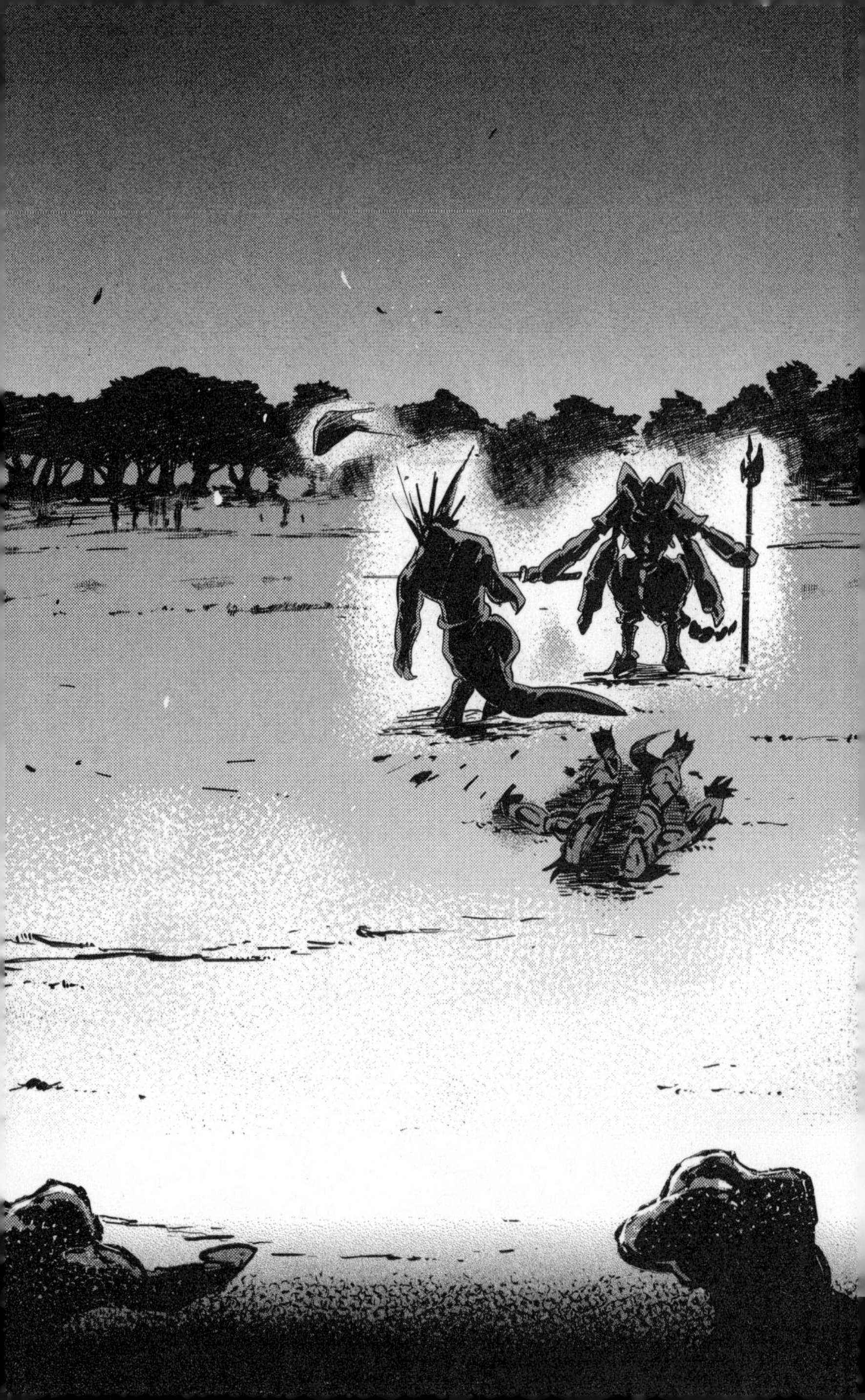

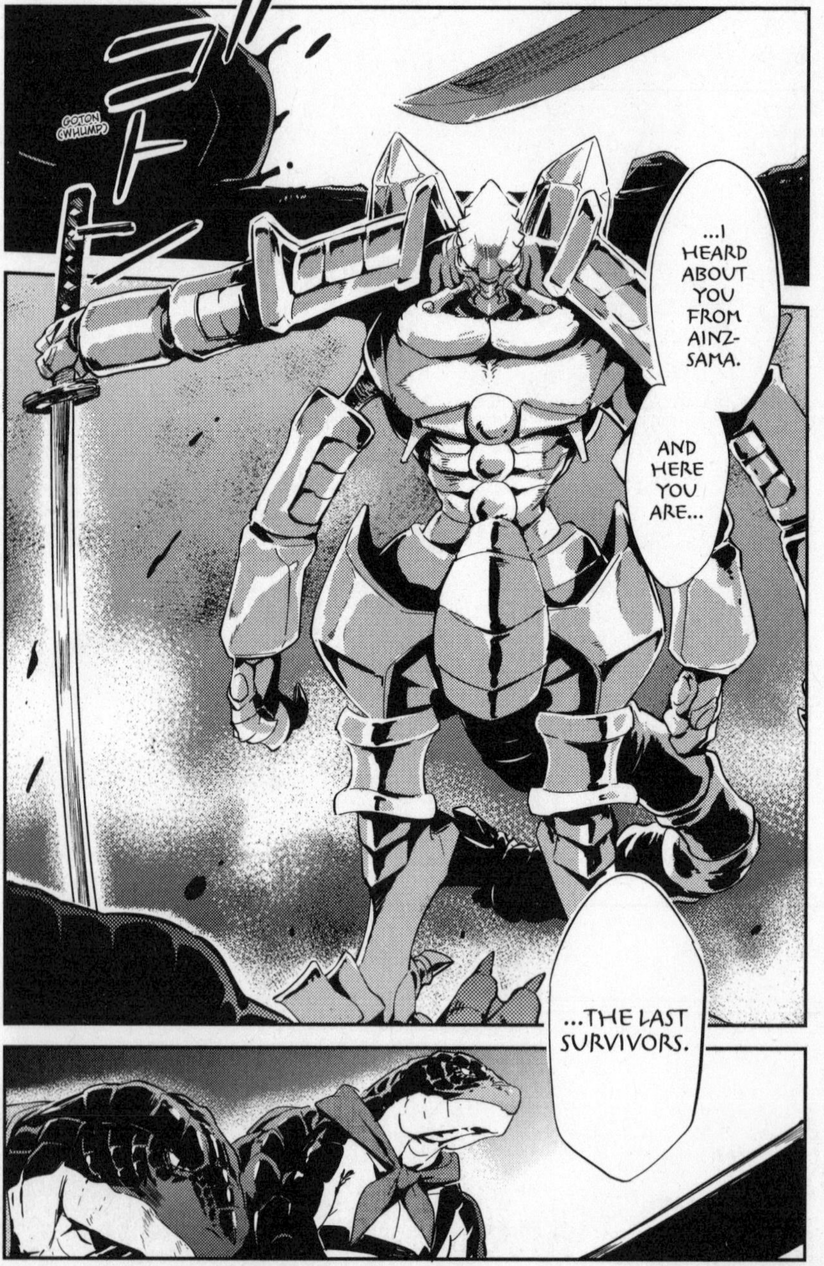
GOTON (WHUMP)
...I HEARD ABOUT YOU FROM AINZ-SAMA.
AND HERE YOU ARE...
...THE LAST SURVIVORS.

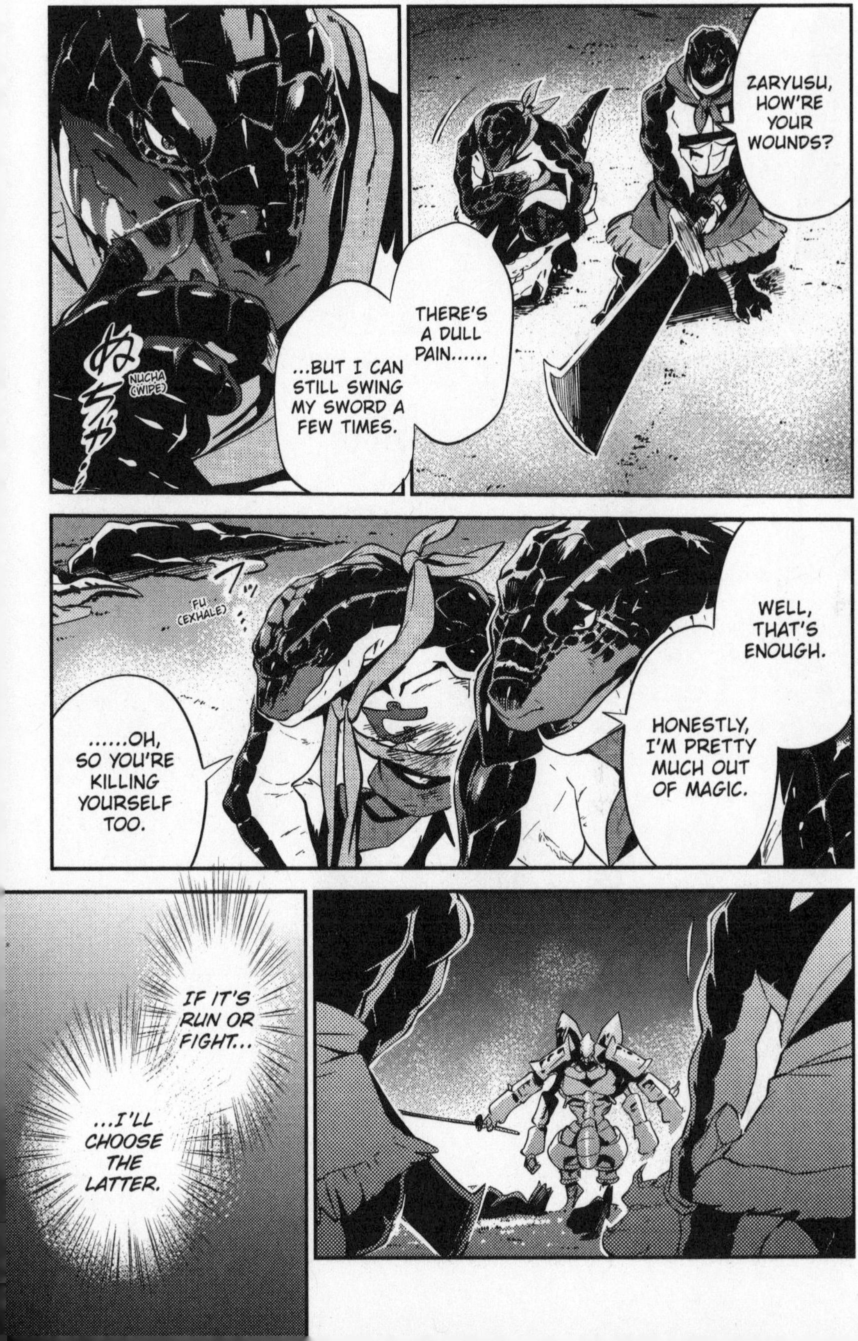
ZARYUSU, HOW'RE YOUR WOUNDS?
THERE'S A DULL PAIN......
...BUT I CAN STILL SWING MY SWORD A FEW TIMES.
NUCHA (WIPE)
WELL, THAT'S ENOUGH.
HONESTLY, I'M PRETTY MUCH OUT OF MAGIC.
FU (EXHALE)
......OH, SO YOU'RE KILLING YOURSELF TOO.
IF IT'S RUN OR FIGHT...
...I'LL CHOOSE THE LATTER.

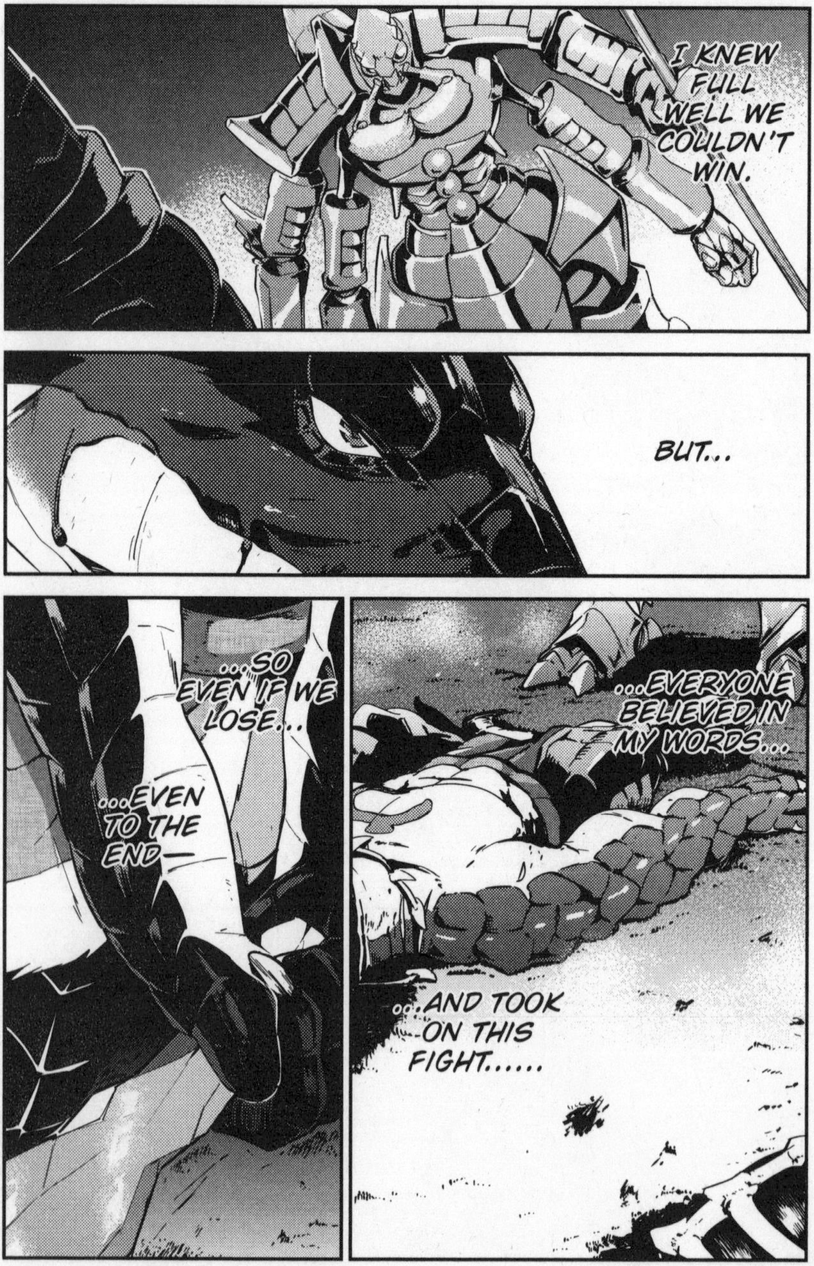
I KNEW FULL WELL WE COULDN'T WIN.
BUT...
...EVERYONE BELIEVED IN MY WORDS...
...AND TOOK ON THIS FIGHT......
...SO EVEN IF WE LOSE...
...EVEN TO THE END—

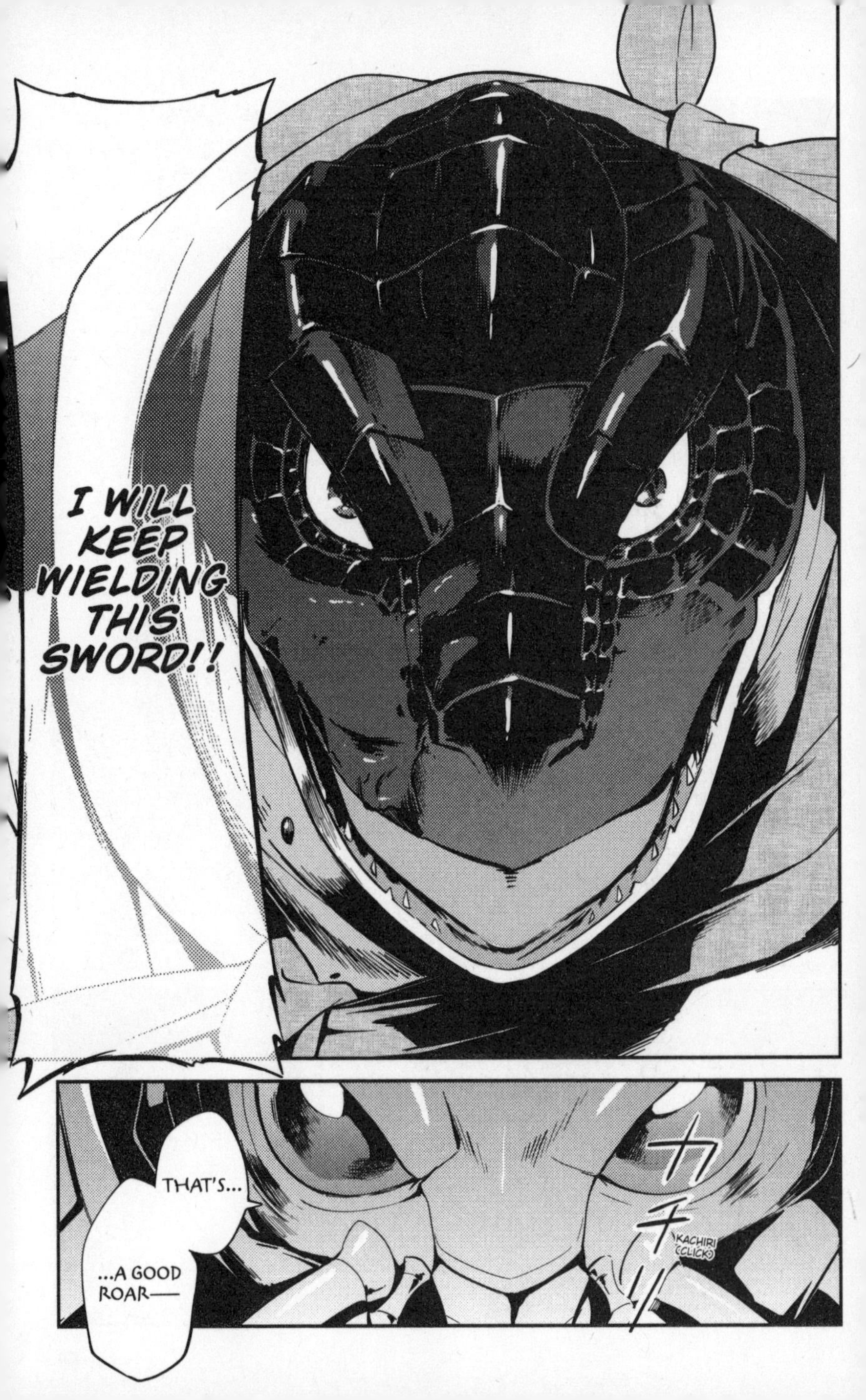
I WILL KEEP WIELDING THIS SWORD!!
THAT'S...
...A GOOD ROAR—
KACHIRI (CLICK)

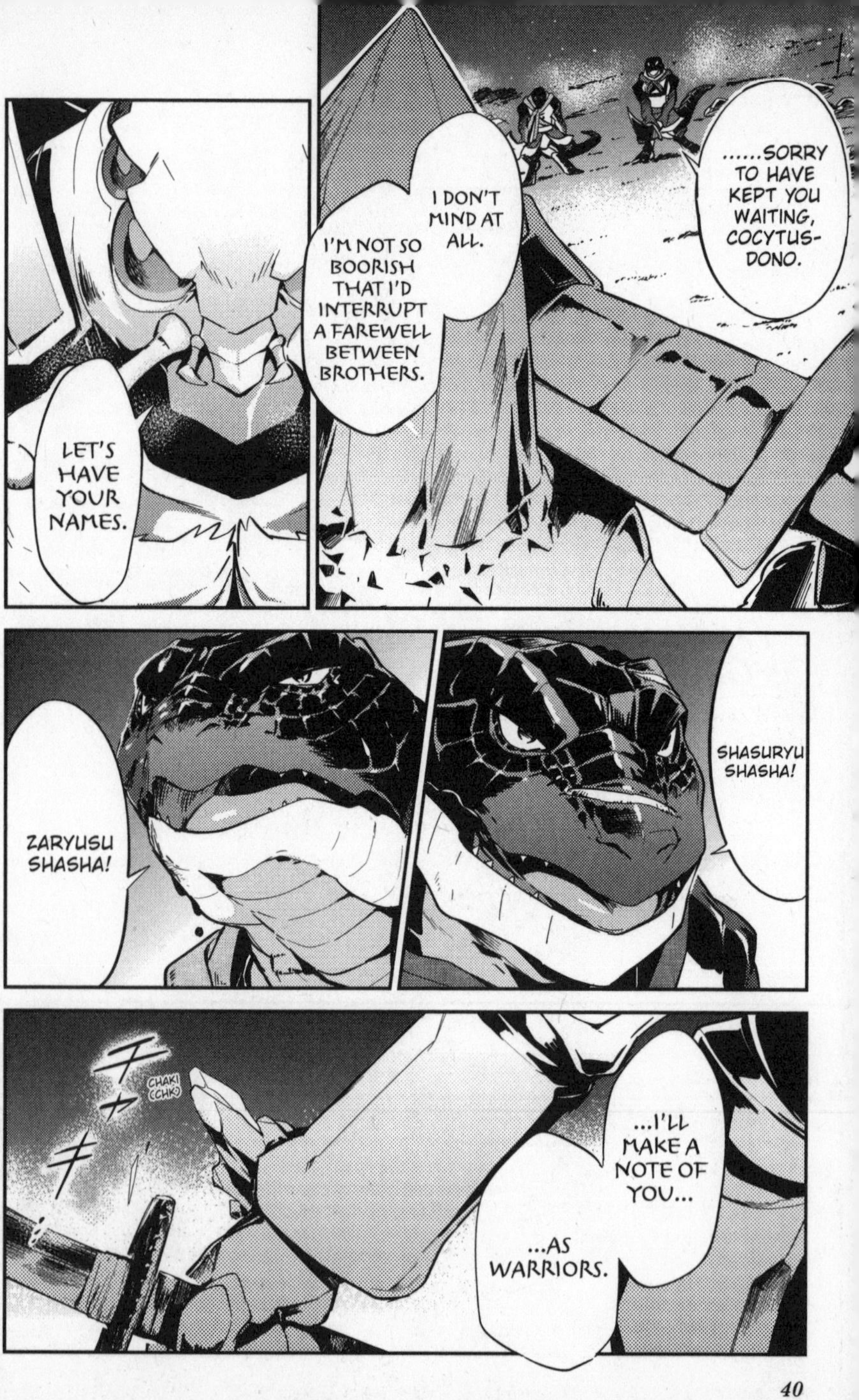
......SORRY TO HAVE KEPT YOU WAITING, COCYTUS-DONO.
I DON'T MIND AT ALL.
I'M NOT SO BOORISH THAT I'D INTERRUPT A FAREWELL BETWEEN BROTHERS.
LET'S HAVE YOUR NAMES.
SHASURYU SHASHA!
ZARYUSU SHASHA!
...I'LL MAKE A NOTE OF YOU...
...AS WARRIORS.
CHAKI (CHK)

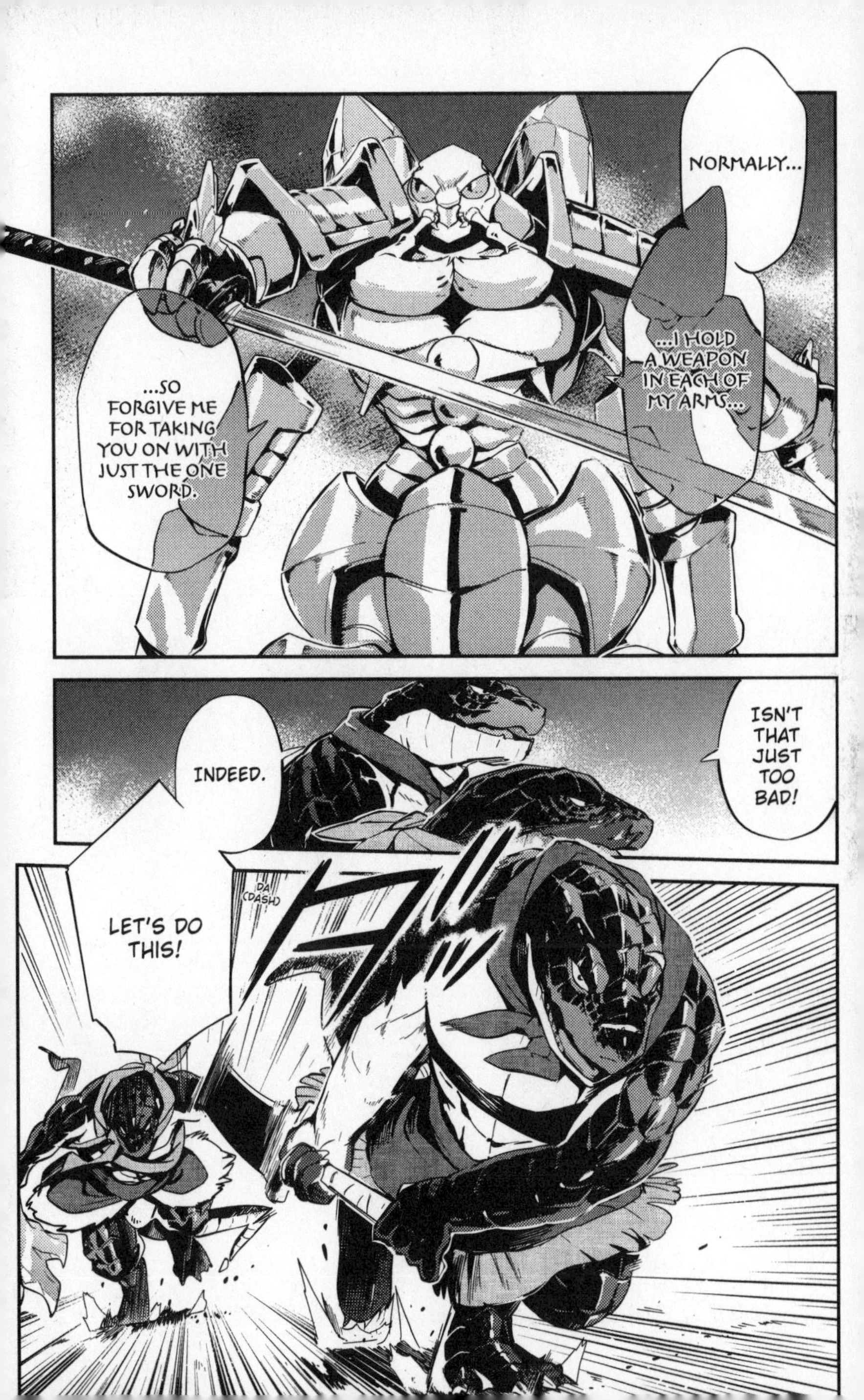
NORMALLY...
...I HOLD A WEAPON IN EACH OF MY ARMS...
...SO FORGIVE ME FOR TAKING YOU ON WITH JUST THE ONE SWORD.
ISN'T THAT JUST TOO BAD!
INDEED.
DA (DASH)
LET'S DO THIS!

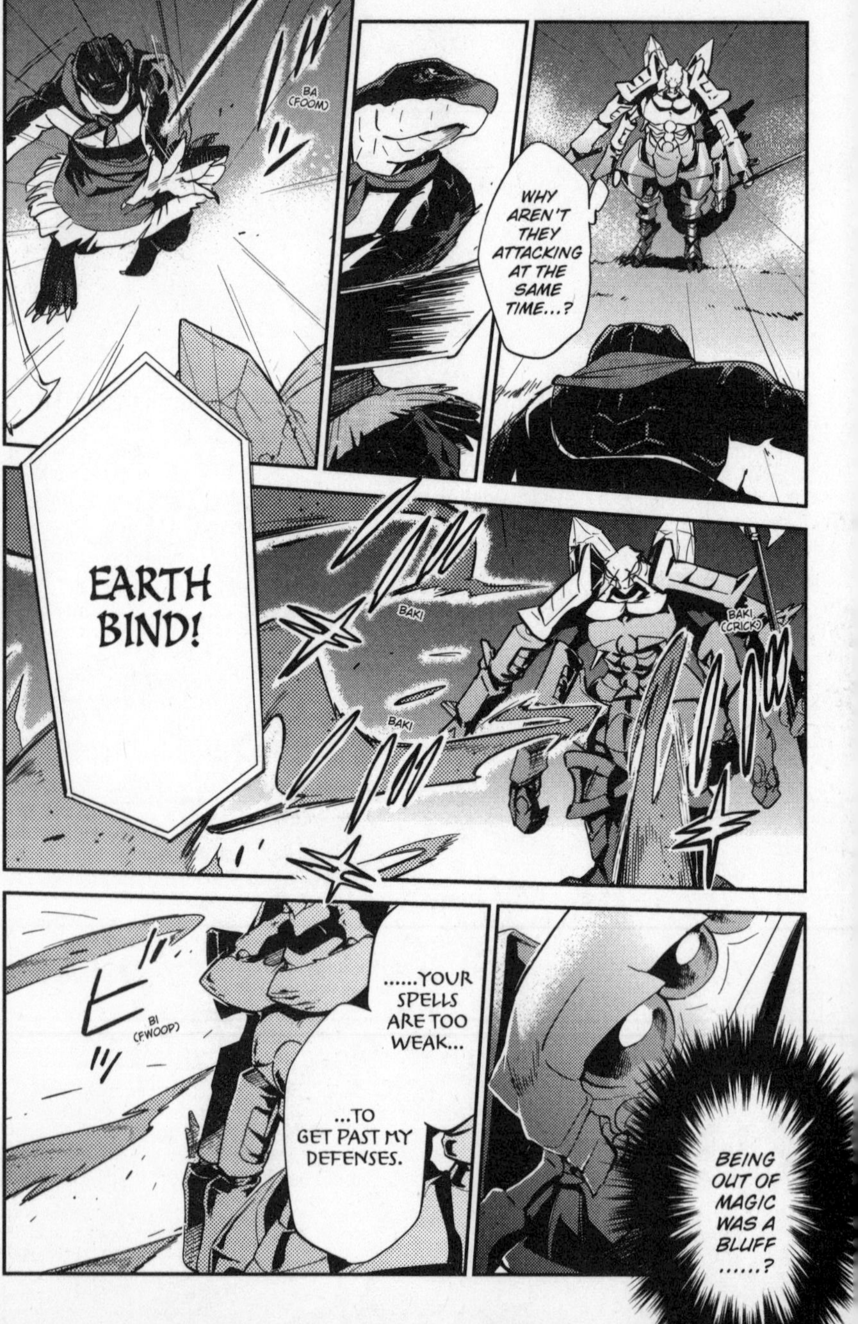
WHY AREN'T THEY ATTACKING AT THE SAME TIME...?
BA (FOOM)
EARTH BIND!
BAKI (CRICK)
BAKI
BAKI
BEING OUT OF MAGIC WAS A BLUFF ......?
......YOUR SPELLS ARE TOO WEAK...
...TO GET PAST MY DEFENSES.
BI (FWOOP)

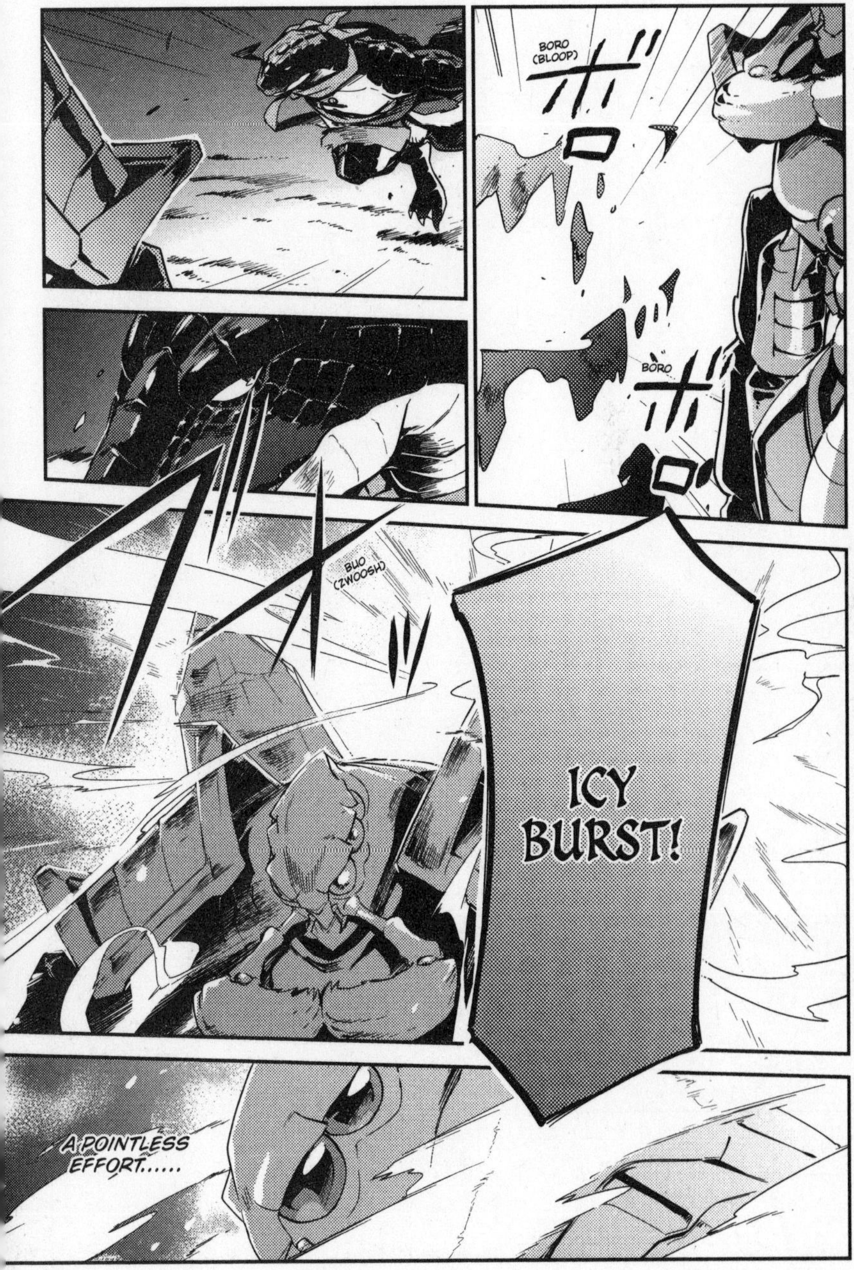
BORO (BLOOP)
BORO
BUO (ZWOOSH)
ICY BURST!
A POINTLESS EFFORT......

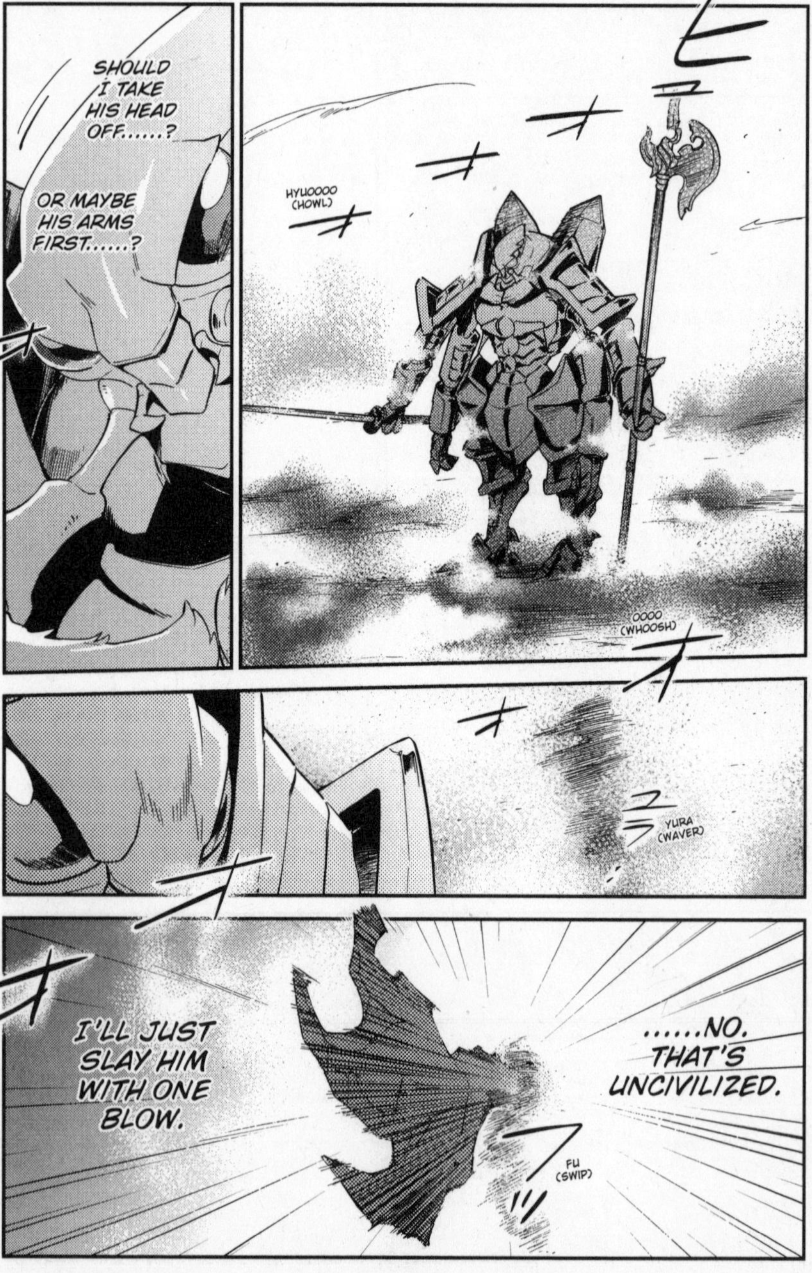
HYUOOOO (HOWL)
OOOO (WHOOSH)
SHOULD I TAKE HIS HEAD OFF......?
OR MAYBE HIS ARMS FIRST......?
YURA (WAVER)
......NO. THAT'S UNCIVILIZED.
FU (SWIP)
I'LL JUST SLAY HIM WITH ONE BLOW.

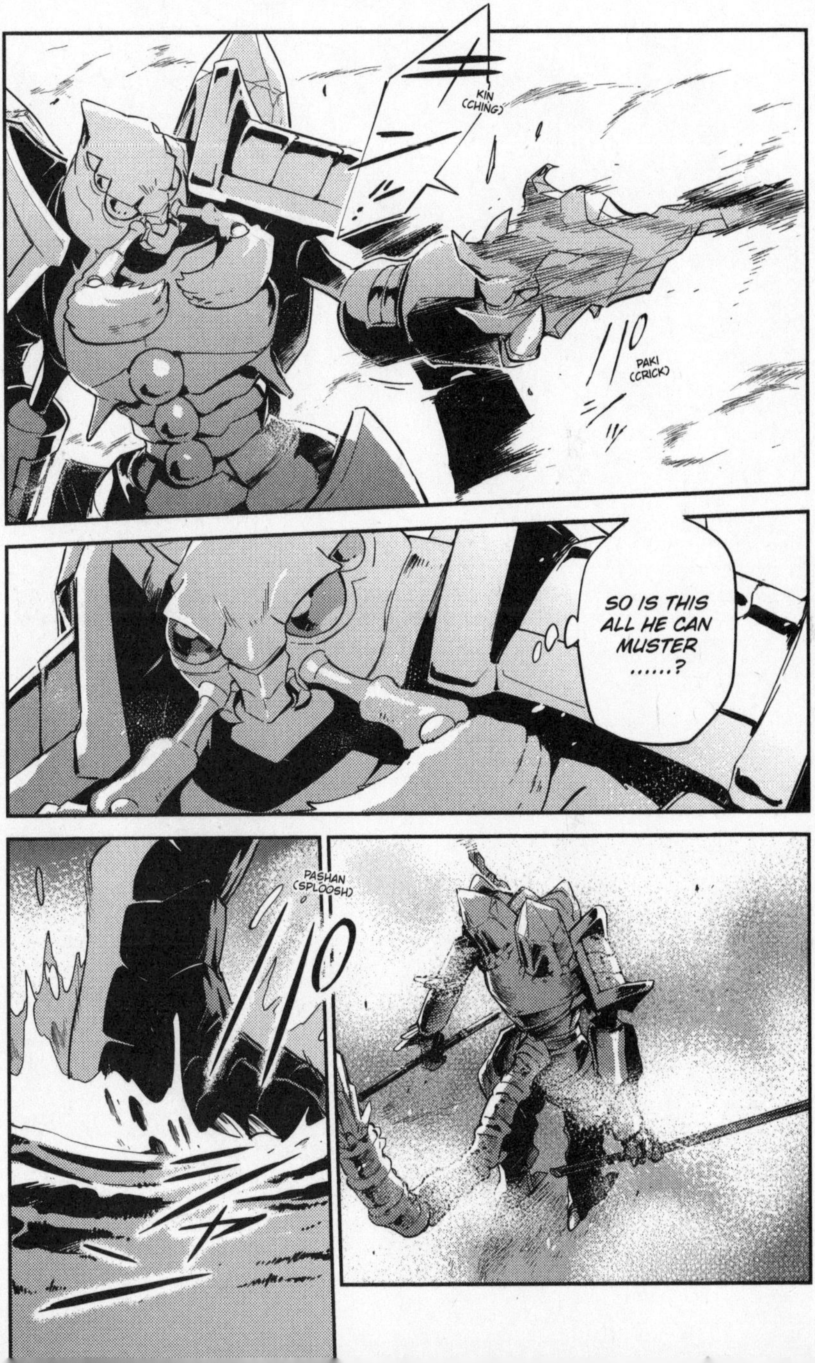
KIN (CHING)
PAKI (CRICK)
SO IS THIS ALL HE CAN MUSTER ......?
PASHAN (SPLOOSH)

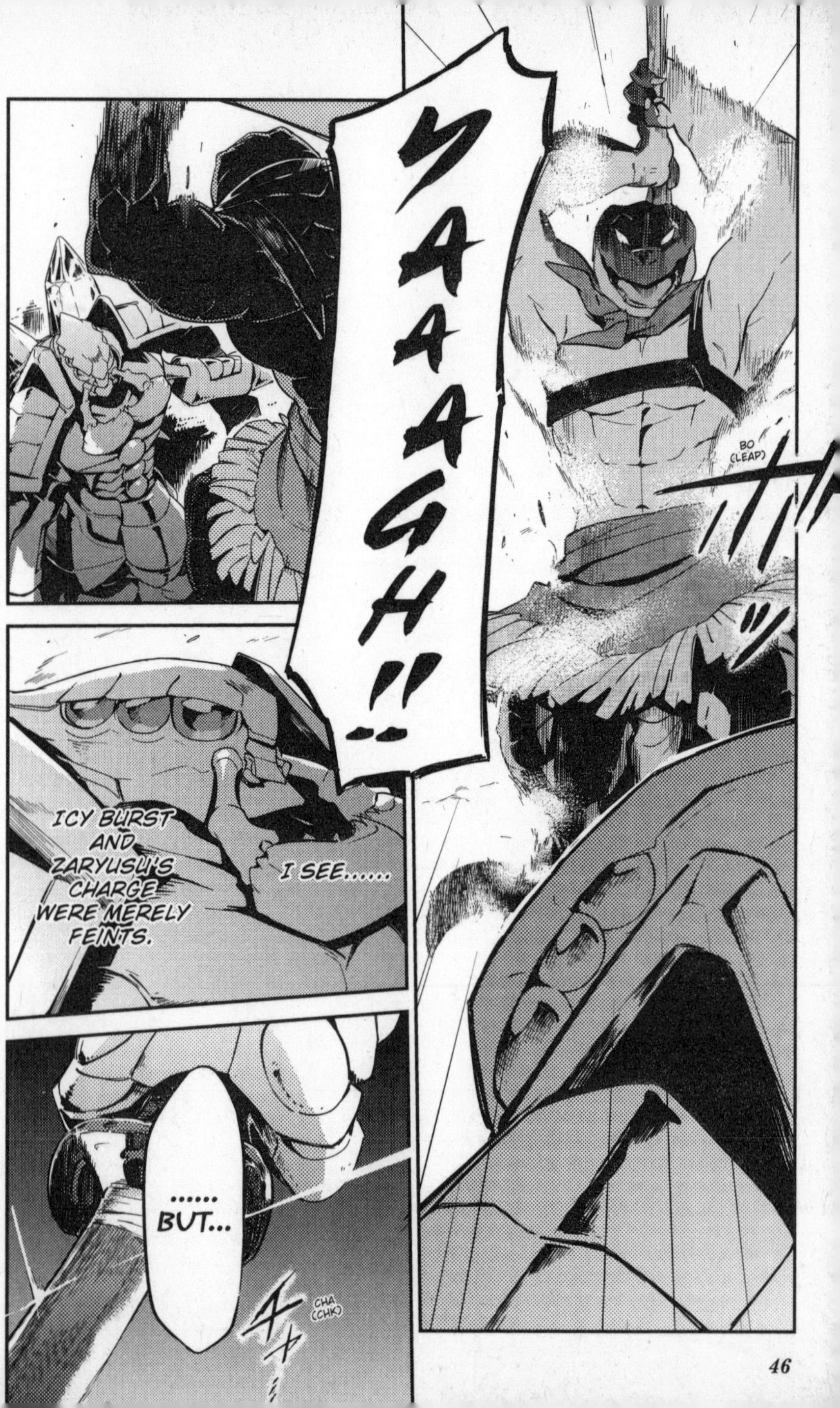
YAAAGH!!
BO (LEAP)
I SEE......
ICY BURST AND ZARYUSU'S CHARGE WERE MERELY FEINTS.
...... BUT...
CHA (CHK)

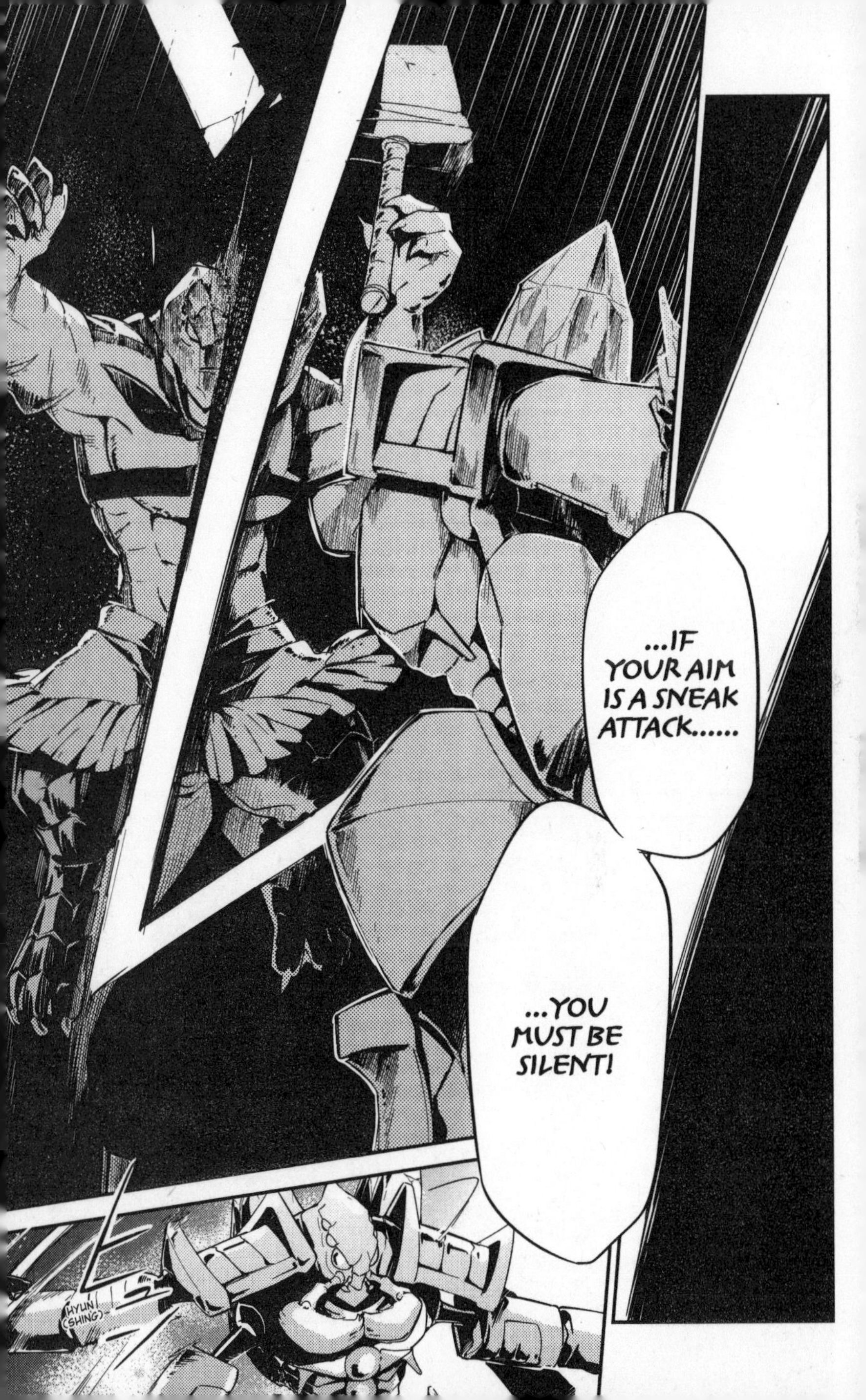
...IF YOUR AIM IS A SNEAK ATTACK......
...YOU MUST BE SILENT!
HYUN (SHING)

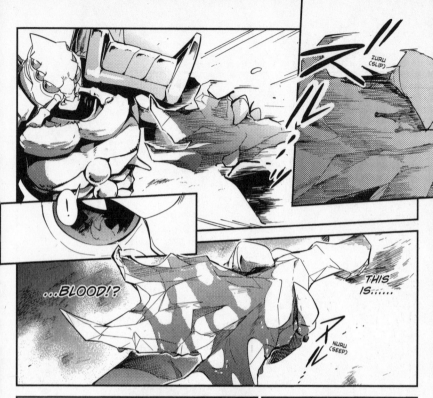

ZURU
(SLIP)

...BLOOD!?

THIS IS......

NURU
(SEEP)

HE MADE HIS EARLIER ATTACK LIGHTER...

GUGU
(SHOVE)

...SO I'D THINK IT'D BE EASY TO CATCH THE SWORD......!

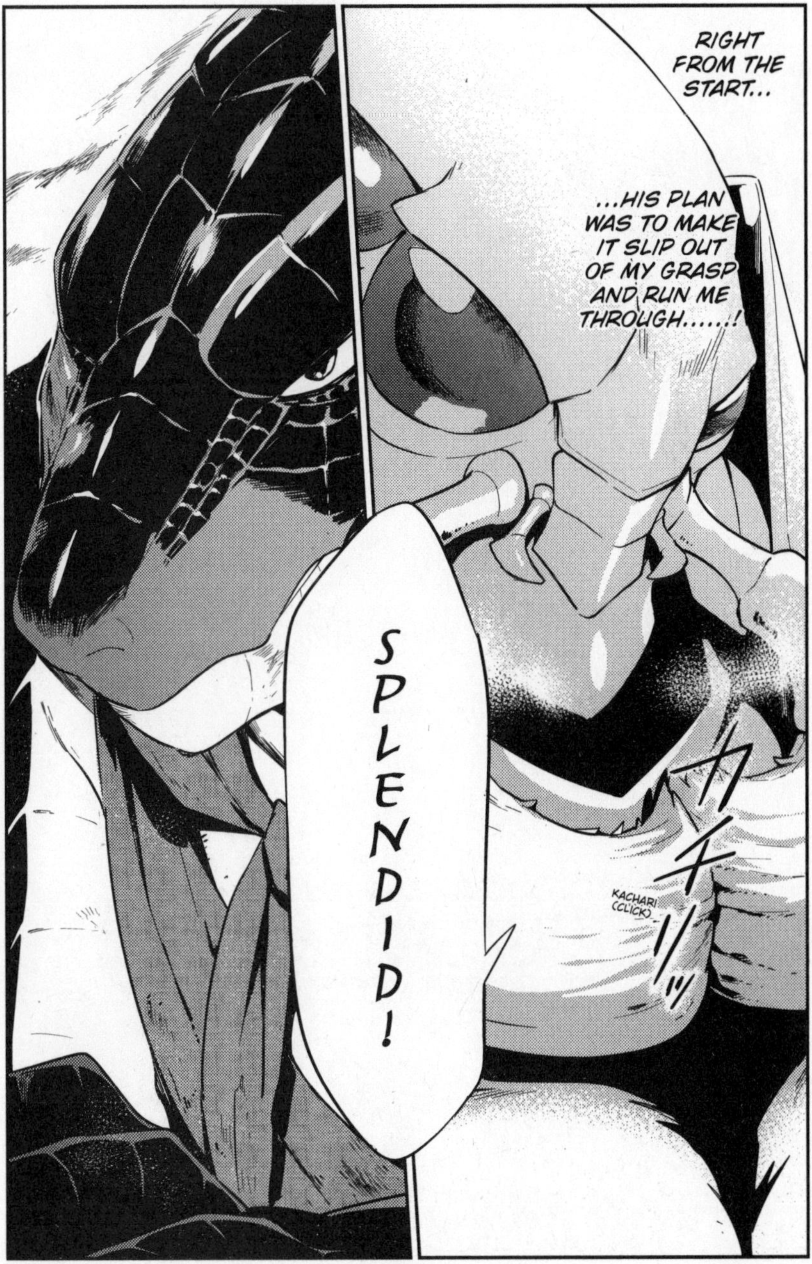
RIGHT FROM THE START...
...HIS PLAN WAS TO MAKE IT SLIP OUT OF MY GRASP AND RUN ME THROUGH......!
SPLENDID!
KACHARI (CLICK)

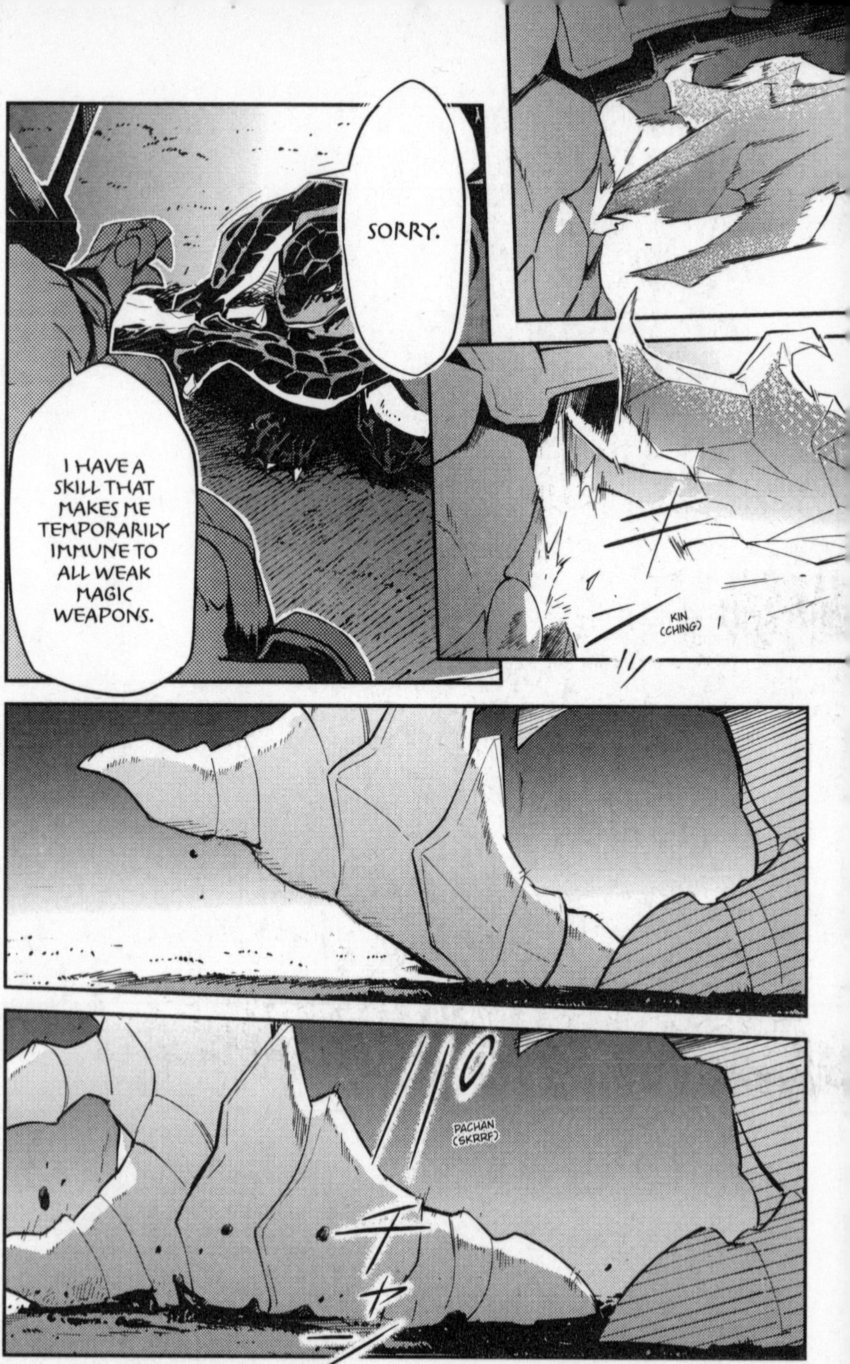
KIN
(CHING)
SORRY.
I HAVE A SKILL THAT MAKES ME TEMPORARILY IMMUNE TO ALL WEAK MAGIC WEAPONS.
PACHAN
(SKRRF)

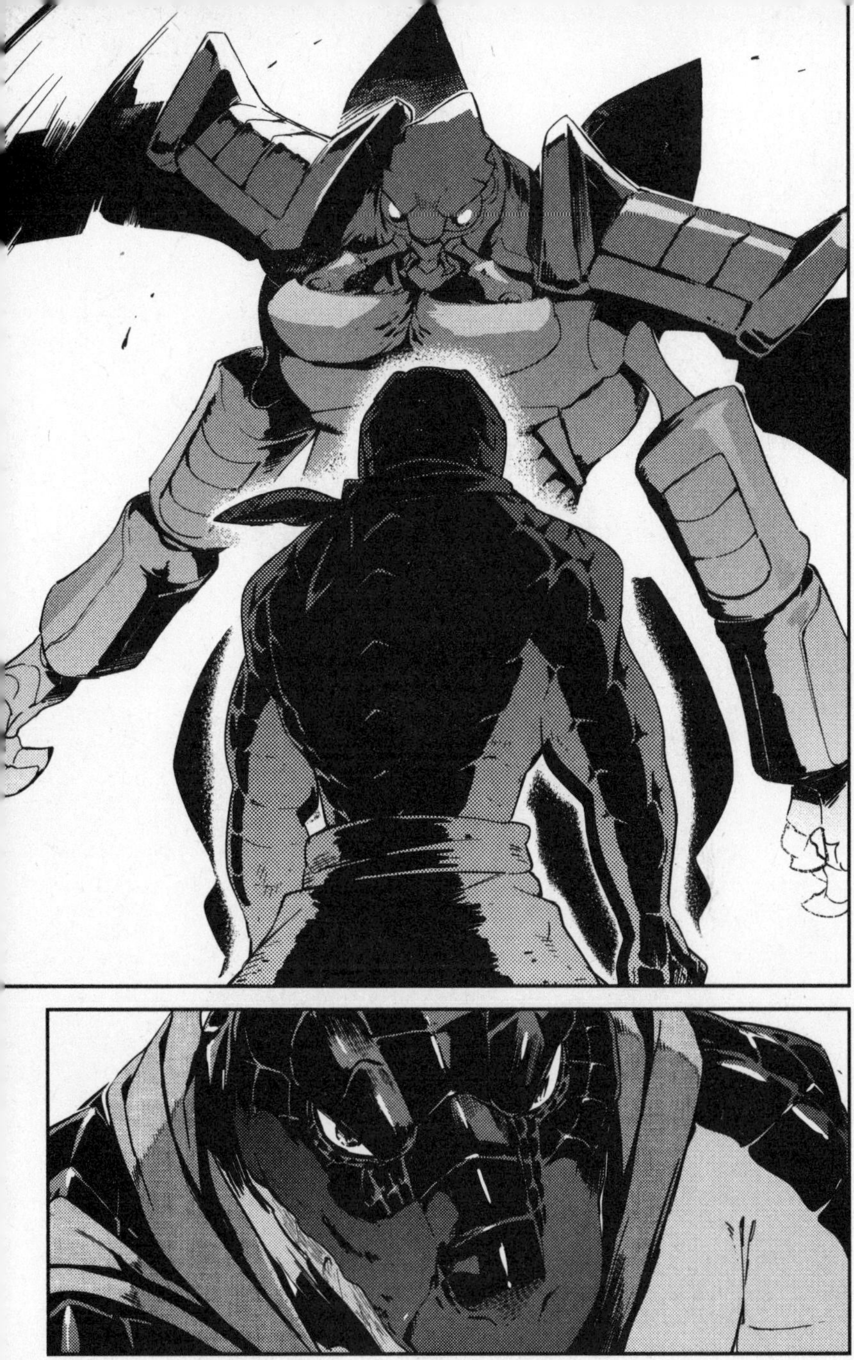

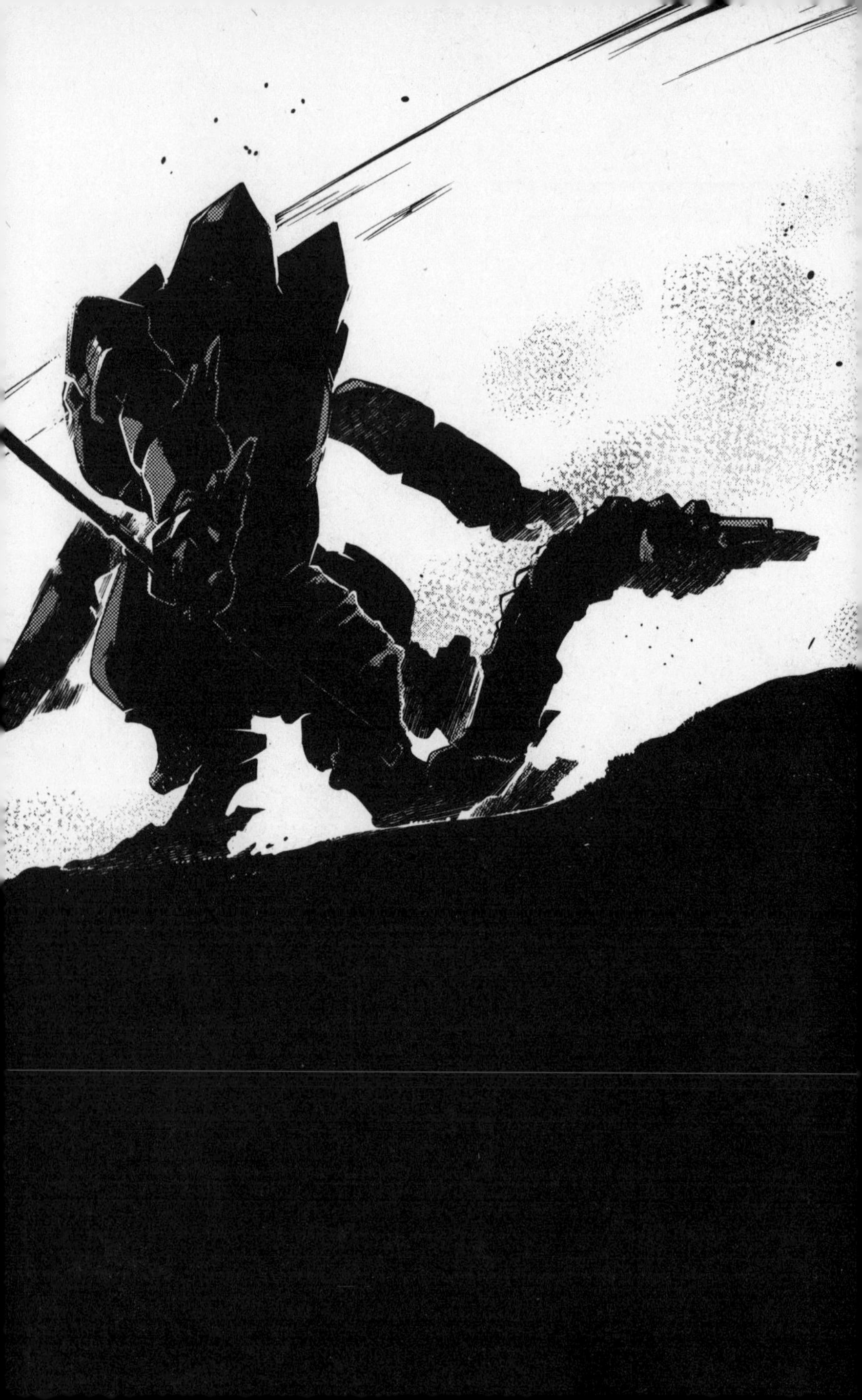

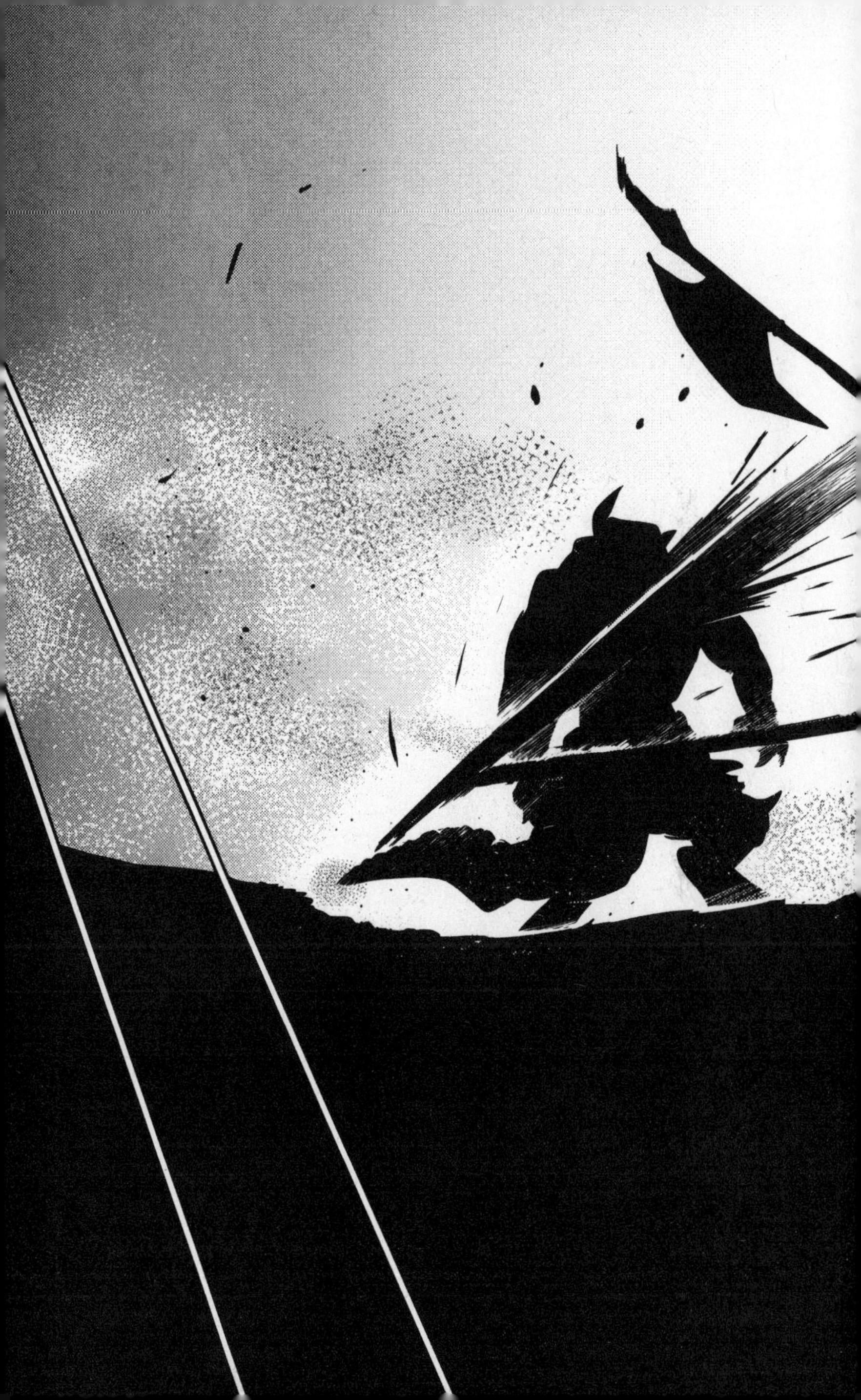

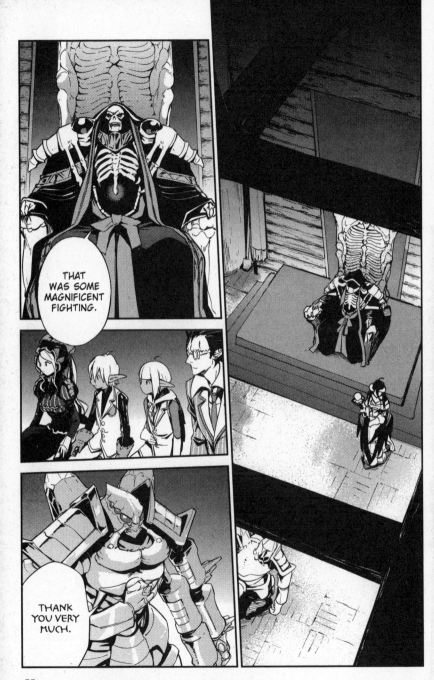

THAT WAS SOME MAGNIFICENT FIGHTING.

THANK YOU VERY MUCH.

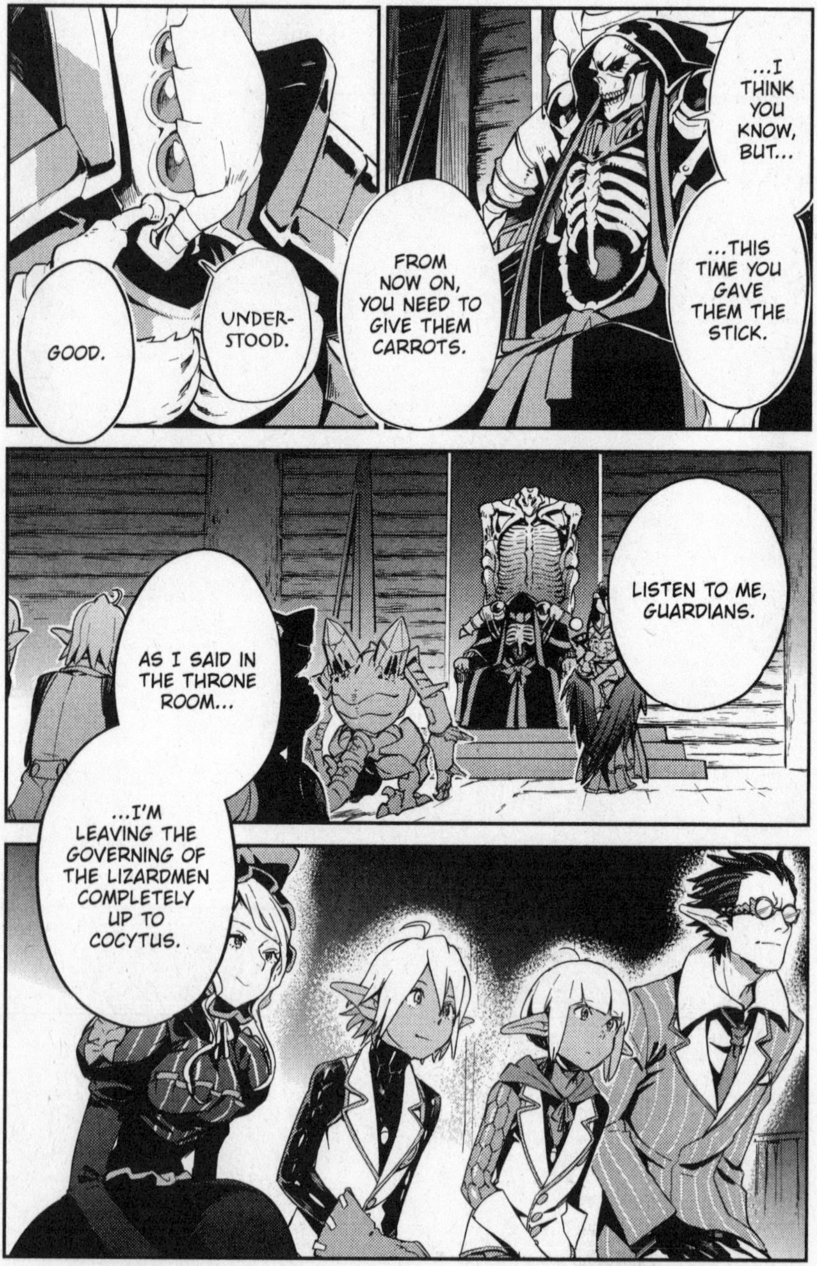
...I THINK YOU KNOW, BUT...
...THIS TIME YOU GAVE THEM THE STICK.
FROM NOW ON, YOU NEED TO GIVE THEM CARROTS.
UNDER-STOOD.
GOOD.
LISTEN TO ME, GUARDIANS.
AS I SAID IN THE THRONE ROOM...
...I'M LEAVING THE GOVERNING OF THE LIZARDMEN COMPLETELY UP TO COCYTUS.

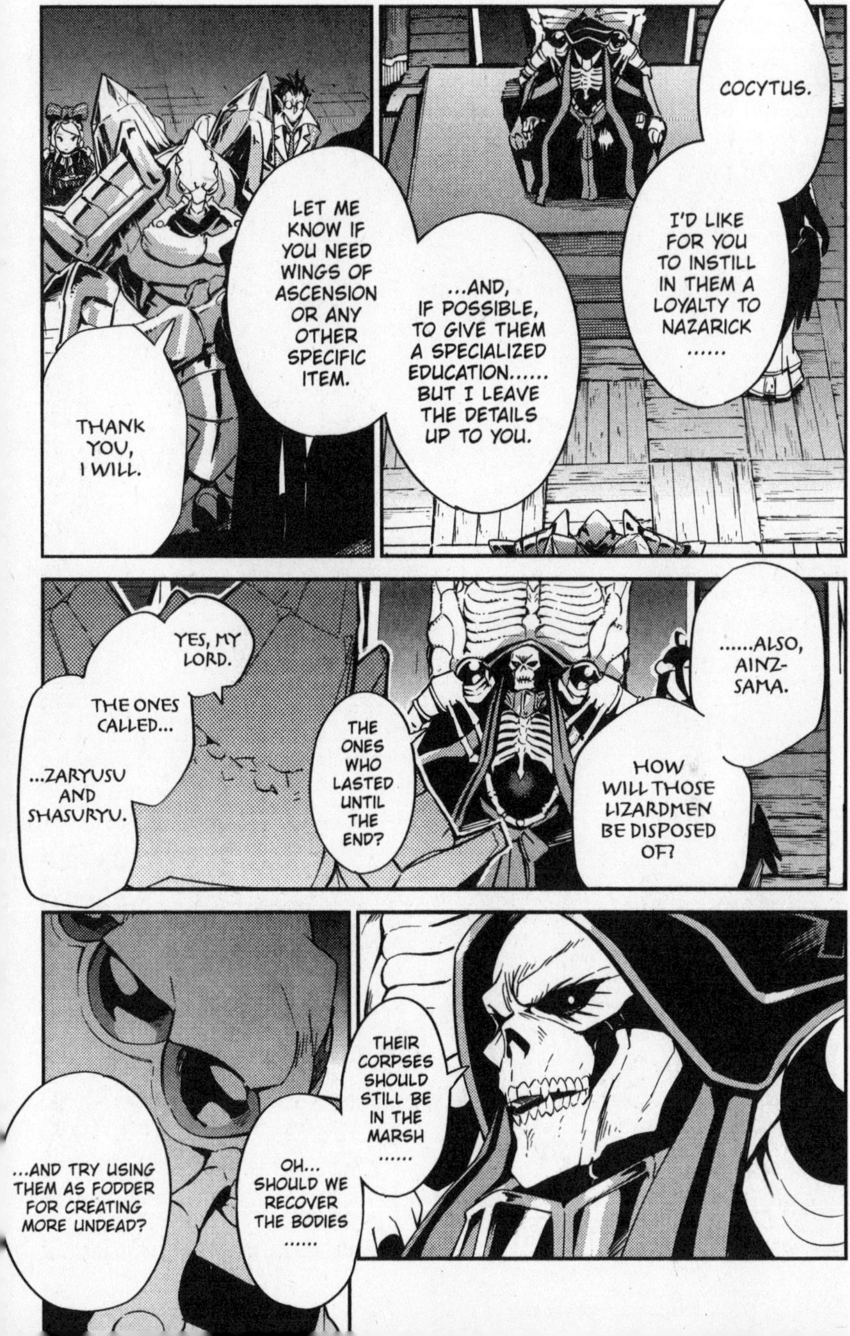
COCYTUS.
I'D LIKE FOR YOU TO INSTILL IN THEM A LOYALTY TO NAZARICK ......
...AND, IF POSSIBLE, TO GIVE THEM A SPECIALIZED EDUCATION...... BUT I LEAVE THE DETAILS UP TO YOU.
LET ME KNOW IF YOU NEED WINGS OF ASCENSION OR ANY OTHER SPECIFIC ITEM.
THANK YOU, I WILL.
......ALSO, AINZ-SAMA.
HOW WILL THOSE LIZARDMEN BE DISPOSED OF?
THE ONES WHO LASTED UNTIL THE END?
YES, MY LORD.
THE ONES CALLED...
...ZARYUSU AND SHASURYU.
THEIR CORPSES SHOULD STILL BE IN THE MARSH ......
OH... SHOULD WE RECOVER THE BODIES ......
...AND TRY USING THEM AS FODDER FOR CREATING MORE UNDEAD?

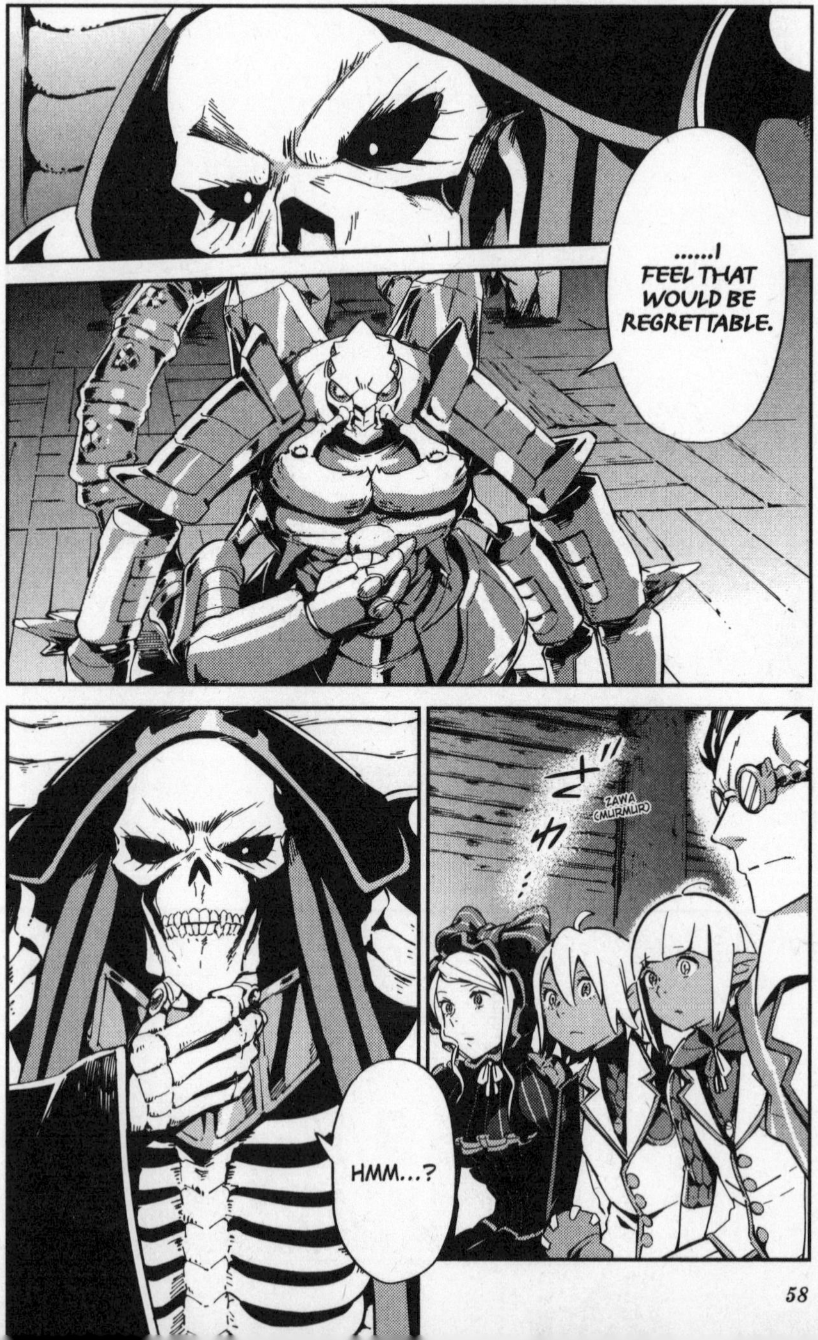
......I FEEL THAT WOULD BE REGRETTABLE.
ZAWA (MURMUR)
HMM...?

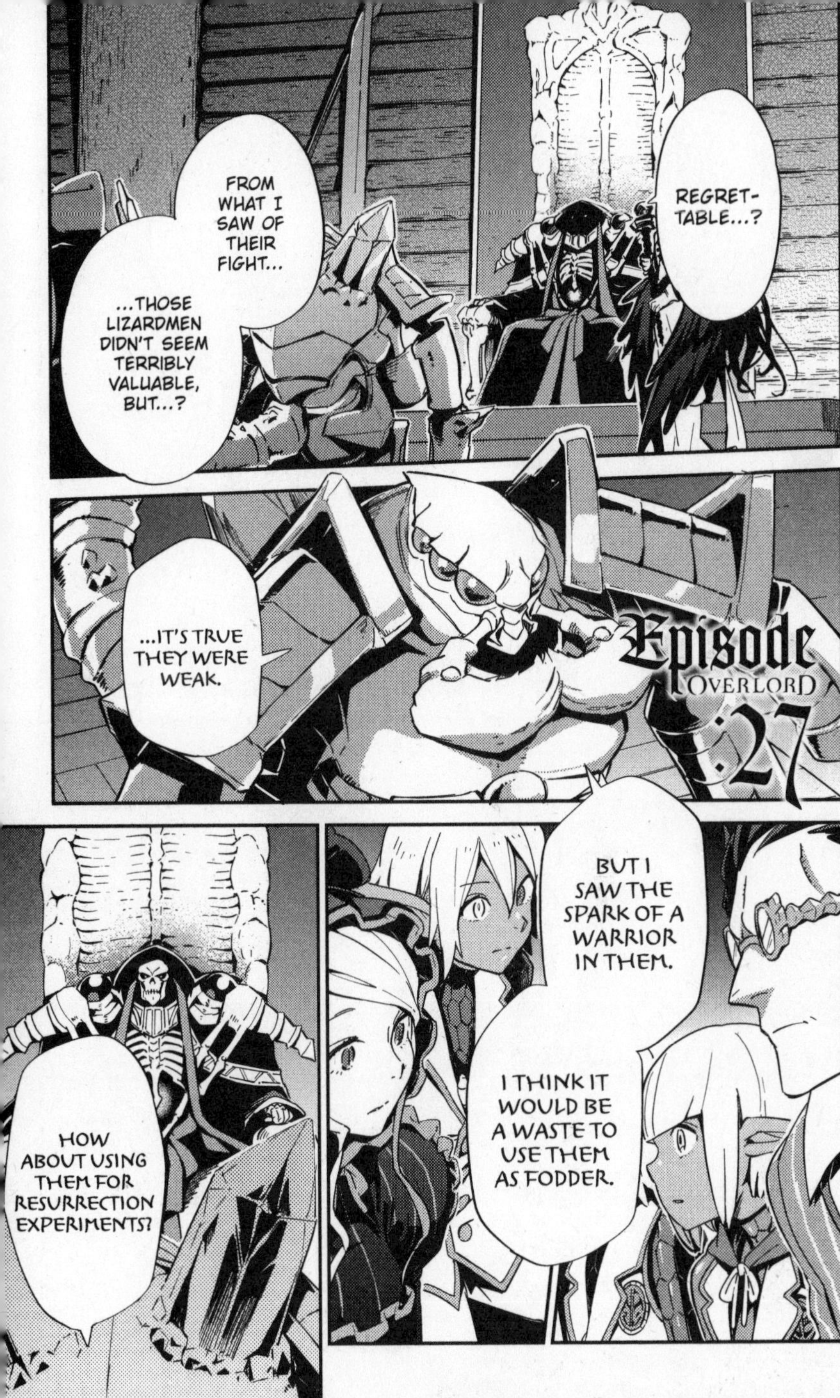
REGRET-TABLE...?
FROM WHAT I SAW OF THEIR FIGHT...
...THOSE LIZARDMEN DIDN'T SEEM TERRIBLY VALUABLE, BUT...?
Episode
OVERLORD
:27
...IT'S TRUE THEY WERE WEAK.
BUT I SAW THE SPARK OF A WARRIOR IN THEM.
I THINK IT WOULD BE A WASTE TO USE THEM AS FODDER.
HOW ABOUT USING THEM FOR RESURRECTION EXPERIMENTS?

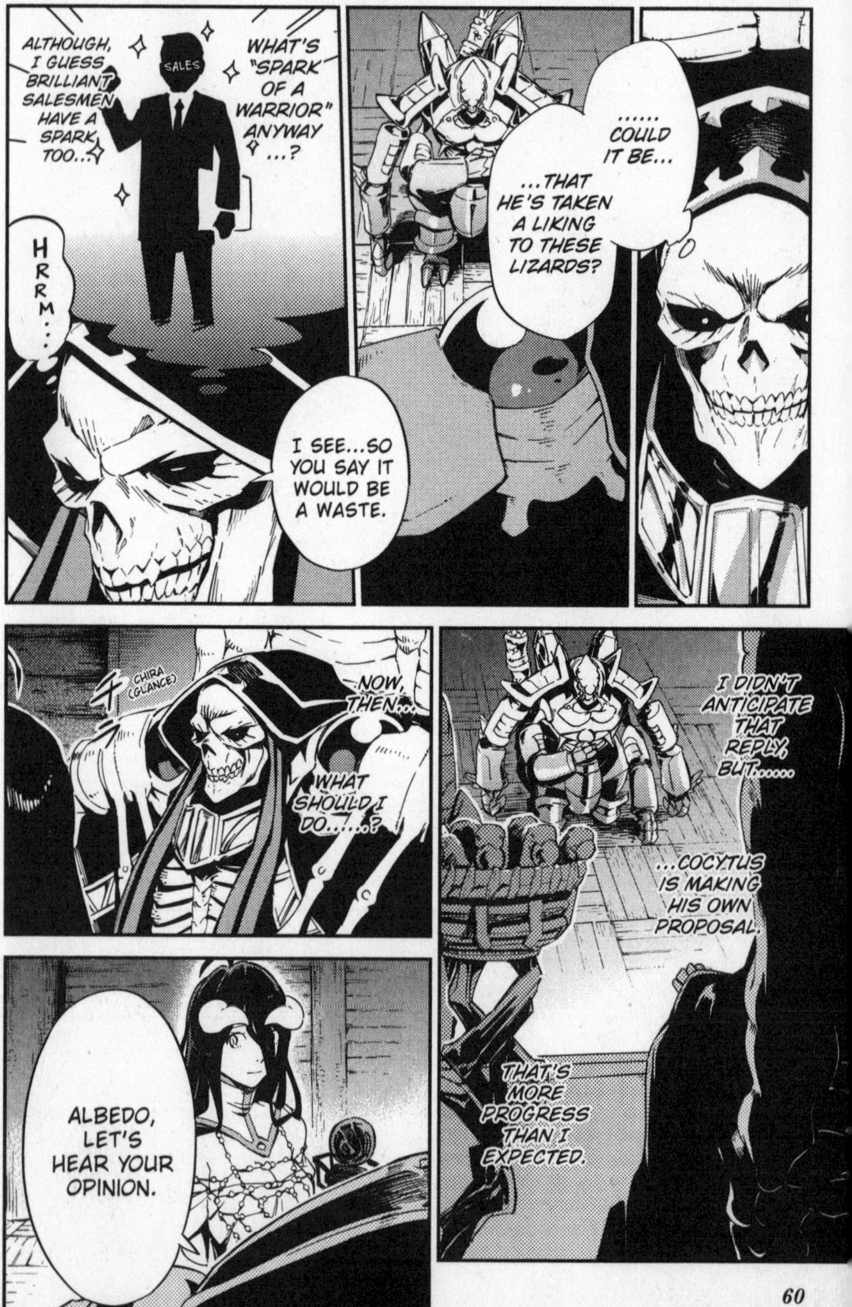
......COULD IT BE...
...THAT HE'S TAKEN A LIKING TO THESE LIZARDS?
I SEE...SO YOU SAY IT WOULD BE A WASTE.
WHAT'S "SPARK OF A WARRIOR" ANYWAY...?
SALES
ALTHOUGH, I GUESS BRILLIANT SALESMEN HAVE A SPARK TOO...
HRRM...
I DIDN'T ANTICIPATE THAT REPLY, BUT......
...COCYTUS IS MAKING HIS OWN PROPOSAL.
THAT'S MORE PROGRESS THAN I EXPECTED.
NOW, THEN...
CHIRA (GLANCE)
WHAT SHOULD I DO......?
ALBEDO, LET'S HEAR YOUR OPINION.

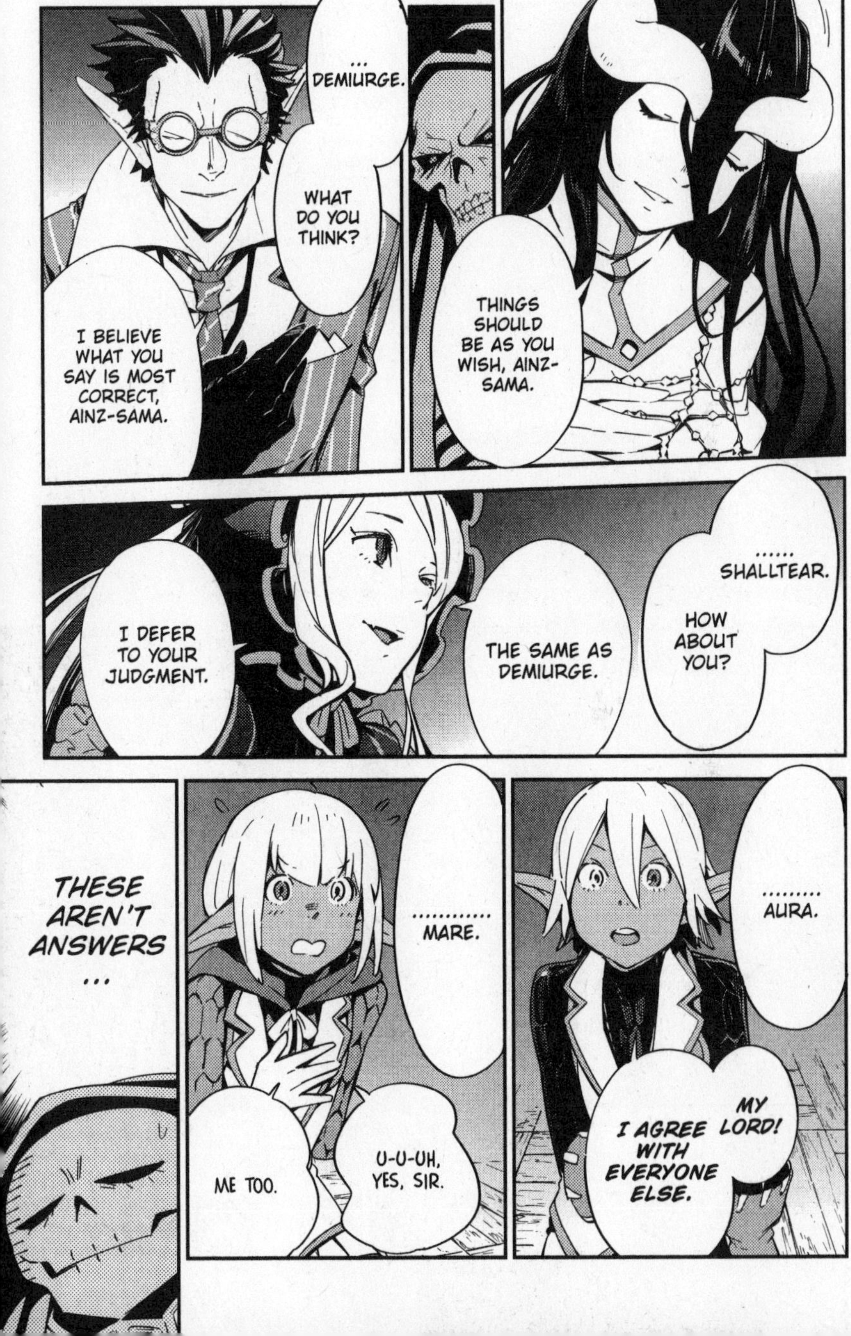
THINGS SHOULD BE AS YOU WISH, AINZ-SAMA.
... DEMIURGE.
WHAT DO YOU THINK?
I BELIEVE WHAT YOU SAY IS MOST CORRECT, AINZ-SAMA.
...... SHALLTEAR.
HOW ABOUT YOU?
THE SAME AS DEMIURGE.
I DEFER TO YOUR JUDGMENT.
.... AURA.
MY LORD!
I AGREE WITH EVERYONE ELSE.
.... MARE.
U-U-UH, YES, SIR.
ME TOO.
THESE AREN'T ANSWERS ...

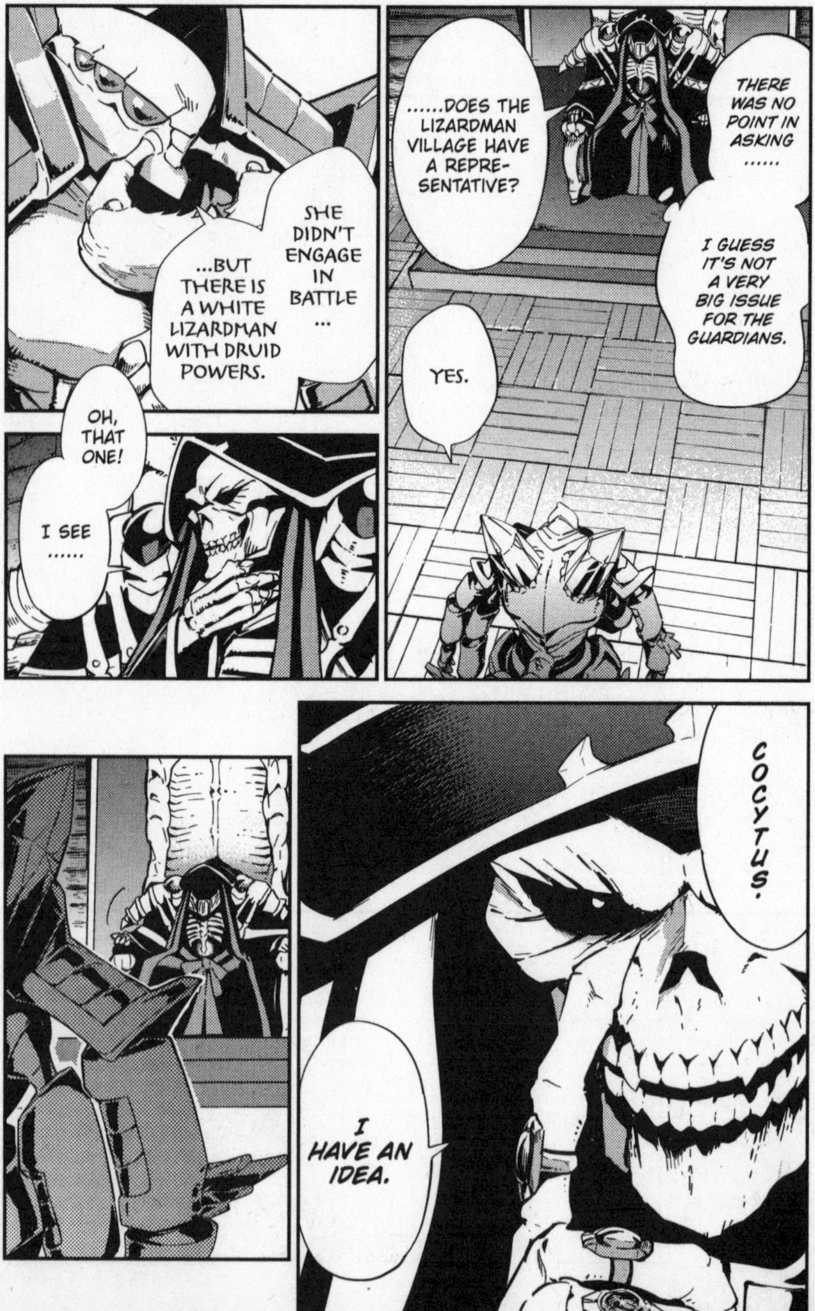
THERE WAS NO POINT IN ASKING......
......DOES THE LIZARDMAN VILLAGE HAVE A REPRESENTATIVE?
I GUESS IT'S NOT A VERY BIG ISSUE FOR THE GUARDIANS.
YES.
SHE DIDN'T ENGAGE IN BATTLE...
...BUT THERE IS A WHITE LIZARDMAN WITH DRUID POWERS.
OH, THAT ONE!
I SEE......
COCYTUS.
I HAVE AN IDEA.

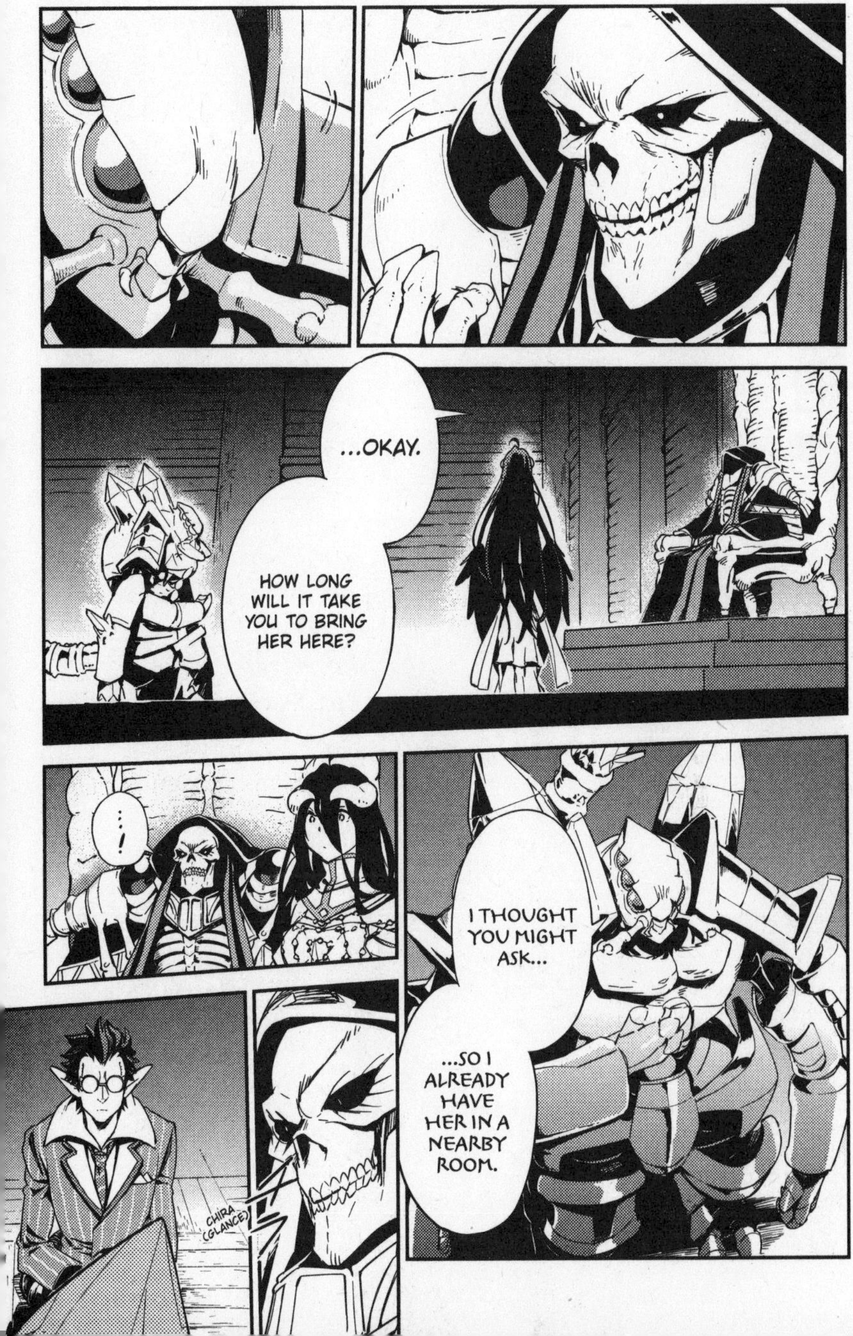
...OKAY.
HOW LONG WILL IT TAKE YOU TO BRING HER HERE?
I THOUGHT YOU MIGHT ASK...
...SO I ALREADY HAVE HER IN A NEARBY ROOM.
...!
CHIRA (GLANCE)

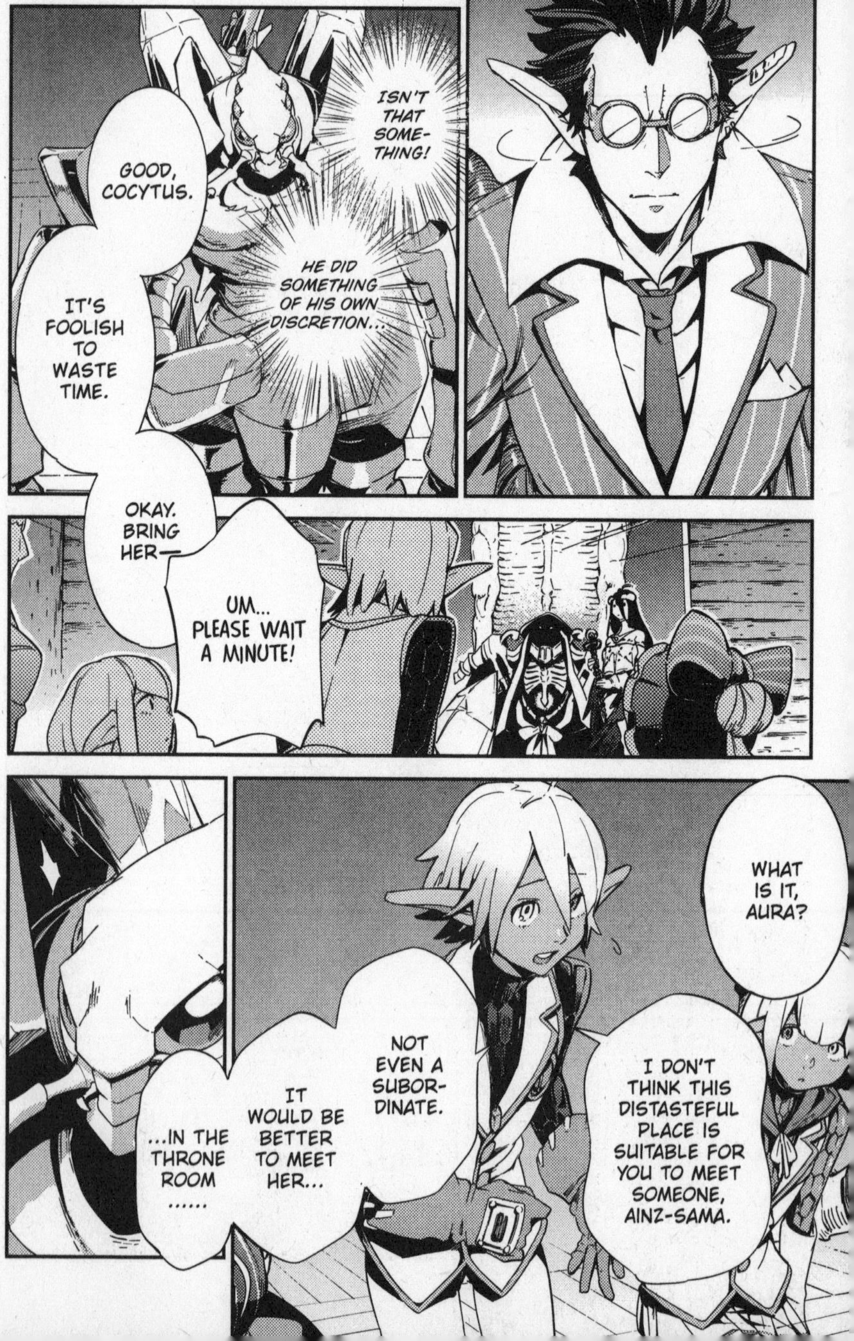
ISN'T THAT SOMETHING!
HE DID SOMETHING OF HIS OWN DISCRETION...
GOOD, COCYTUS.
IT'S FOOLISH TO WASTE TIME.
OKAY. BRING HER—
UM... PLEASE WAIT A MINUTE!
WHAT IS IT, AURA?
I DON'T THINK THIS DISTASTEFUL PLACE IS SUITABLE FOR YOU TO MEET SOMEONE, AINZ-SAMA.
NOT EVEN A SUBORDINATE.
IT WOULD BE BETTER TO MEET HER...
...IN THE THRONE ROOM ......

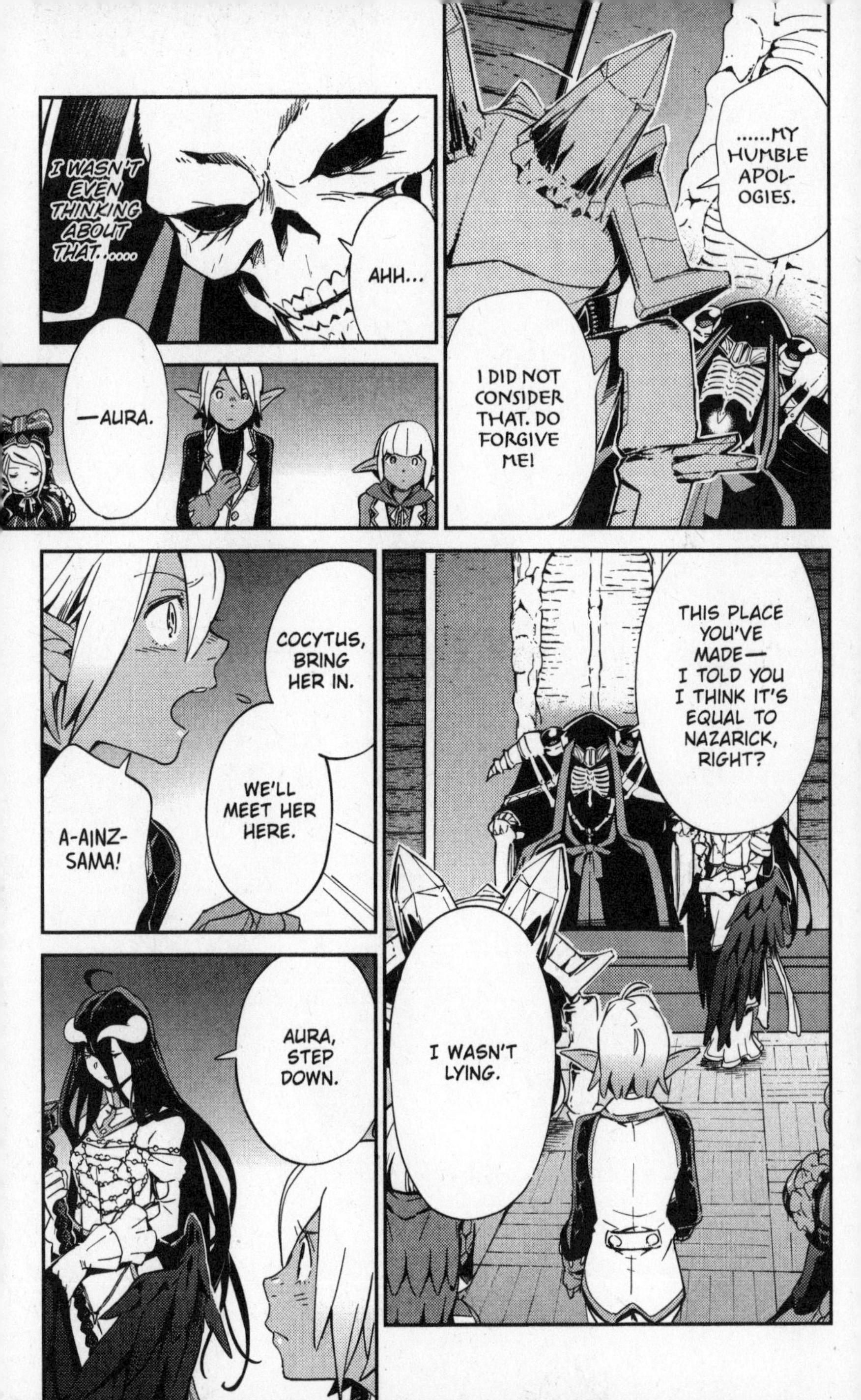
......MY HUMBLE APOLOGIES.
I DID NOT CONSIDER THAT. DO FORGIVE ME!
AHH...
I WASN'T EVEN THINKING ABOUT THAT......
—AURA.
THIS PLACE YOU'VE MADE—I TOLD YOU I THINK IT'S EQUAL TO NAZARICK, RIGHT?
I WASN'T LYING.
COCYTUS, BRING HER IN.
WE'LL MEET HER HERE.
A-AINZ-SAMA!
AURA, STEP DOWN.

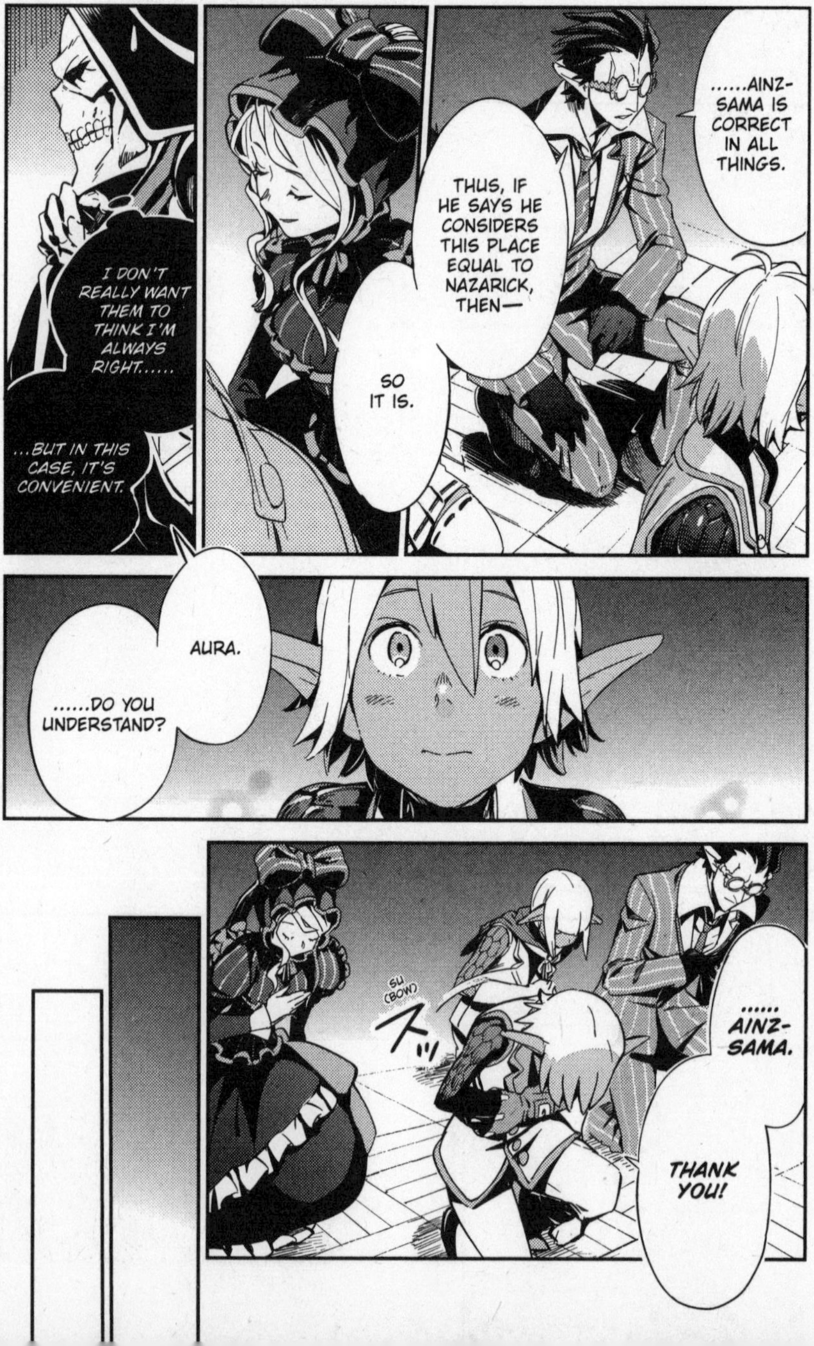
......AINZ-SAMA IS CORRECT IN ALL THINGS.
THUS, IF HE SAYS HE CONSIDERS THIS PLACE EQUAL TO NAZARICK, THEN—
SO IT IS.
I DON'T REALLY WANT THEM TO THINK I'M ALWAYS RIGHT......
...BUT IN THIS CASE, IT'S CONVENIENT.
AURA.
......DO YOU UNDERSTAND?
......AINZ-SAMA.
SU (BOW)
THANK YOU!

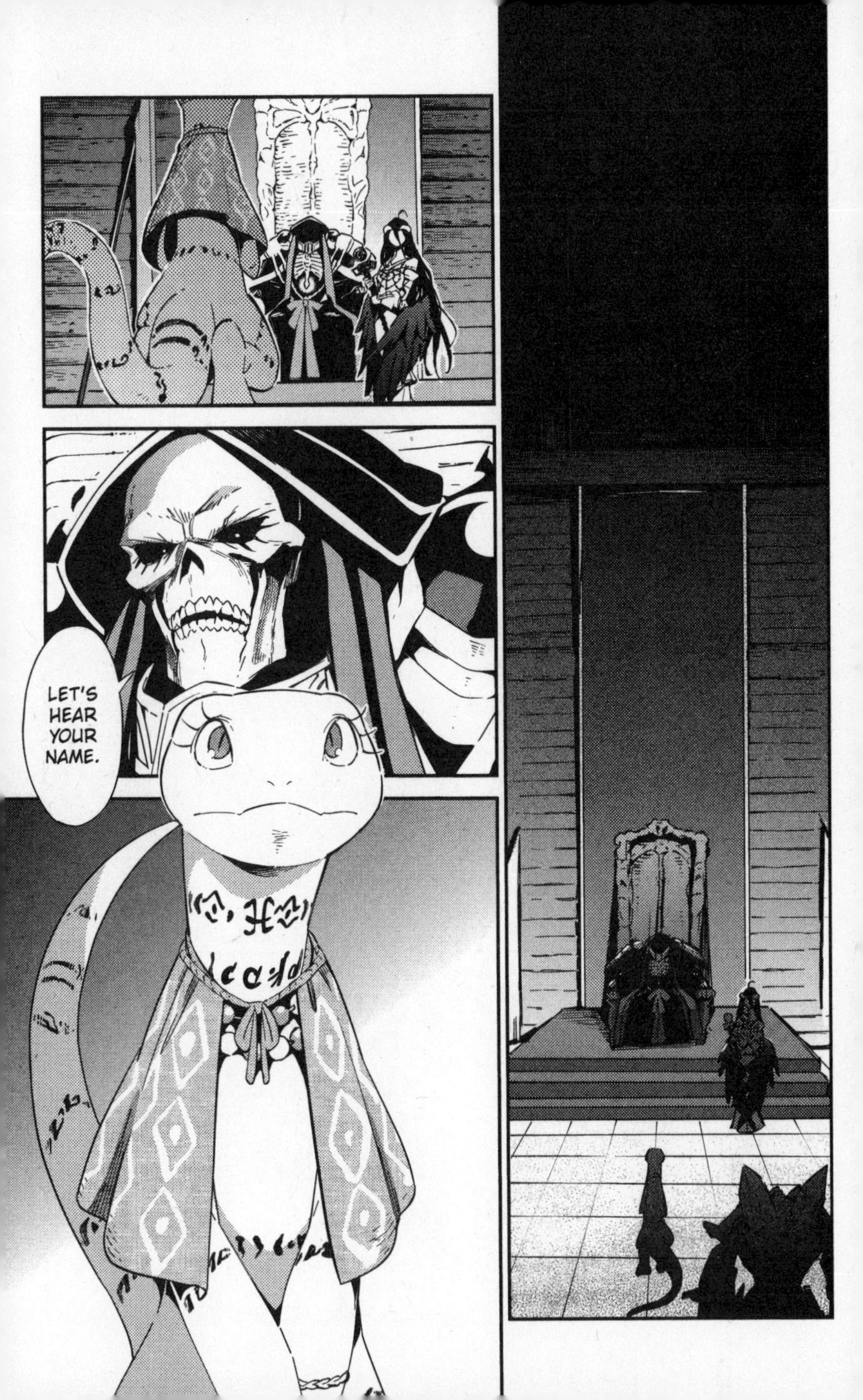
LET'S HEAR YOUR NAME.

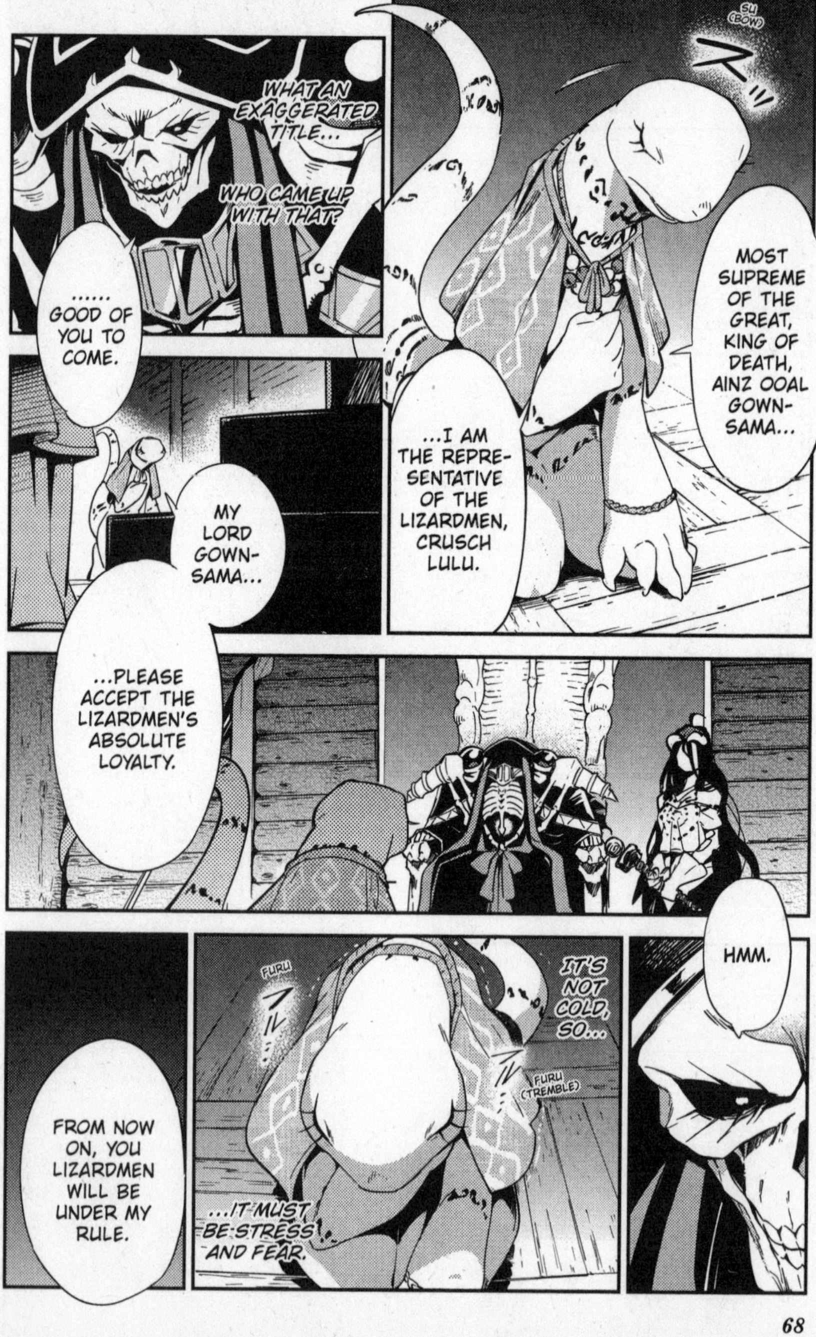
SU (BOW)
MOST SUPREME OF THE GREAT, KING OF DEATH, AINZ OOAL GOWN-SAMA...
...I AM THE REPRESENTATIVE OF THE LIZARDMEN, CRUSCH LULU.
WHAT AN EXAGGERATED TITLE...
WHO CAME UP WITH THAT?
...... GOOD OF YOU TO COME.
MY LORD GOWN-SAMA...
...PLEASE ACCEPT THE LIZARDMEN'S ABSOLUTE LOYALTY.
HMM.
IT'S NOT COLD, SO...
FURU
FURU (TREMBLE)
...IT MUST BE STRESS AND FEAR.
FROM NOW ON, YOU LIZARDMEN WILL BE UNDER MY RULE.

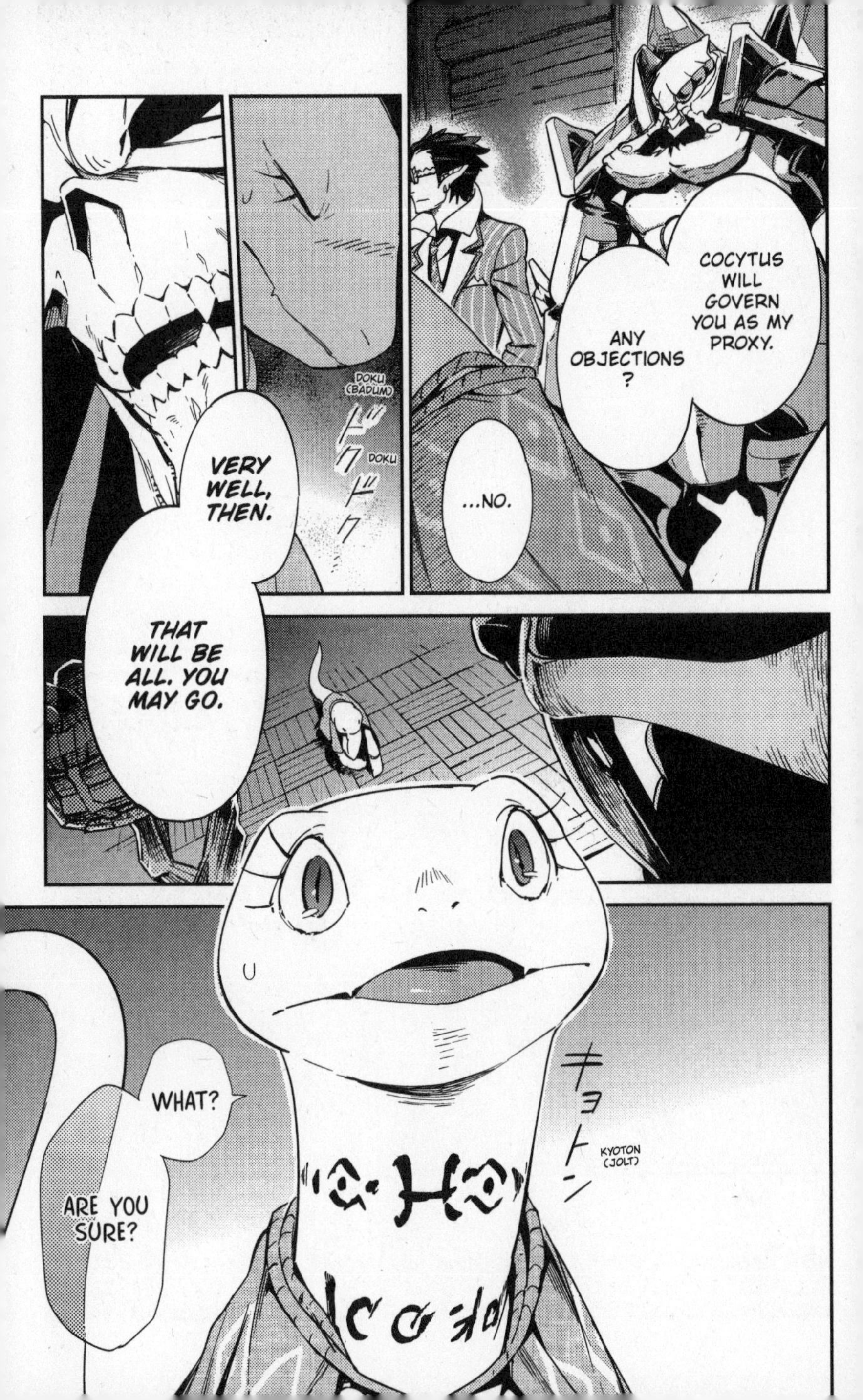
COCYTUS WILL GOVERN YOU AS MY PROXY.
ANY OBJECTIONS?
...NO.
DOKU (BADUM)
DOKU
VERY WELL, THEN.
THAT WILL BE ALL. YOU MAY GO.
KYOTON (JOLT)
WHAT?
ARE YOU SURE?

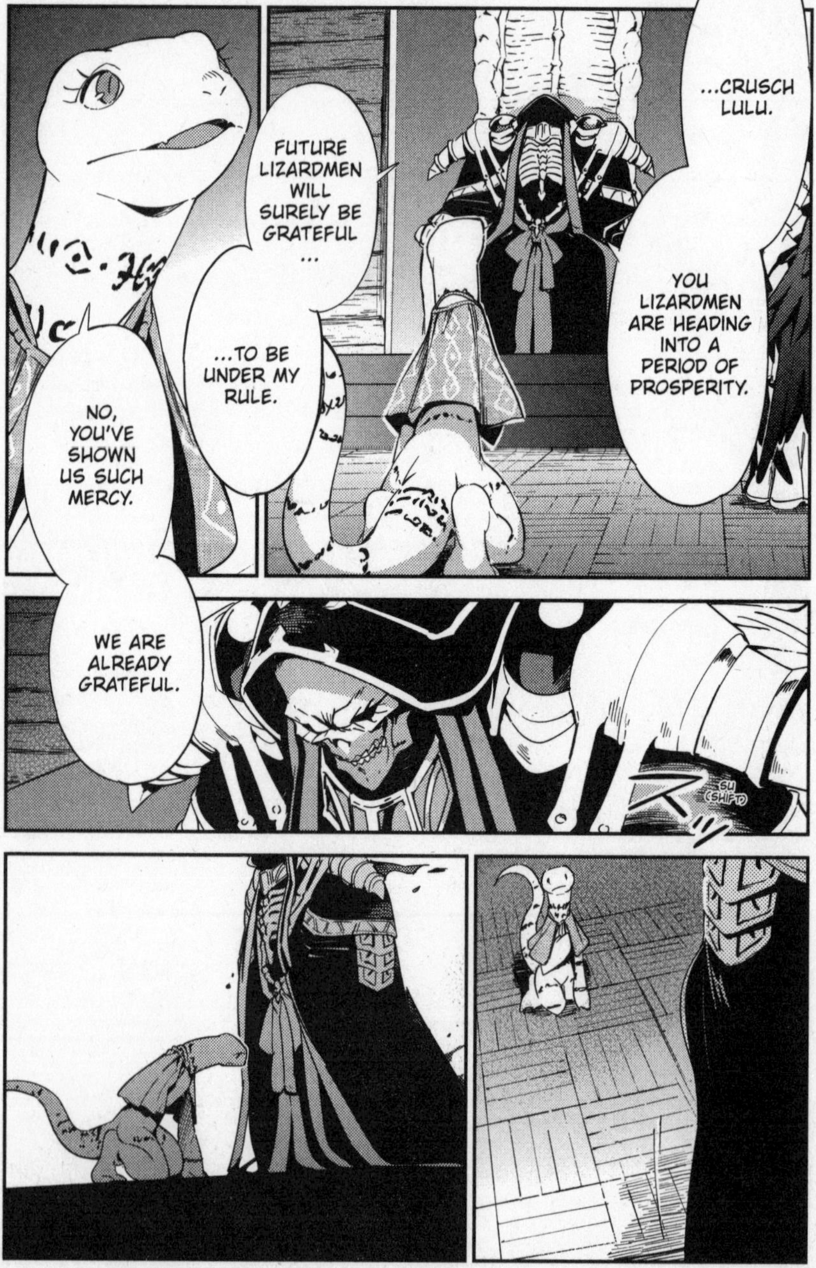
...CRUSCH LULU.
YOU LIZARDMEN ARE HEADING INTO A PERIOD OF PROSPERITY.
FUTURE LIZARDMEN WILL SURELY BE GRATEFUL...
...TO BE UNDER MY RULE.
NO, YOU'VE SHOWN US SUCH MERCY.
WE ARE ALREADY GRATEFUL.
SU (SHIFT)

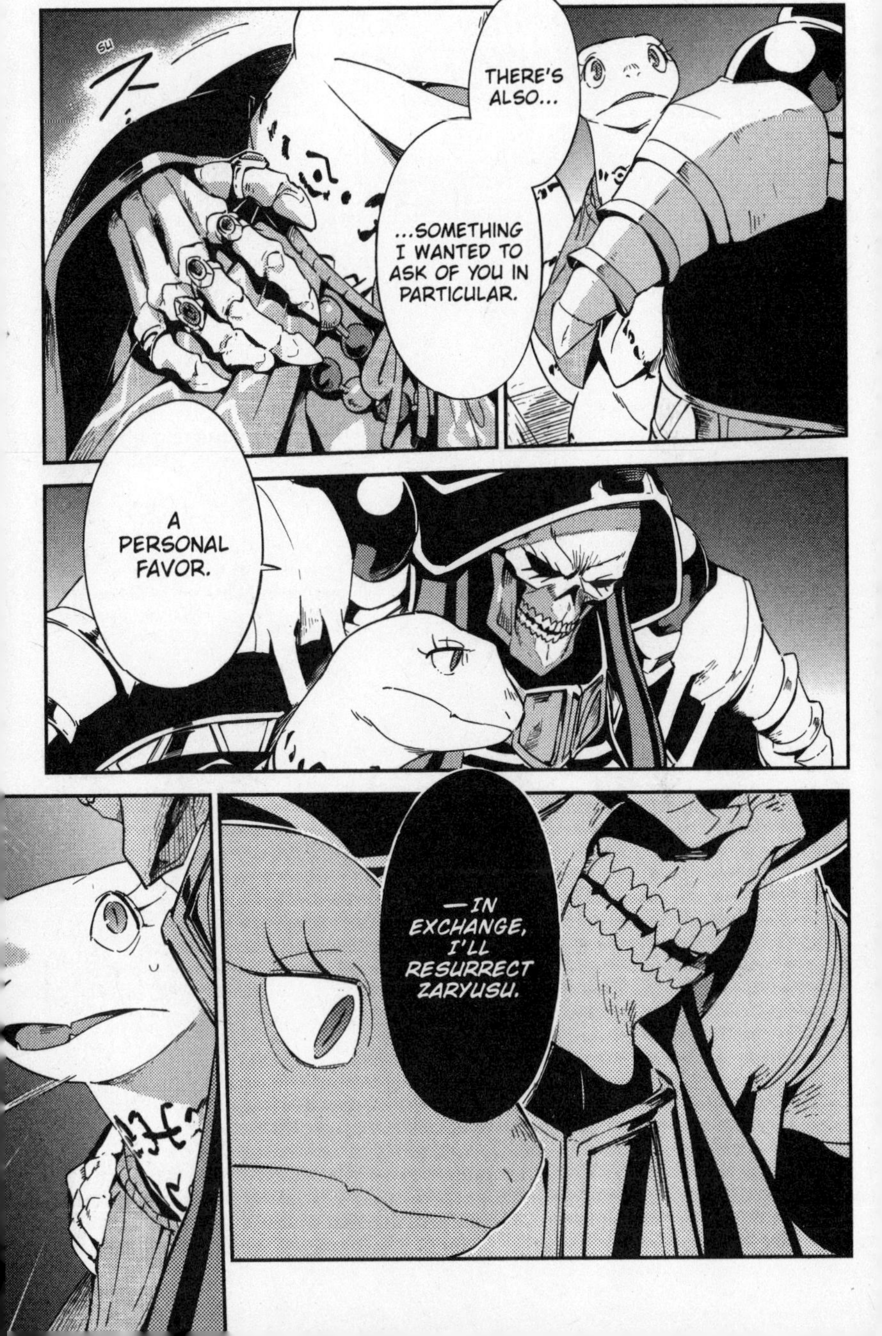
THERE'S ALSO...
...SOMETHING I WANTED TO ASK OF YOU IN PARTICULAR.
SU
A PERSONAL FAVOR.
—IN EXCHANGE, I'LL RESURRECT ZARYUSU.

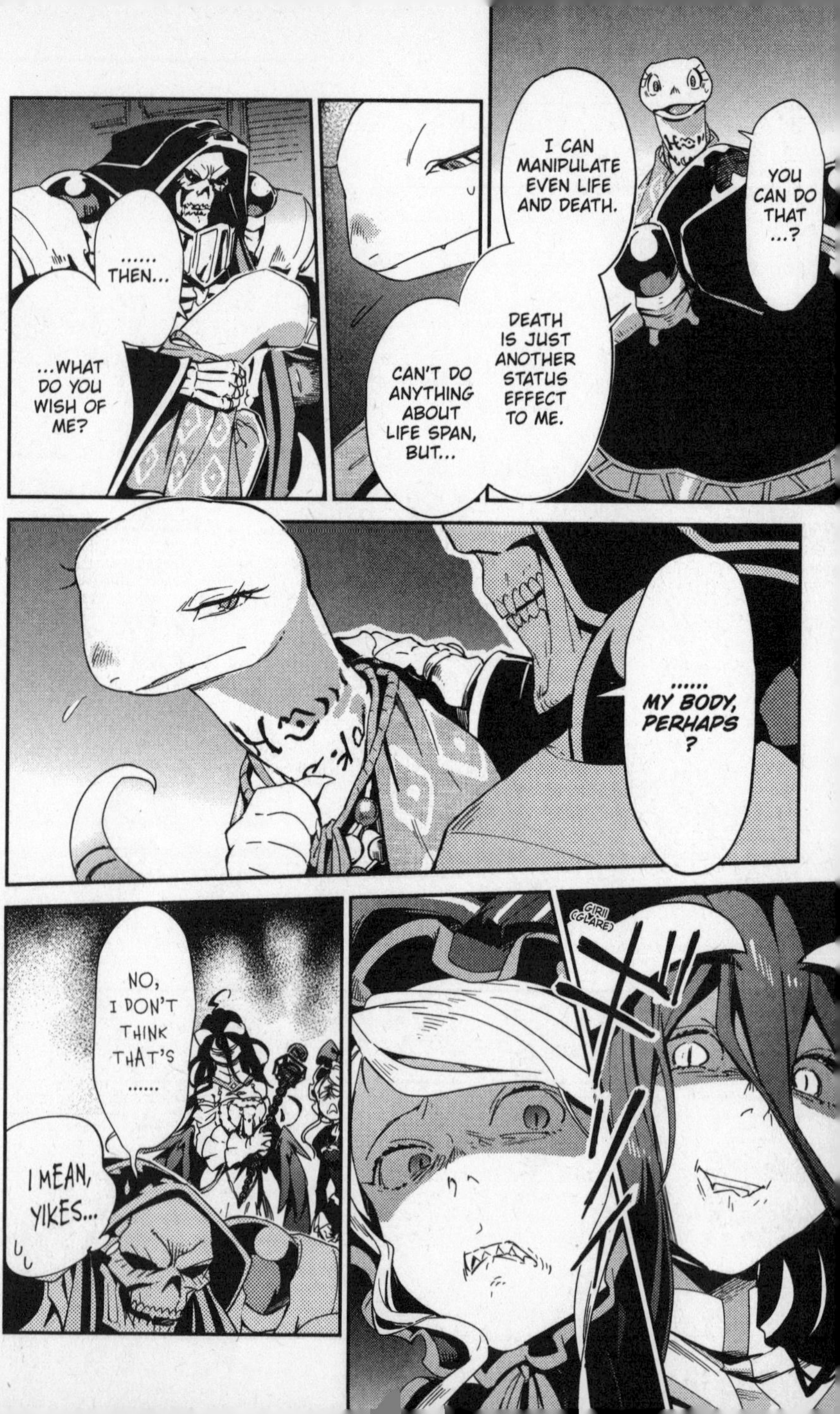
YOU CAN DO THAT ...?
I CAN MANIPULATE EVEN LIFE AND DEATH.
DEATH IS JUST ANOTHER STATUS EFFECT TO ME.
CAN'T DO ANYTHING ABOUT LIFE SPAN, BUT...
...... THEN...
...WHAT DO YOU WISH OF ME?
...... MY BODY, PERHAPS?
GIRII (GLARE)
NO, I DON'T THINK THAT'S ......
I MEAN, YIKES...

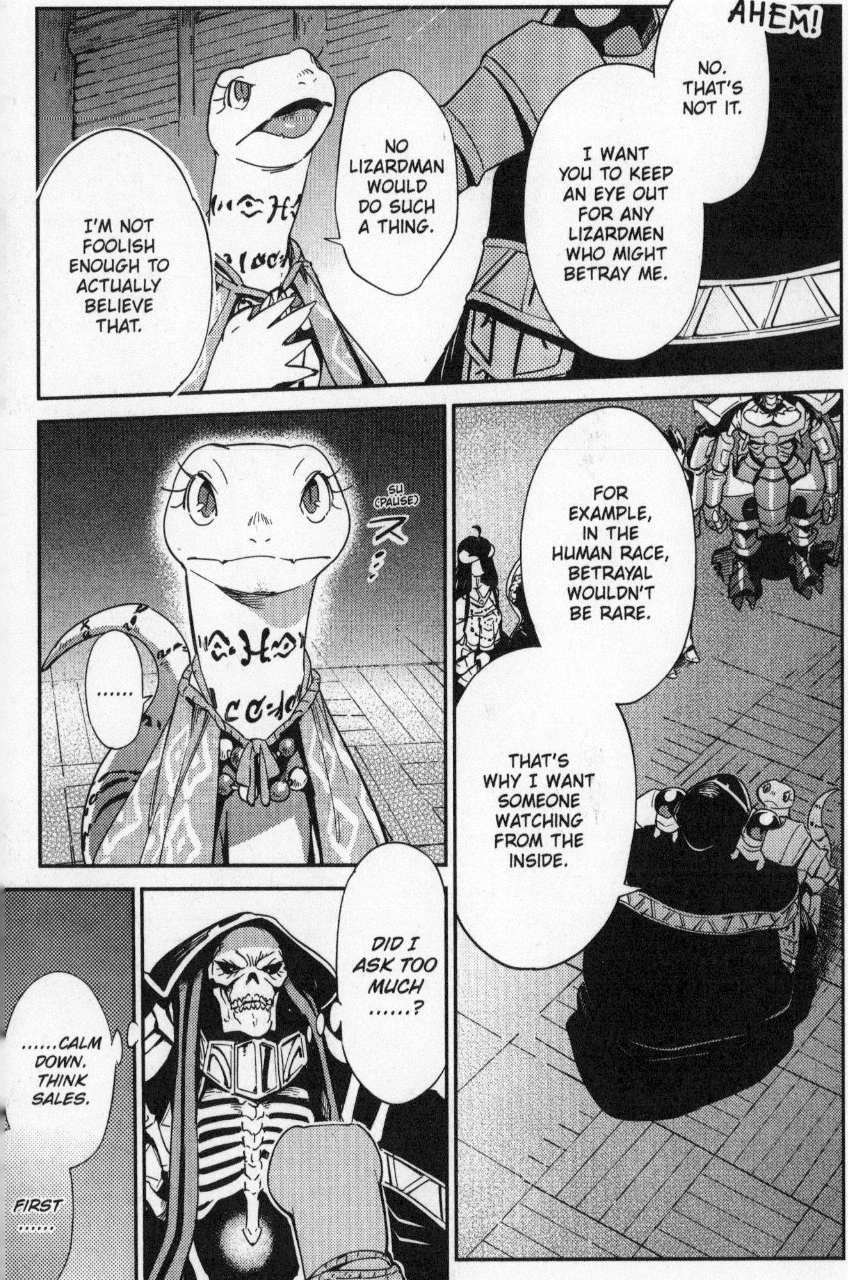
AHEM!
NO. THAT'S NOT IT.
I WANT YOU TO KEEP AN EYE OUT FOR ANY LIZARDMEN WHO MIGHT BETRAY ME.
NO LIZARDMAN WOULD DO SUCH A THING.
I'M NOT FOOLISH ENOUGH TO ACTUALLY BELIEVE THAT.
FOR EXAMPLE, IN THE HUMAN RACE, BETRAYAL WOULDN'T BE RARE.
THAT'S WHY I WANT SOMEONE WATCHING FROM THE INSIDE.
SU (PAUSE)
ス…
......
DID I ASK TOO MUCH ......?
......CALM DOWN. THINK SALES.
FIRST ......

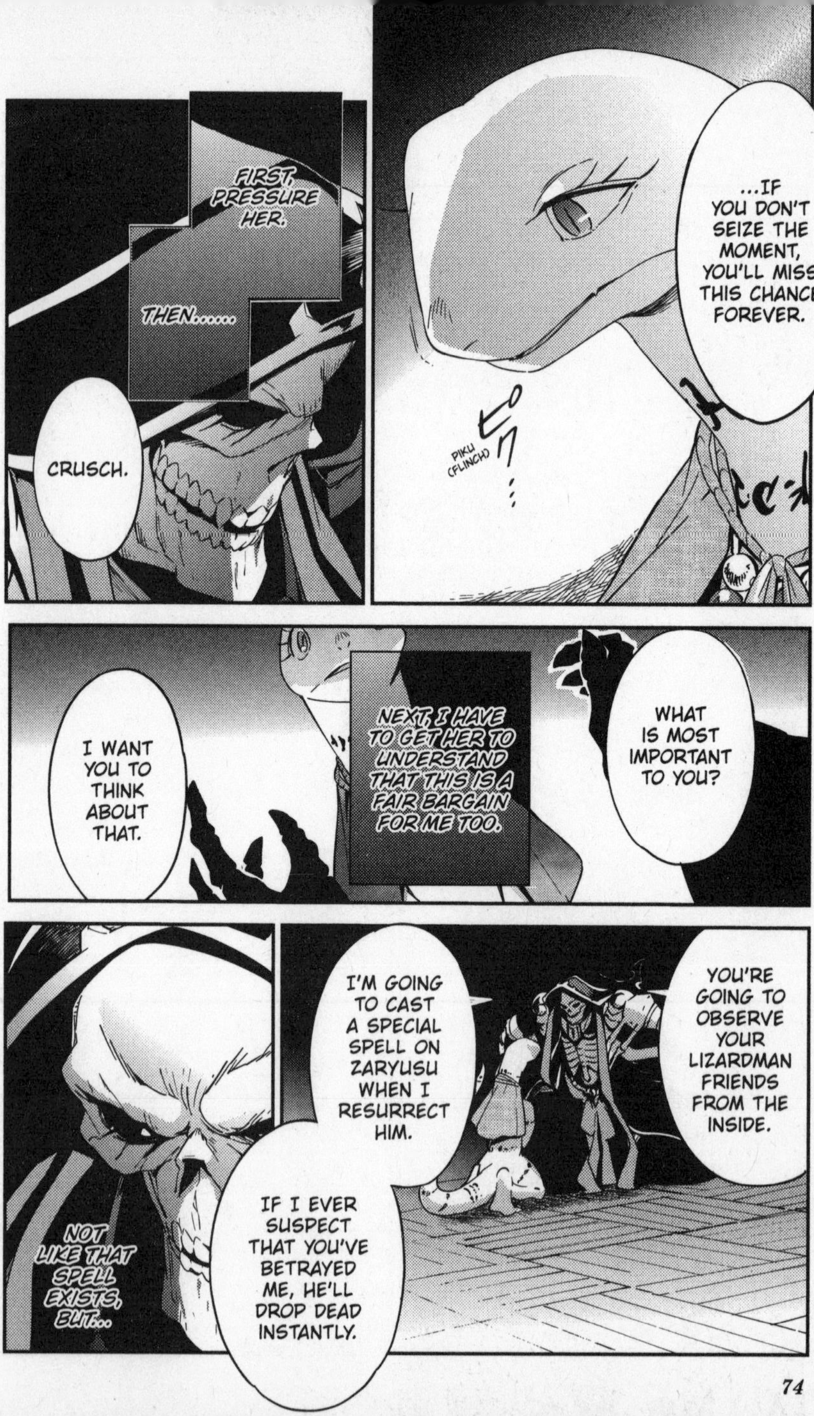
...IF YOU DON'T SEIZE THE MOMENT, YOU'LL MISS THIS CHANCE FOREVER.
PIKU (FLINCH)
FIRST, PRESSURE HER.
THEN......
CRUSCH.
WHAT IS MOST IMPORTANT TO YOU?
NEXT, I HAVE TO GET HER TO UNDERSTAND THAT THIS IS A FAIR BARGAIN FOR ME TOO.
I WANT YOU TO THINK ABOUT THAT.
YOU'RE GOING TO OBSERVE YOUR LIZARDMAN FRIENDS FROM THE INSIDE.
I'M GOING TO CAST A SPECIAL SPELL ON ZARYUSU WHEN I RESURRECT HIM.
IF I EVER SUSPECT THAT YOU'VE BETRAYED ME, HE'LL DROP DEAD INSTANTLY.
NOT LIKE THAT SPELL EXISTS, BUT...

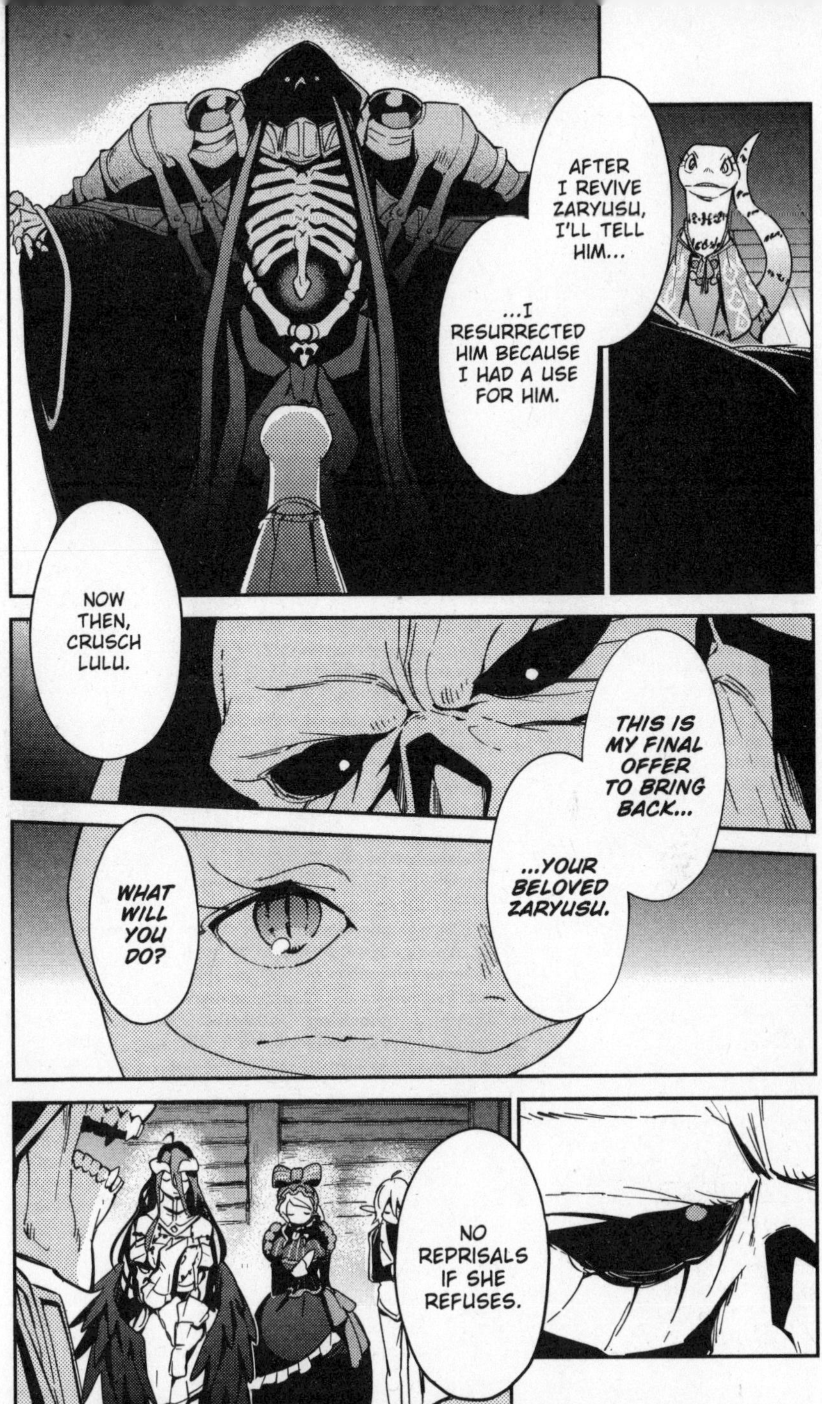
AFTER I REVIVE ZARYUSU, I'LL TELL HIM...
...I RESURRECTED HIM BECAUSE I HAD A USE FOR HIM.
NOW THEN, CRUSCH LULU.
THIS IS MY FINAL OFFER TO BRING BACK...
...YOUR BELOVED ZARYUSU.
WHAT WILL YOU DO?
NO REPRISALS IF SHE REFUSES.

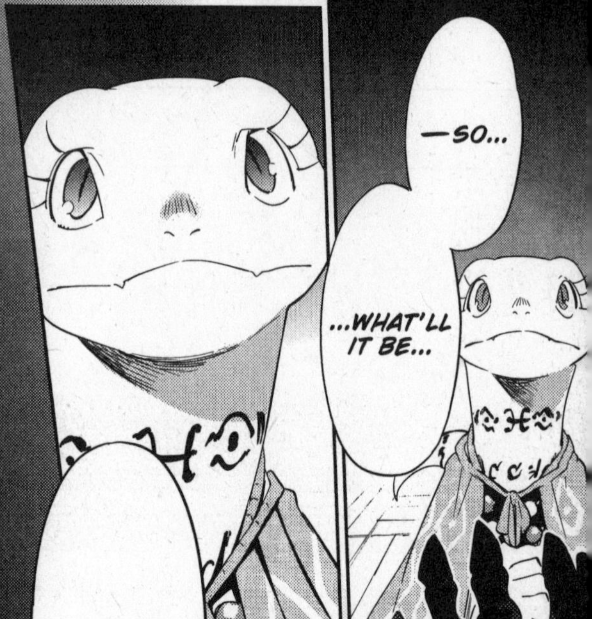
—SO...
...WHAT'LL IT BE...
...CRUSCH LULU?

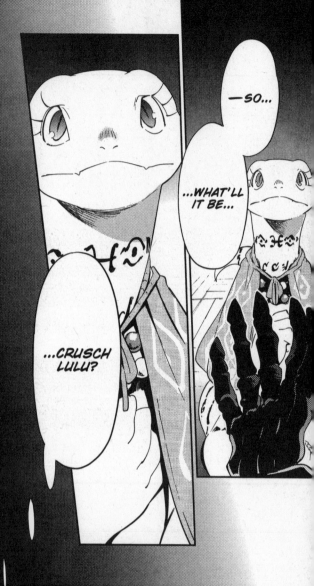

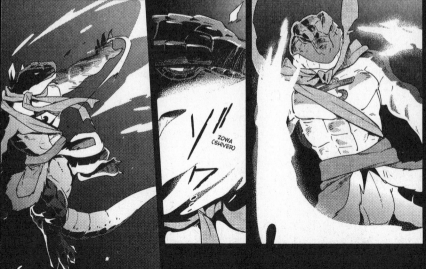

ZOWA
(SHIVER)

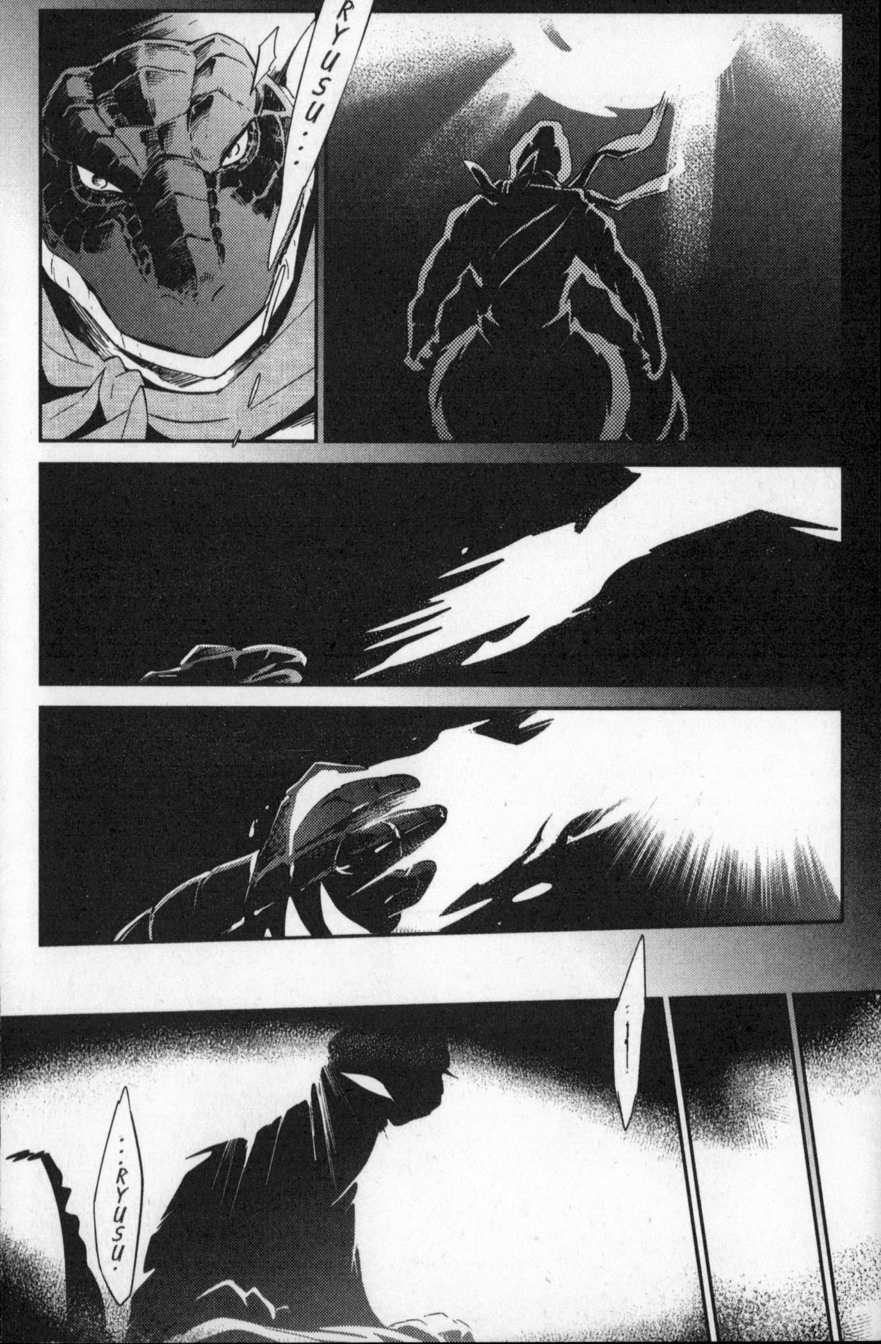
ZARYUSU...
...!
...RYUSU.

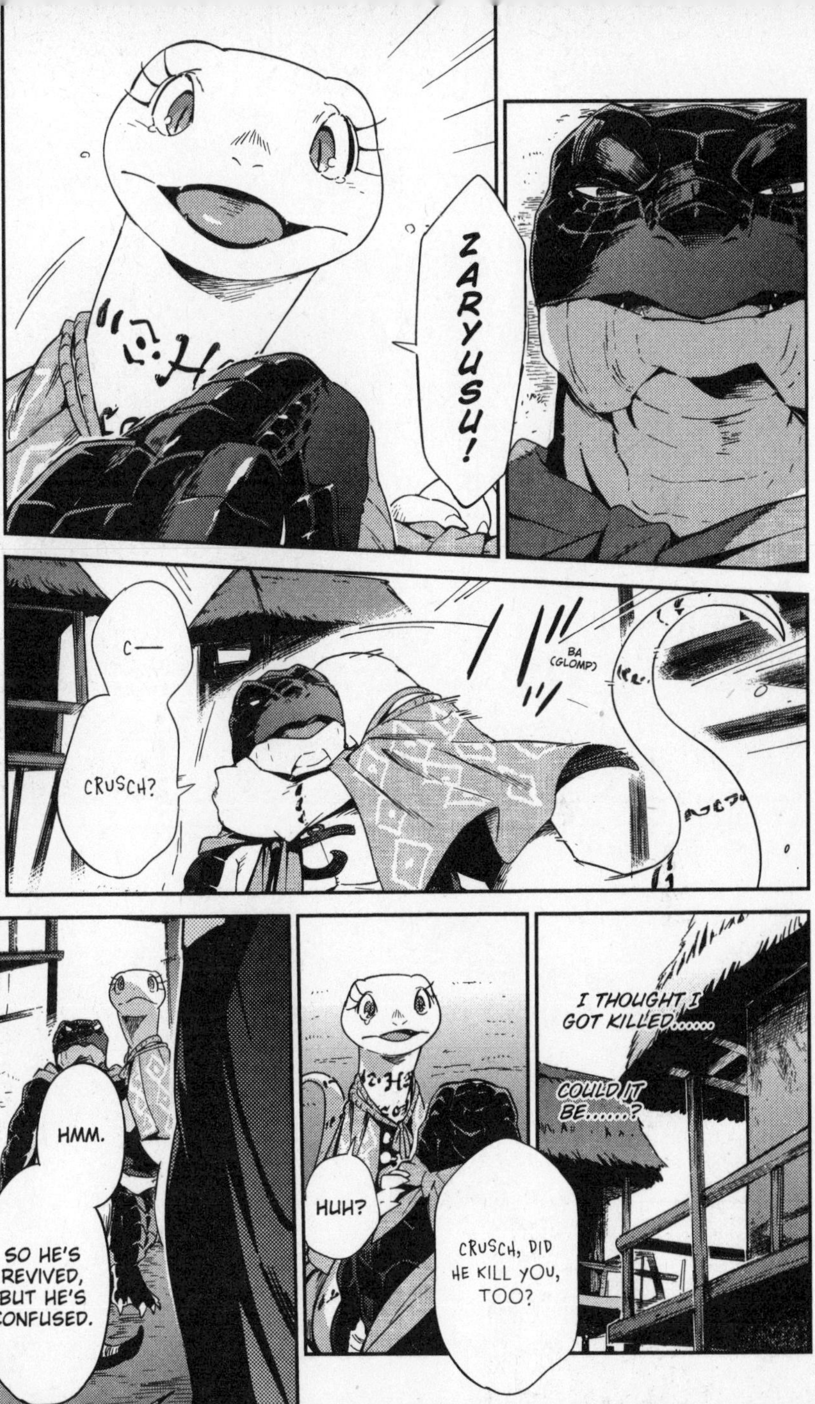

ZARYUSU!
BA (GLOMP)
C—
CRUSCH?
I THOUGHT I GOT KILLED......
COULD IT BE......?
CRUSCH, DID HE KILL YOU, TOO?
HUH?
HMM.
SO HE'S REVIVED, BUT HE'S CONFUSED.

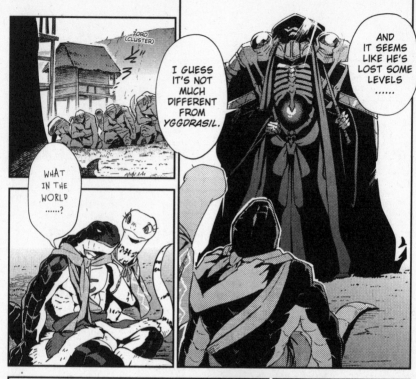

AND IT SEEMS LIKE HE'S LOST SOME LEVELS......
I GUESS IT'S NOT MUCH DIFFERENT FROM *YGGDRASIL*.
ZORO (CLUSTER)
WHAT IN THE WORLD......?
HMM. YOU MAY LEAVE US, LIZARD-MEN.
DON'T ENTER THE VILLAGE UNTIL I GIVE YOU PERMISSION.
PASHA (SPLOOSH)
PASHA
PASHA

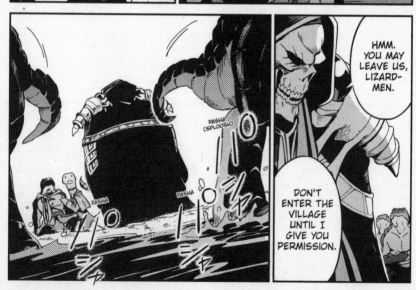

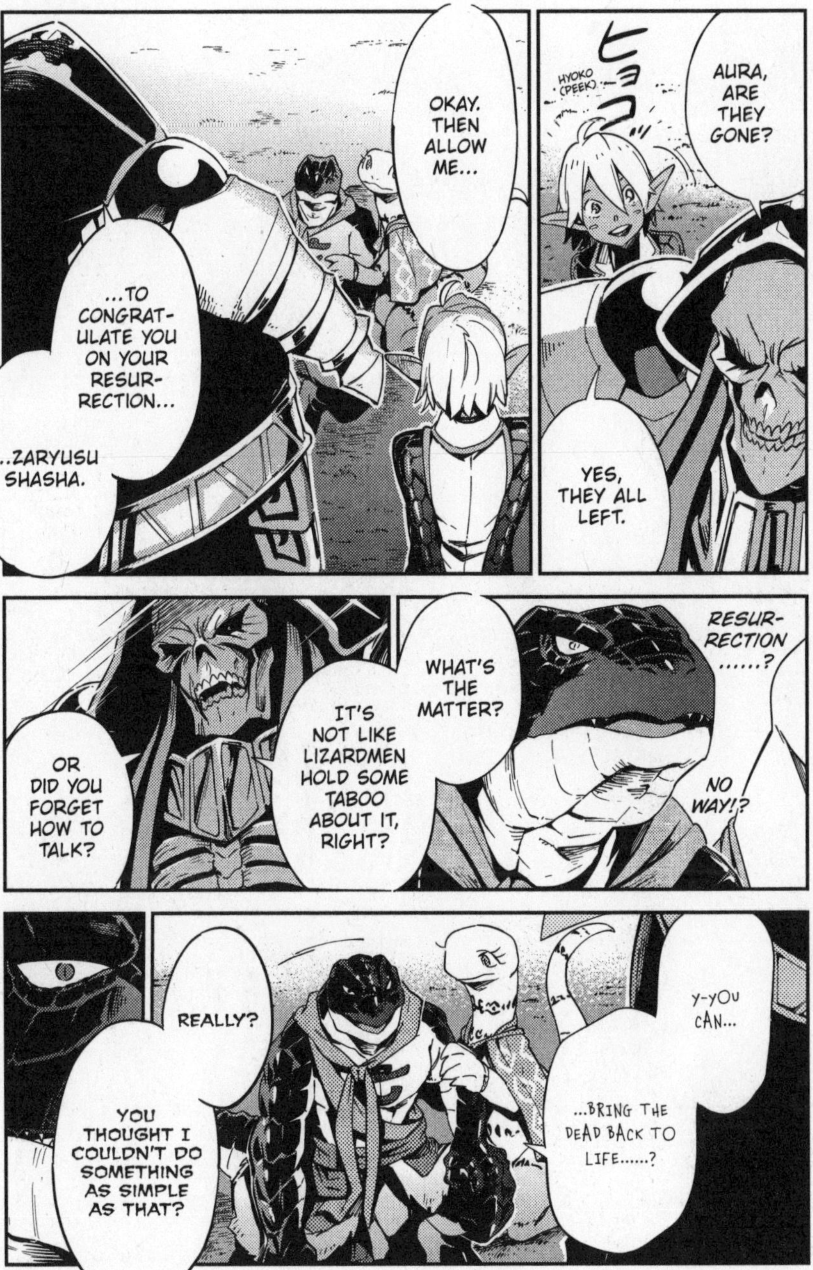
ヒョコ
HYOKO (PEEK)
AURA, ARE THEY GONE?
YES, THEY ALL LEFT.
OKAY. THEN ALLOW ME...
...TO CONGRATULATE YOU ON YOUR RESURRECTION...
...ZARYUSU SHASHA.
RESURRECTION......?
NO WAY!?
WHAT'S THE MATTER?
IT'S NOT LIKE LIZARDMEN HOLD SOME TABOO ABOUT IT, RIGHT?
OR DID YOU FORGET HOW TO TALK?
Y-YOU CAN...
...BRING THE DEAD BACK TO LIFE......?
REALLY?
YOU THOUGHT I COULDN'T DO SOMETHING AS SIMPLE AS THAT?

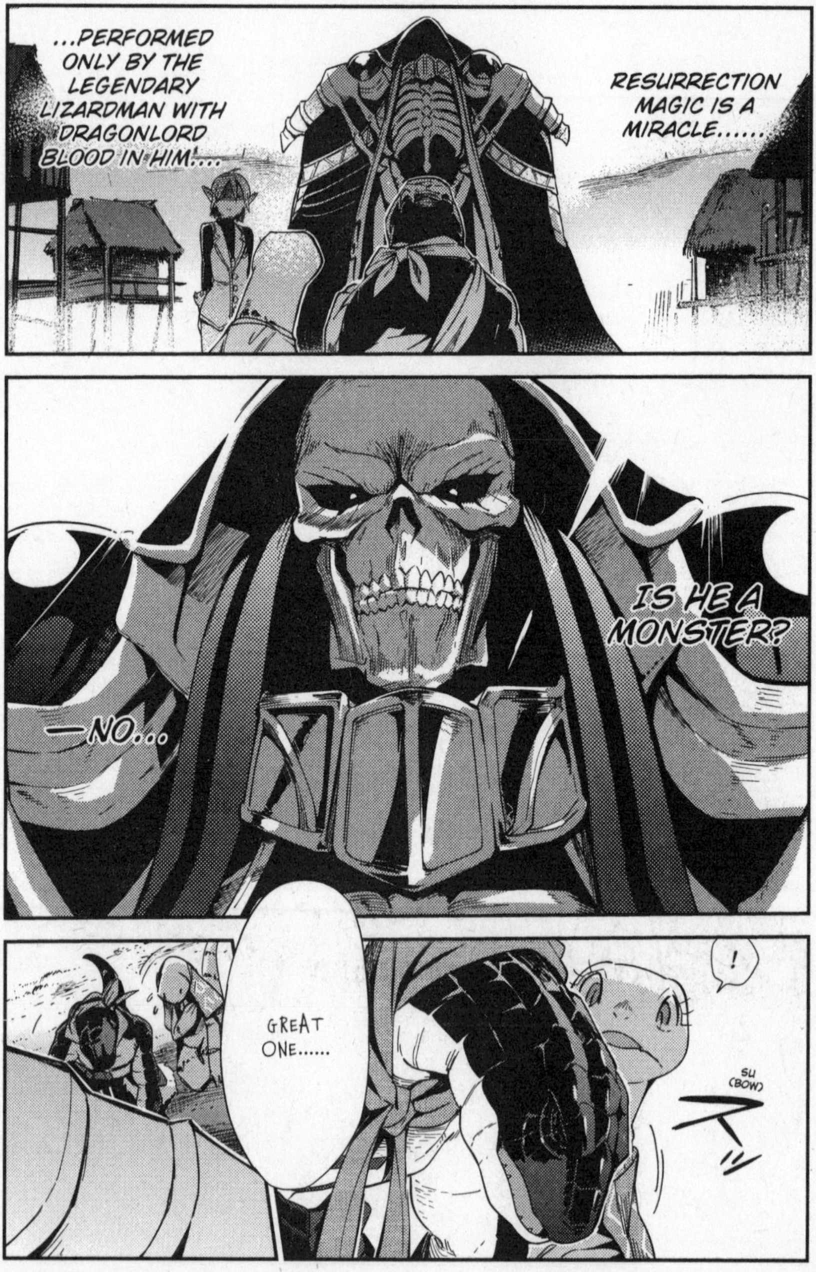
RESURRECTION MAGIC IS A MIRACLE......
...PERFORMED ONLY BY THE LEGENDARY LIZARDMAN WITH DRAGONLORD BLOOD IN HIM....
IS HE A MONSTER?
—NO...
!
SU (BOW)
GREAT ONE......

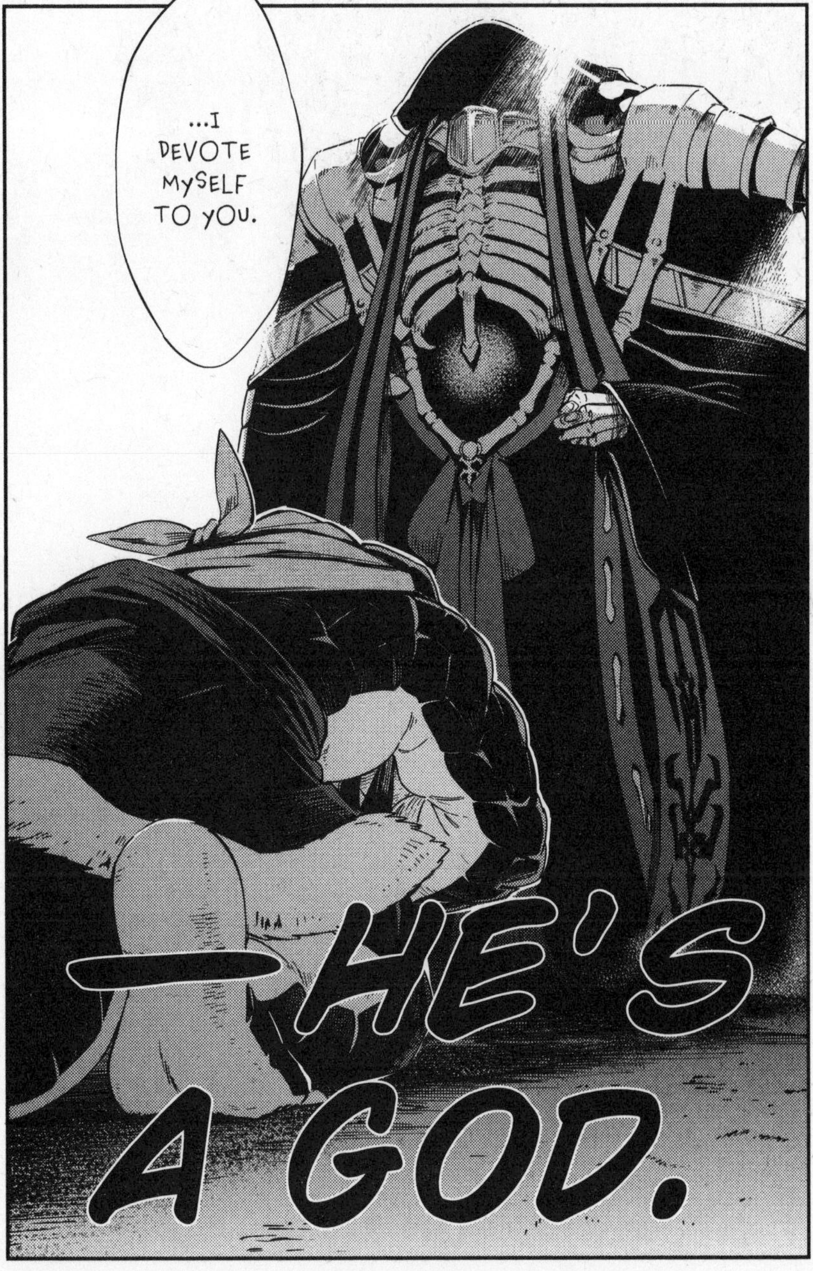
...I DEVOTE MYSELF TO YOU.
—HE'S A GOD.

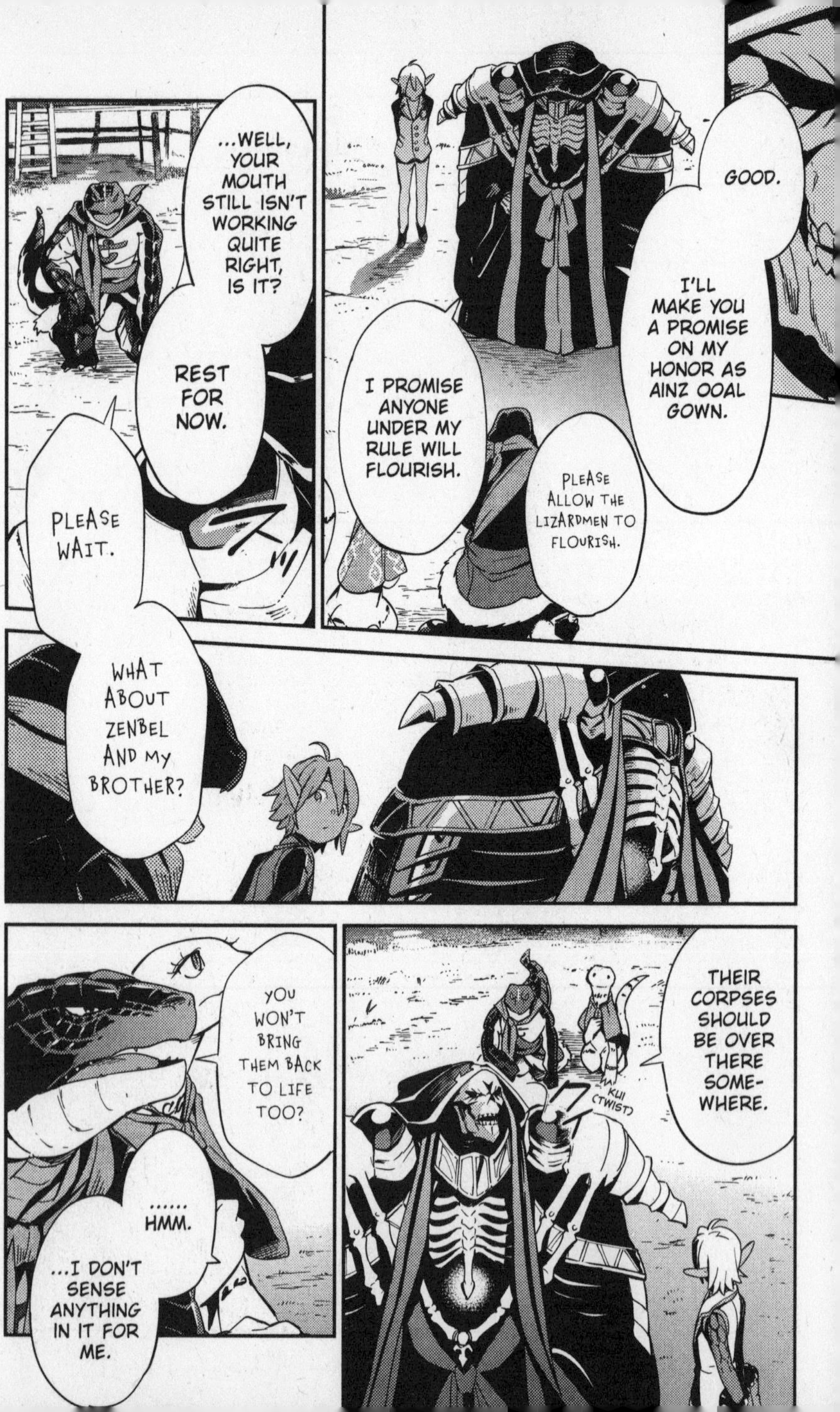
GOOD.
I'LL MAKE YOU A PROMISE ON MY HONOR AS AINZ OOAL GOWN.
PLEASE ALLOW THE LIZARDMEN TO FLOURISH.
I PROMISE ANYONE UNDER MY RULE WILL FLOURISH.
...WELL, YOUR MOUTH STILL ISN'T WORKING QUITE RIGHT, IS IT?
REST FOR NOW.
PLEASE WAIT.
WHAT ABOUT ZENBEL AND MY BROTHER?
THEIR CORPSES SHOULD BE OVER THERE SOME-WHERE.
KUI (TWIST)
YOU WON'T BRING THEM BACK TO LIFE TOO?
...... HMM.
...I DON'T SENSE ANYTHING IN IT FOR ME.

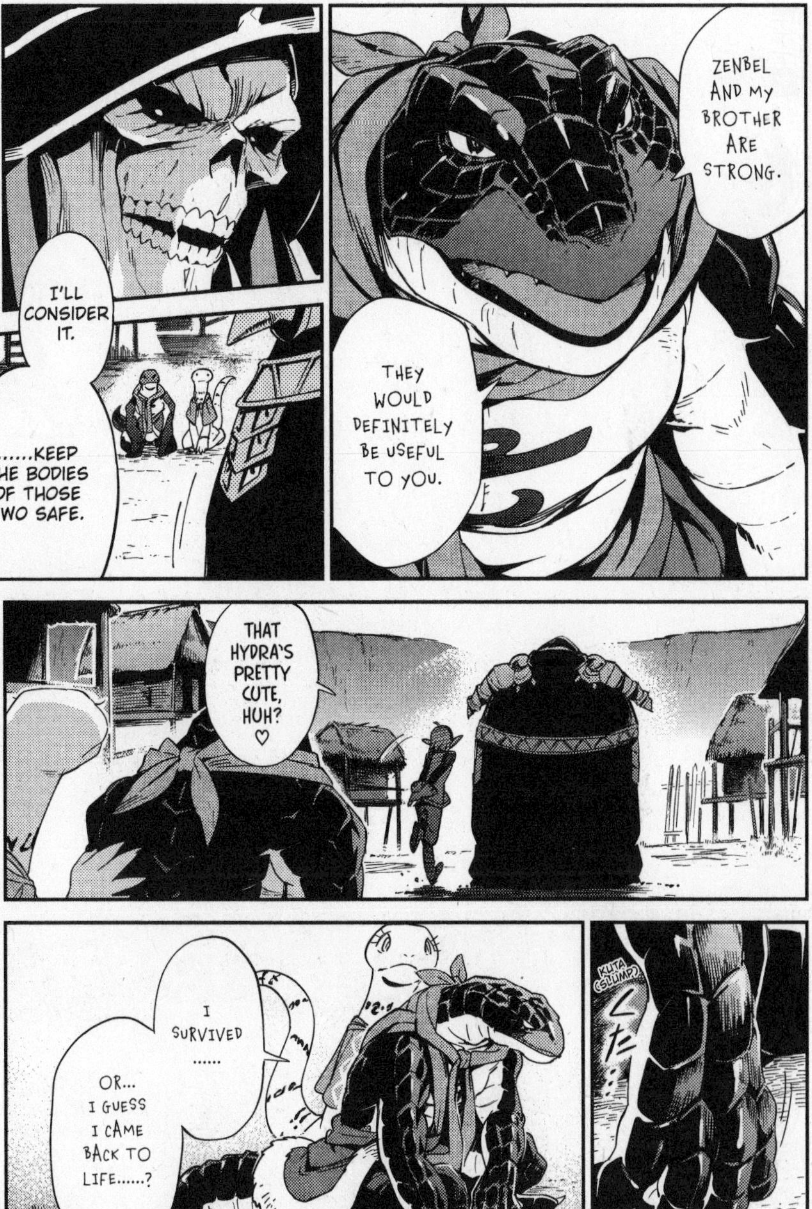
ZENBEL AND MY BROTHER ARE STRONG.
THEY WOULD DEFINITELY BE USEFUL TO YOU.
I'LL CONSIDER IT.
......KEEP THE BODIES OF THOSE TWO SAFE.
THAT HYDRA'S PRETTY CUTE, HUH? ♡
KUTA (SLUMP)
くた…
I SURVIVED ......
OR... I GUESS I CAME BACK TO LIFE......?

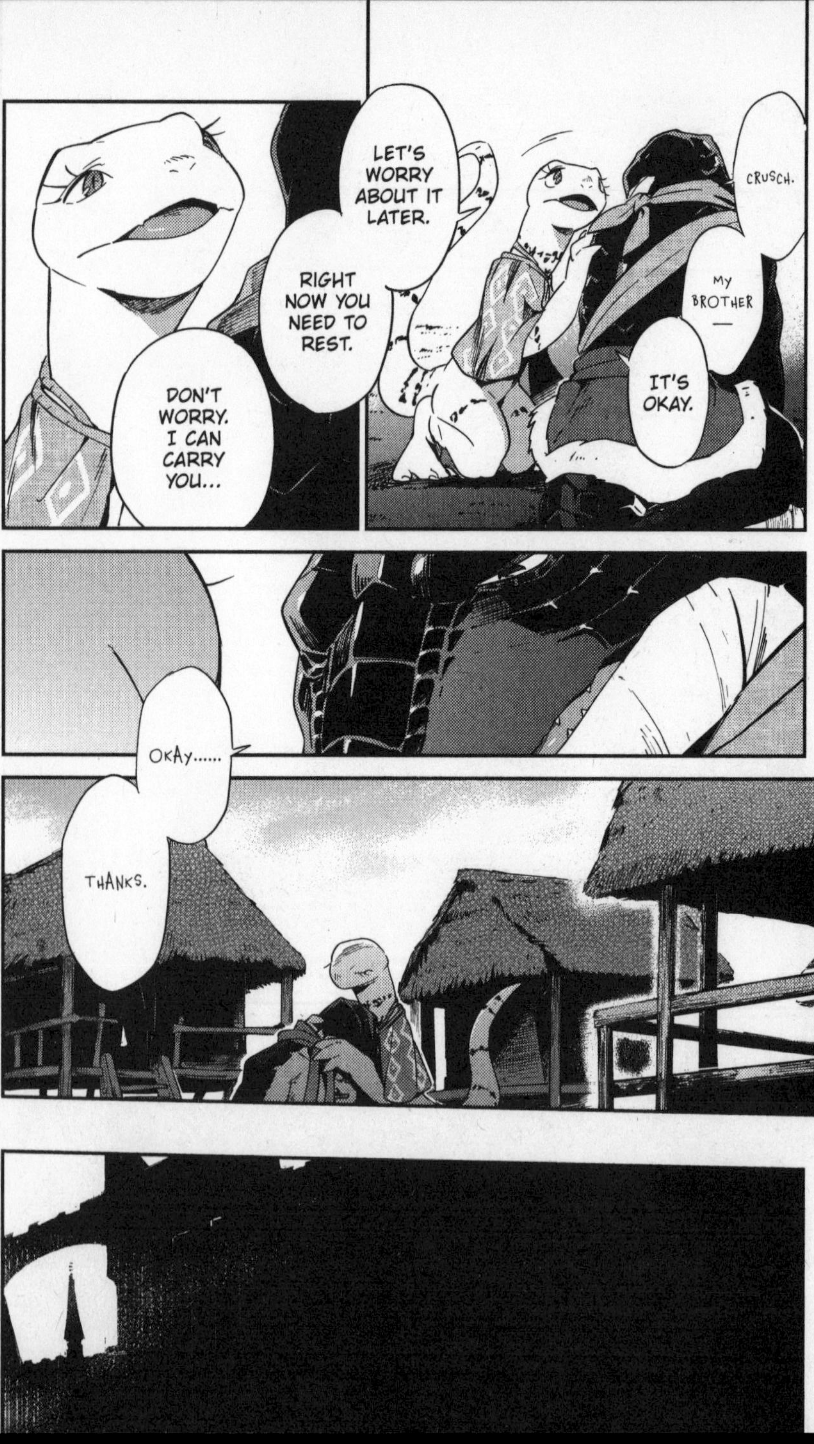
CRUSCH.
MY BROTHER —
IT'S OKAY.
LET'S WORRY ABOUT IT LATER.
RIGHT NOW YOU NEED TO REST.
DON'T WORRY. I CAN CARRY YOU...
OKAY......
THANKS.

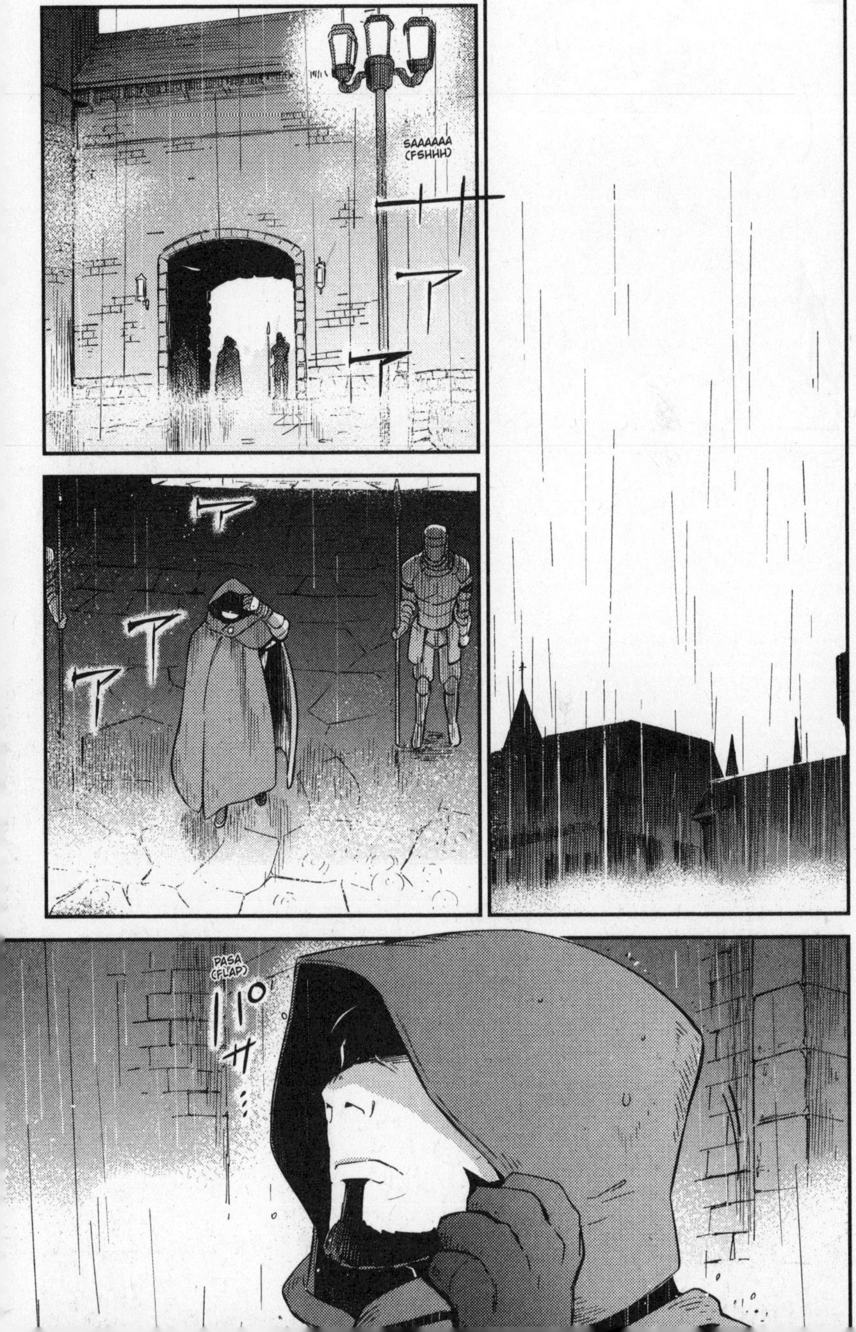
SAAAAAA (FSHHH)
PASA (FLAP)

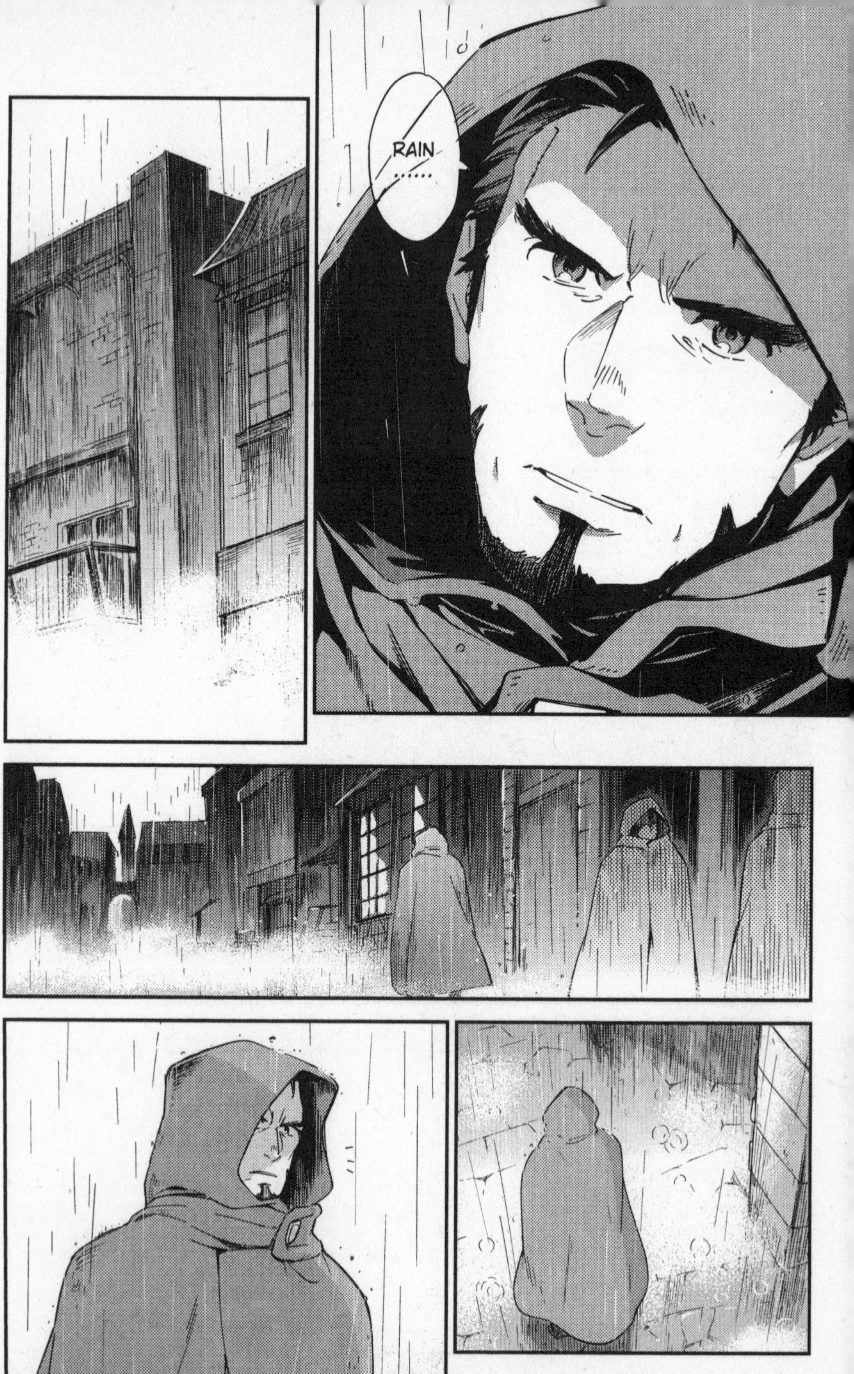
RAIN ....

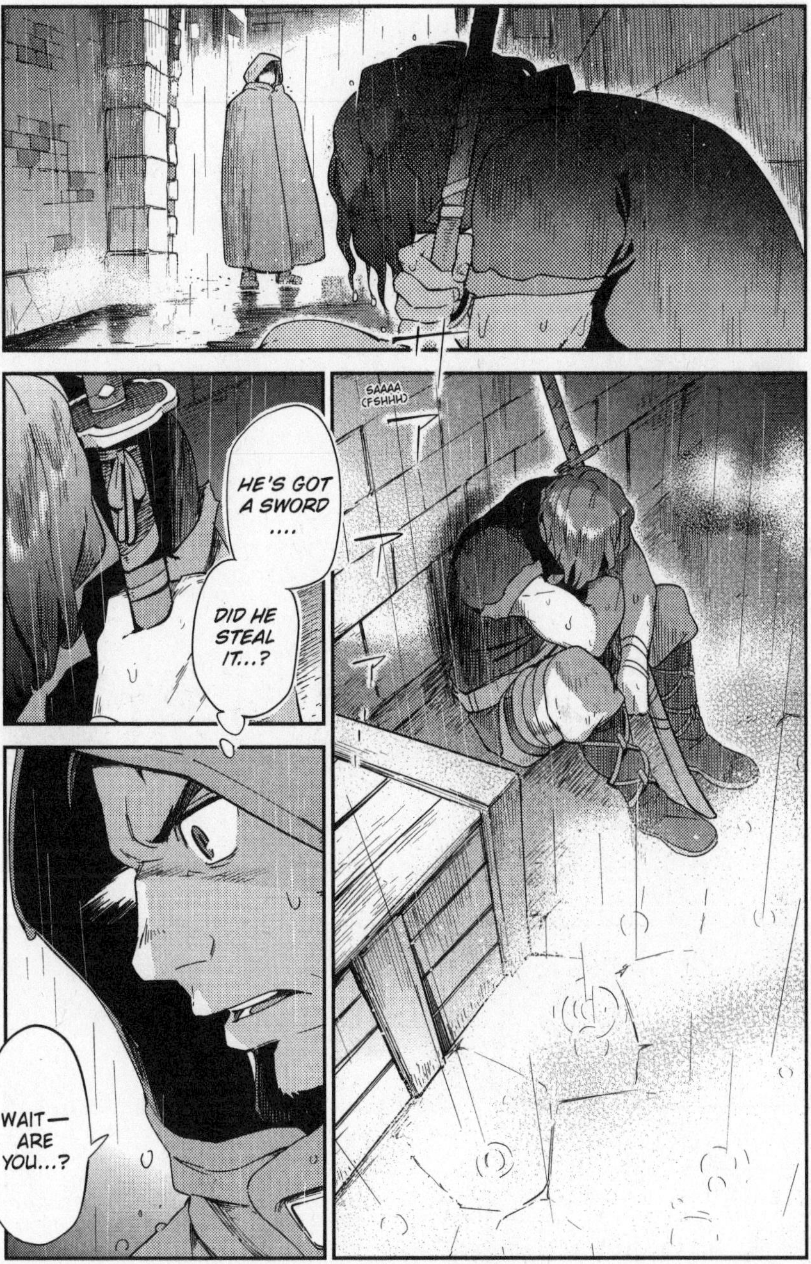
SAAAA (FSHHH)
HE'S GOT A SWORD ....
DID HE STEAL IT...?
WAIT— ARE YOU...?

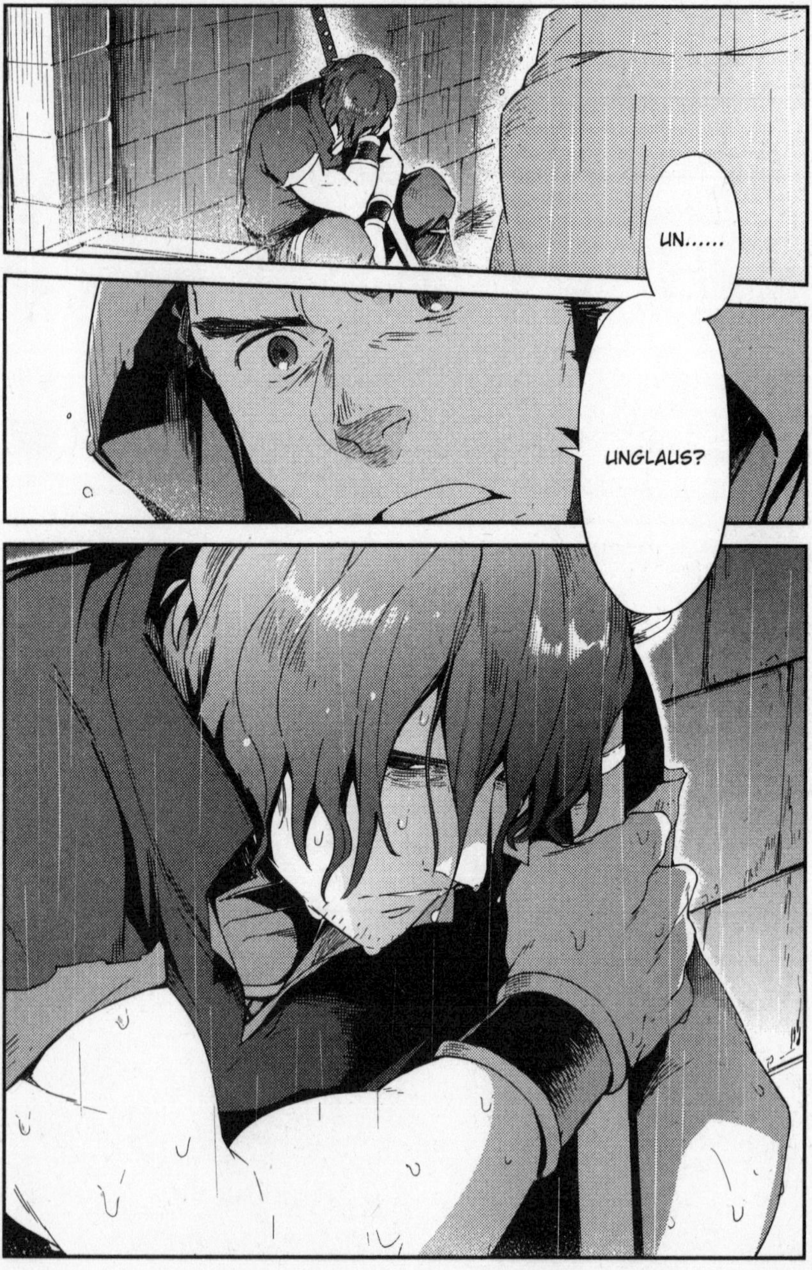
UN......
UNGLAUS?

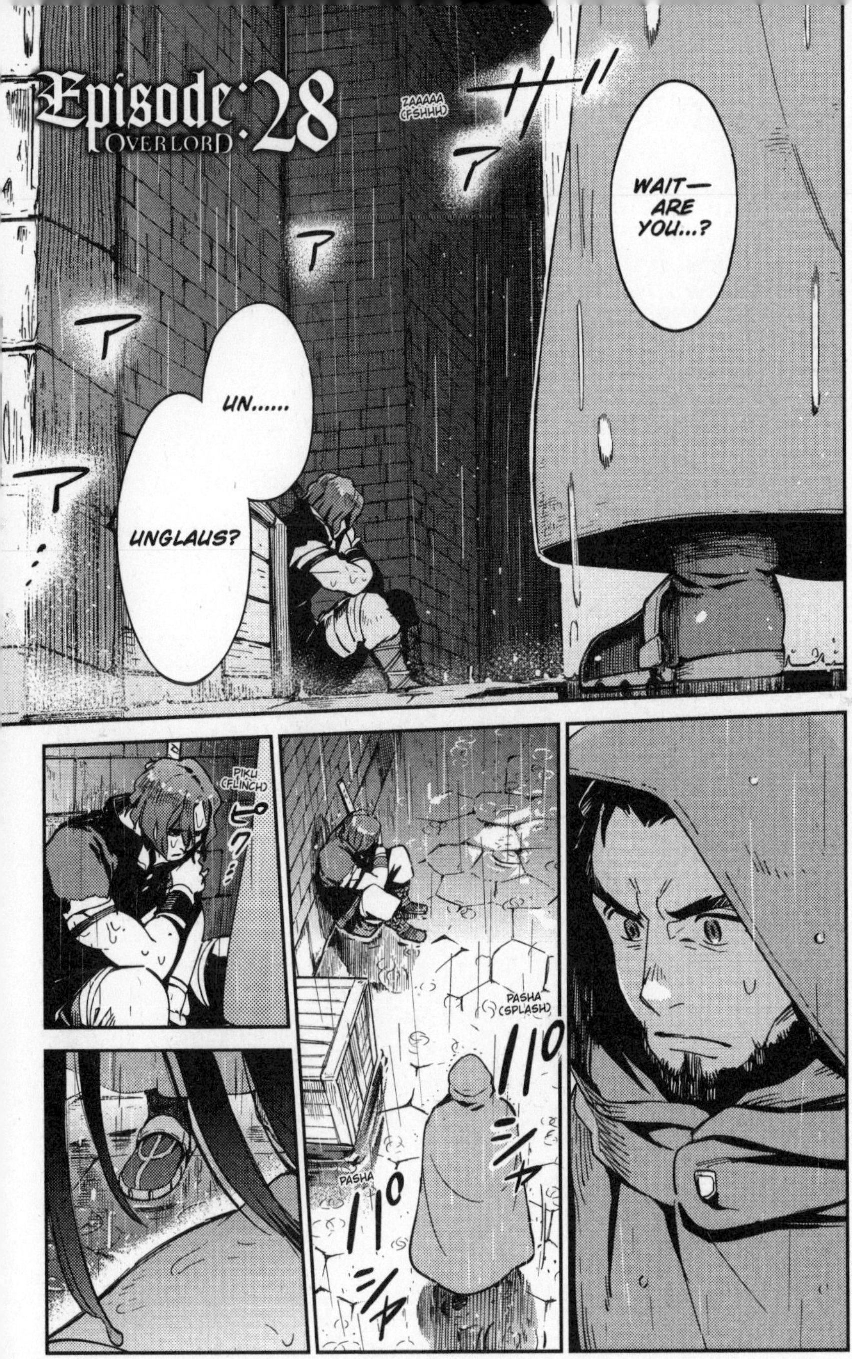
Episode:28
OVERLORD
ZAAAAA (FSHHH)
WAIT— ARE YOU...?
UN...... UNGLAUS?
PASHA (SPLASH)
PASHA
PIKU (FLINCH)

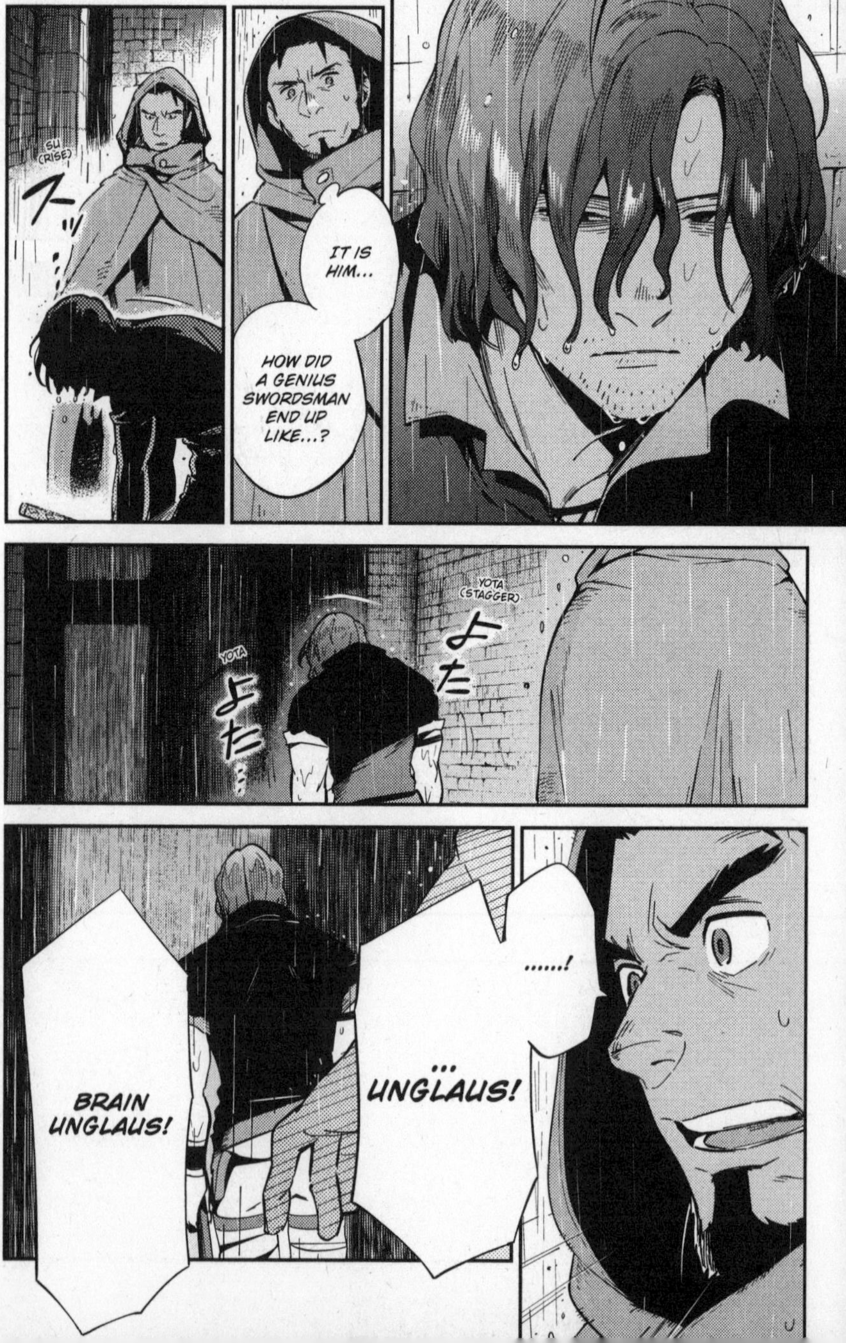

IT IS HIM...
HOW DID A GENIUS SWORDSMAN END UP LIKE...?
SU (RISE)
スッ
YOTA (STAGGER)
よた
YOTA
よた…
......!
...UNGLÄUS!
BRAIN UNGLAUS!

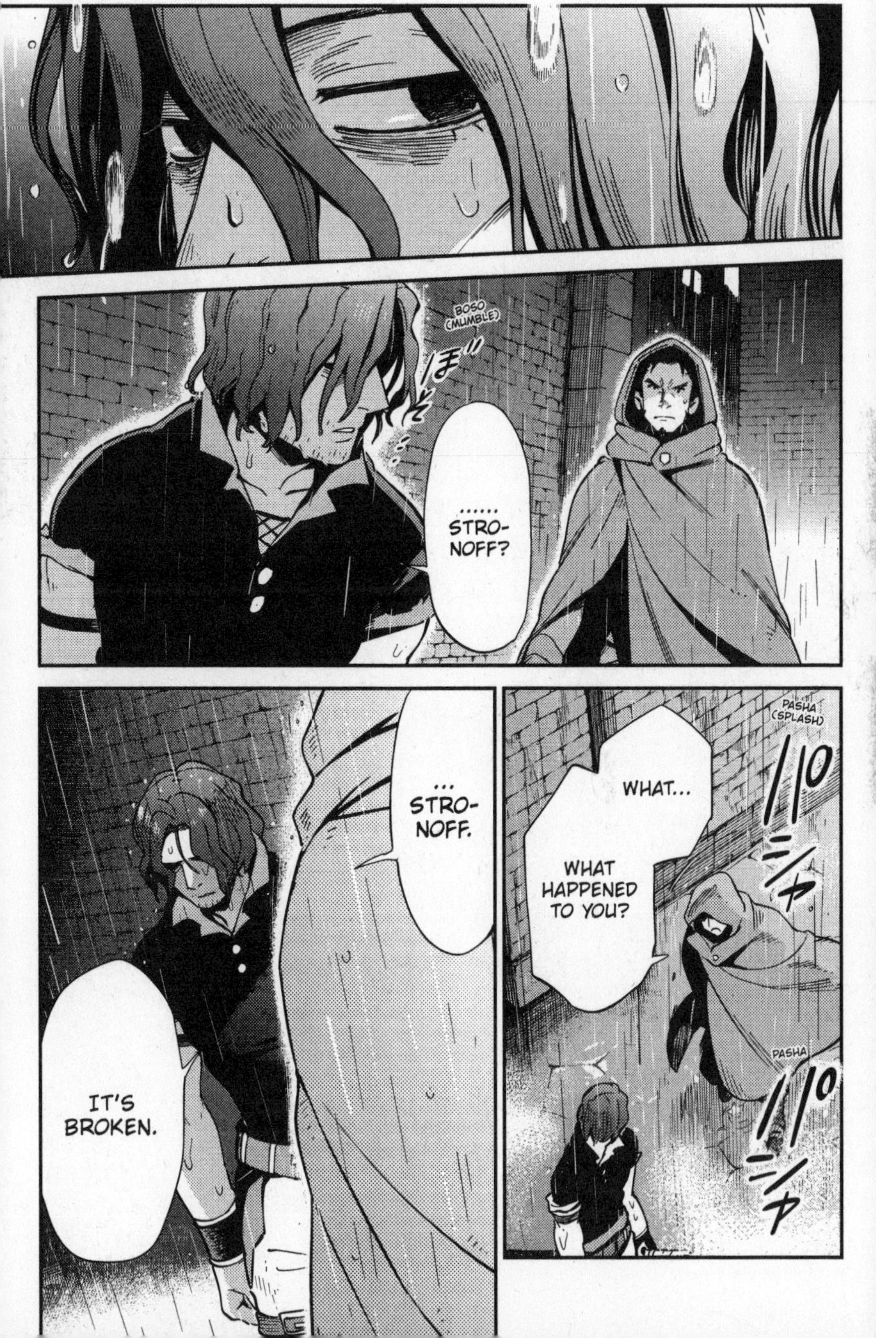
BOSO (MUMBLE)
...... STRO-NOFF?
PASHA (SPLASH)
WHAT...
WHAT HAPPENED TO YOU?
PASHA
... STRO-NOFF.
IT'S BROKEN.

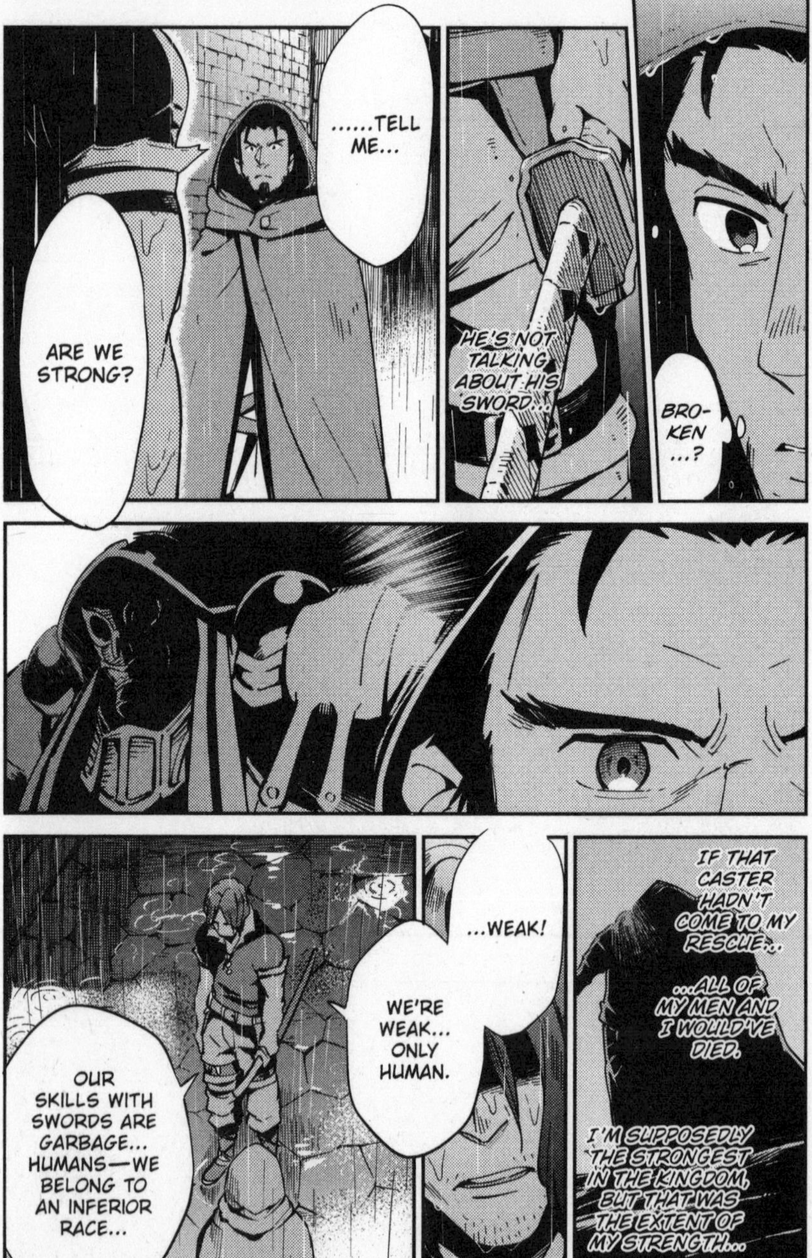
BRO-KEN...?
HE'S NOT TALKING ABOUT HIS SWORD...
......TELL ME...
ARE WE STRONG?
IF THAT CASTER HADN'T COME TO MY RESCUE...
...ALL OF MY MEN AND I WOULD'VE DIED.
I'M SUPPOSEDLY THE STRONGEST IN THE KINGDOM, BUT THAT WAS THE EXTENT OF MY STRENGTH...
...WEAK!
WE'RE WEAK... ONLY HUMAN.
OUR SKILLS WITH SWORDS ARE GARBAGE... HUMANS—WE BELONG TO AN INFERIOR RACE...

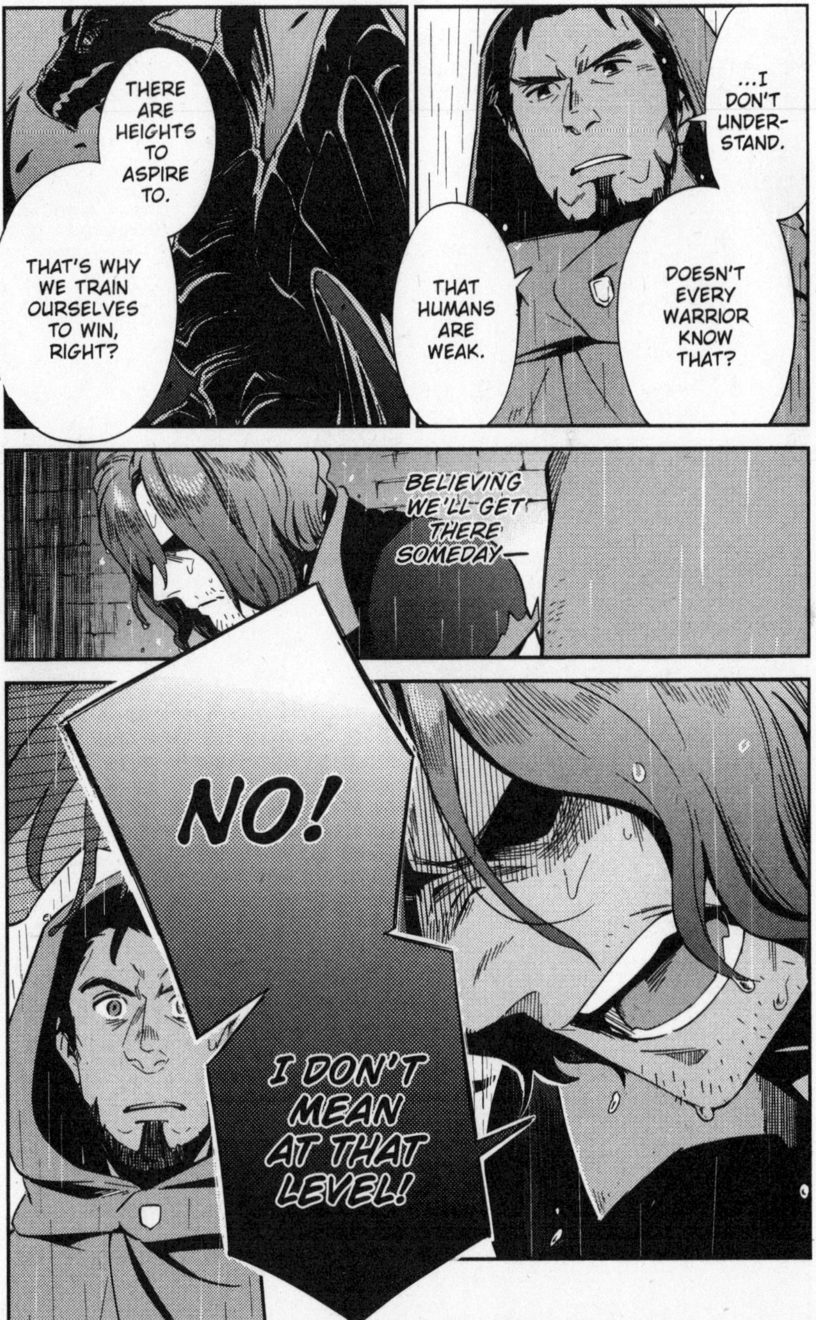
...I DON'T UNDER-STAND.
DOESN'T EVERY WARRIOR KNOW THAT?
THAT HUMANS ARE WEAK.
THERE ARE HEIGHTS TO ASPIRE TO.
THAT'S WHY WE TRAIN OURSELVES TO WIN, RIGHT?
BELIEVING WE'LL GET THERE SOMEDAY—
NO!
I DON'T MEAN AT THAT LEVEL!

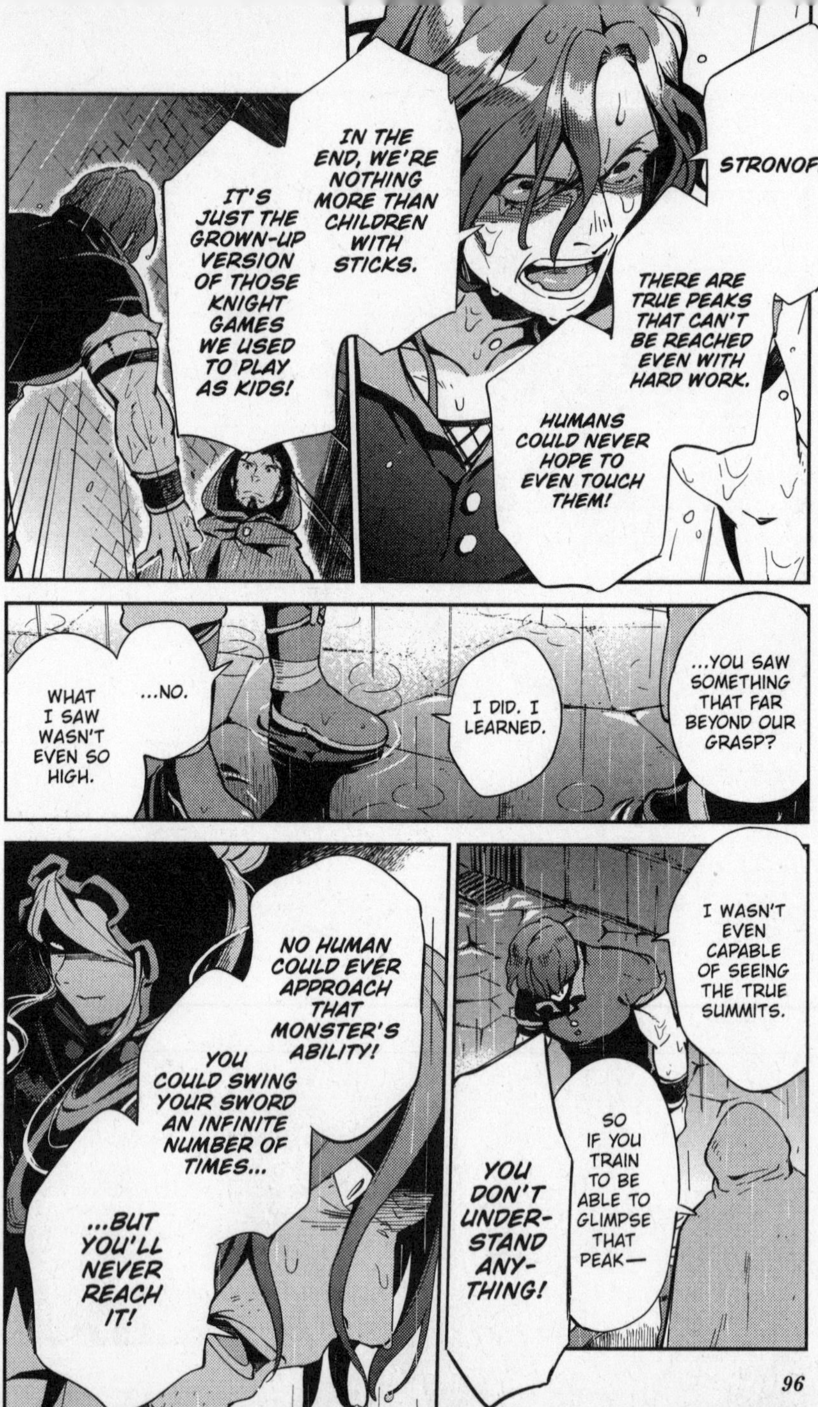
STRONOFF!
THERE ARE TRUE PEAKS THAT CAN'T BE REACHED EVEN WITH HARD WORK.
HUMANS COULD NEVER HOPE TO EVEN TOUCH THEM!
IN THE END, WE'RE NOTHING MORE THAN CHILDREN WITH STICKS.
IT'S JUST THE GROWN-UP VERSION OF THOSE KNIGHT GAMES WE USED TO PLAY AS KIDS!
...YOU SAW SOMETHING THAT FAR BEYOND OUR GRASP?
I DID. I LEARNED.
...NO.
WHAT I SAW WASN'T EVEN SO HIGH.
I WASN'T EVEN CAPABLE OF SEEING THE TRUE SUMMITS.
SO IF YOU TRAIN TO BE ABLE TO GLIMPSE THAT PEAK—
YOU DON'T UNDER-STAND ANY-THING!
NO HUMAN COULD EVER APPROACH THAT MONSTER'S ABILITY!
YOU COULD SWING YOUR SWORD AN INFINITE NUMBER OF TIMES...
...BUT YOU'LL NEVER REACH IT!

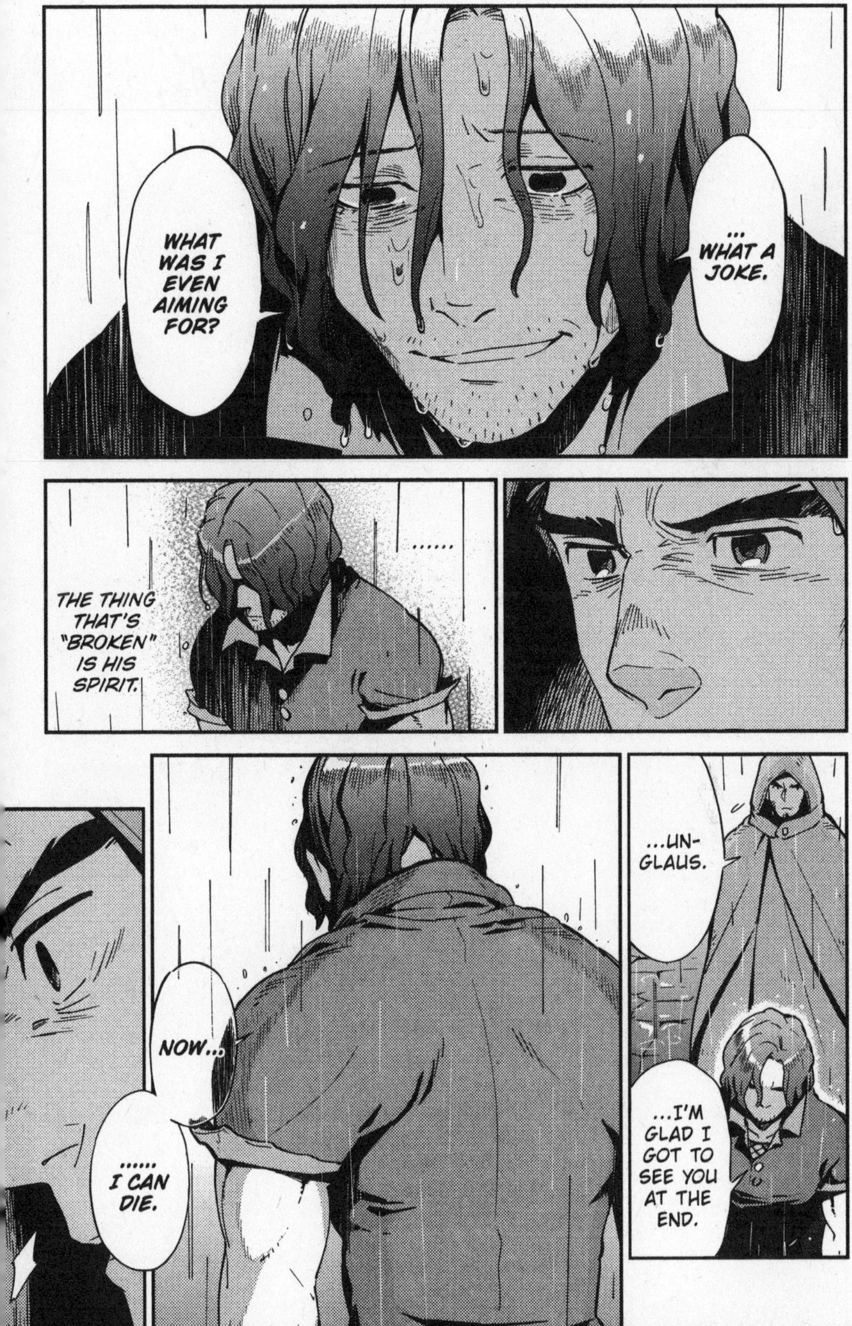
...WHAT A JOKE.
WHAT WAS I EVEN AIMING FOR?
......
THE THING THAT'S "BROKEN" IS HIS SPIRIT.
...UN-GLAUS.
...I'M GLAD I GOT TO SEE YOU AT THE END.
NOW...
...... I CAN DIE.

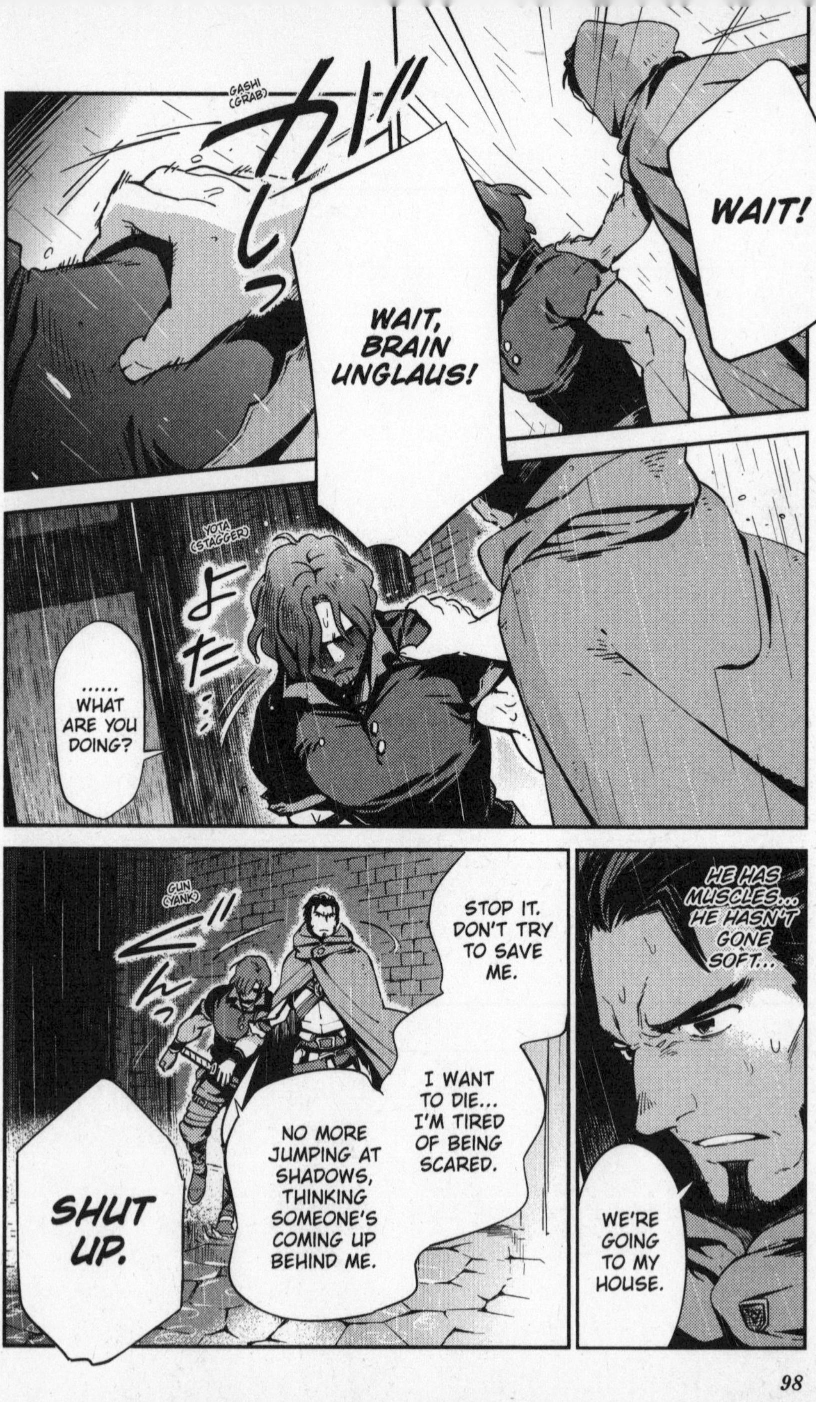
WAIT!
WAIT, BRAIN UNGLAUS!
GASHI (GRAB)
YOTA (STAGGER)
...... WHAT ARE YOU DOING?
HE HAS MUSCLES... HE HASN'T GONE SOFT...
WE'RE GOING TO MY HOUSE.
STOP IT. DON'T TRY TO SAVE ME.
I WANT TO DIE... I'M TIRED OF BEING SCARED.
NO MORE JUMPING AT SHADOWS, THINKING SOMEONE'S COMING UP BEHIND ME.
GUN (YANK)
SHUT UP.

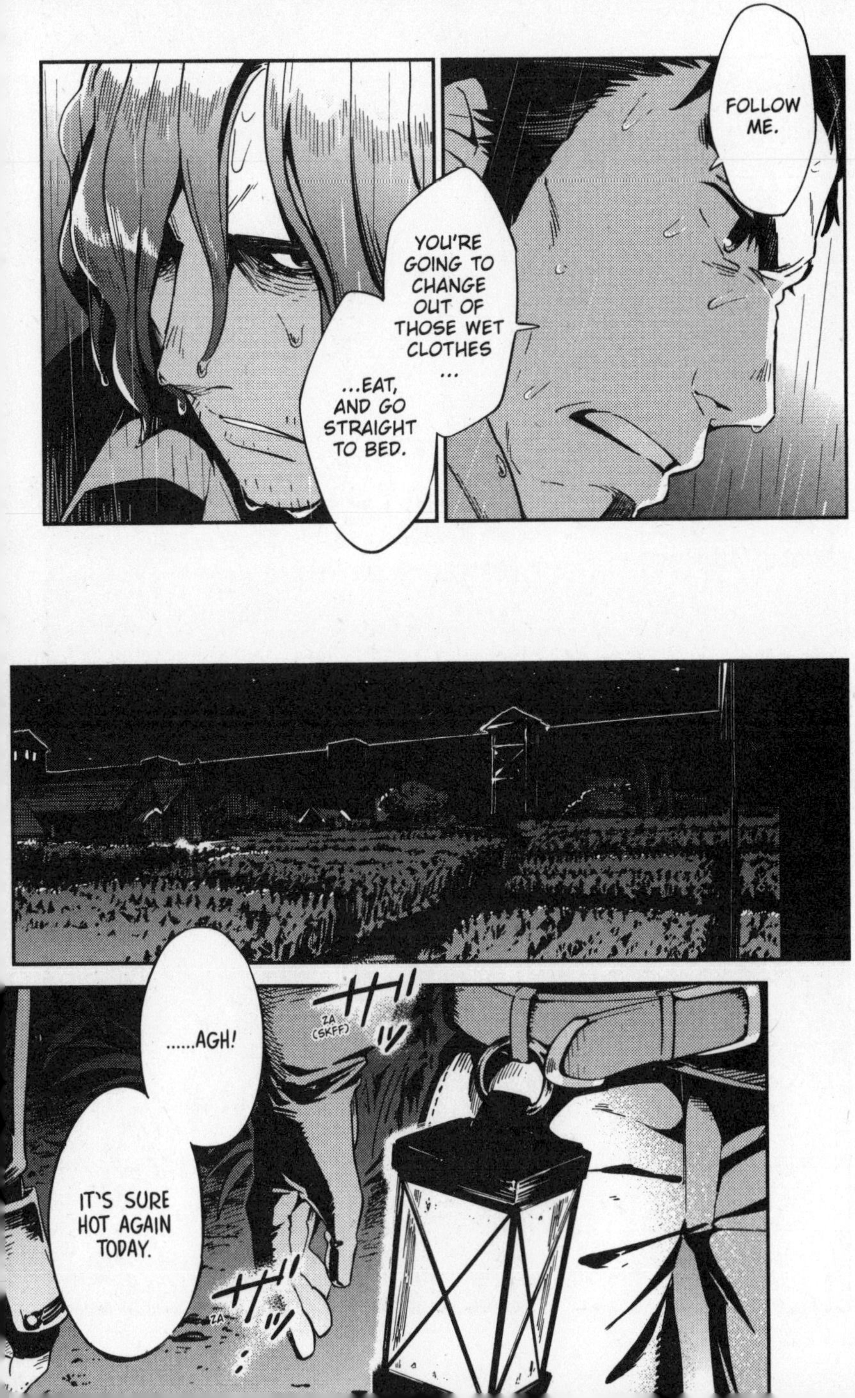
FOLLOW ME.
YOU'RE GOING TO CHANGE OUT OF THOSE WET CLOTHES ...
...EAT, AND GO STRAIGHT TO BED.
ZA (SKFF)
......AGH!
IT'S SURE HOT AGAIN TODAY.
ZA

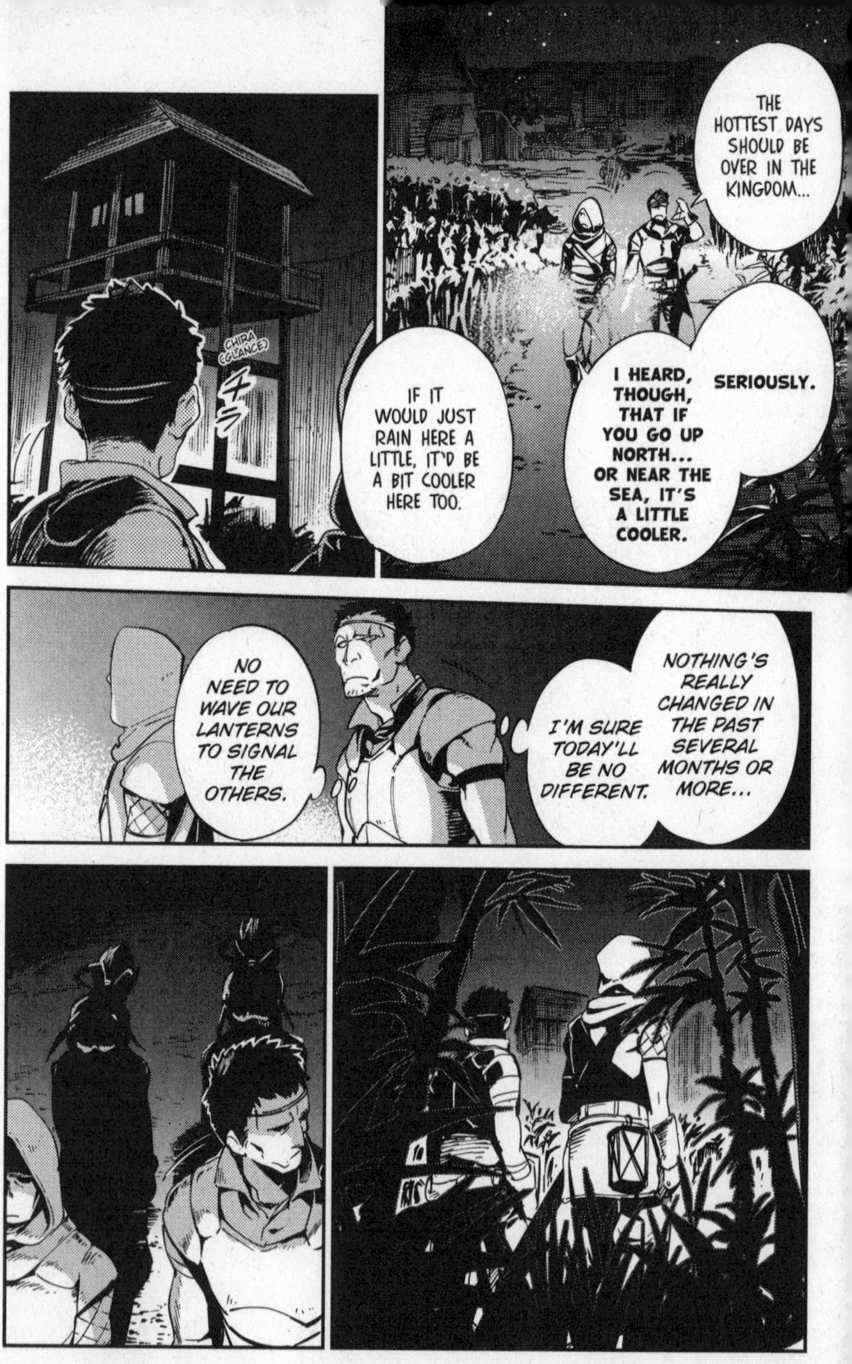
THE HOTTEST DAYS SHOULD BE OVER IN THE KINGDOM...
SERIOUSLY.
I HEARD, THOUGH, THAT IF YOU GO UP NORTH... OR NEAR THE SEA, IT'S A LITTLE COOLER.
IF IT WOULD JUST RAIN HERE A LITTLE, IT'D BE A BIT COOLER HERE TOO.
CHIRA (GLANCE)
NOTHING'S REALLY CHANGED IN THE PAST SEVERAL MONTHS OR MORE...
I'M SURE TODAY'LL BE NO DIFFERENT.
NO NEED TO WAVE OUR LANTERNS TO SIGNAL THE OTHERS.

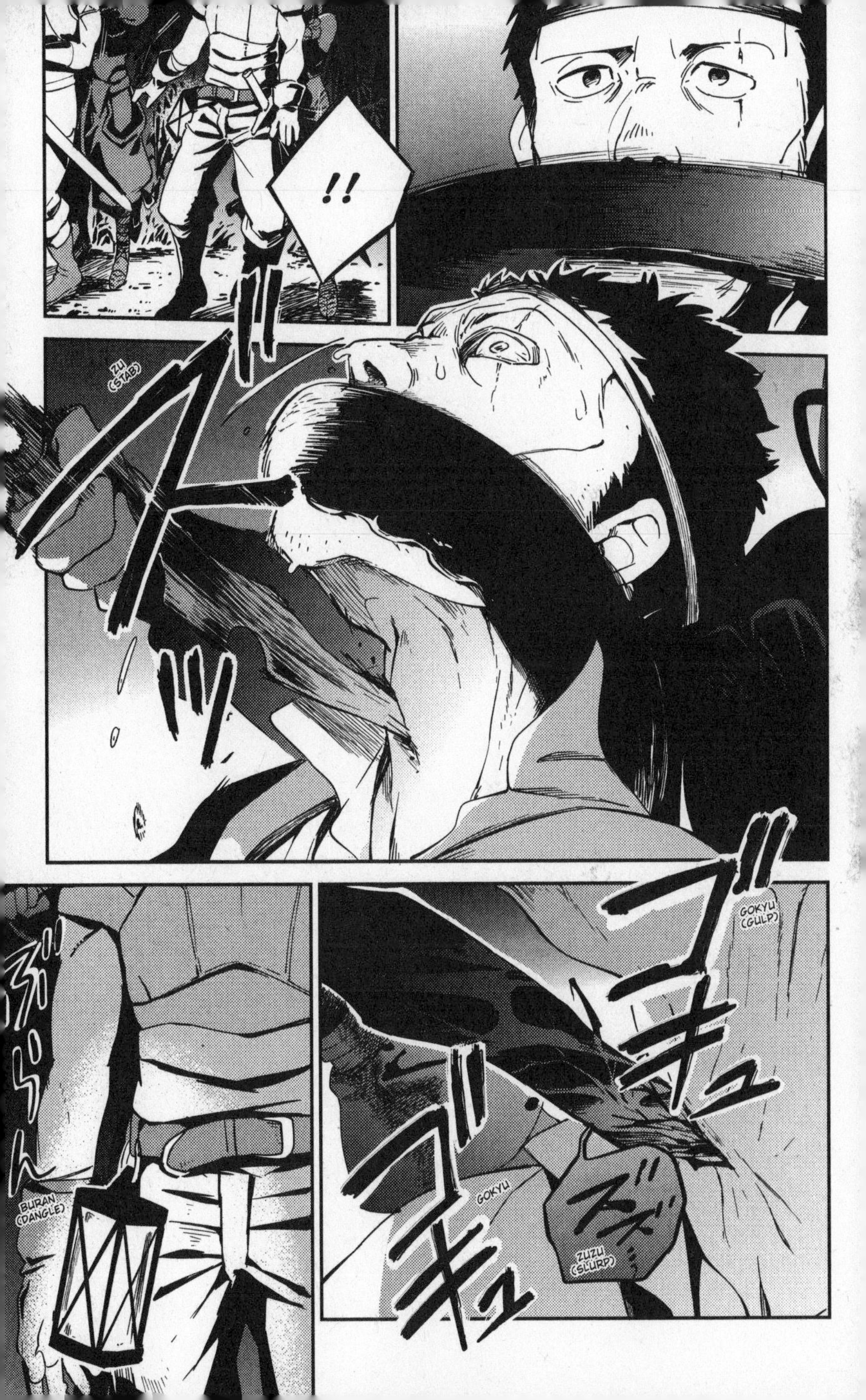
!!
ZU (STAB)
GOKYU (GULP)
GOKYU
ZUZU (SLURP)
BURAN (DANGLE)

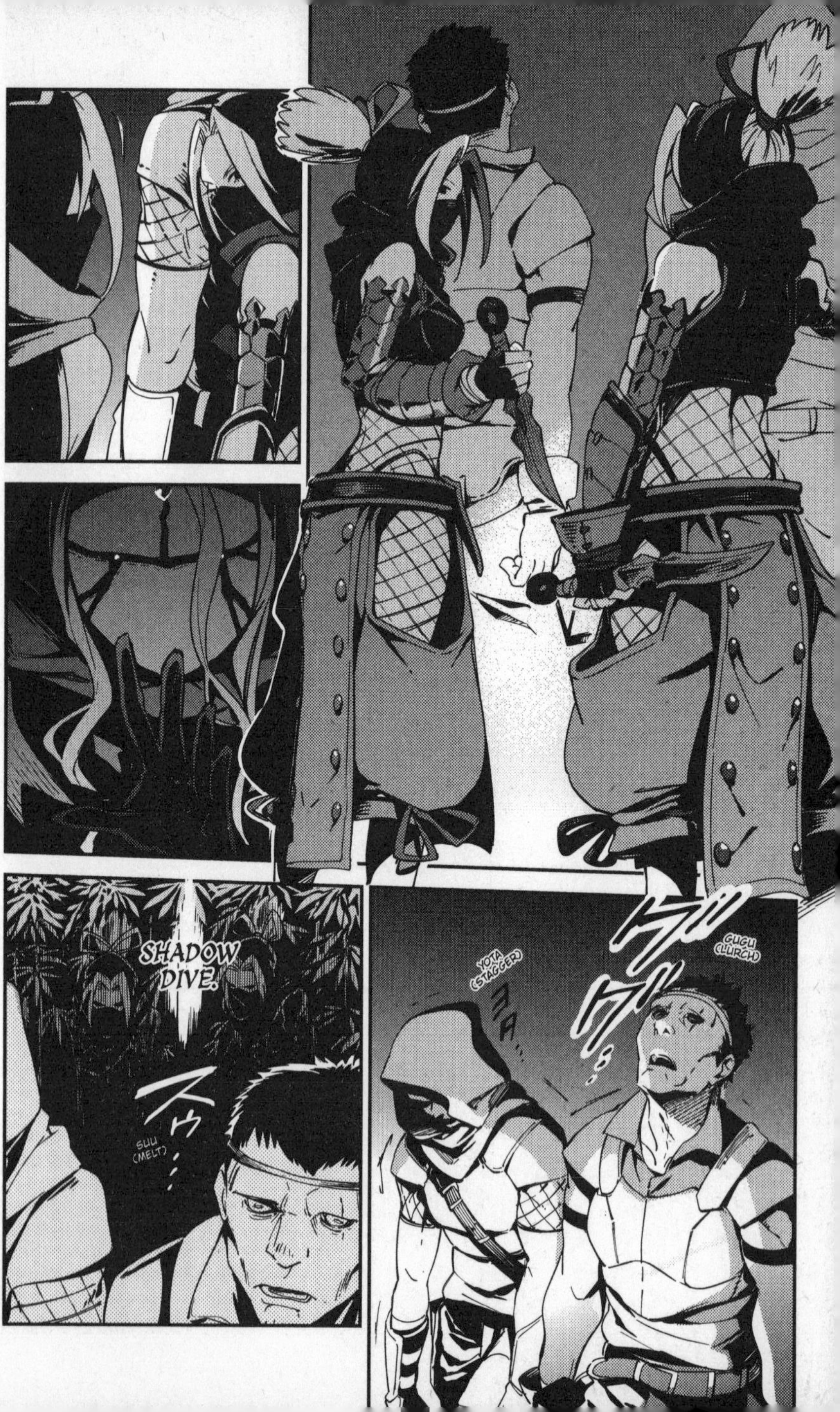
GUGU (LURCH)
YOTA (STAGGER)
SHADOW DIVE.
SUU (MELT)

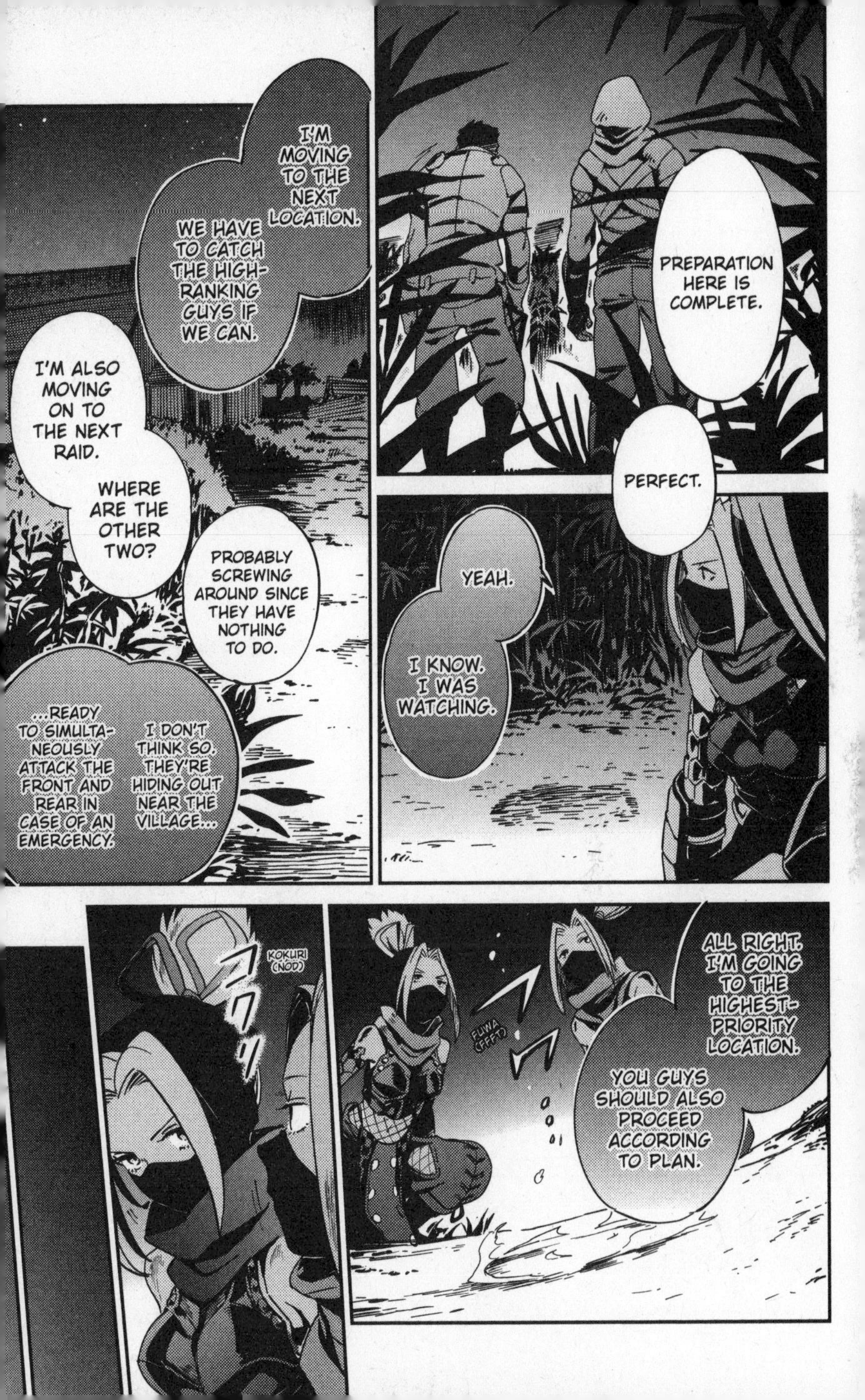
PREPARATION HERE IS COMPLETE.
PERFECT.
YEAH.
I KNOW. I WAS WATCHING.
I'M MOVING TO THE NEXT LOCATION.
WE HAVE TO CATCH THE HIGH-RANKING GUYS IF WE CAN.
I'M ALSO MOVING ON TO THE NEXT RAID.
WHERE ARE THE OTHER TWO?
PROBABLY SCREWING AROUND SINCE THEY HAVE NOTHING TO DO.
I DON'T THINK SO. THEY'RE HIDING OUT NEAR THE VILLAGE...
...READY TO SIMULTANEOUSLY ATTACK THE FRONT AND REAR IN CASE OF AN EMERGENCY.
ALL RIGHT. I'M GOING TO THE HIGHEST-PRIORITY LOCATION.
YOU GUYS SHOULD ALSO PROCEED ACCORDING TO PLAN.
FUWA (PFFT)
KOKURI (NOD)

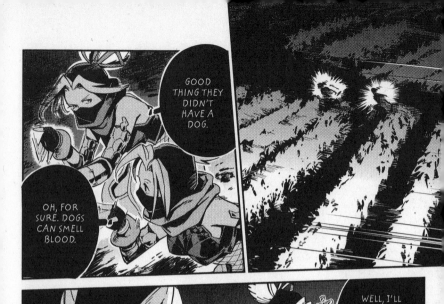

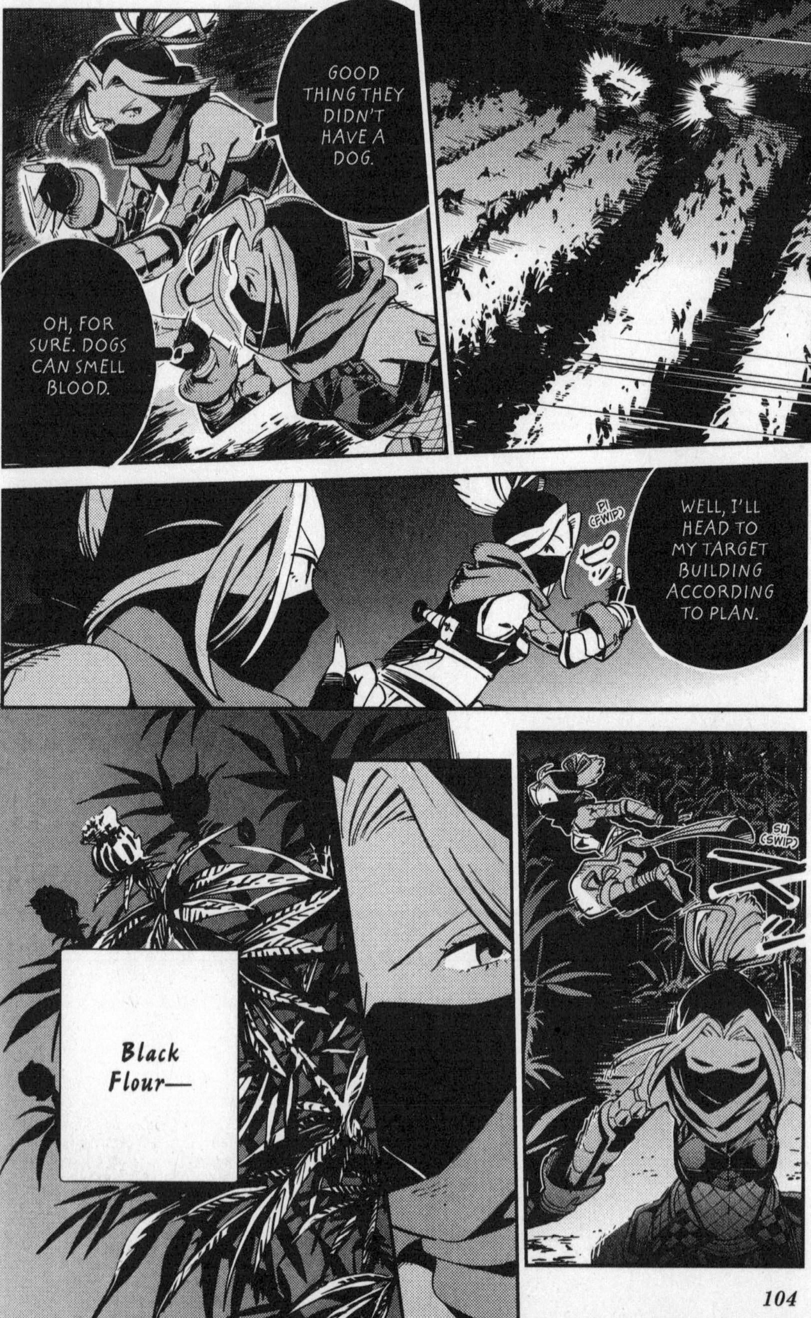
GOOD THING THEY DIDN'T HAVE A DOG.
OH, FOR SURE. DOGS CAN SMELL BLOOD.
WELL, I'LL HEAD TO MY TARGET BUILDING ACCORDING TO PLAN.
PI (FWIP)
SU (SWIP)
Black Flour—

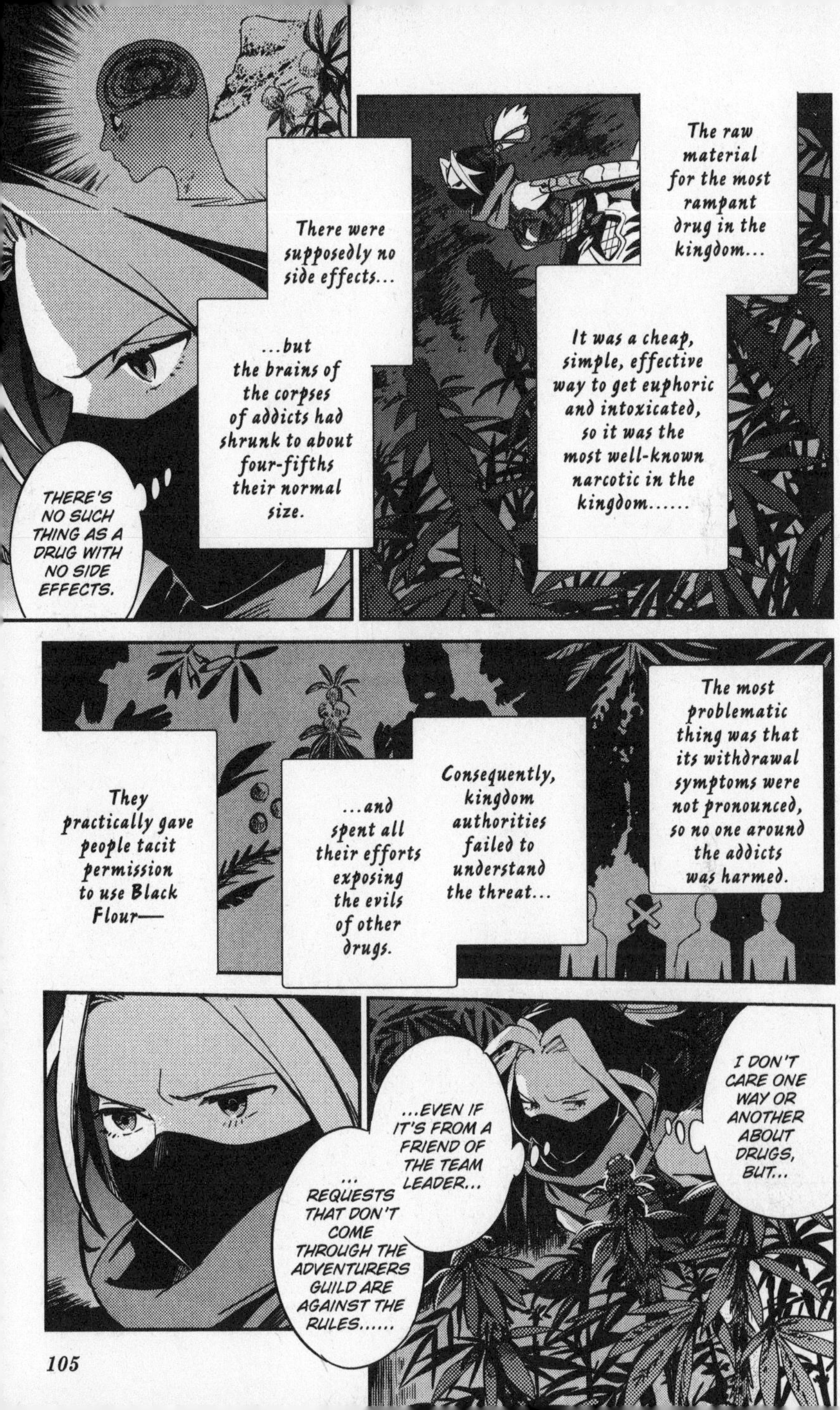
The raw material for the most rampant drug in the kingdom...
It was a cheap, simple, effective way to get euphoric and intoxicated, so it was the most well-known narcotic in the kingdom......
There were supposedly no side effects...
...but the brains of the corpses of addicts had shrunk to about four-fifths their normal size.
THERE'S NO SUCH THING AS A DRUG WITH NO SIDE EFFECTS.
The most problematic thing was that its withdrawal symptoms were not pronounced, so no one around the addicts was harmed.
Consequently, kingdom authorities failed to understand the threat...
...and spent all their efforts exposing the evils of other drugs.
They practically gave people tacit permission to use Black Flour—
I DON'T CARE ONE WAY OR ANOTHER ABOUT DRUGS, BUT...
...EVEN IF IT'S FROM A FRIEND OF THE TEAM LEADER...
... REQUESTS THAT DON'T COME THROUGH THE ADVENTURERS GUILD ARE AGAINST THE RULES......

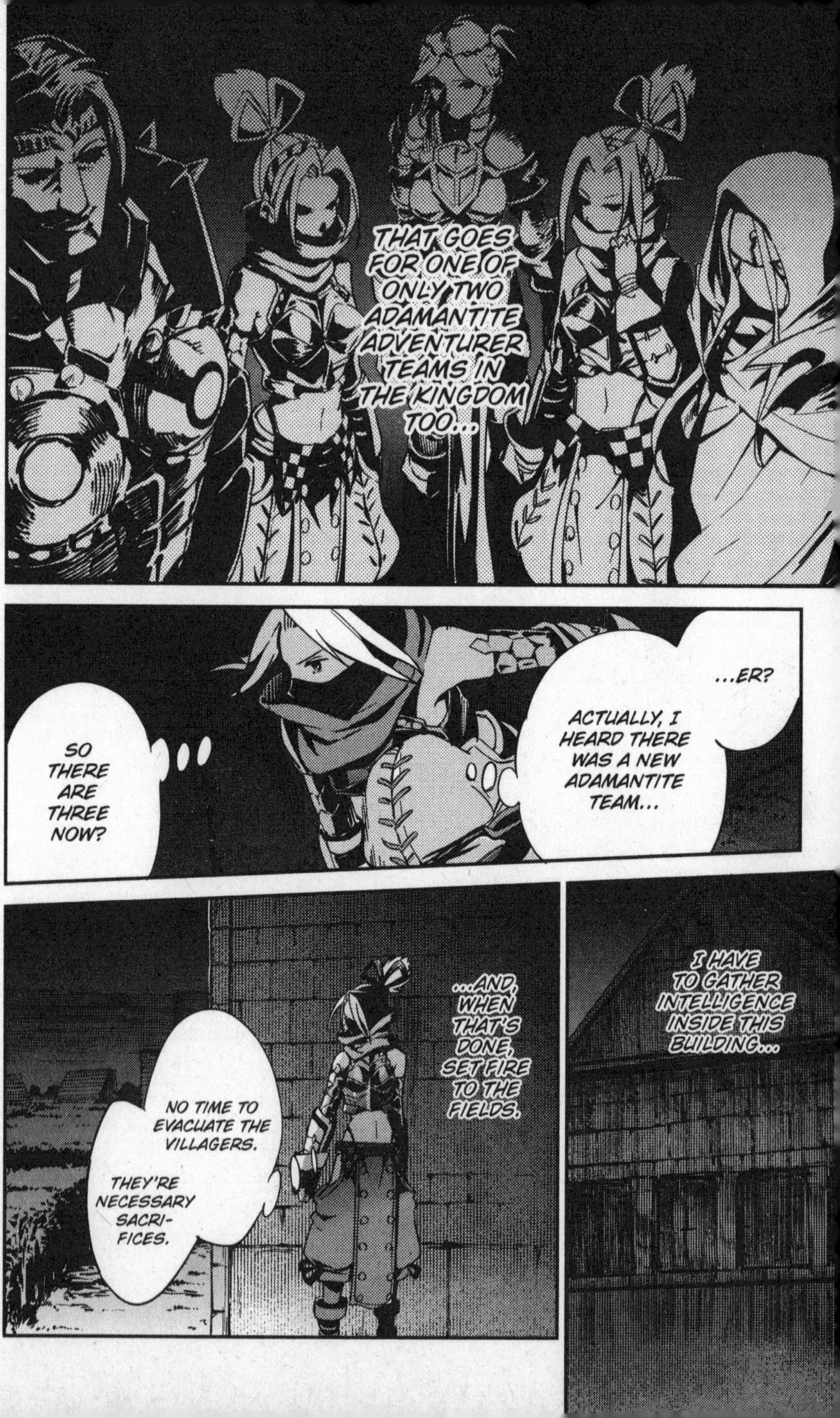
THAT GOES FOR ONE OF ONLY TWO ADAMANTITE ADVENTURER TEAMS IN THE KINGDOM TOO...
...ER?
ACTUALLY, I HEARD THERE WAS A NEW ADAMANTITE TEAM...
SO THERE ARE THREE NOW?
I HAVE TO GATHER INTELLIGENCE INSIDE THIS BUILDING...
...AND, WHEN THAT'S DONE, SET FIRE TO THE FIELDS.
NO TIME TO EVACUATE THE VILLAGERS.
THEY'RE NECESSARY SACRI-FICES.

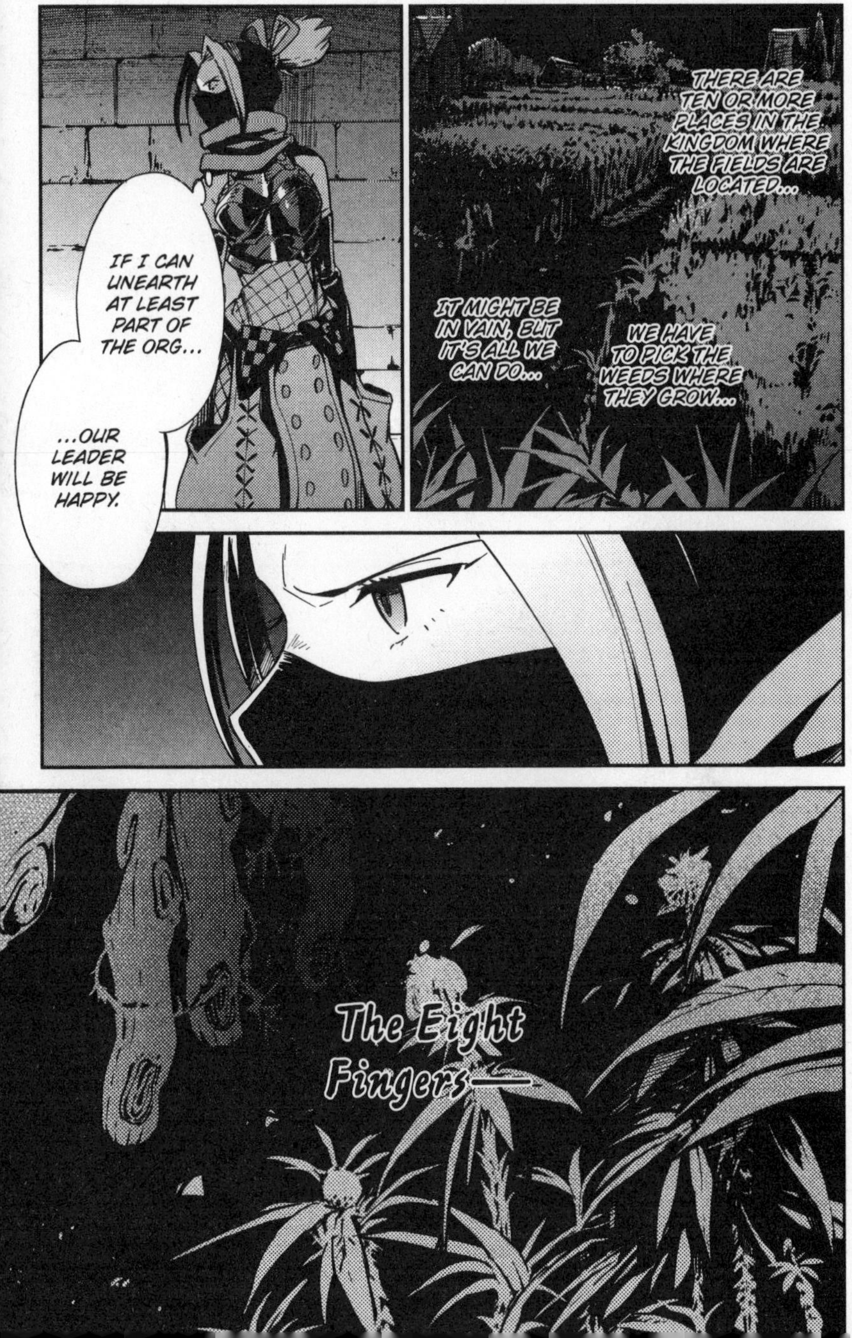
THERE ARE TEN OR MORE PLACES IN THE KINGDOM WHERE THE FIELDS ARE LOCATED...
WE HAVE TO PICK THE WEEDS WHERE THEY GROW...
IT MIGHT BE IN VAIN, BUT IT'S ALL WE CAN DO...
IF I CAN UNEARTH AT LEAST PART OF THE ORG...
...OUR LEADER WILL BE HAPPY.
The Eight Fingers——

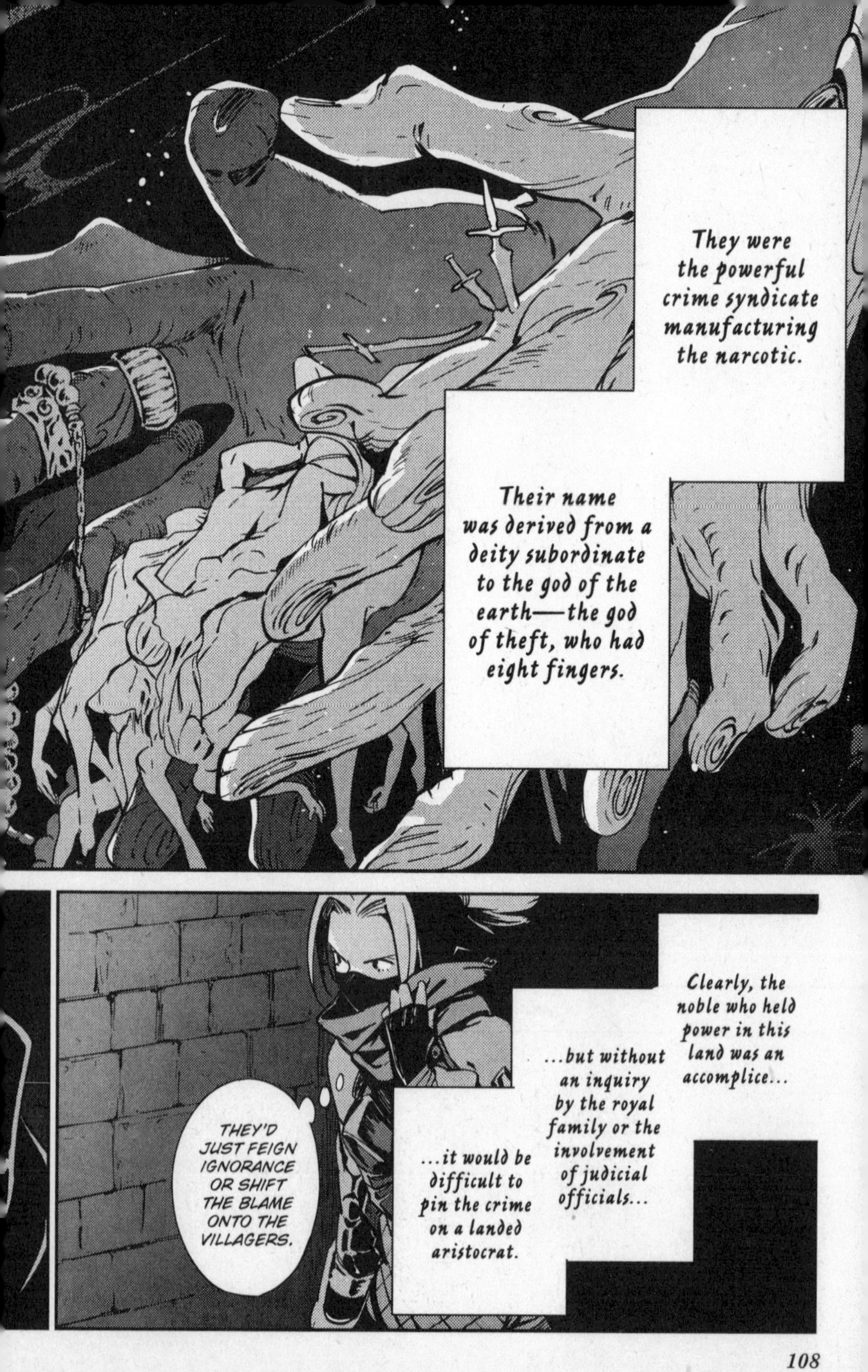

They were the powerful crime syndicate manufacturing the narcotic.
Their name was derived from a deity subordinate to the god of the earth—the god of theft, who had eight fingers.
Clearly, the noble who held power in this land was an accomplice...
...but without an inquiry by the royal family or the involvement of judicial officials...
...it would be difficult to pin the crime on a landed aristocrat.
THEY'D JUST FEIGN IGNORANCE OR SHIFT THE BLAME ONTO THE VILLAGERS.

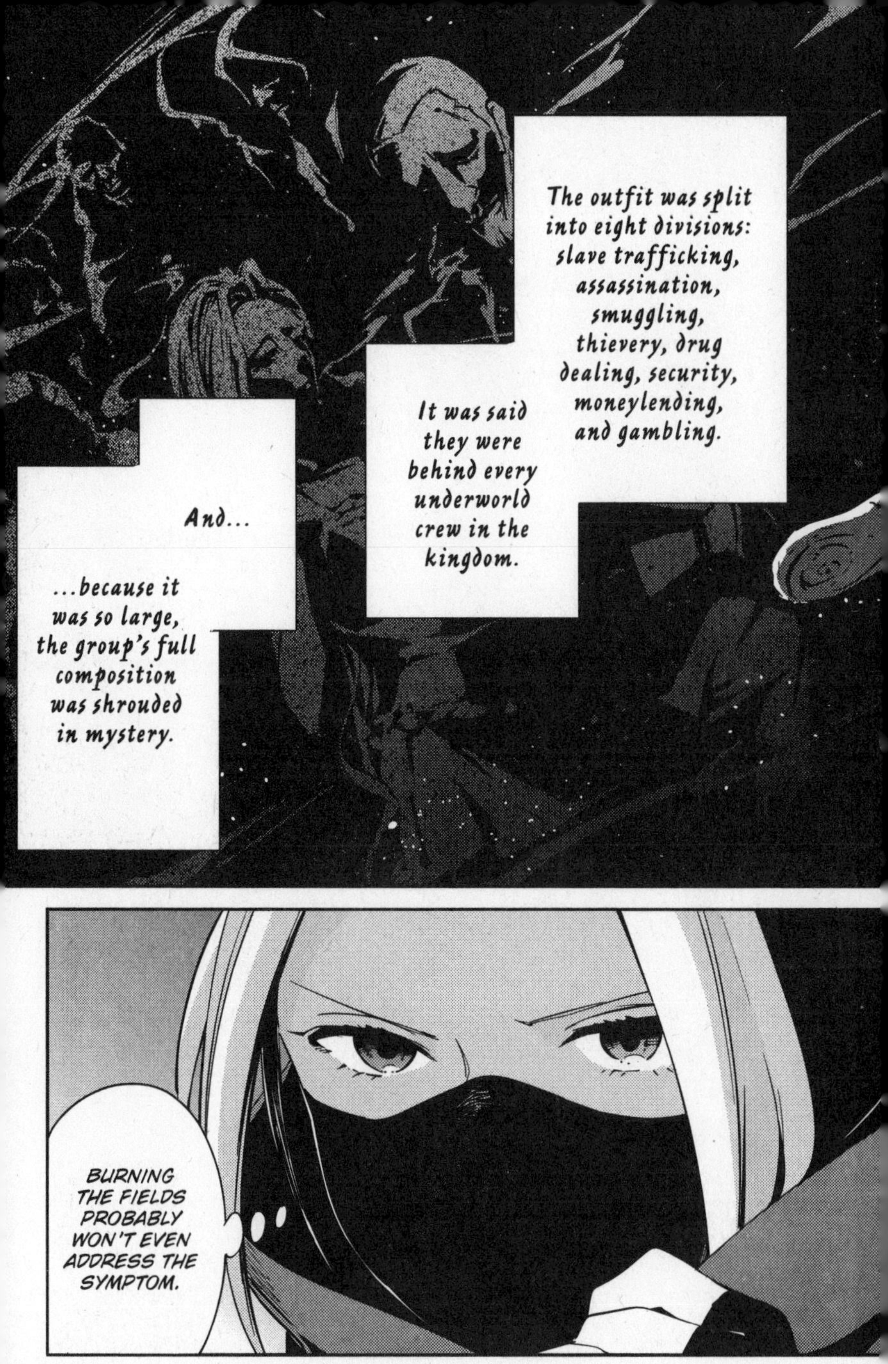

The outfit was split into eight divisions: slave trafficking, assassination, smuggling, thievery, drug dealing, security, moneylending, and gambling.
It was said they were behind every underworld crew in the kingdom.
And...
...because it was so large, the group's full composition was shrouded in mystery.
BURNING THE FIELDS PROBABLY WON'T EVEN ADDRESS THE SYMPTOM.

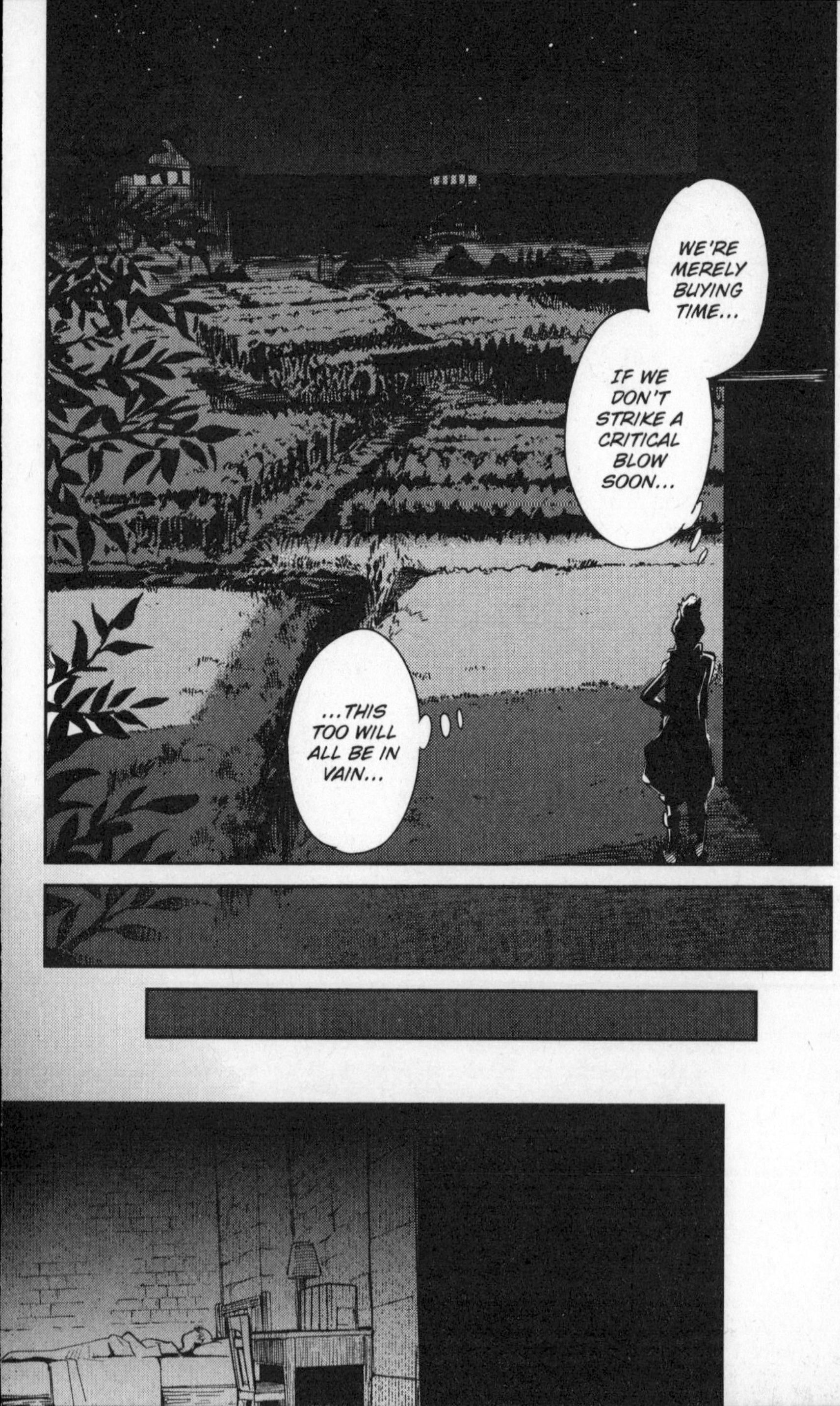
WE'RE MERELY BUYING TIME...
IF WE DON'T STRIKE A CRITICAL BLOW SOON...
...THIS TOO WILL ALL BE IN VAIN...

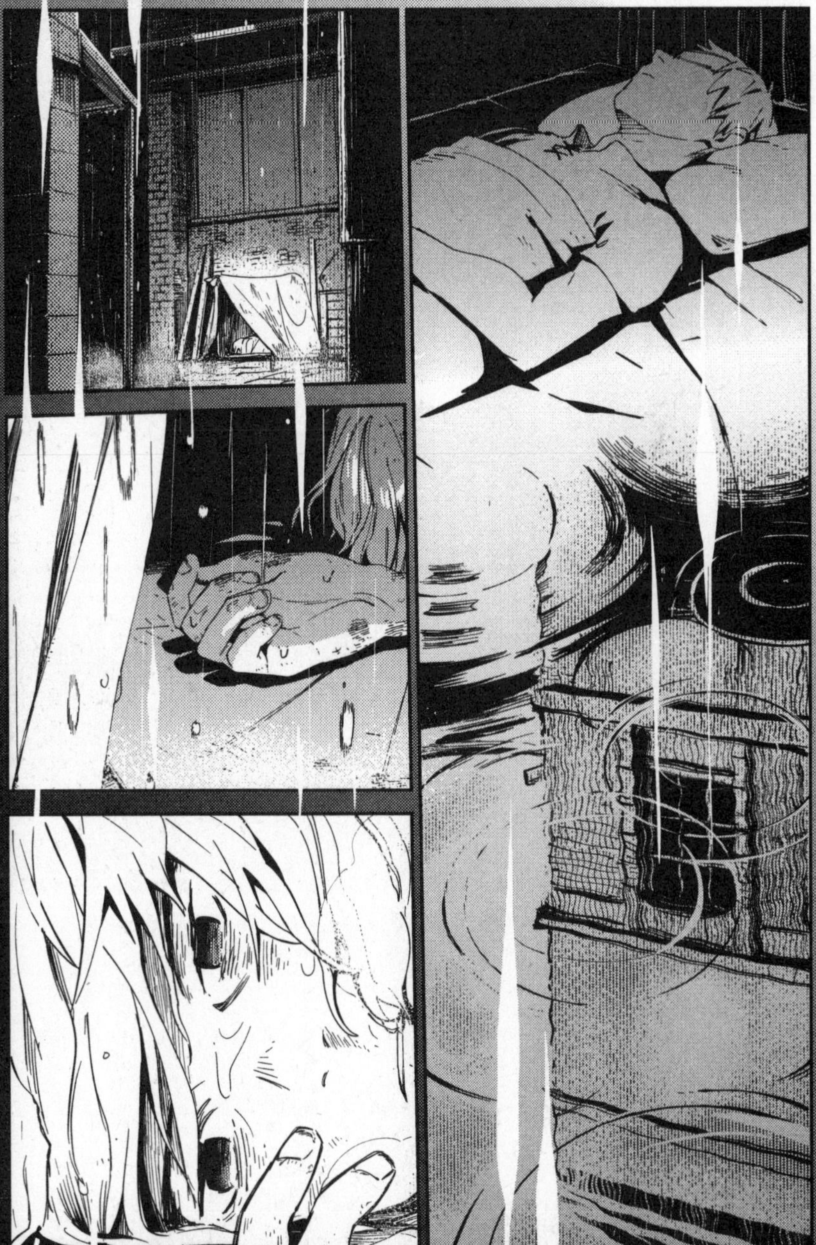

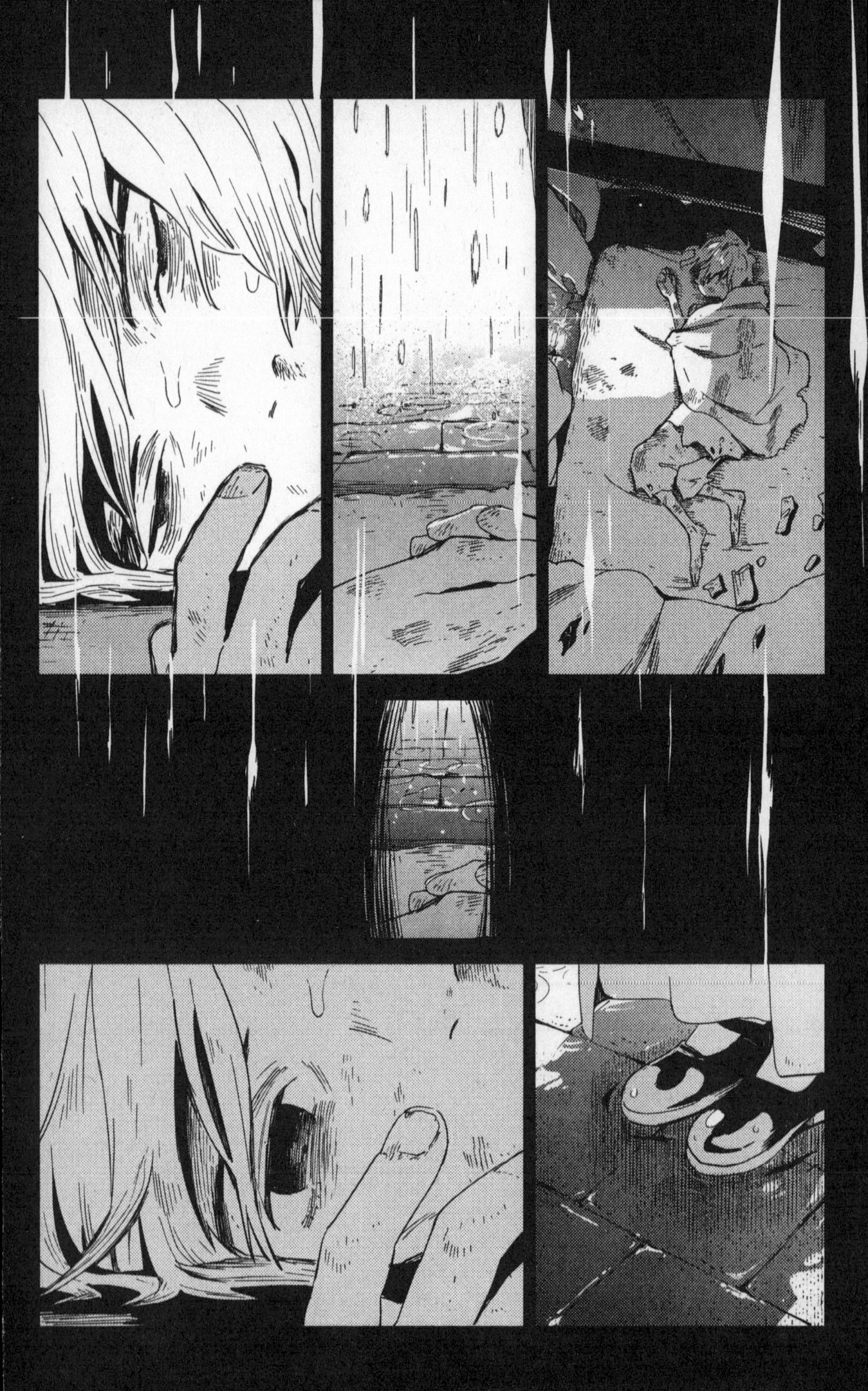

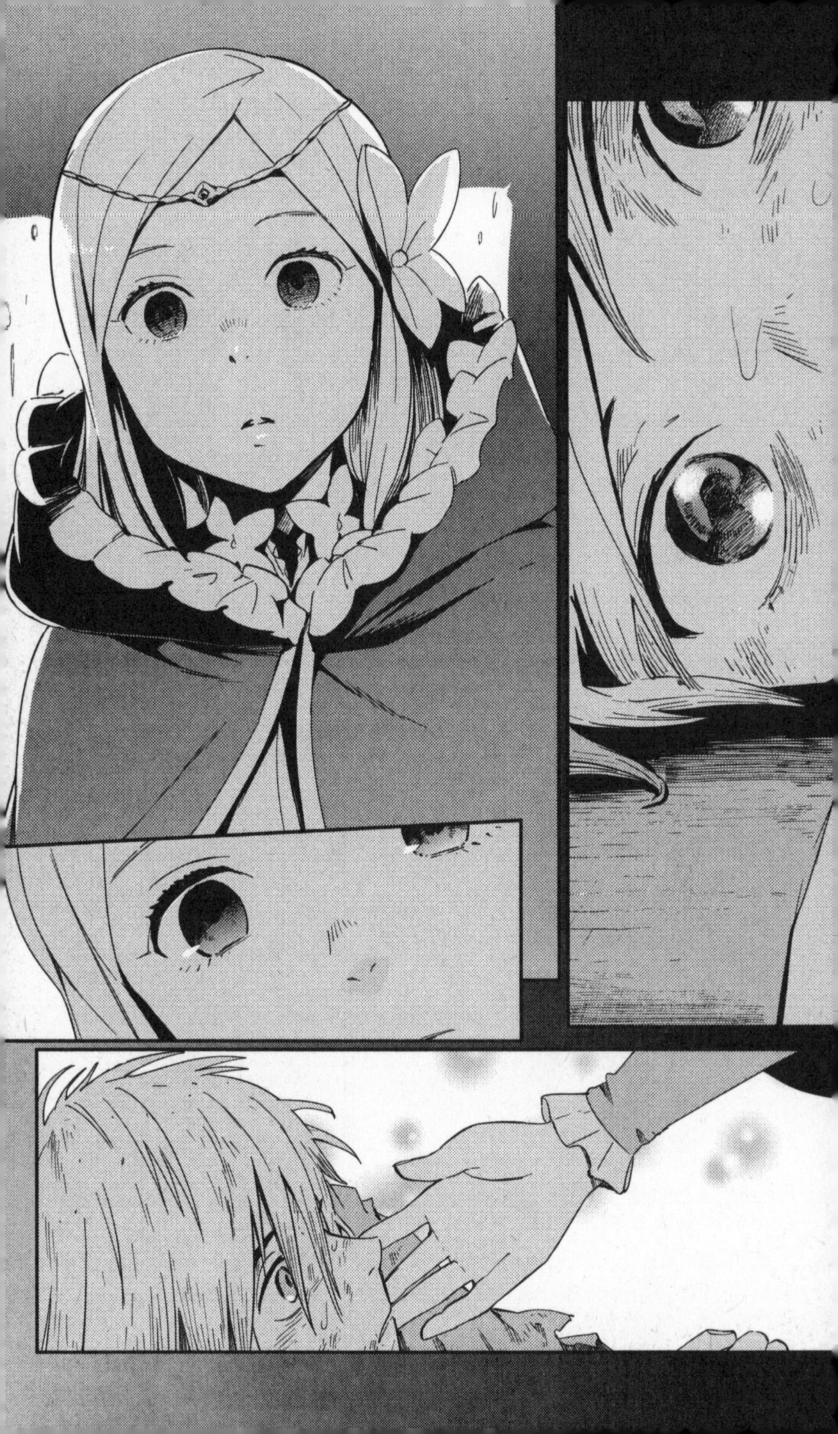

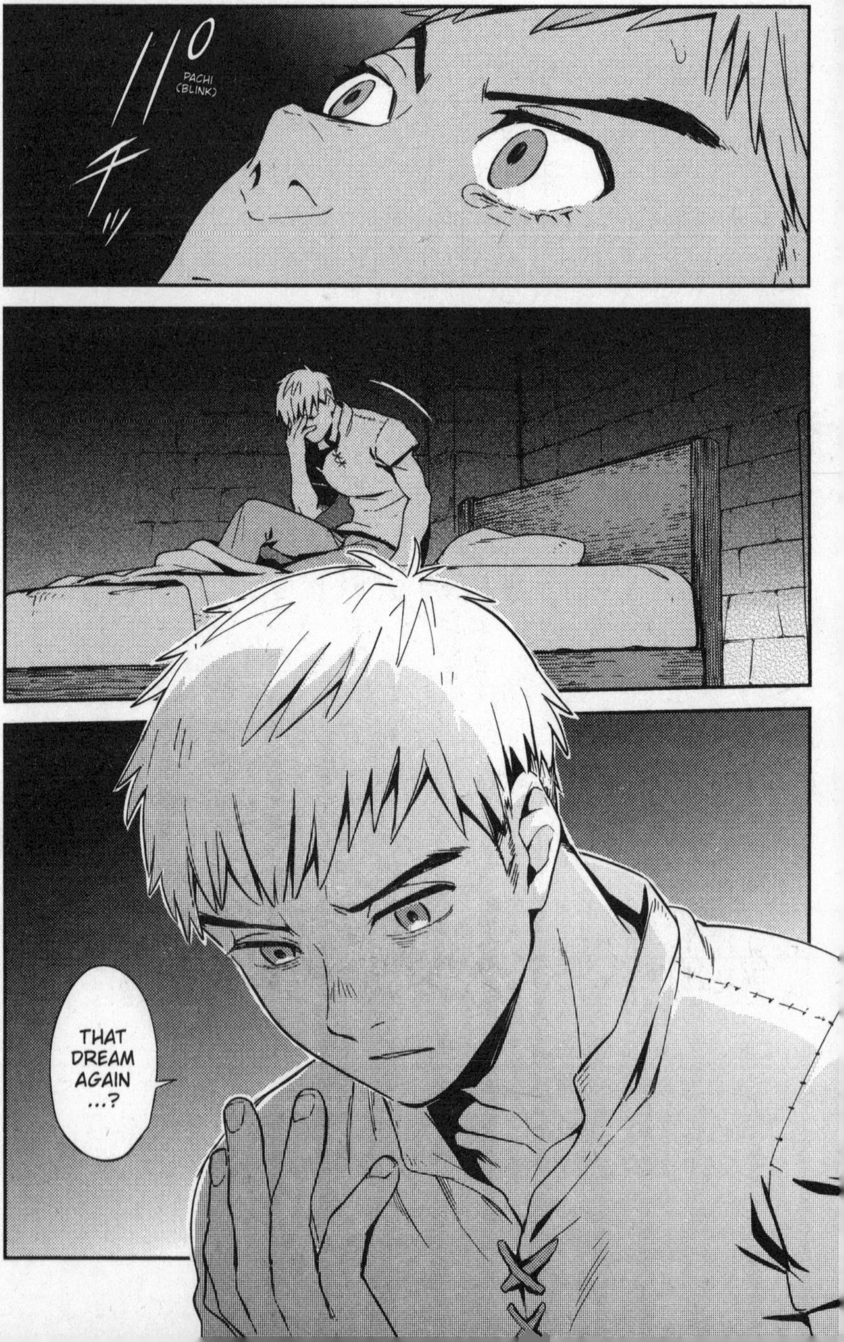
PACHI (BLINK)
THAT DREAM AGAIN ...?

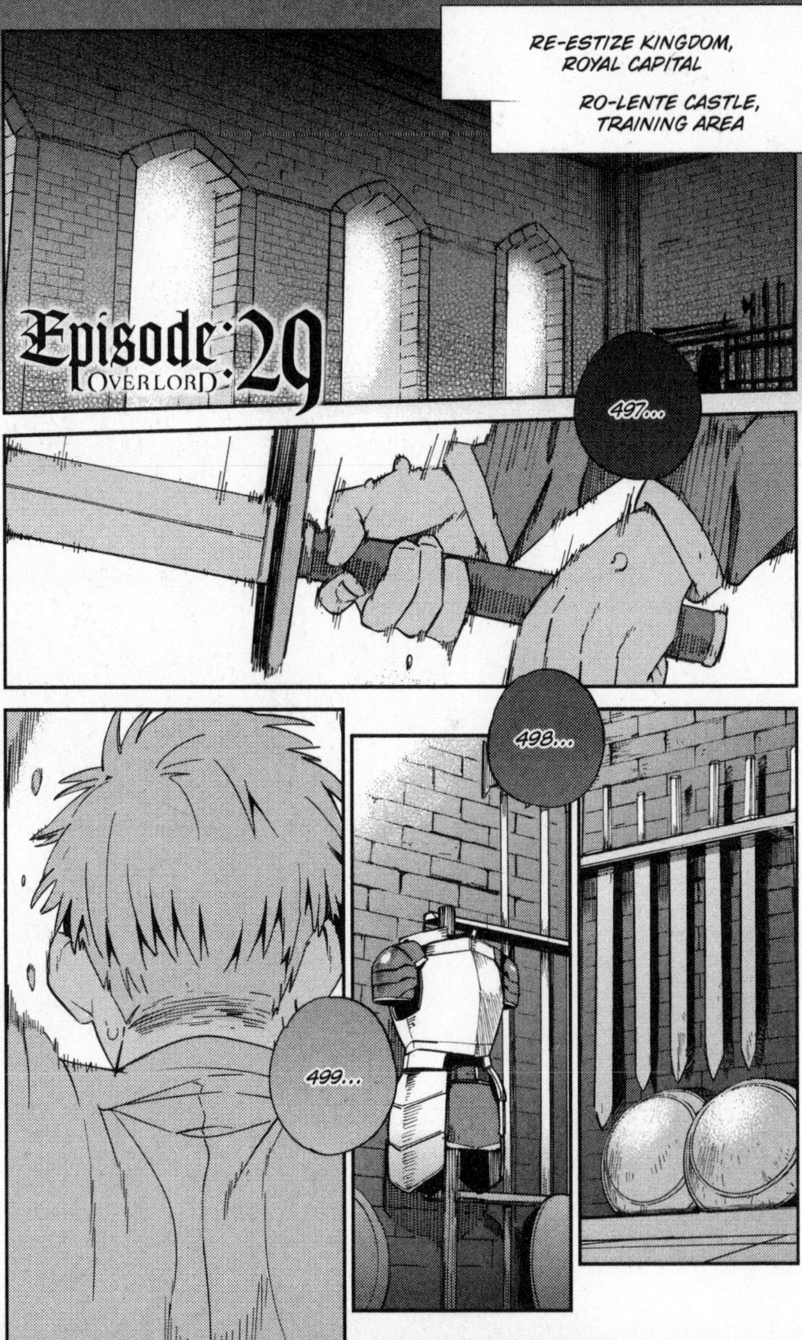
RE-ESTIZE KINGDOM, ROYAL CAPITAL
RO-LENTE CASTLE, TRAINING AREA
Episode:29
OVERLORD
497...
498...
499...

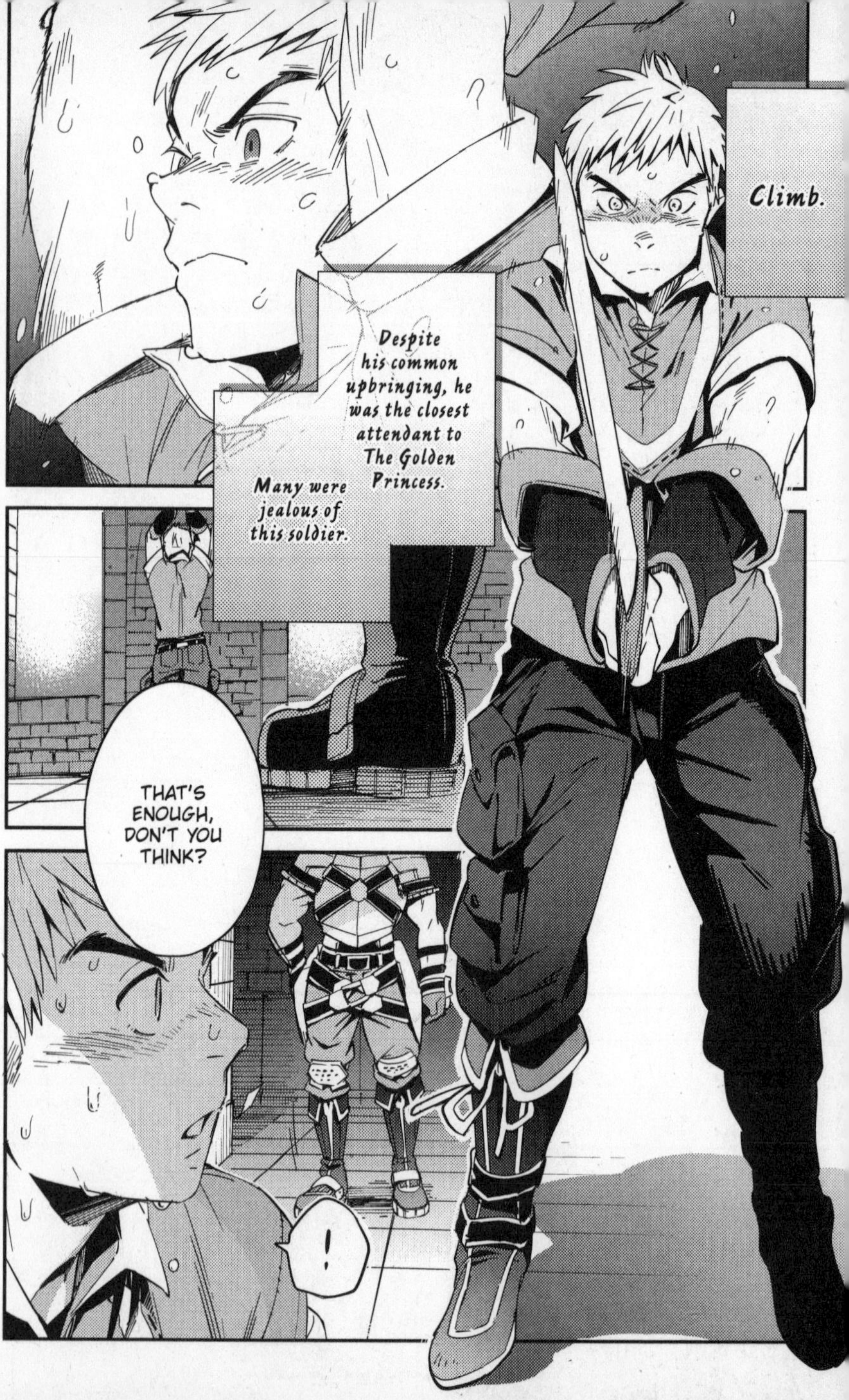
Climb.
Despite his common upbringing, he was the closest attendant to The Golden Princess.
Many were jealous of this soldier.
THAT'S ENOUGH, DON'T YOU THINK?
!

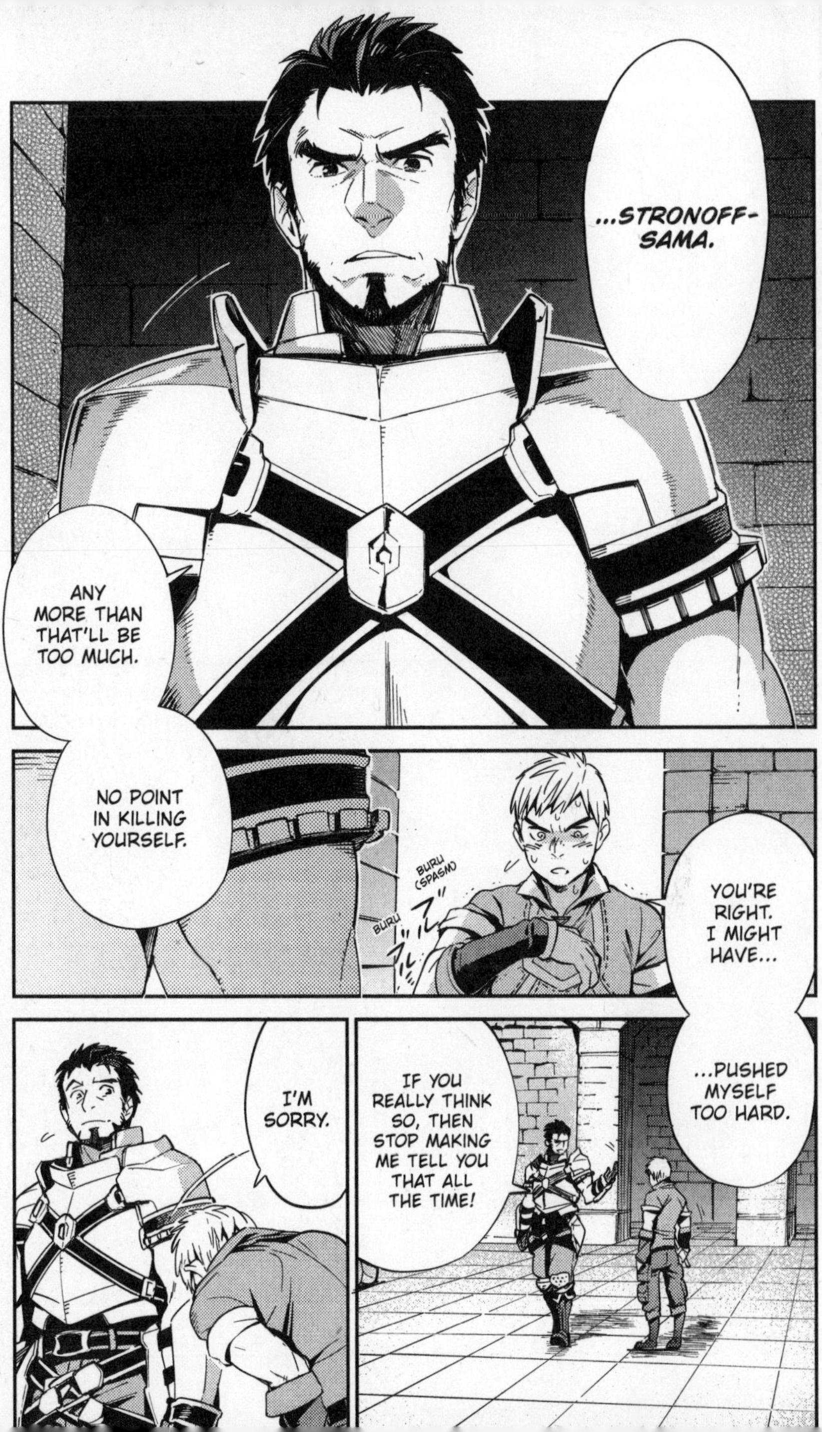
...STRONOFF-SAMA.
ANY MORE THAN THAT'LL BE TOO MUCH.
NO POINT IN KILLING YOURSELF.
BURU (SPASM)
BURU
YOU'RE RIGHT. I MIGHT HAVE...
...PUSHED MYSELF TOO HARD.
IF YOU REALLY THINK SO, THEN STOP MAKING ME TELL YOU THAT ALL THE TIME!
I'M SORRY.

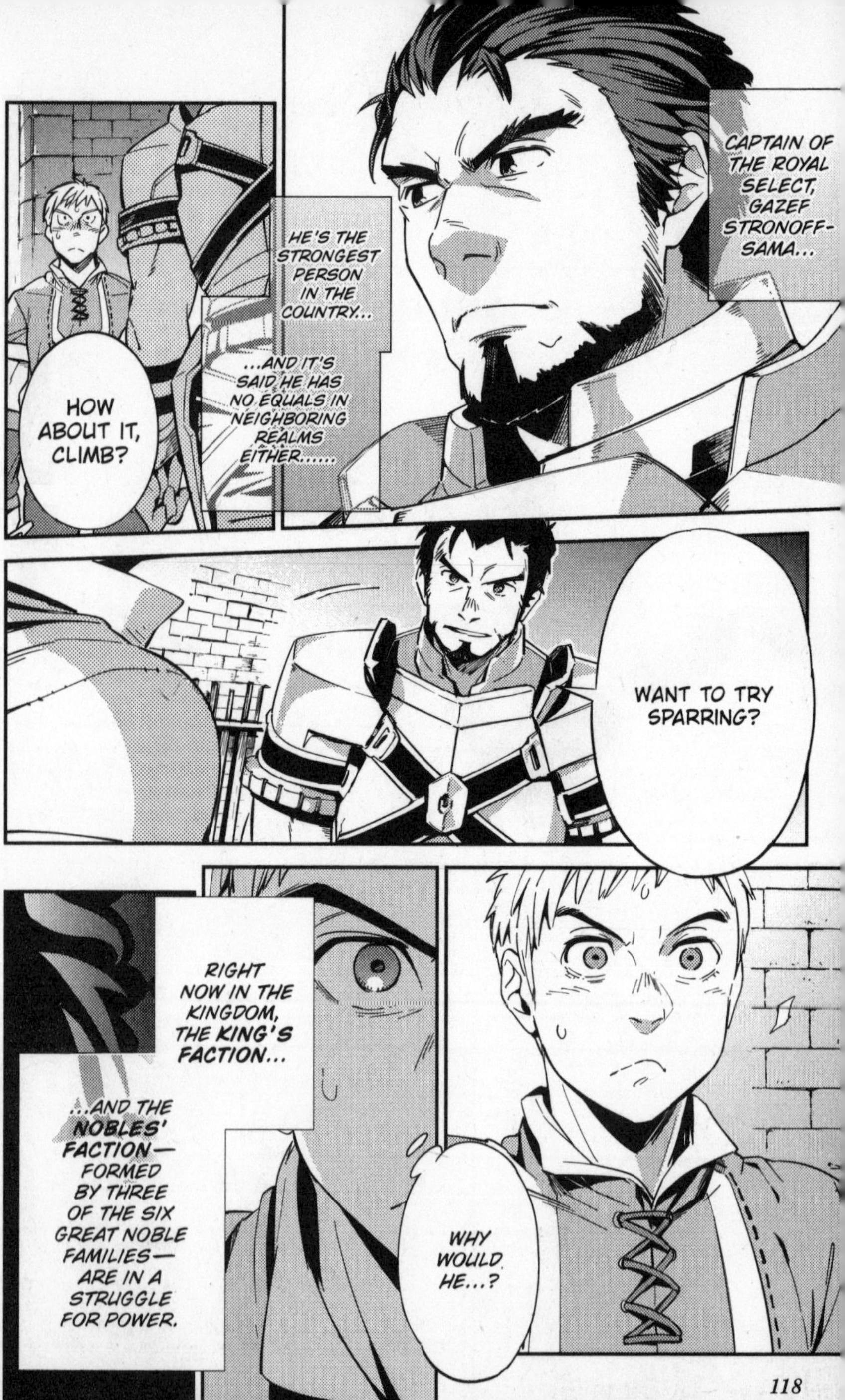
CAPTAIN OF THE ROYAL SELECT, GAZEF STRONOFF-SAMA...
HE'S THE STRONGEST PERSON IN THE COUNTRY...
...AND IT'S SAID HE HAS NO EQUALS IN NEIGHBORING REALMS EITHER......
HOW ABOUT IT, CLIMB?
WANT TO TRY SPARRING?
WHY WOULD HE...?
RIGHT NOW IN THE KINGDOM, THE KING'S FACTION...
...AND THE NOBLES' FACTION—FORMED BY THREE OF THE SIX GREAT NOBLE FAMILIES—ARE IN A STRUGGLE FOR POWER.

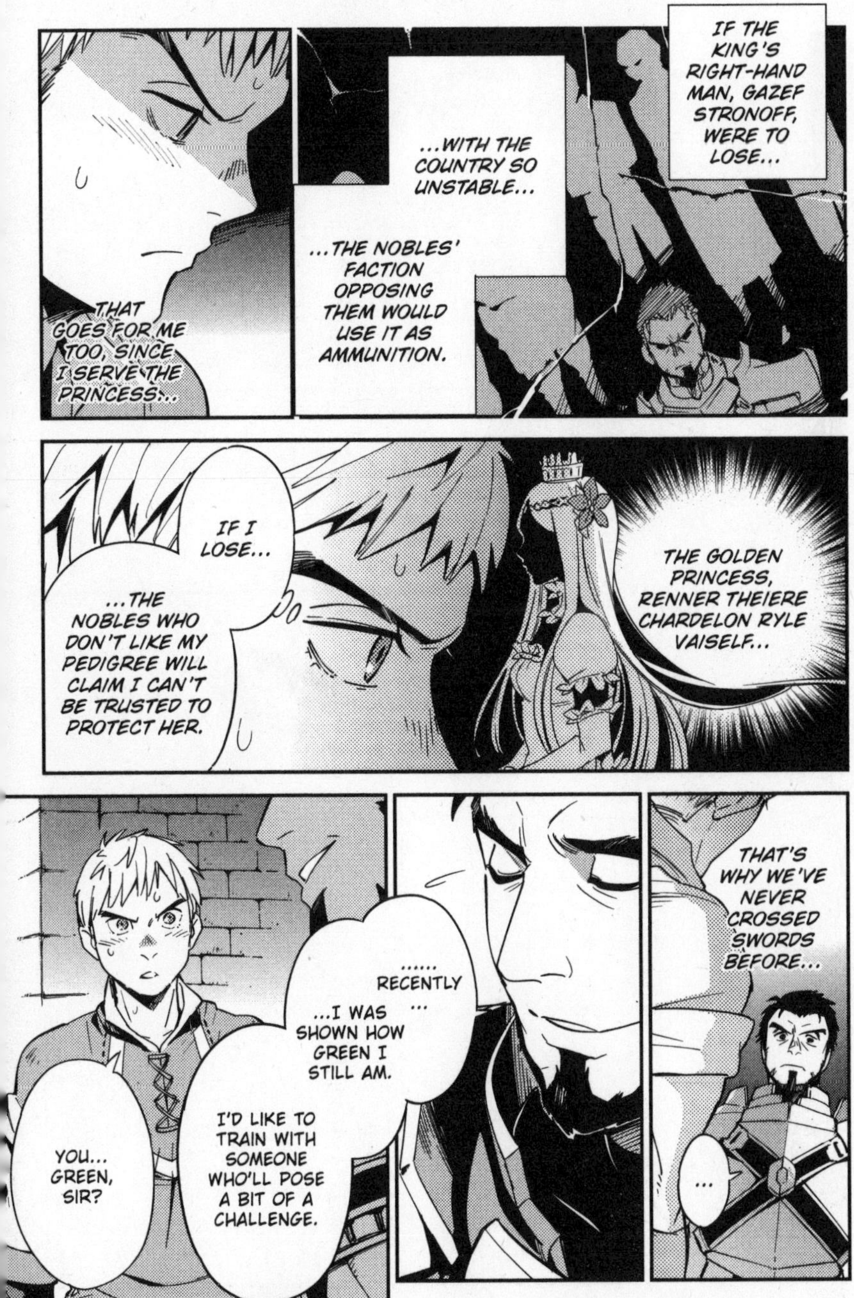
IF THE KING'S RIGHT-HAND MAN, GAZEF STRONOFF, WERE TO LOSE...
...WITH THE COUNTRY SO UNSTABLE...
...THE NOBLES' FACTION OPPOSING THEM WOULD USE IT AS AMMUNITION.
THAT GOES FOR ME TOO, SINCE I SERVE THE PRINCESS...
THE GOLDEN PRINCESS, RENNER THEIERE CHARDELON RYLE VAISELF...
IF I LOSE...
...THE NOBLES WHO DON'T LIKE MY PEDIGREE WILL CLAIM I CAN'T BE TRUSTED TO PROTECT HER.
THAT'S WHY WE'VE NEVER CROSSED SWORDS BEFORE...
...
...... RECENTLY ...
...I WAS SHOWN HOW GREEN I STILL AM.
I'D LIKE TO TRAIN WITH SOMEONE WHO'LL POSE A BIT OF A CHALLENGE.
YOU... GREEN, SIR?

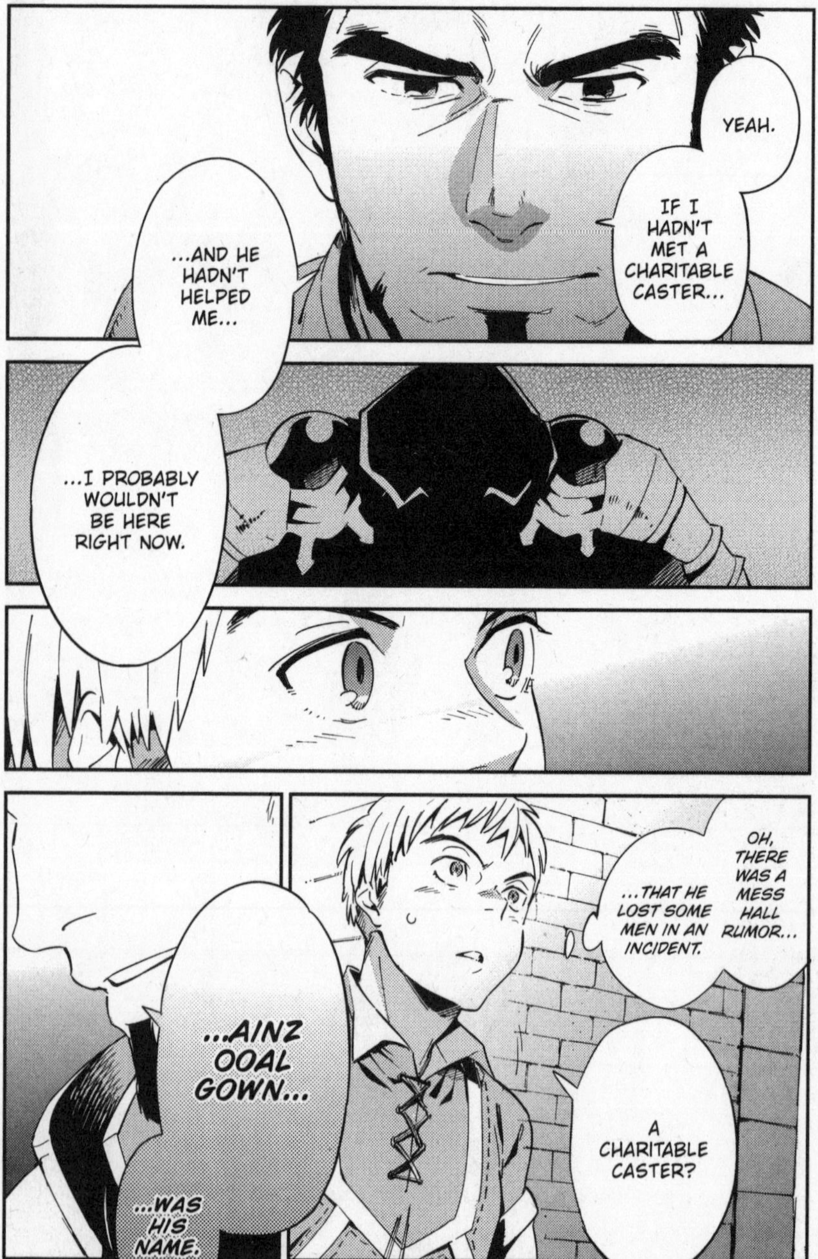

YEAH.
IF I HADN'T MET A CHARITABLE CASTER...
...AND HE HADN'T HELPED ME...
...I PROBABLY WOULDN'T BE HERE RIGHT NOW.
OH, THERE WAS A MESS HALL RUMOR...
...THAT HE LOST SOME MEN IN AN INCIDENT.
A CHARITABLE CASTER?
...AINZ OOAL GOWN...
...WAS HIS NAME.

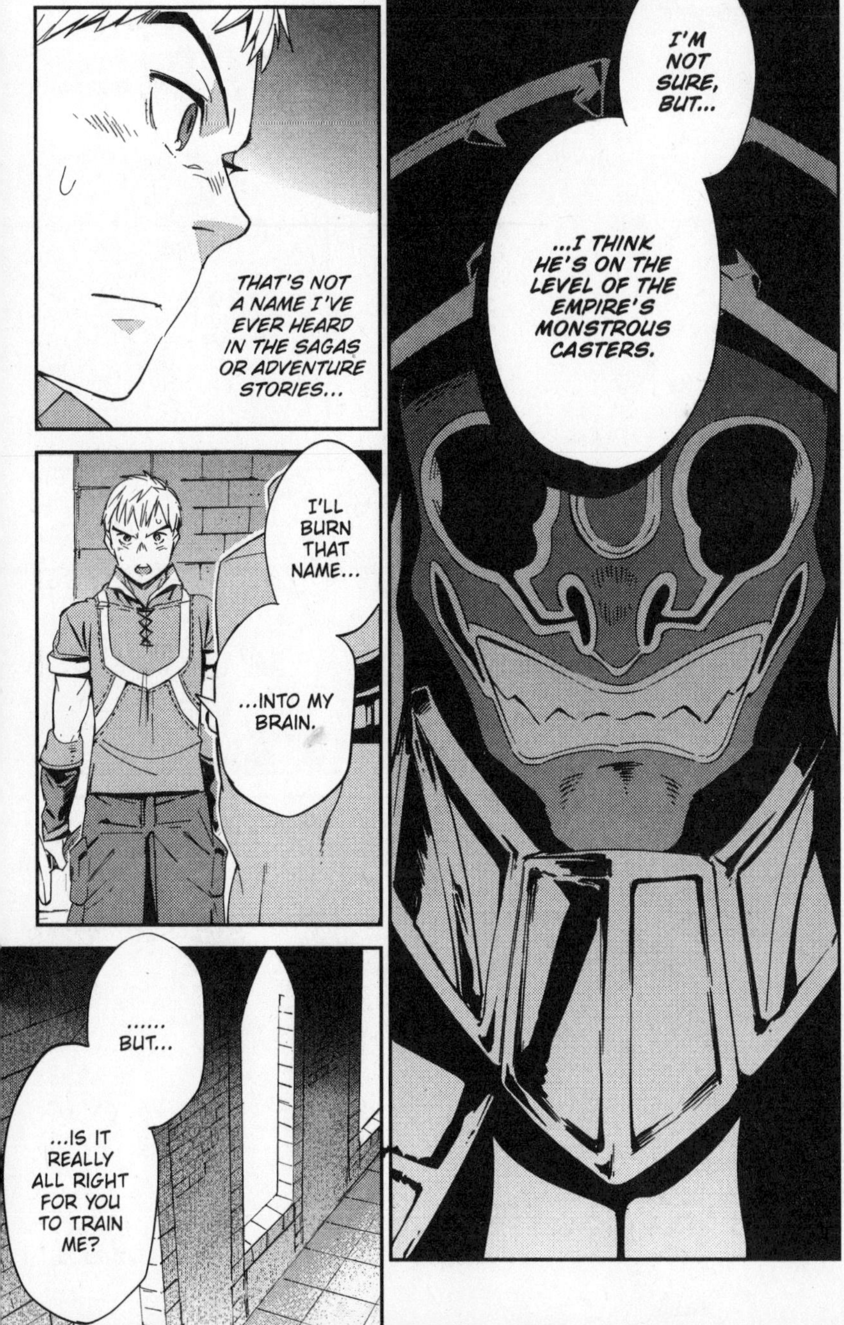
I'M NOT SURE, BUT...
...I THINK HE'S ON THE LEVEL OF THE EMPIRE'S MONSTROUS CASTERS.
THAT'S NOT A NAME I'VE EVER HEARD IN THE SAGAS OR ADVENTURE STORIES...
I'LL BURN THAT NAME...
...INTO MY BRAIN.
...... BUT...
...IS IT REALLY ALL RIGHT FOR YOU TO TRAIN ME?

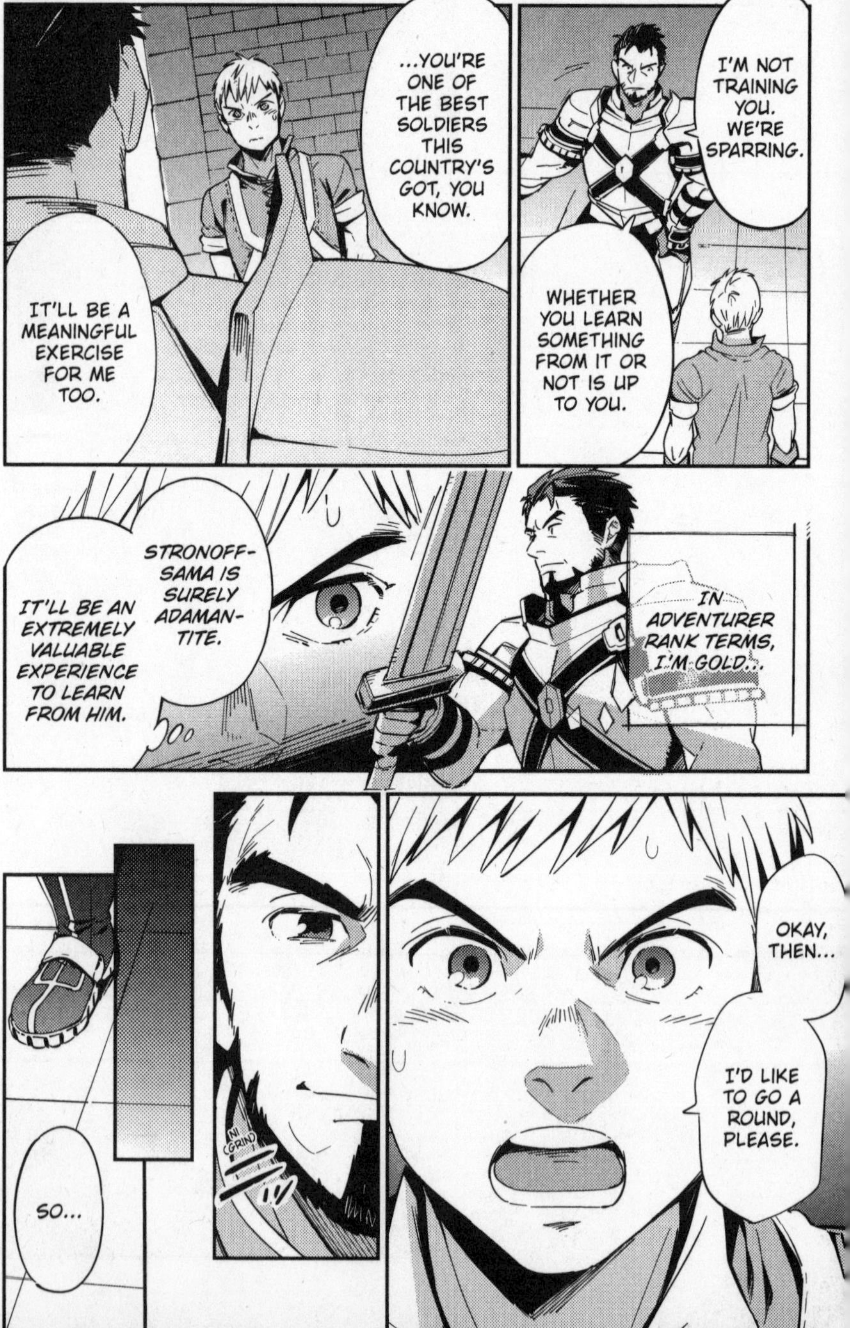
I'M NOT TRAINING YOU. WE'RE SPARRING.
WHETHER YOU LEARN SOMETHING FROM IT OR NOT IS UP TO YOU.
...YOU'RE ONE OF THE BEST SOLDIERS THIS COUNTRY'S GOT, YOU KNOW.
IT'LL BE A MEANINGFUL EXERCISE FOR ME TOO.
IN ADVENTURER RANK TERMS, I'M GOLD...
STRONOFF-SAMA IS SURELY ADAMANTITE.
IT'LL BE AN EXTREMELY VALUABLE EXPERIENCE TO LEARN FROM HIM.
OKAY, THEN...
I'D LIKE TO GO A ROUND, PLEASE.
NI (GRIN)
SO...

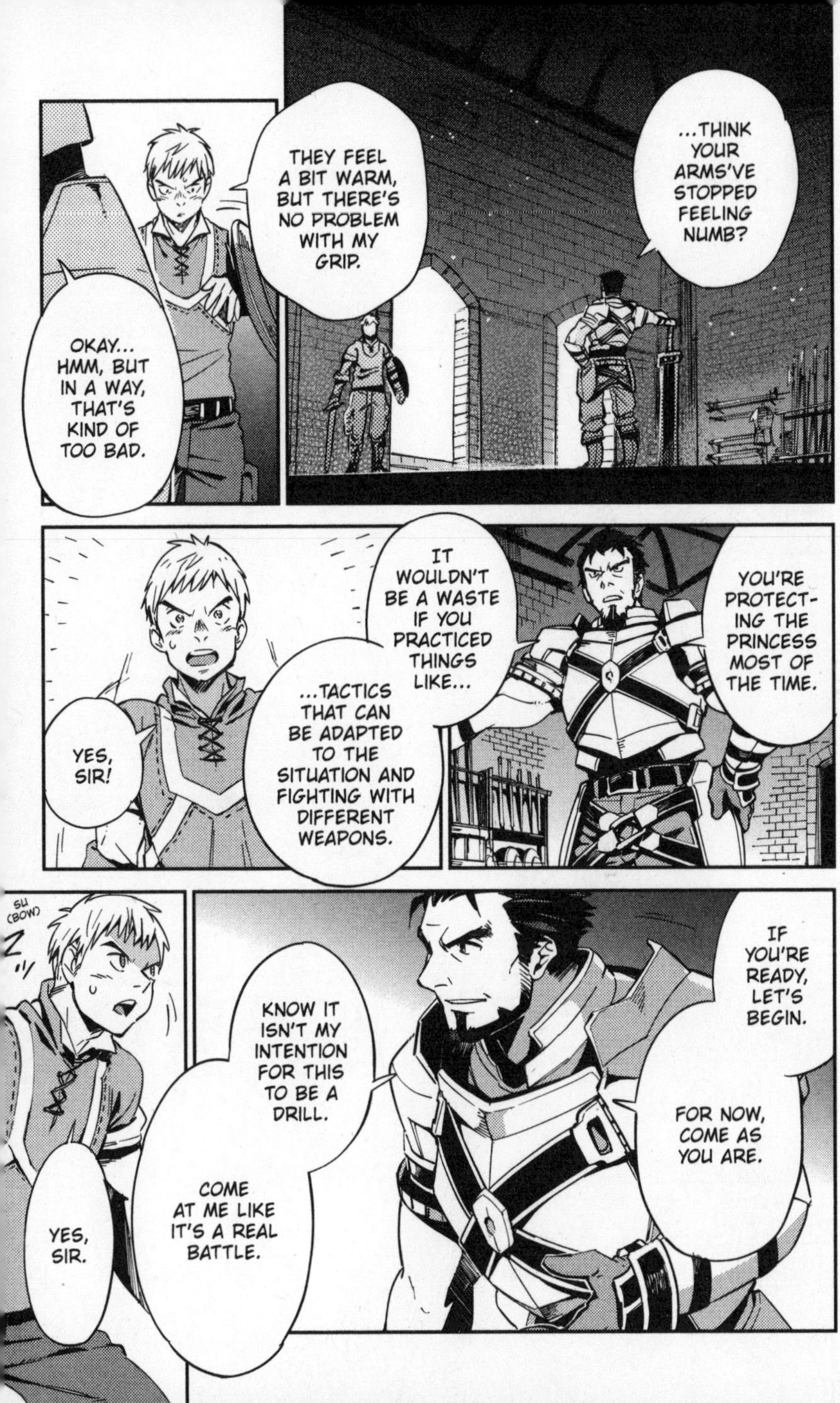
...THINK YOUR ARMS'VE STOPPED FEELING NUMB?
THEY FEEL A BIT WARM, BUT THERE'S NO PROBLEM WITH MY GRIP.
OKAY... HMM, BUT IN A WAY, THAT'S KIND OF TOO BAD.
YOU'RE PROTECT-ING THE PRINCESS MOST OF THE TIME.
IT WOULDN'T BE A WASTE IF YOU PRACTICED THINGS LIKE...
...TACTICS THAT CAN BE ADAPTED TO THE SITUATION AND FIGHTING WITH DIFFERENT WEAPONS.
YES, SIR!
IF YOU'RE READY, LET'S BEGIN.
FOR NOW, COME AS YOU ARE.
KNOW IT ISN'T MY INTENTION FOR THIS TO BE A DRILL.
COME AT ME LIKE IT'S A REAL BATTLE.
SU (BOW)
YES, SIR.

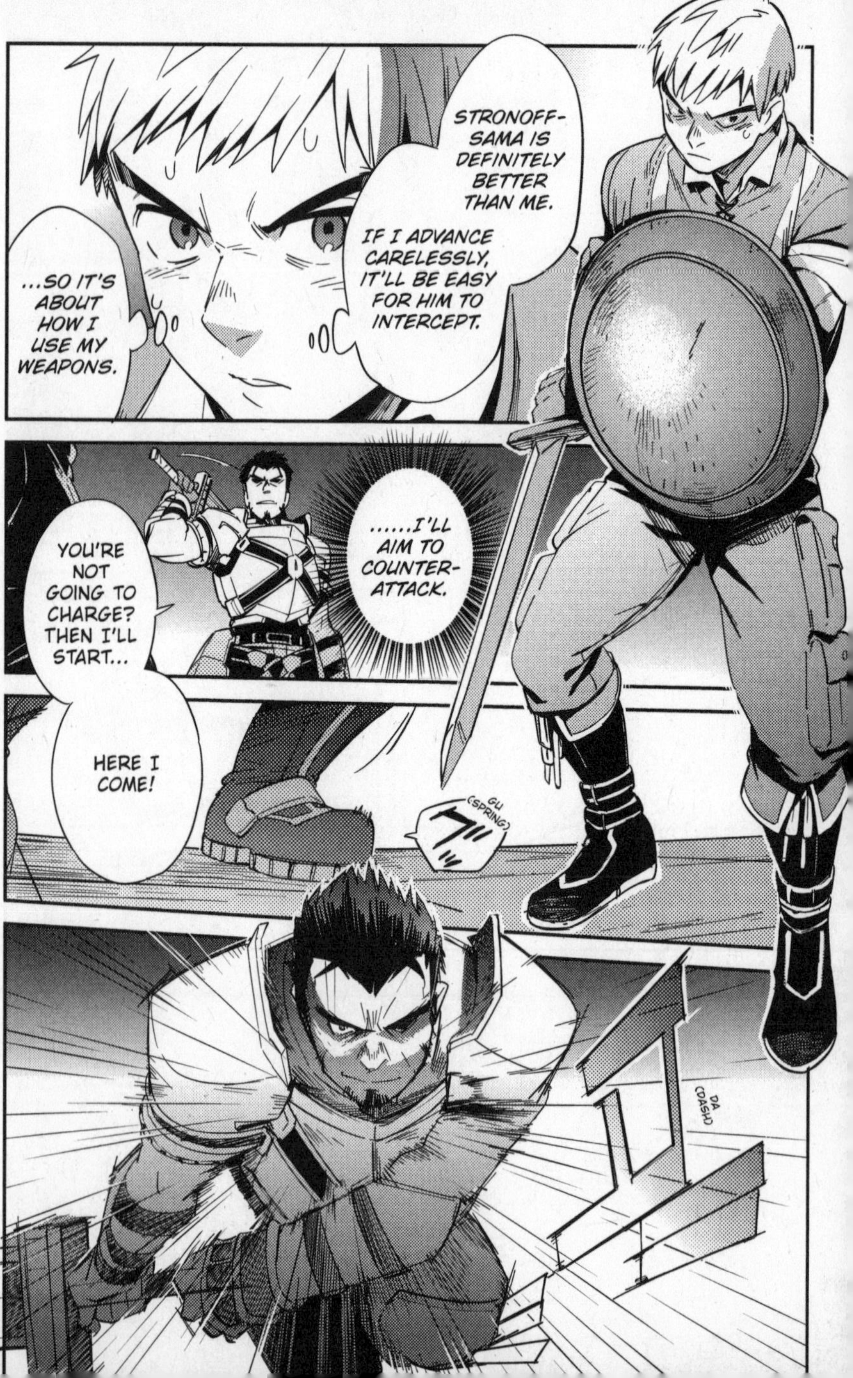
STRONOFF-SAMA IS DEFINITELY BETTER THAN ME.
IF I ADVANCE CARELESSLY, IT'LL BE EASY FOR HIM TO INTERCEPT.
...SO IT'S ABOUT HOW I USE MY WEAPONS.
......I'LL AIM TO COUNTER-ATTACK.
YOU'RE NOT GOING TO CHARGE? THEN I'LL START...
HERE I COME!
GU (SPRING)
DA (DASH)

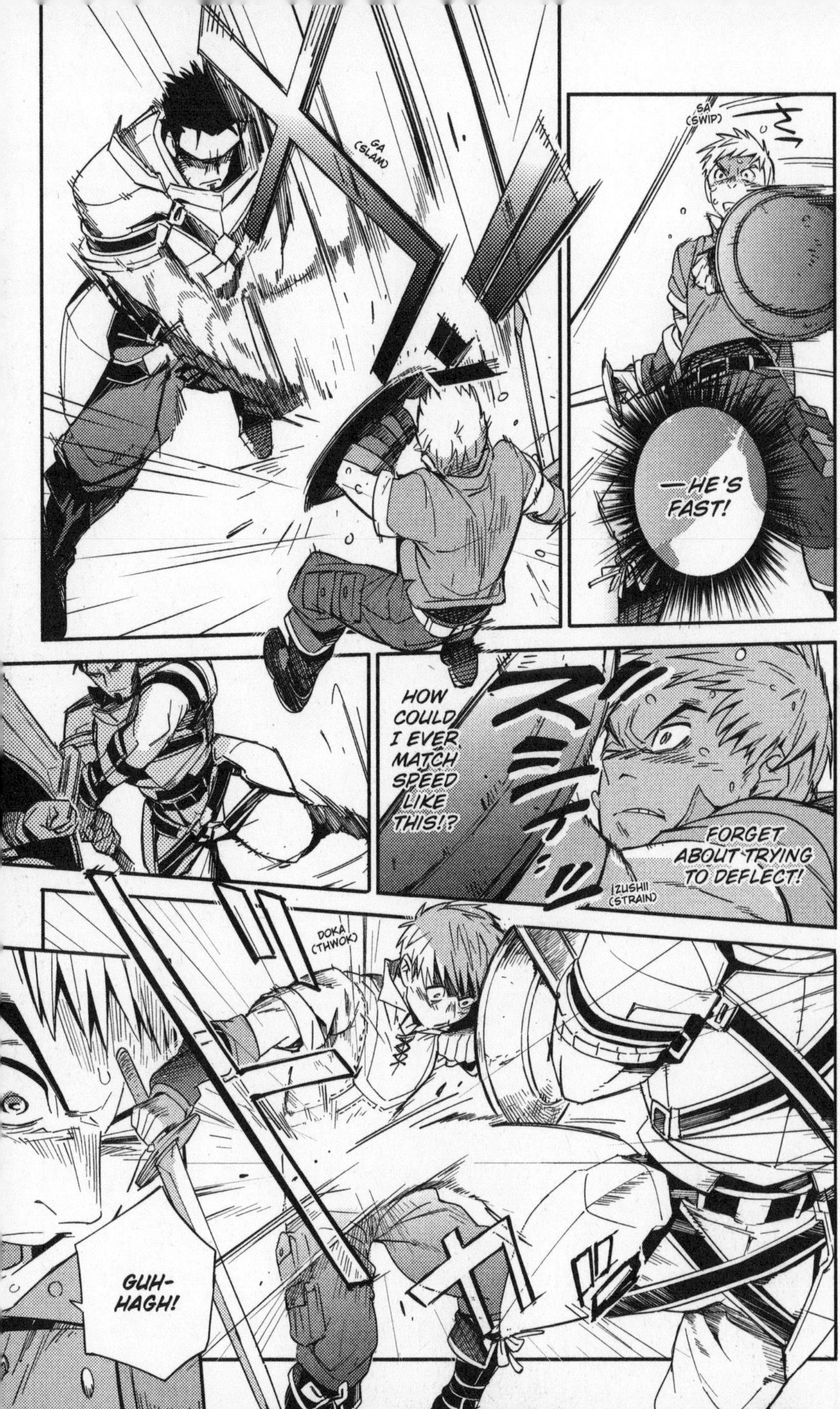
SA (SWIP)
—HE'S FAST!
GA (SLAM)
HOW COULD I EVER MATCH SPEED LIKE THIS!?
FORGET ABOUT TRYING TO DEFLECT!
IZUSHII (STRAIN)
DOKA (THWOK)
GUH-HAGH!

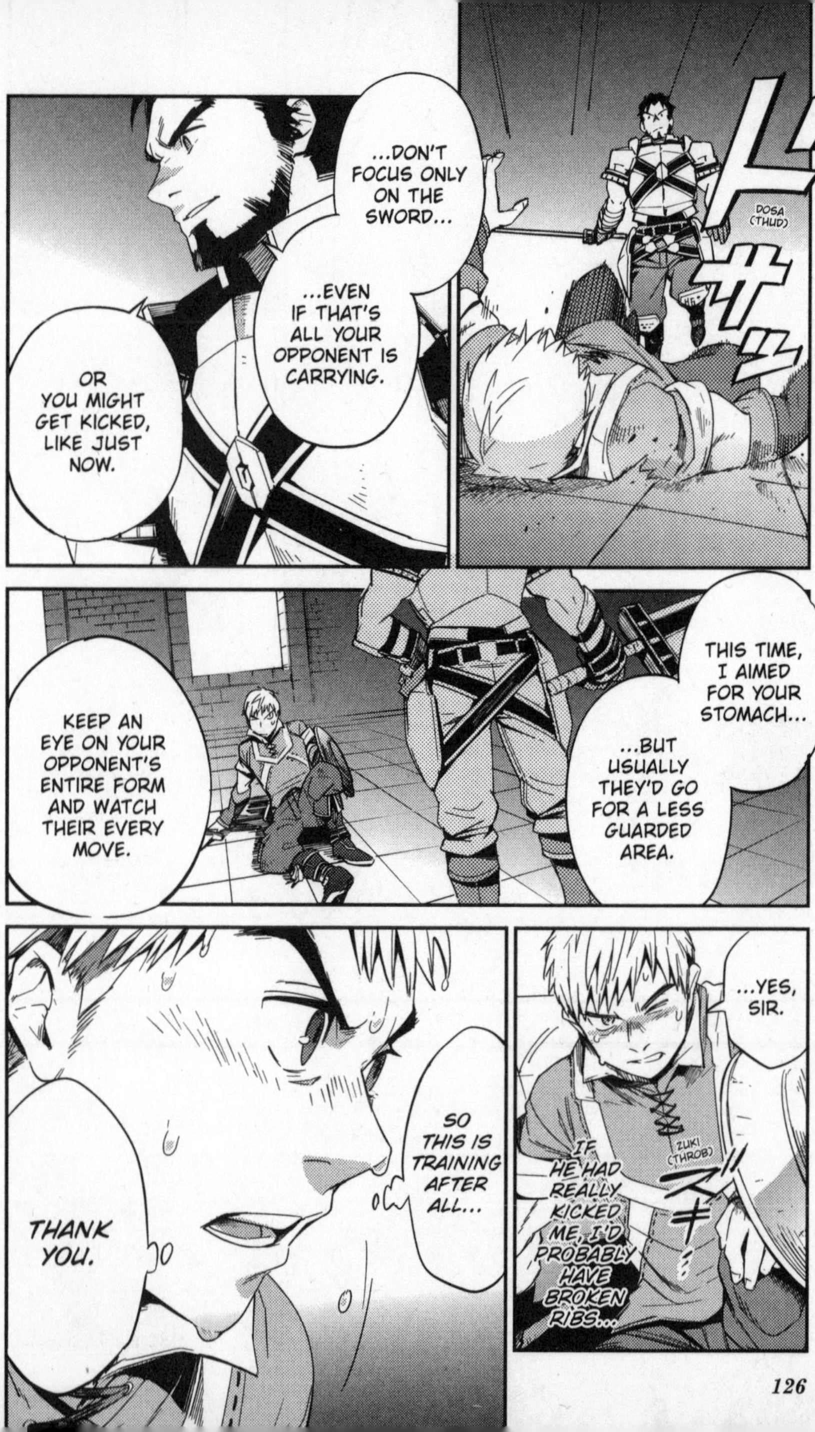
DOSA (THUD)
...DON'T FOCUS ONLY ON THE SWORD...
...EVEN IF THAT'S ALL YOUR OPPONENT IS CARRYING.
OR YOU MIGHT GET KICKED, LIKE JUST NOW.
THIS TIME, I AIMED FOR YOUR STOMACH...
...BUT USUALLY THEY'D GO FOR A LESS GUARDED AREA.
KEEP AN EYE ON YOUR OPPONENT'S ENTIRE FORM AND WATCH THEIR EVERY MOVE.
...YES, SIR.
ZUKI (THROB)
IF HE HAD REALLY KICKED ME, I'D PROBABLY HAVE BROKEN RIBS...
SO THIS IS TRAINING AFTER ALL...
THANK YOU.

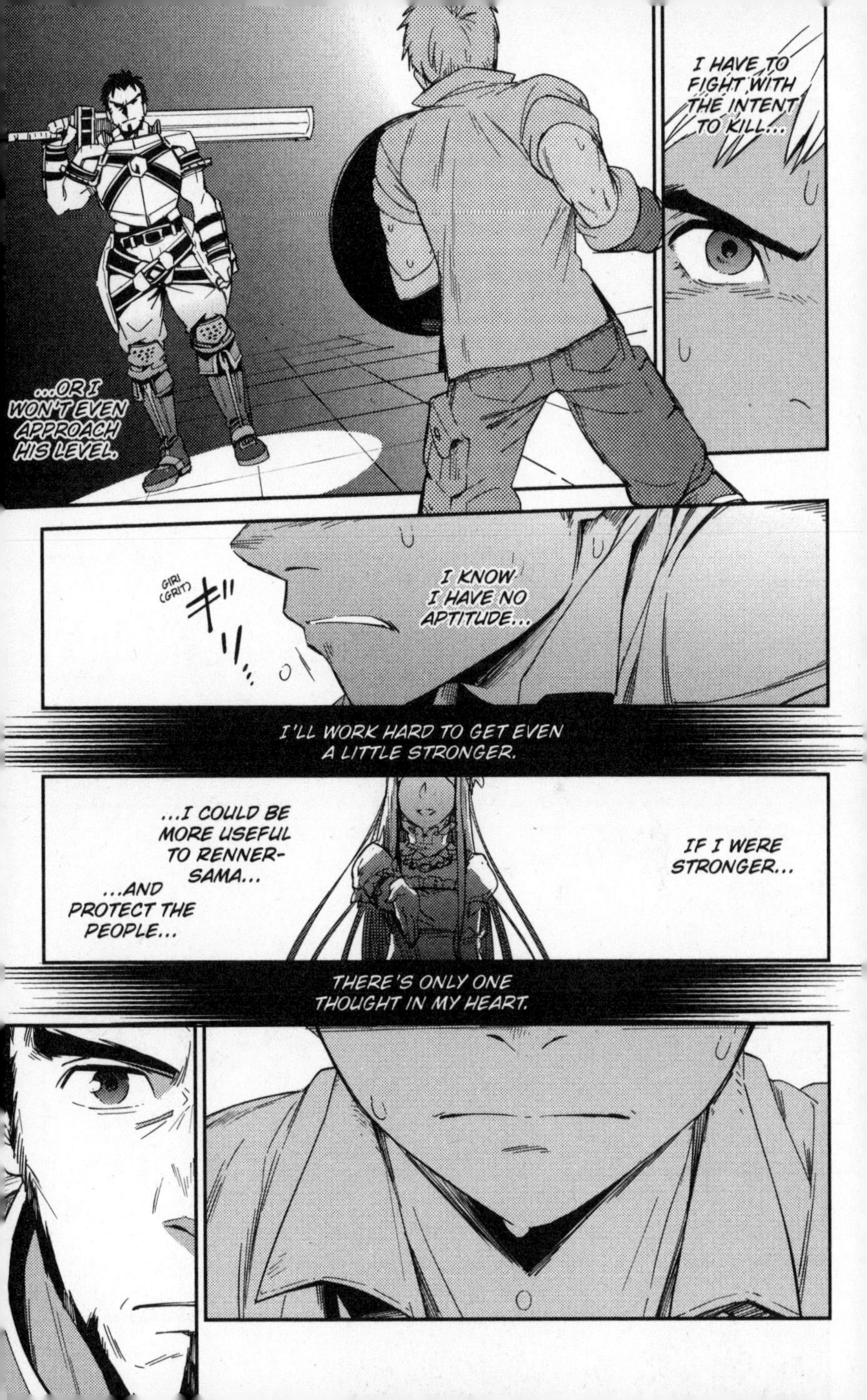
I HAVE TO FIGHT WITH THE INTENT TO KILL...
...OR I WON'T EVEN APPROACH HIS LEVEL.
I KNOW I HAVE NO APTITUDE...
GIRI (GRIT)
I'LL WORK HARD TO GET EVEN A LITTLE STRONGER.
IF I WERE STRONGER...
...I COULD BE MORE USEFUL TO RENNER-SAMA...
...AND PROTECT THE PEOPLE...
THERE'S ONLY ONE THOUGHT IN MY HEART.

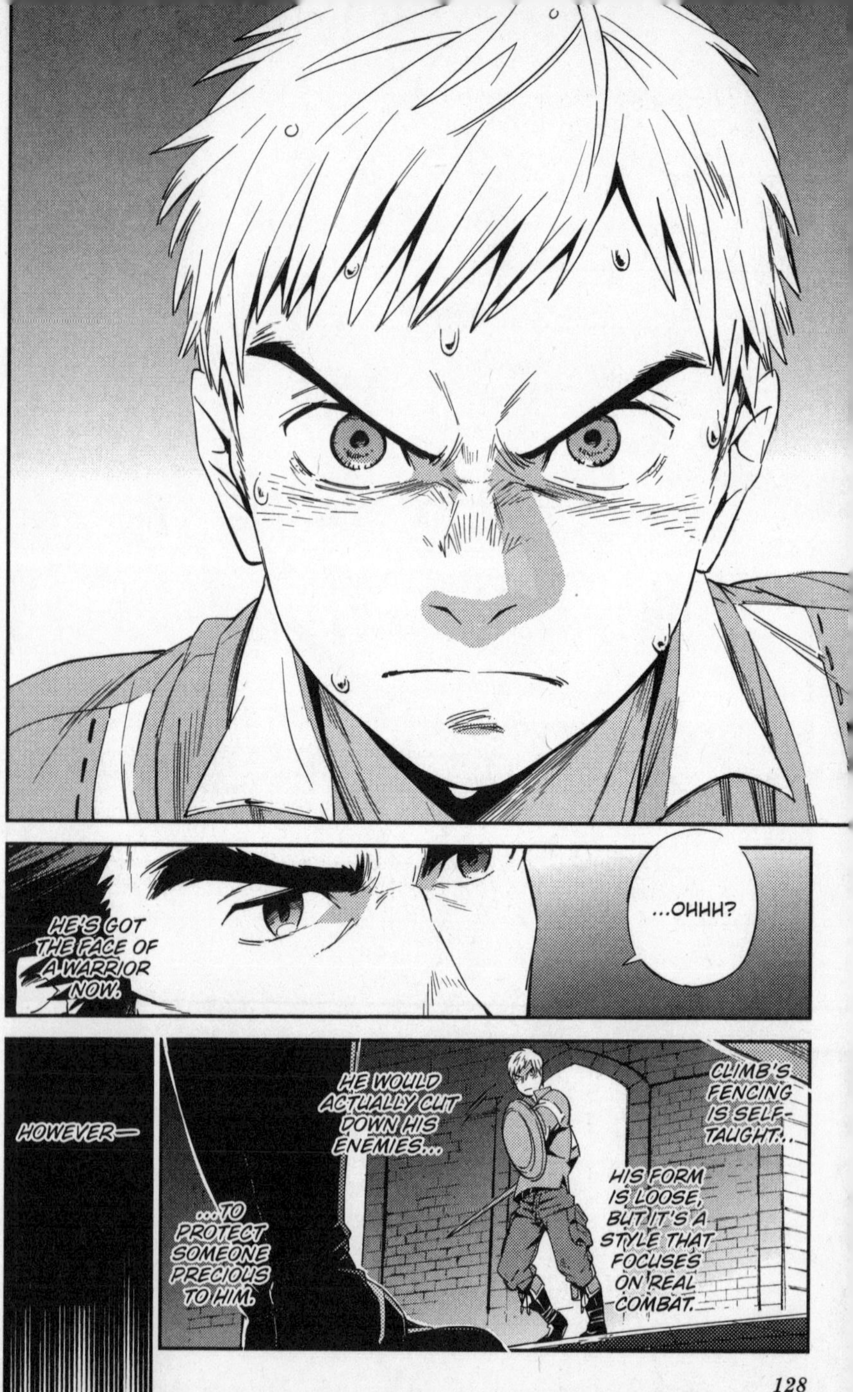
...OHHH?
HE'S GOT THE FACE OF A WARRIOR NOW.
CLIMB'S FENCING IS SELF-TAUGHT...
HIS FORM IS LOOSE, BUT IT'S A STYLE THAT FOCUSES ON REAL COMBAT.
HE WOULD ACTUALLY CUT DOWN HIS ENEMIES...
...TO PROTECT SOMEONE PRECIOUS TO HIM.
HOWEVER—

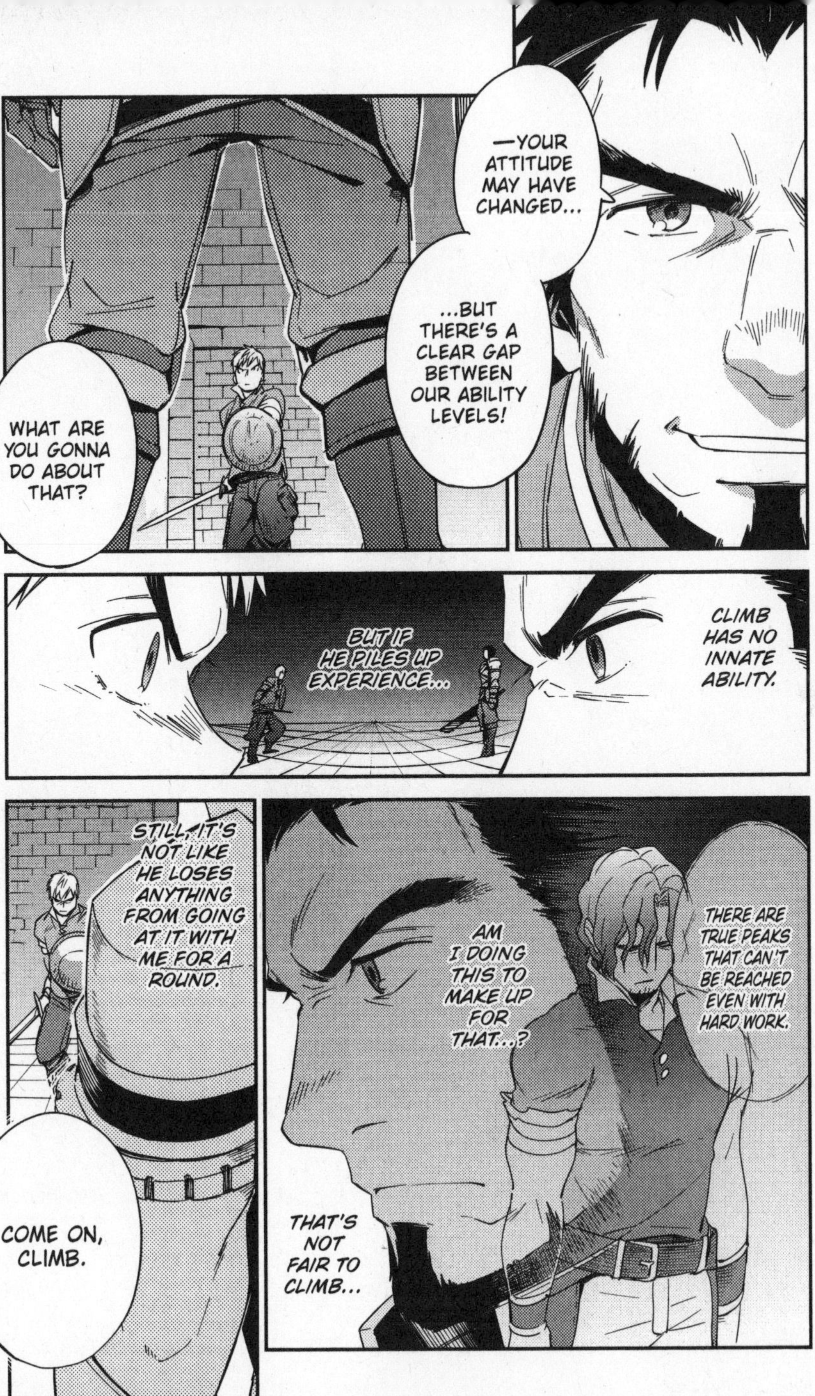
—YOUR ATTITUDE MAY HAVE CHANGED...
...BUT THERE'S A CLEAR GAP BETWEEN OUR ABILITY LEVELS!
WHAT ARE YOU GONNA DO ABOUT THAT?
CLIMB HAS NO INNATE ABILITY.
BUT IF HE PILES UP EXPERIENCE...
THERE ARE TRUE PEAKS THAT CAN'T BE REACHED EVEN WITH HARD WORK.
AM I DOING THIS TO MAKE UP FOR THAT...?
THAT'S NOT FAIR TO CLIMB...
STILL, IT'S NOT LIKE HE LOSES ANYTHING FROM GOING AT IT WITH ME FOR A ROUND.
COME ON, CLIMB.

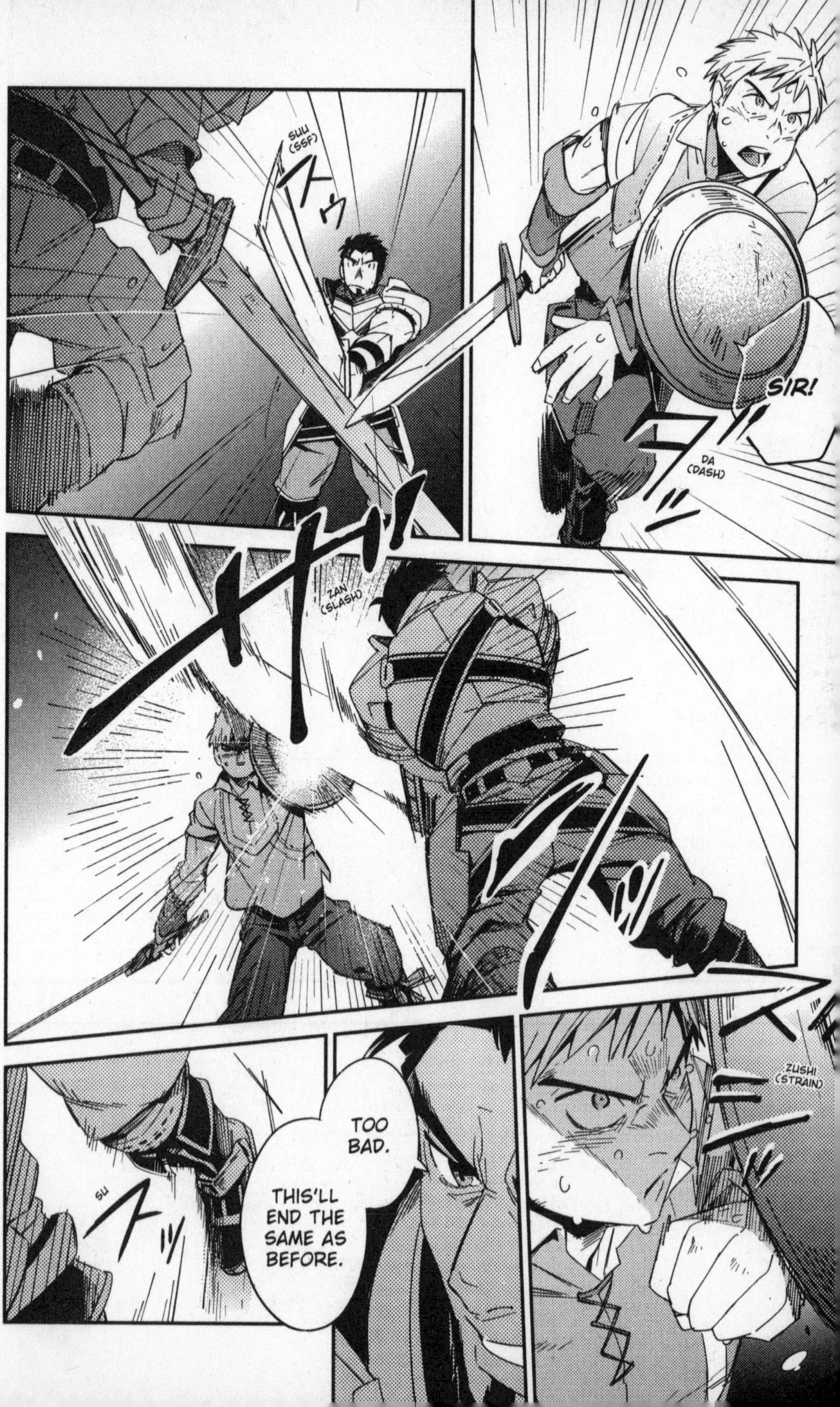
SIR!
DA (DASH)
SUU (SSF)
ZAN (SLASH)
ZUSHI (STRAIN)
TOO BAD.
THIS'LL END THE SAME AS BEFORE.
SU

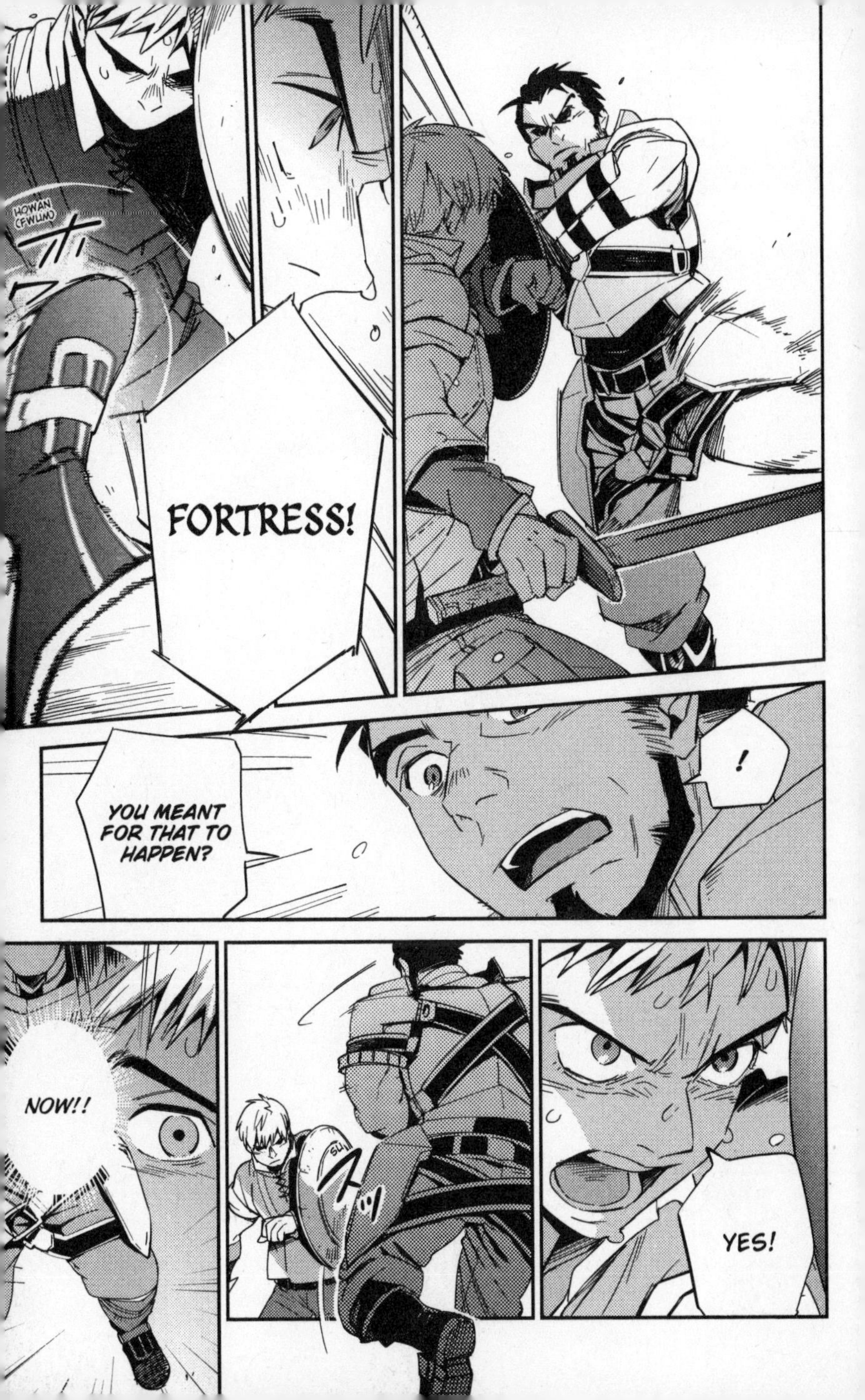
FORTRESS!
HOWAN (FWUN)
!
YOU MEANT FOR THAT TO HAPPEN?
YES!
SU
NOW!!

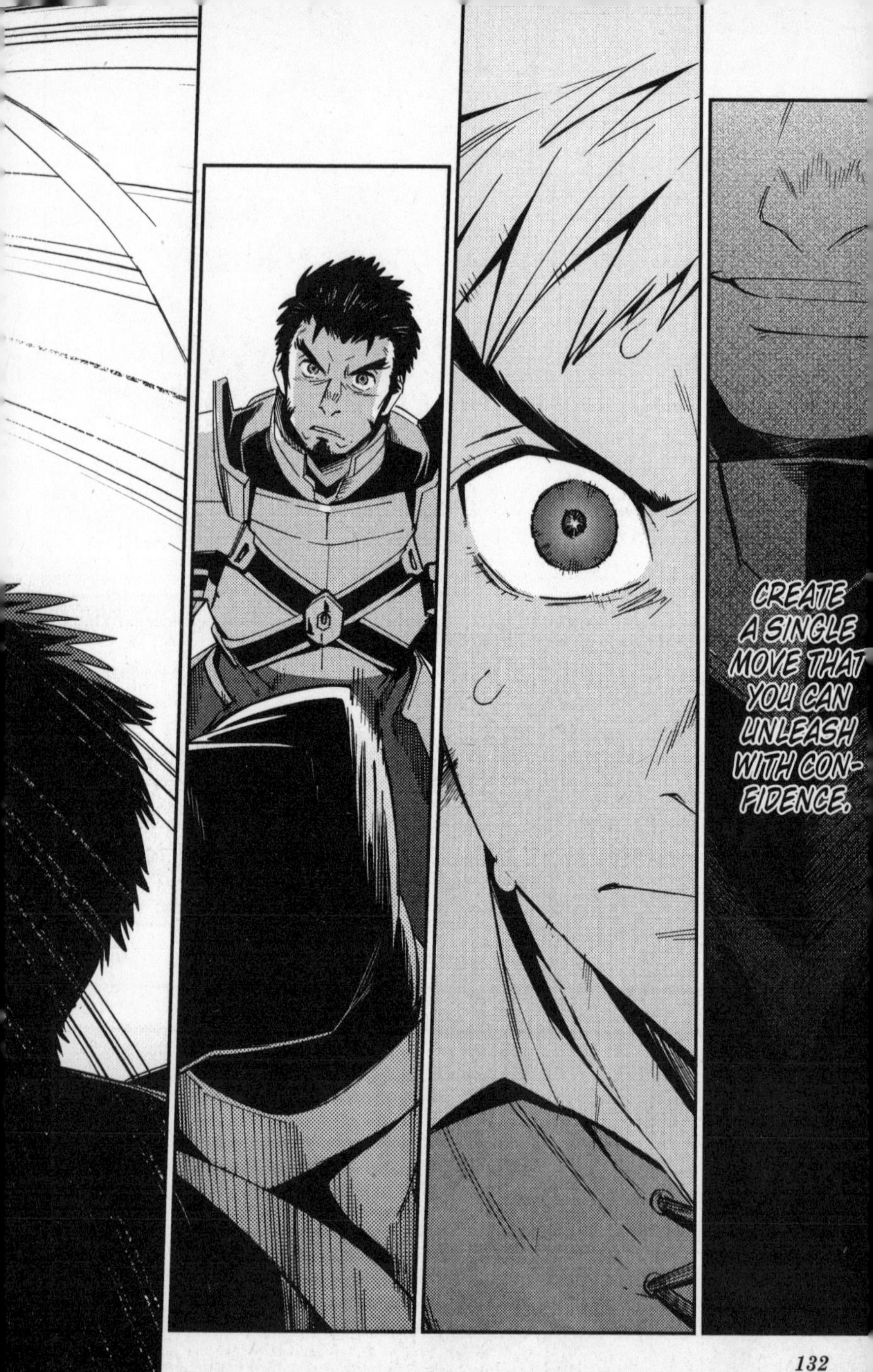
CREATE A SINGLE MOVE THAT YOU CAN UNLEASH WITH CON-FIDENCE.

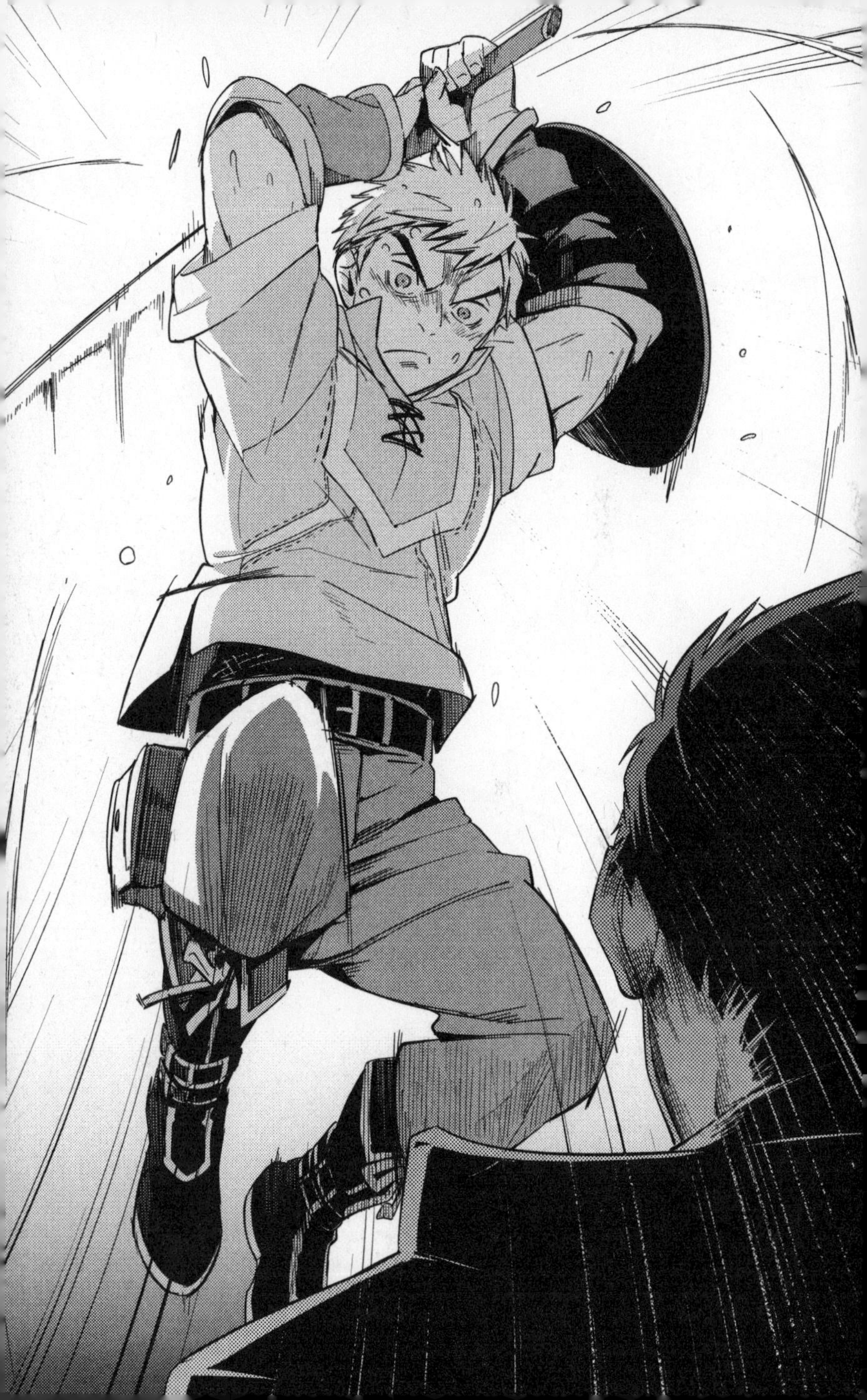

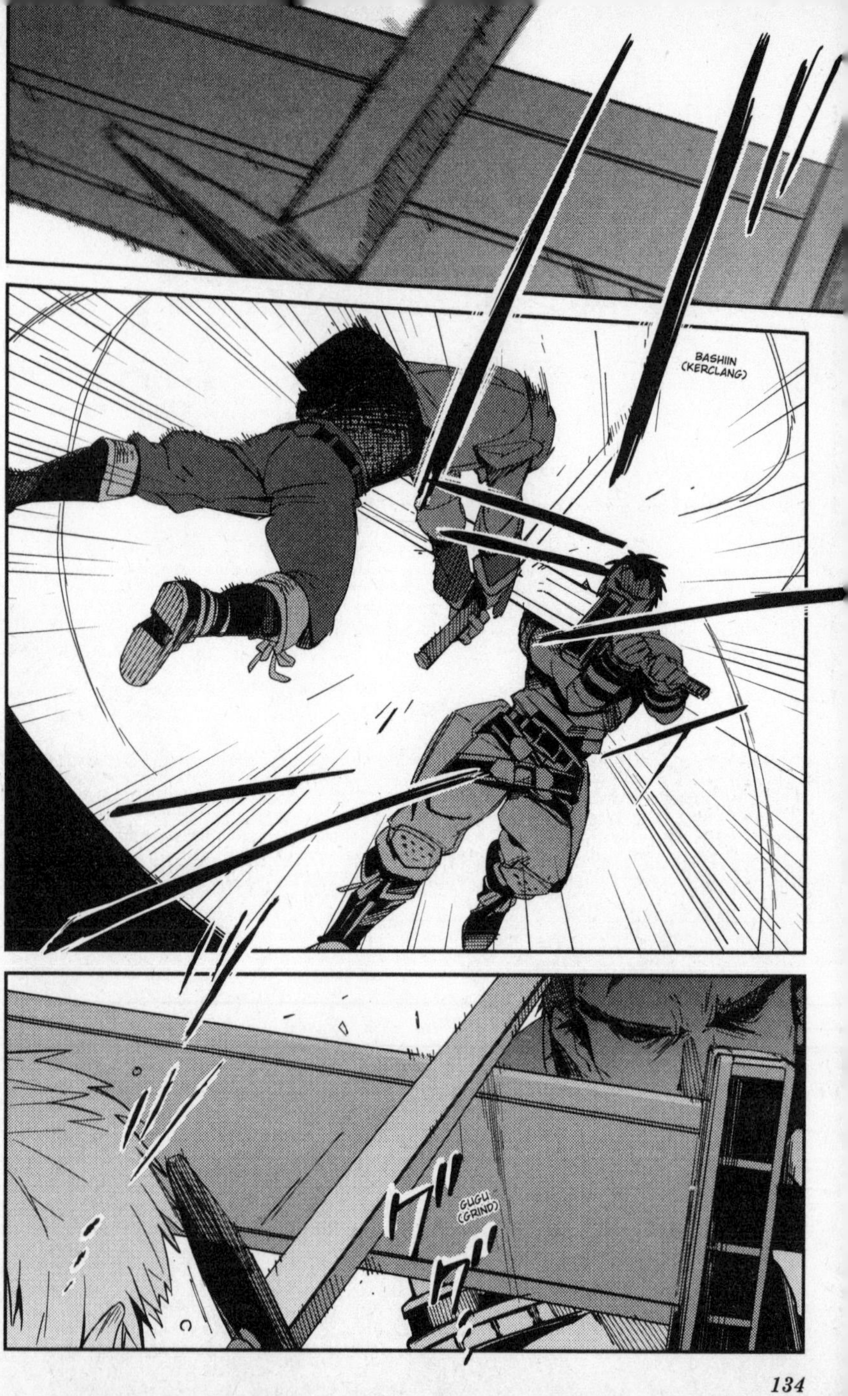
BASHIIN
(KERCLANG)
GUGU
(GRIND)

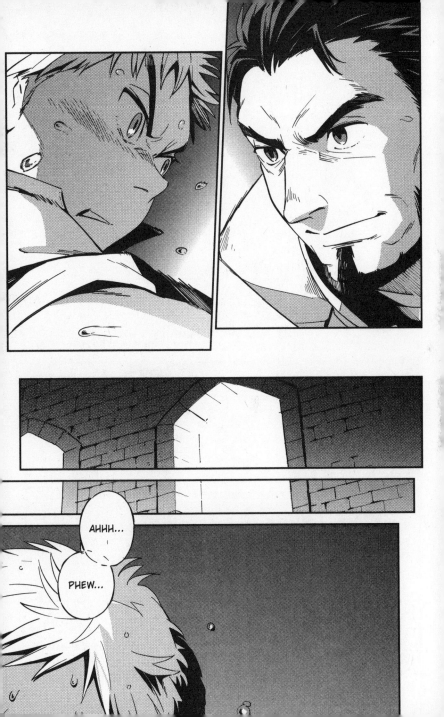

AHHH...

PHEW...

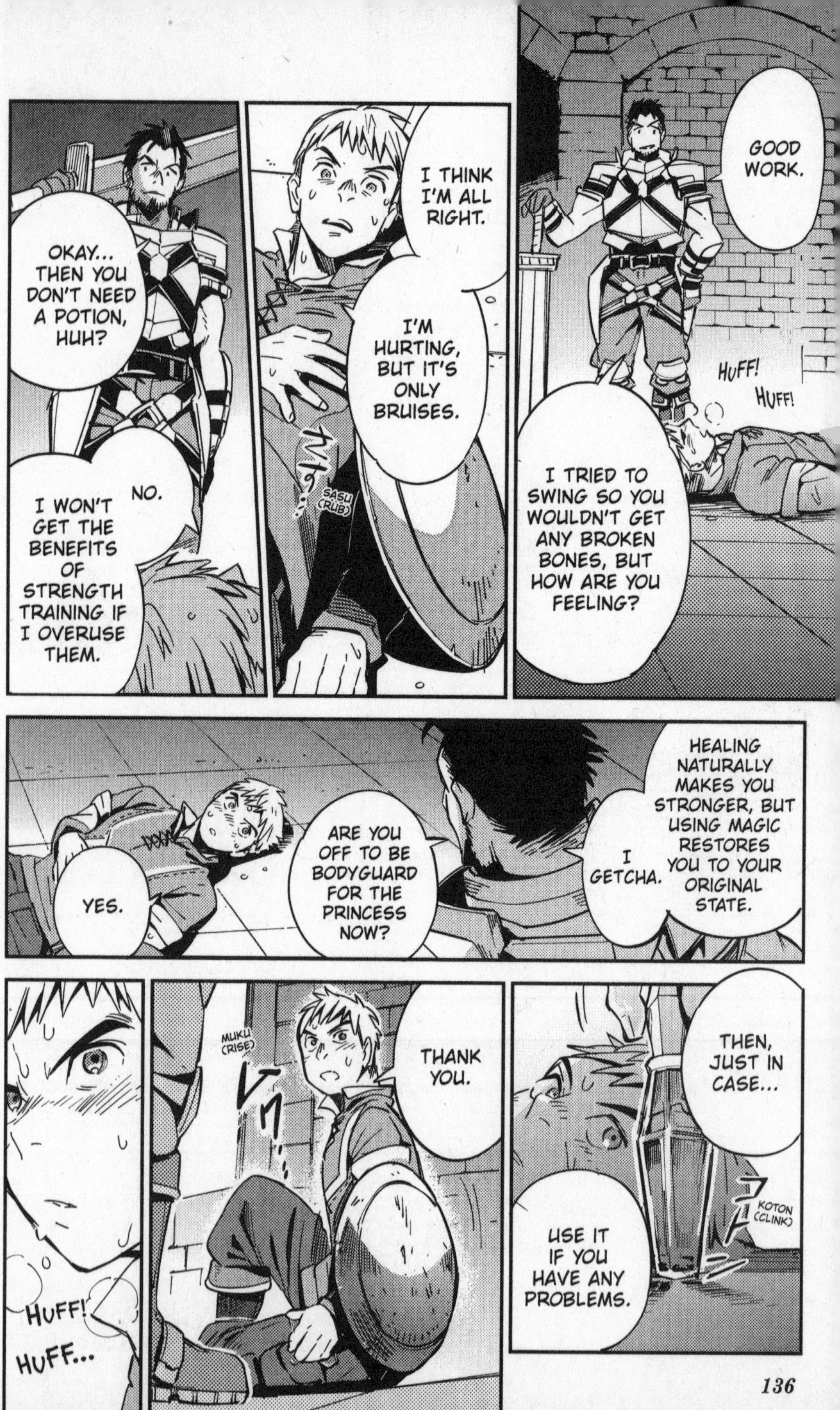
GOOD WORK.
HUFF! HUFF!
I TRIED TO SWING SO YOU WOULDN'T GET ANY BROKEN BONES, BUT HOW ARE YOU FEELING?
I THINK I'M ALL RIGHT.
I'M HURTING, BUT IT'S ONLY BRUISES.
SASU (RUB)
OKAY... THEN YOU DON'T NEED A POTION, HUH?
NO.
I WON'T GET THE BENEFITS OF STRENGTH TRAINING IF I OVERUSE THEM.
HEALING NATURALLY MAKES YOU STRONGER, BUT USING MAGIC RESTORES YOU TO YOUR ORIGINAL STATE.
I GETCHA.
ARE YOU OFF TO BE BODYGUARD FOR THE PRINCESS NOW?
YES.
THEN, JUST IN CASE...
KOTON (CLINK)
USE IT IF YOU HAVE ANY PROBLEMS.
THANK YOU.
MUKU (RISE)
HUFF! HUFF...

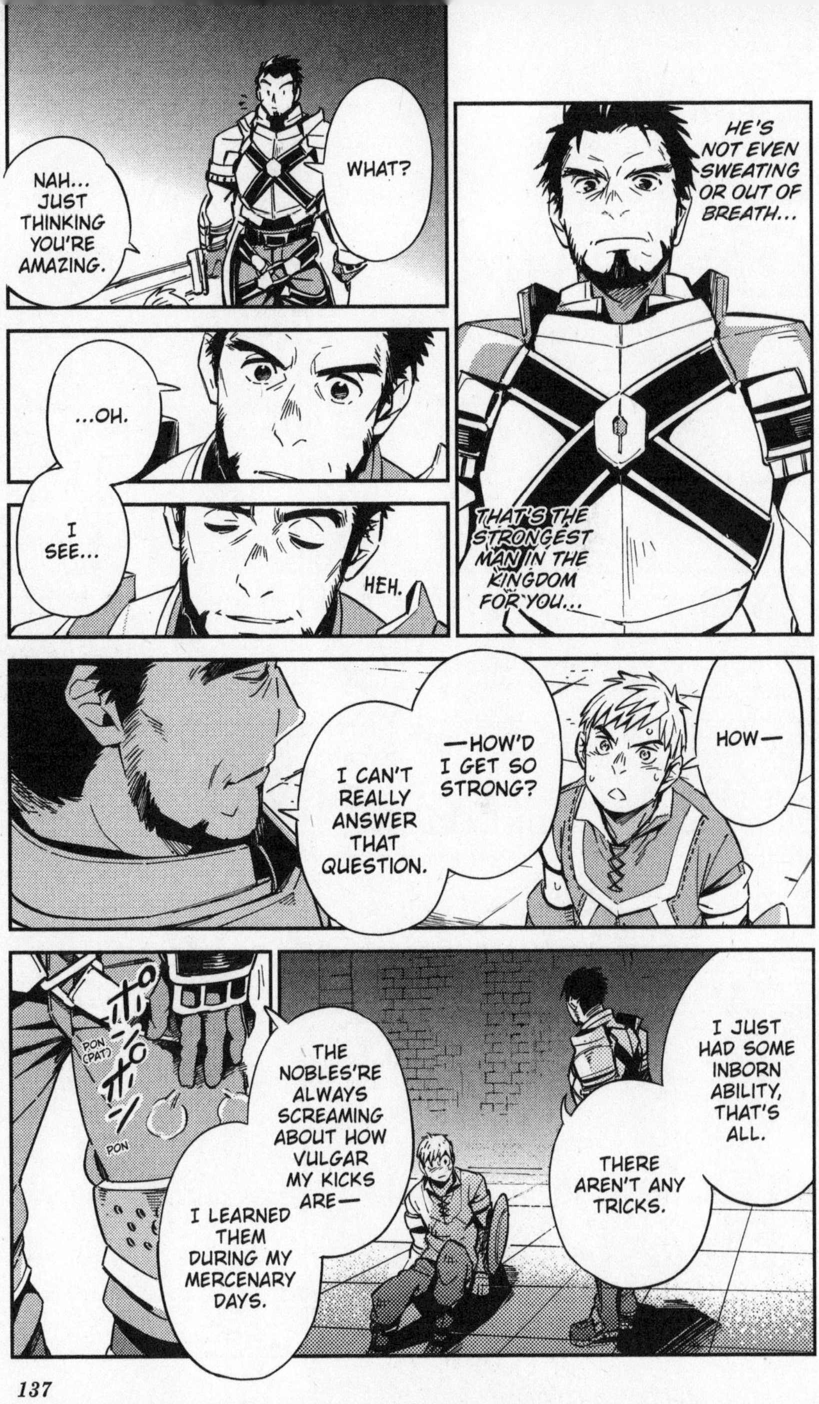
HE'S NOT EVEN SWEATING OR OUT OF BREATH...
THAT'S THE STRONGEST MAN IN THE KINGDOM FOR YOU...
WHAT?
NAH... JUST THINKING YOU'RE AMAZING.
...OH.
I SEE...
HEH.
HOW—
—HOW'D I GET SO STRONG?
I CAN'T REALLY ANSWER THAT QUESTION.
I JUST HAD SOME INBORN ABILITY, THAT'S ALL.
THERE AREN'T ANY TRICKS.
THE NOBLES'RE ALWAYS SCREAMING ABOUT HOW VULGAR MY KICKS ARE—
I LEARNED THEM DURING MY MERCENARY DAYS.
PON (PAT)
PON

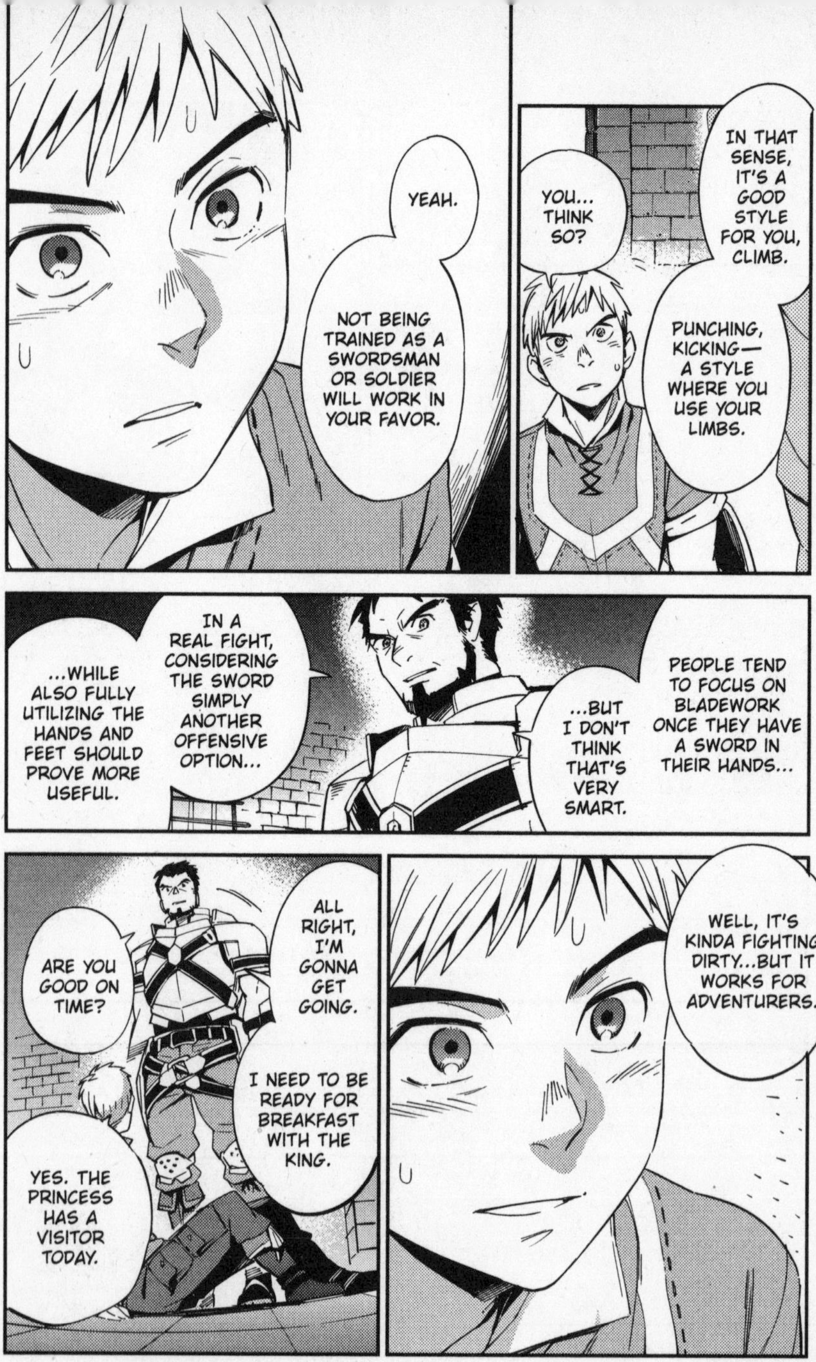
IN THAT SENSE, IT'S A GOOD STYLE FOR YOU, CLIMB.
YOU... THINK SO?
PUNCHING, KICKING— A STYLE WHERE YOU USE YOUR LIMBS.
YEAH.
NOT BEING TRAINED AS A SWORDSMAN OR SOLDIER WILL WORK IN YOUR FAVOR.
PEOPLE TEND TO FOCUS ON BLADEWORK ONCE THEY HAVE A SWORD IN THEIR HANDS...
...BUT I DON'T THINK THAT'S VERY SMART.
IN A REAL FIGHT, CONSIDERING THE SWORD SIMPLY ANOTHER OFFENSIVE OPTION...
...WHILE ALSO FULLY UTILIZING THE HANDS AND FEET SHOULD PROVE MORE USEFUL.
WELL, IT'S KINDA FIGHTING DIRTY...BUT IT WORKS FOR ADVENTURERS.
ALL RIGHT, I'M GONNA GET GOING.
ARE YOU GOOD ON TIME?
I NEED TO BE READY FOR BREAKFAST WITH THE KING.
YES. THE PRINCESS HAS A VISITOR TODAY.

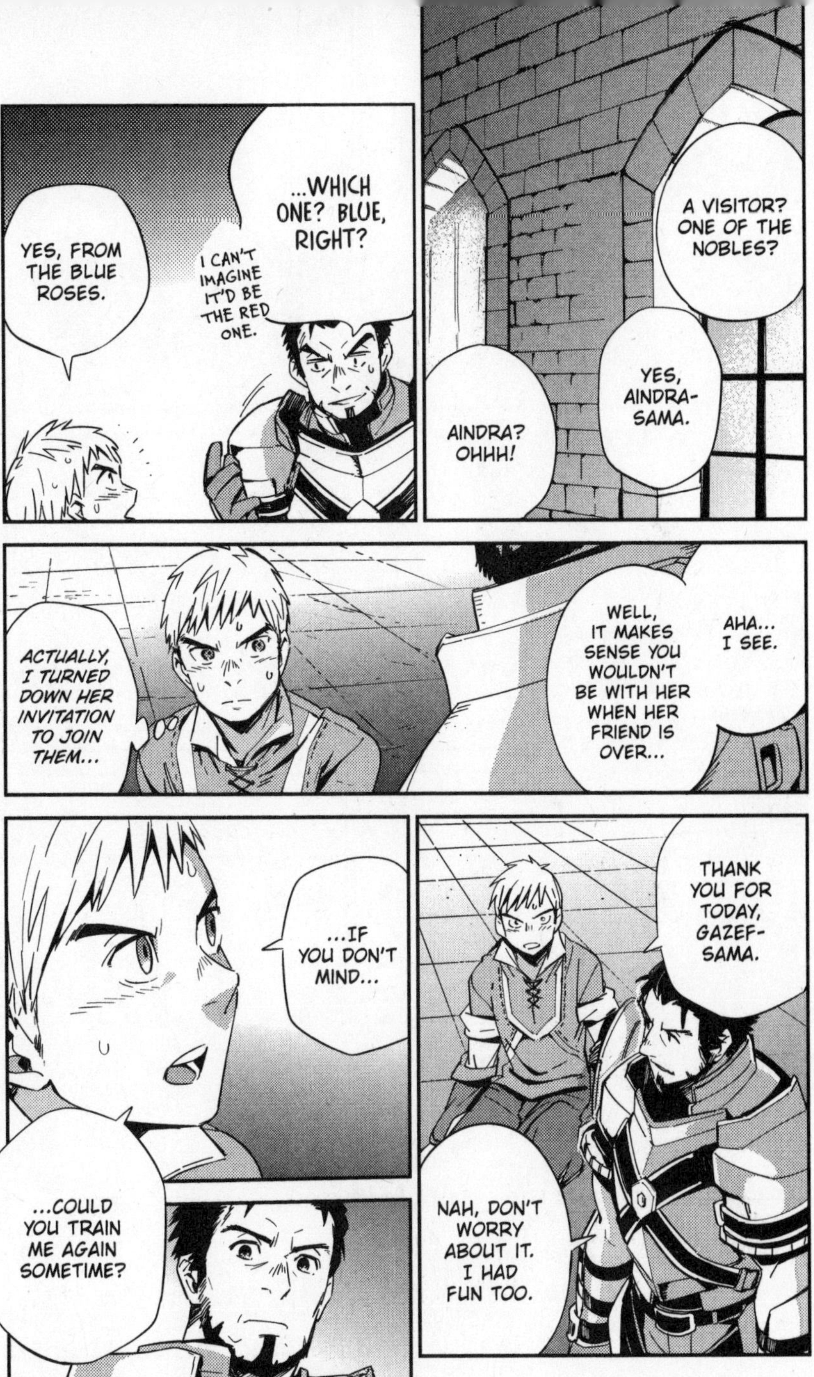
A VISITOR? ONE OF THE NOBLES?
YES, AINDRA-SAMA.
AINDRA? OHHH!
...WHICH ONE? BLUE, RIGHT?
I CAN'T IMAGINE IT'D BE THE RED ONE.
YES, FROM THE BLUE ROSES.
AHA... I SEE.
WELL, IT MAKES SENSE YOU WOULDN'T BE WITH HER WHEN HER FRIEND IS OVER...
ACTUALLY, I TURNED DOWN HER INVITATION TO JOIN THEM...
THANK YOU FOR TODAY, GAZEF-SAMA.
NAH, DON'T WORRY ABOUT IT. I HAD FUN TOO.
...IF YOU DON'T MIND...
...COULD YOU TRAIN ME AGAIN SOMETIME?

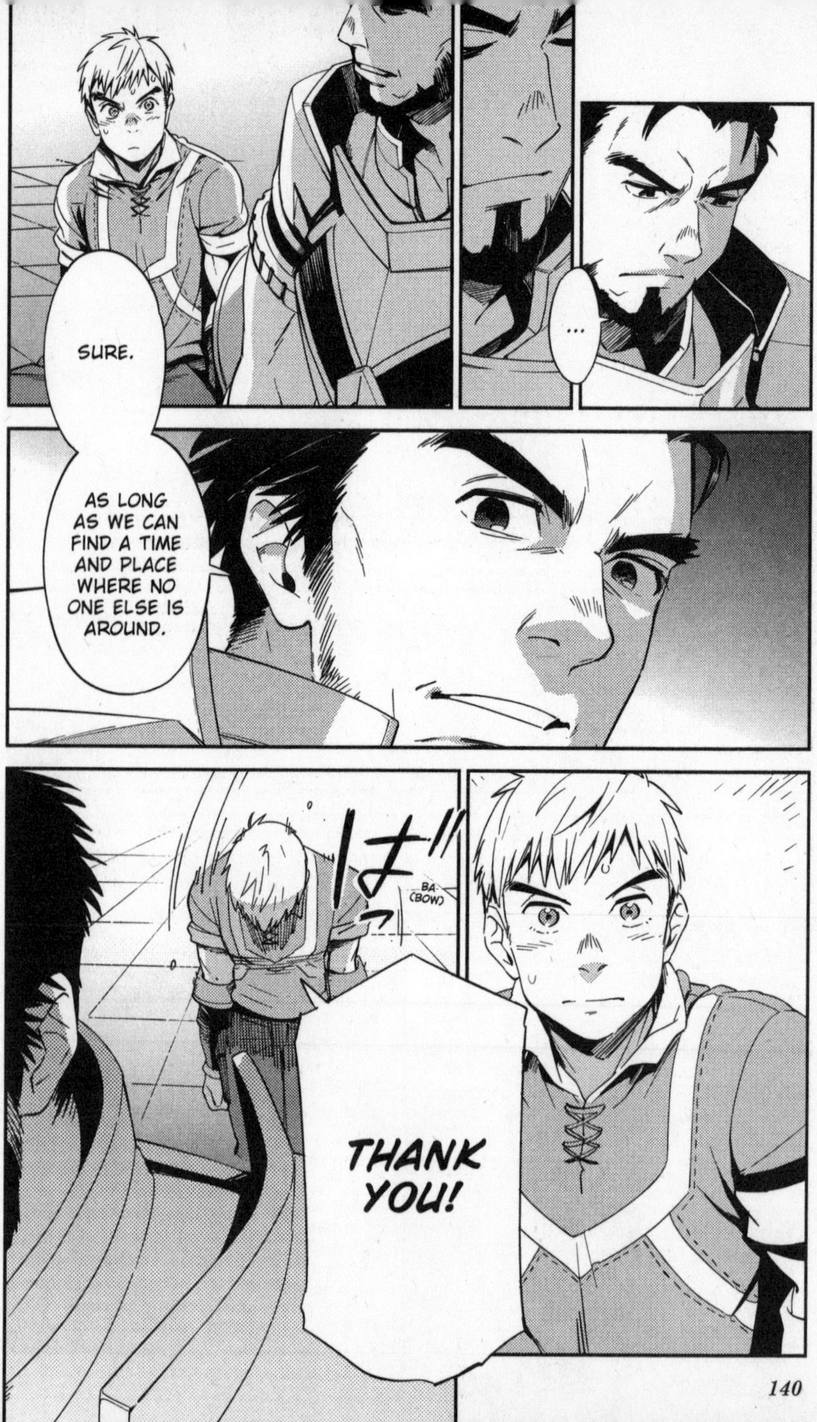
...
SURE.
AS LONG AS WE CAN FIND A TIME AND PLACE WHERE NO ONE ELSE IS AROUND.
BA (BOW)
THANK YOU!

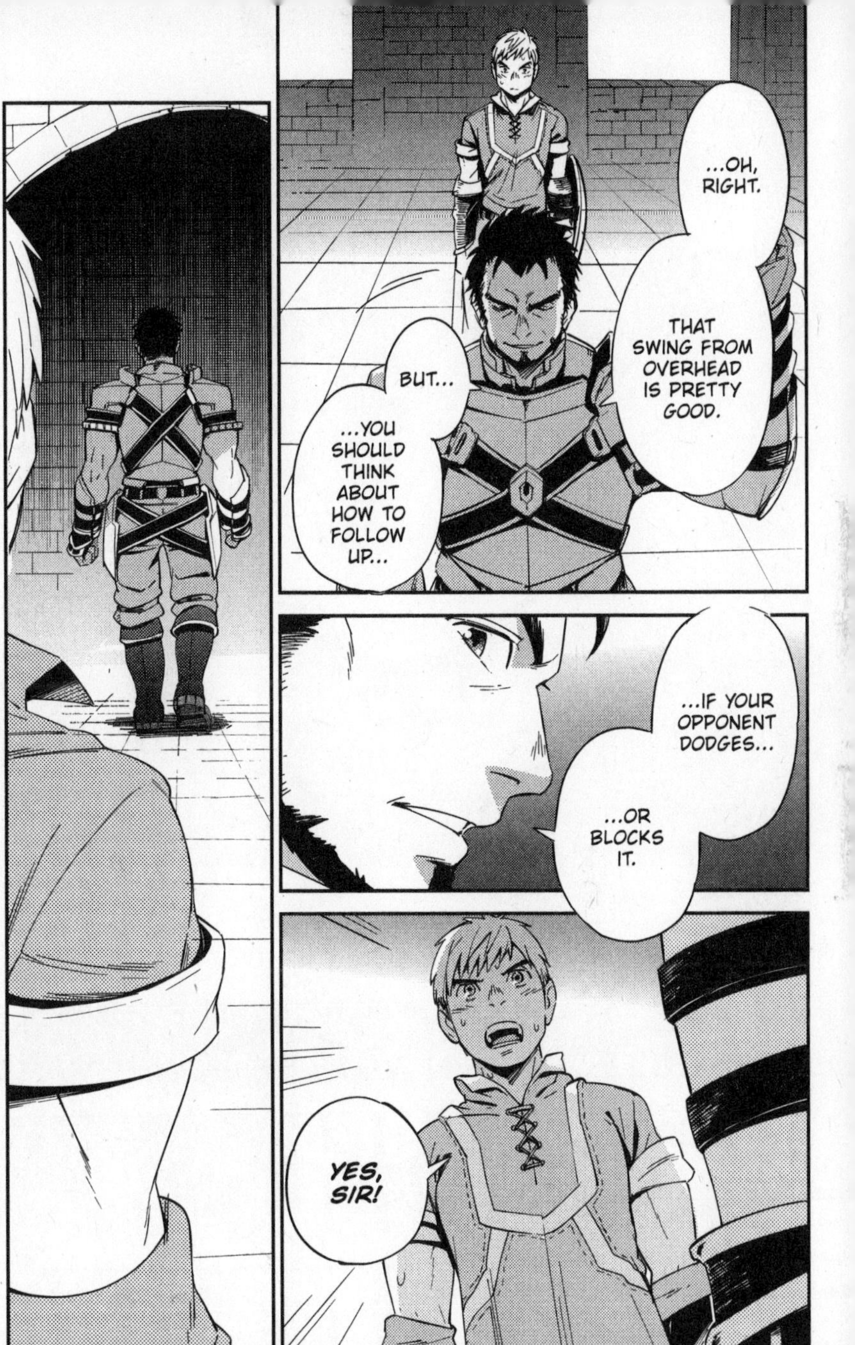
...OH, RIGHT.
THAT SWING FROM OVERHEAD IS PRETTY GOOD.
BUT...
...YOU SHOULD THINK ABOUT HOW TO FOLLOW UP...
...IF YOUR OPPONENT DODGES...
...OR BLOCKS IT.
YES, SIR!

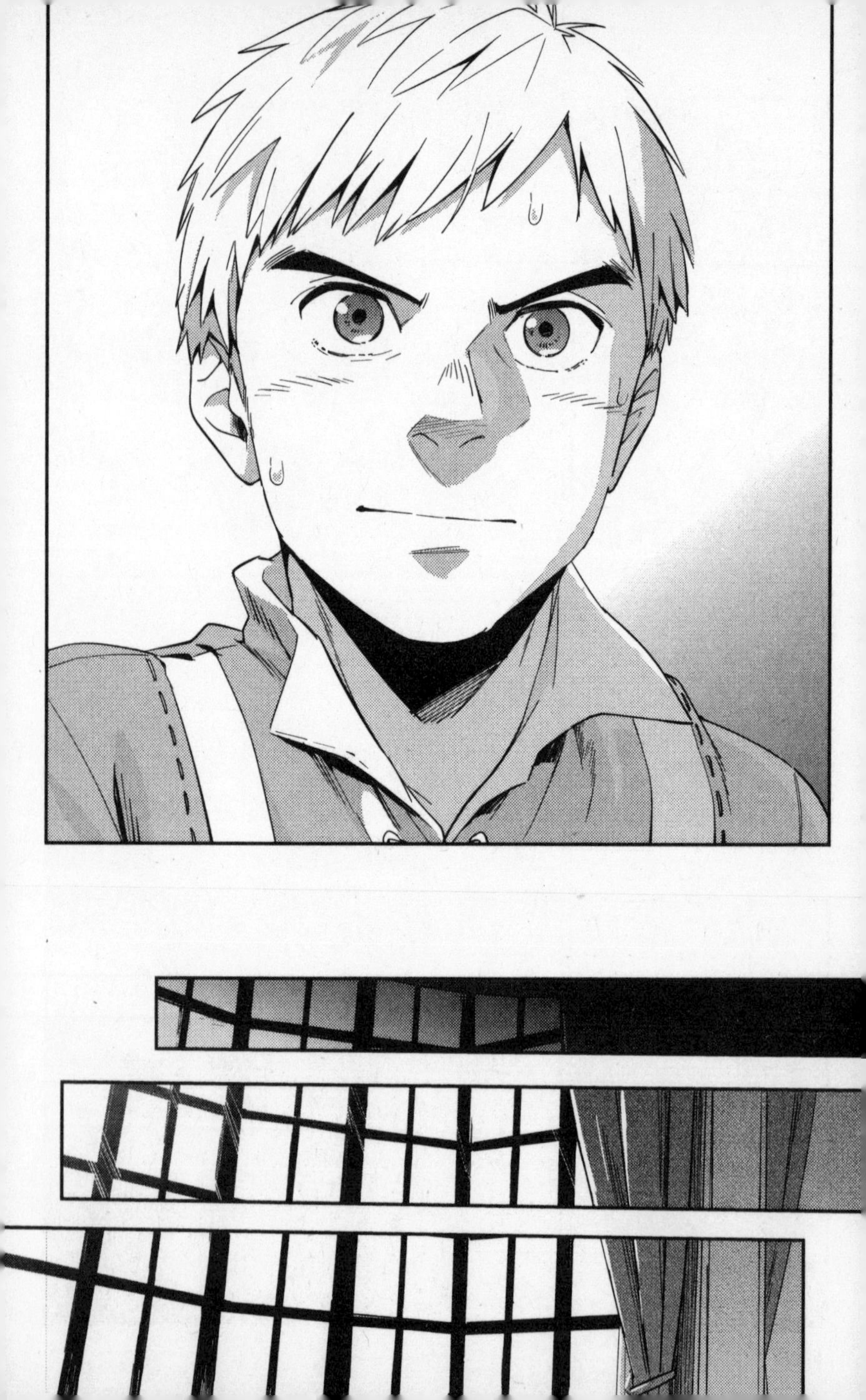

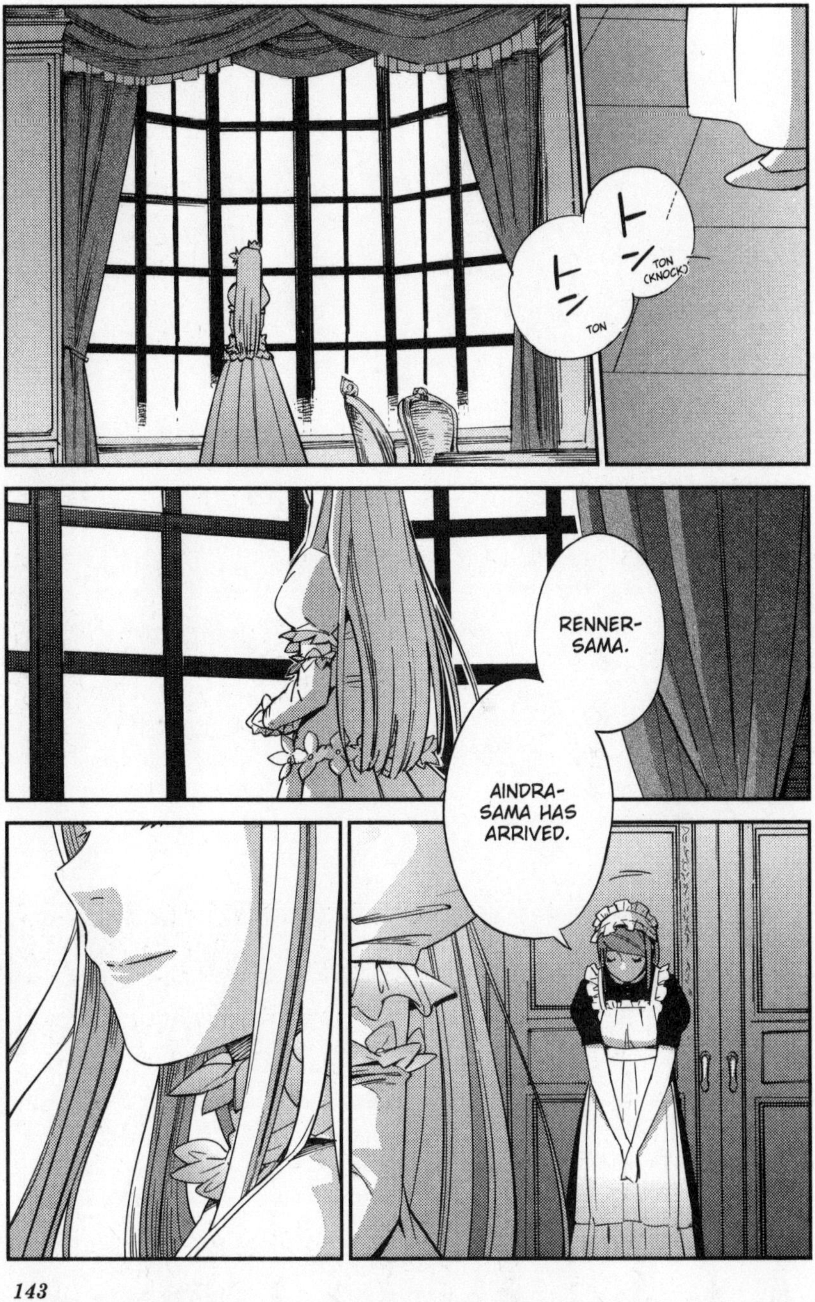
トン
TON (KNOCK)
トン
TON
RENNER-SAMA.
AINDRA-SAMA HAS ARRIVED.

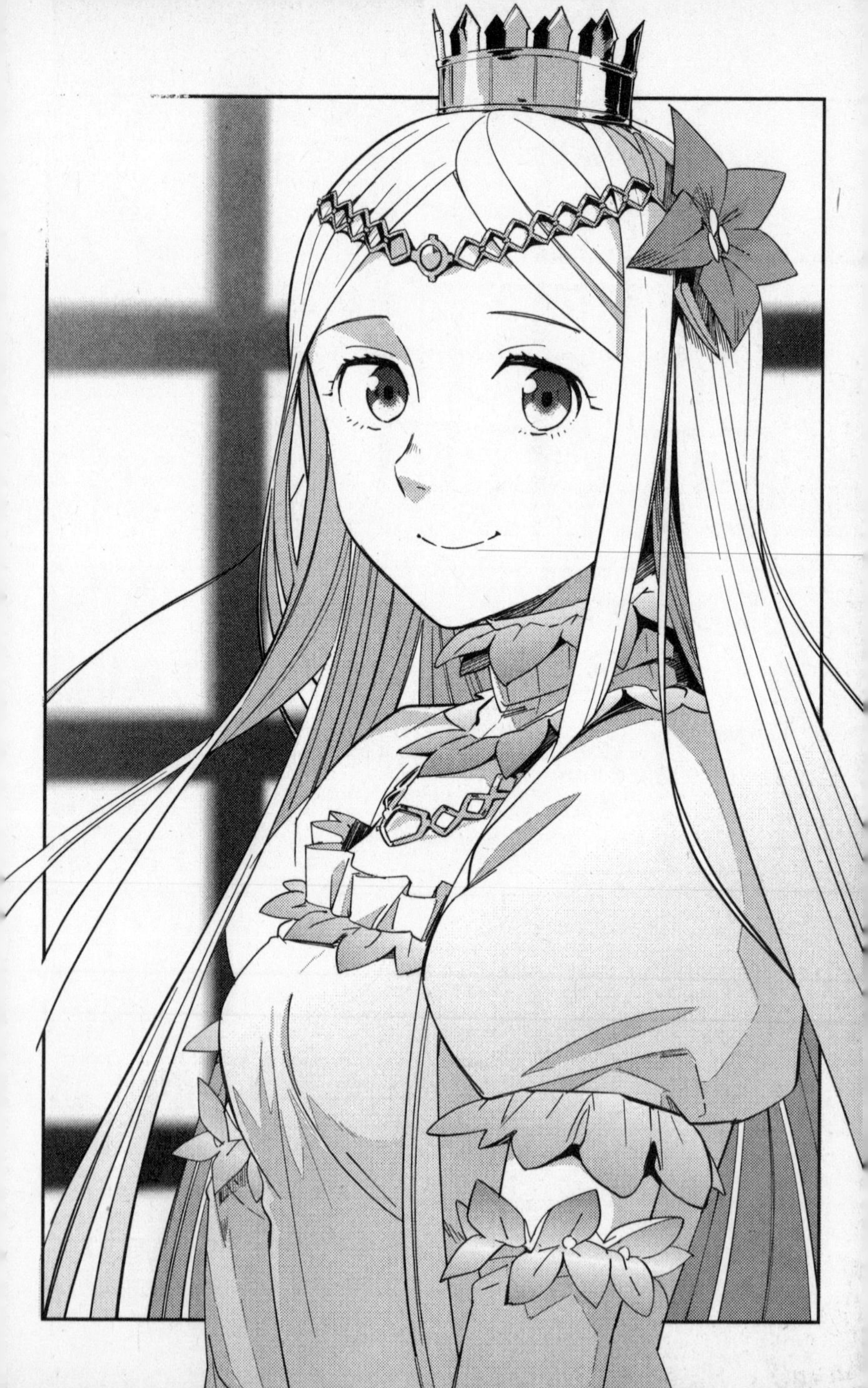

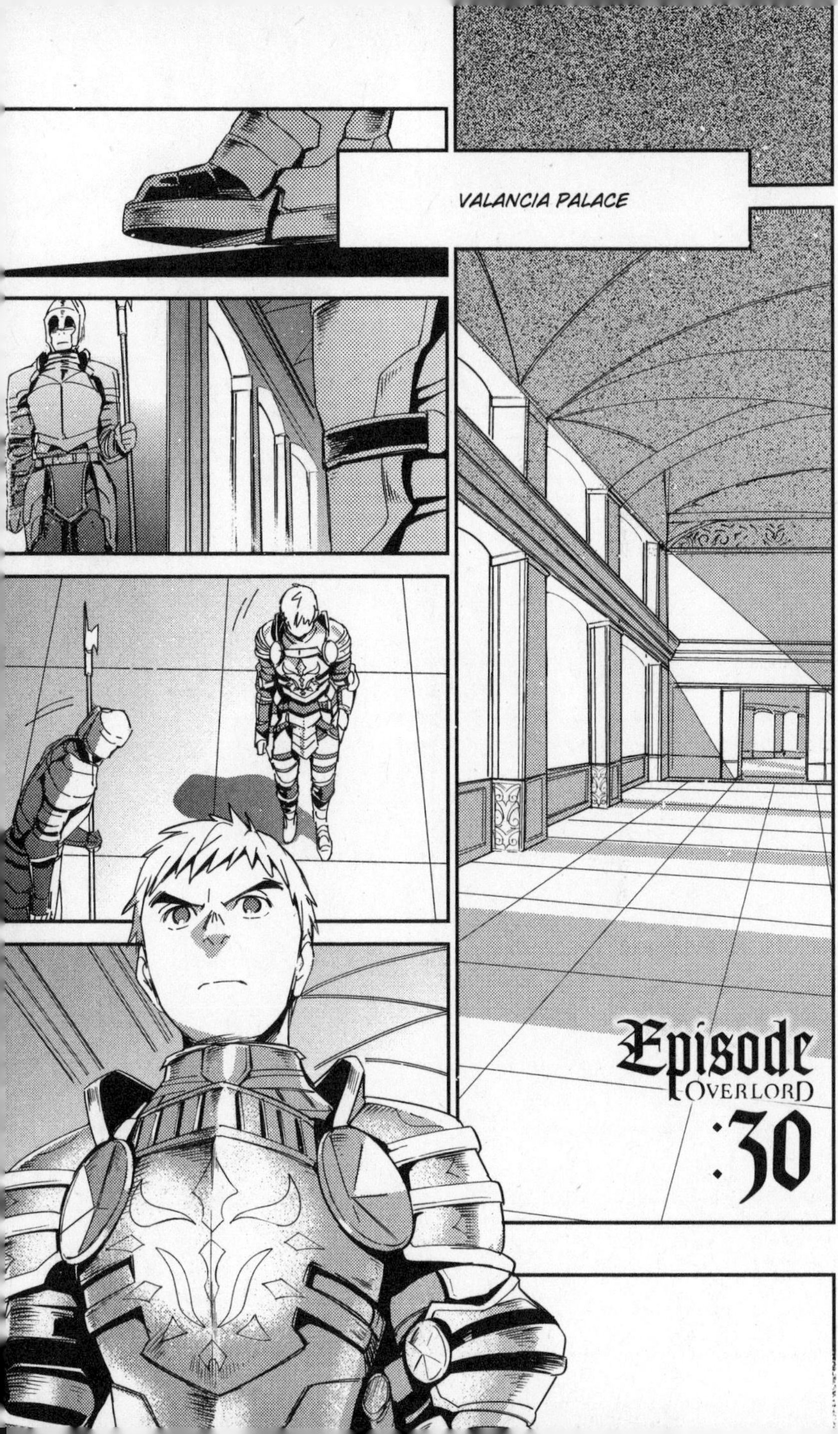
VALANCIA PALACE
Episode
OVERLORD
:30

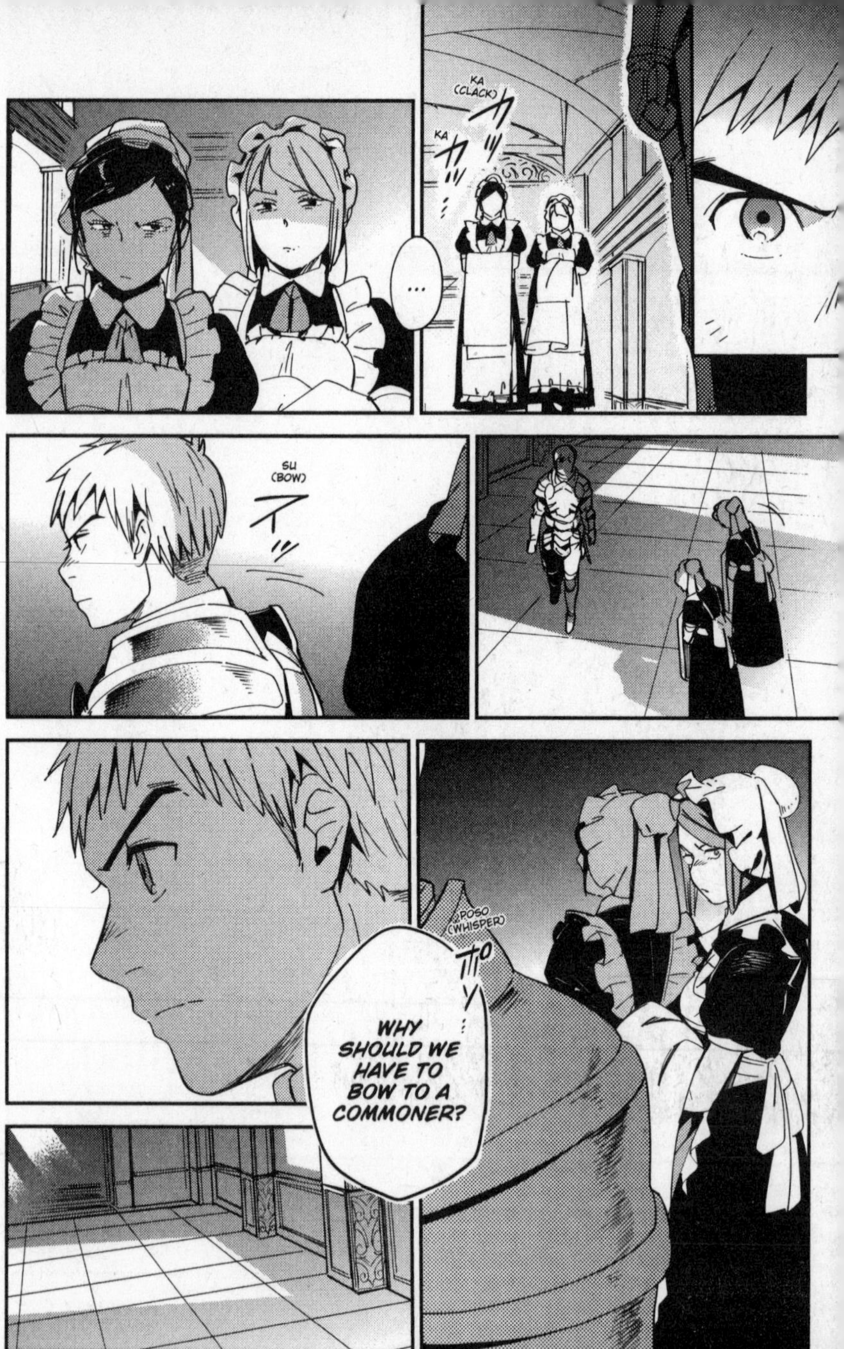
KA (CLACK)
KA
...
SU (BOW)
POSO (WHISPER)
WHY SHOULD WE HAVE TO BOW TO A COMMONER?

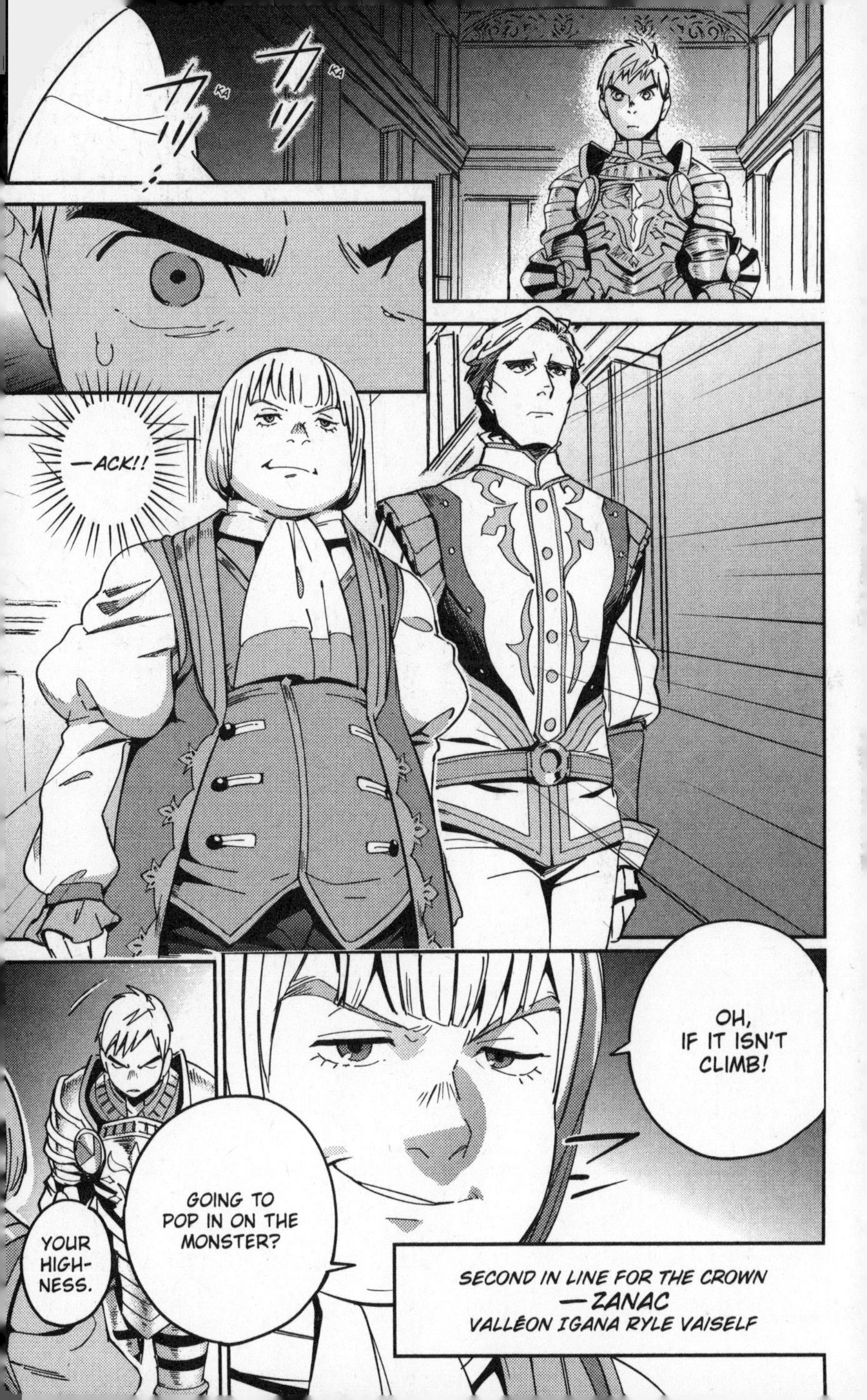
KA
KA
—ACK!!
OH, IF IT ISN'T CLIMB!
GOING TO POP IN ON THE MONSTER?
SECOND IN LINE FOR THE CROWN —ZANAC VALLÉON IGANA RYLE VAISELF
YOUR HIGHNESS.

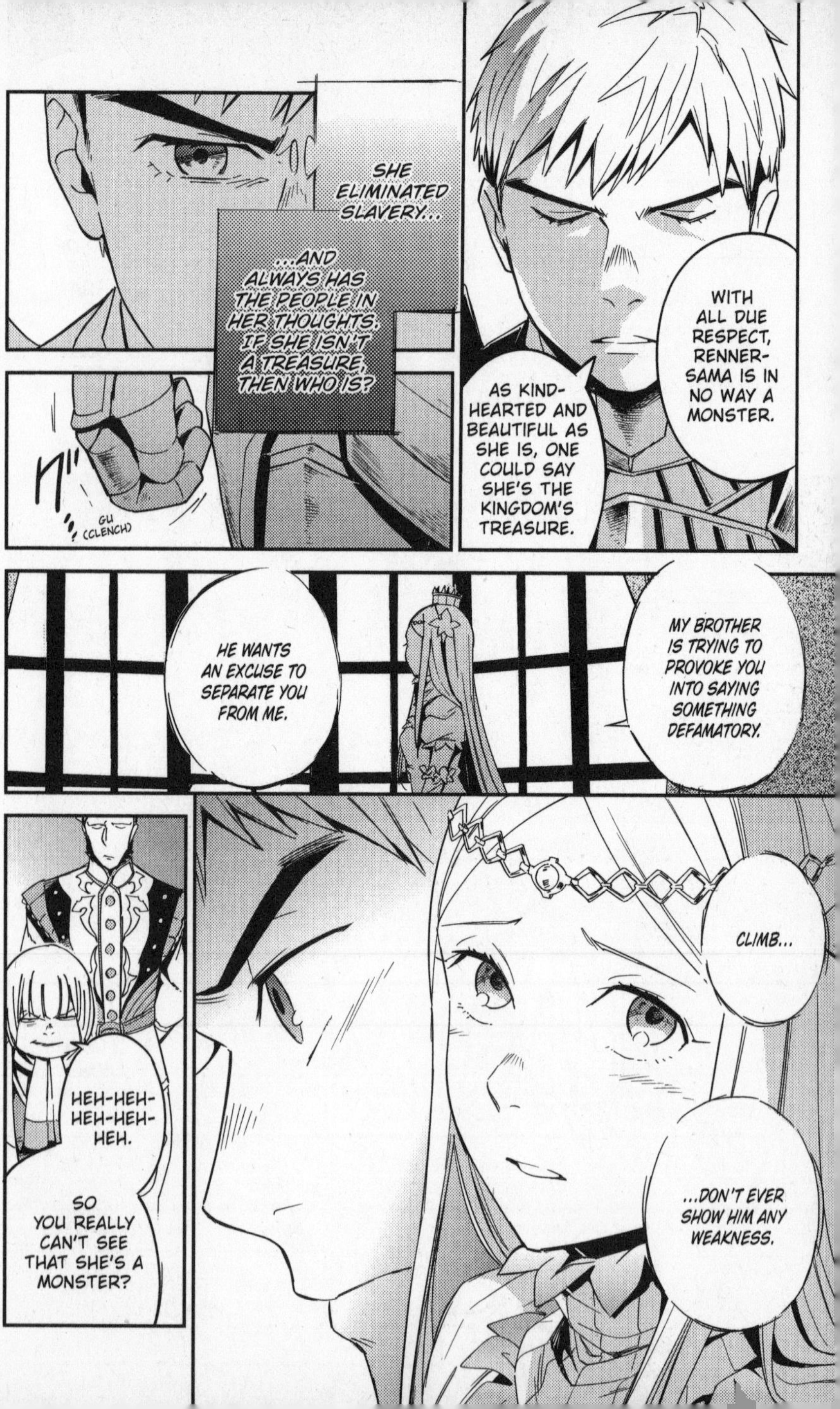
WITH ALL DUE RESPECT, RENNER-SAMA IS IN NO WAY A MONSTER.
AS KIND-HEARTED AND BEAUTIFUL AS SHE IS, ONE COULD SAY SHE'S THE KINGDOM'S TREASURE.
SHE ELIMINATED SLAVERY...
...AND ALWAYS HAS THE PEOPLE IN HER THOUGHTS. IF SHE ISN'T A TREASURE, THEN WHO IS?
GU (CLENCH)
MY BROTHER IS TRYING TO PROVOKE YOU INTO SAYING SOMETHING DEFAMATORY.
HE WANTS AN EXCUSE TO SEPARATE YOU FROM ME.
CLIMB...
...DON'T EVER SHOW HIM ANY WEAKNESS.
HEH-HEH-HEH-HEH-HEH.
SO YOU REALLY CAN'T SEE THAT SHE'S A MONSTER?

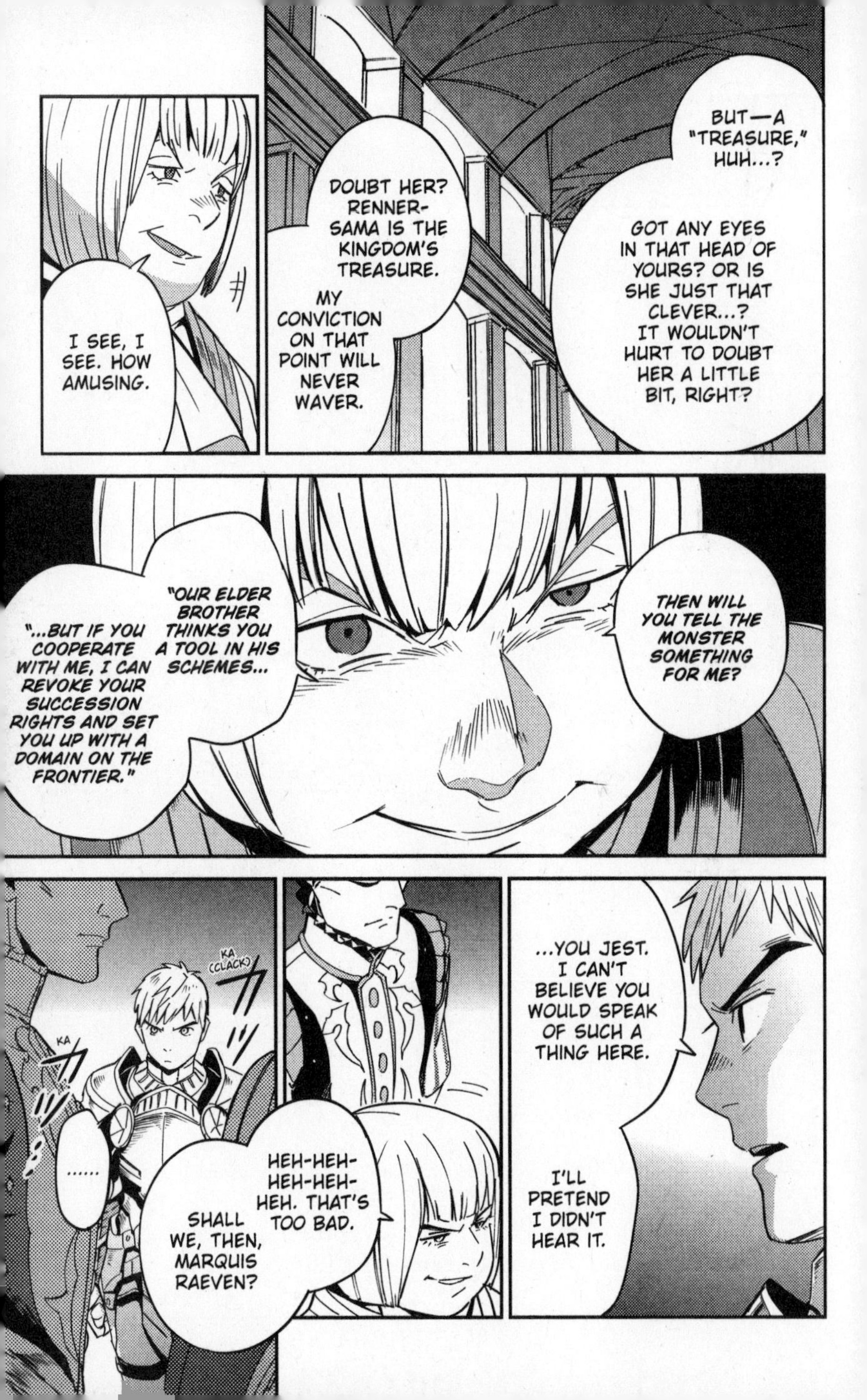
BUT—A "TREASURE," HUH...?
GOT ANY EYES IN THAT HEAD OF YOURS? OR IS SHE JUST THAT CLEVER...? IT WOULDN'T HURT TO DOUBT HER A LITTLE BIT, RIGHT?
DOUBT HER? RENNER-SAMA IS THE KINGDOM'S TREASURE.
MY CONVICTION ON THAT POINT WILL NEVER WAVER.
I SEE, I SEE. HOW AMUSING.
THEN WILL YOU TELL THE MONSTER SOMETHING FOR ME?
"OUR ELDER BROTHER THINKS YOU A TOOL IN HIS SCHEMES...
"...BUT IF YOU COOPERATE WITH ME, I CAN REVOKE YOUR SUCCESSION RIGHTS AND SET YOU UP WITH A DOMAIN ON THE FRONTIER."
...YOU JEST. I CAN'T BELIEVE YOU WOULD SPEAK OF SUCH A THING HERE.
I'LL PRETEND I DIDN'T HEAR IT.
HEH-HEH-HEH-HEH-HEH. THAT'S TOO BAD.
SHALL WE, THEN, MARQUIS RAEVEN?
KA (CLACK)
KA
......

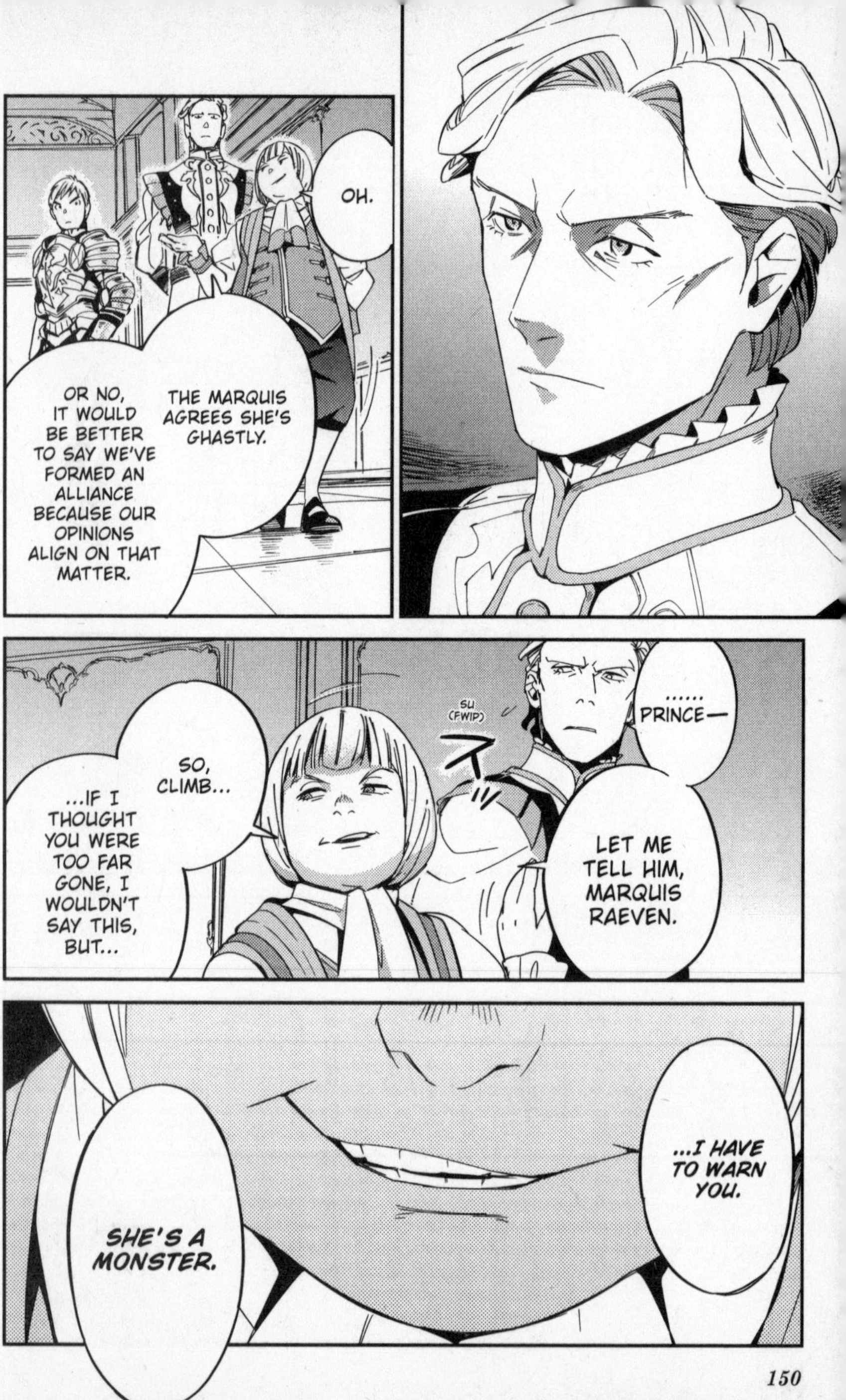
OH.
THE MARQUIS AGREES SHE'S GHASTLY.
OR NO, IT WOULD BE BETTER TO SAY WE'VE FORMED AN ALLIANCE BECAUSE OUR OPINIONS ALIGN ON THAT MATTER.
...... PRINCE—
SU (FWIP)
LET ME TELL HIM, MARQUIS RAEVEN.
SO, CLIMB...
...IF I THOUGHT YOU WERE TOO FAR GONE, I WOULDN'T SAY THIS, BUT...
...I HAVE TO WARN YOU.
SHE'S A MONSTER.

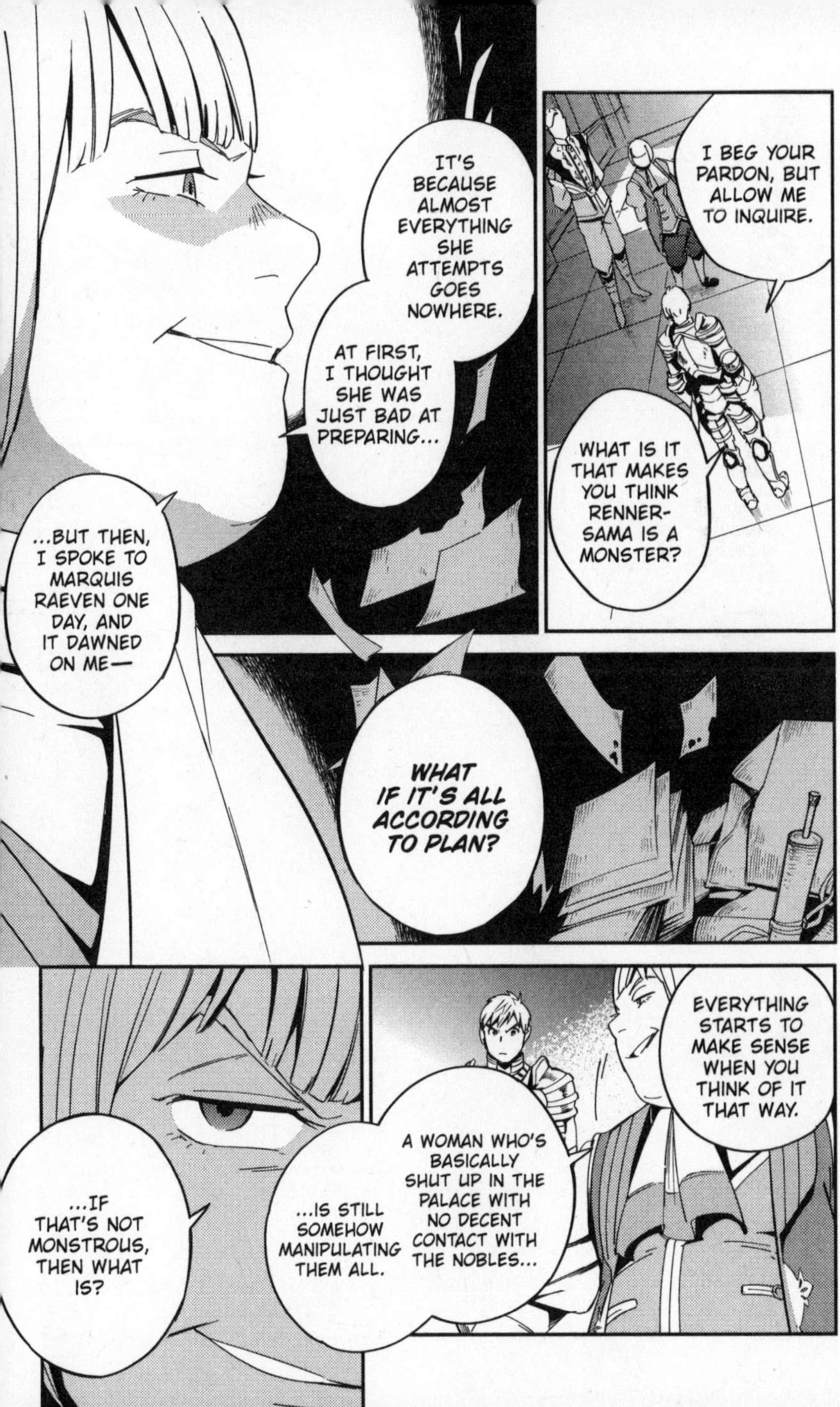
I BEG YOUR PARDON, BUT ALLOW ME TO INQUIRE.
WHAT IS IT THAT MAKES YOU THINK RENNER-SAMA IS A MONSTER?
IT'S BECAUSE ALMOST EVERYTHING SHE ATTEMPTS GOES NOWHERE.
AT FIRST, I THOUGHT SHE WAS JUST BAD AT PREPARING...
...BUT THEN, I SPOKE TO MARQUIS RAEVEN ONE DAY, AND IT DAWNED ON ME—
WHAT IF IT'S ALL ACCORDING TO PLAN?
EVERYTHING STARTS TO MAKE SENSE WHEN YOU THINK OF IT THAT WAY.
A WOMAN WHO'S BASICALLY SHUT UP IN THE PALACE WITH NO DECENT CONTACT WITH THE NOBLES...
...IS STILL SOMEHOW MANIPULATING THEM ALL.
...IF THAT'S NOT MONSTROUS, THEN WHAT IS?

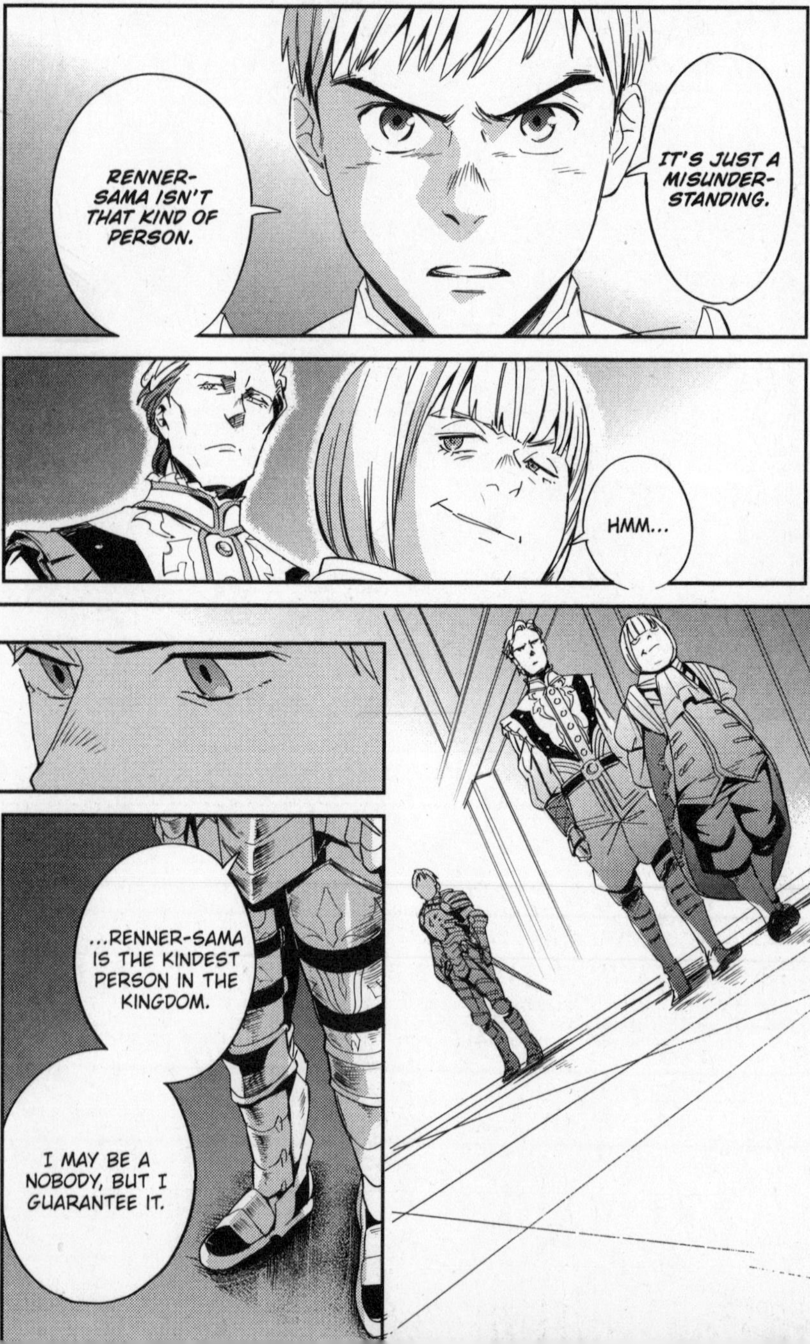
IT'S JUST A MISUNDER-STANDING.
RENNER-SAMA ISN'T THAT KIND OF PERSON.
HMM...
...RENNER-SAMA IS THE KINDEST PERSON IN THE KINGDOM.
I MAY BE A NOBODY, BUT I GUARANTEE IT.

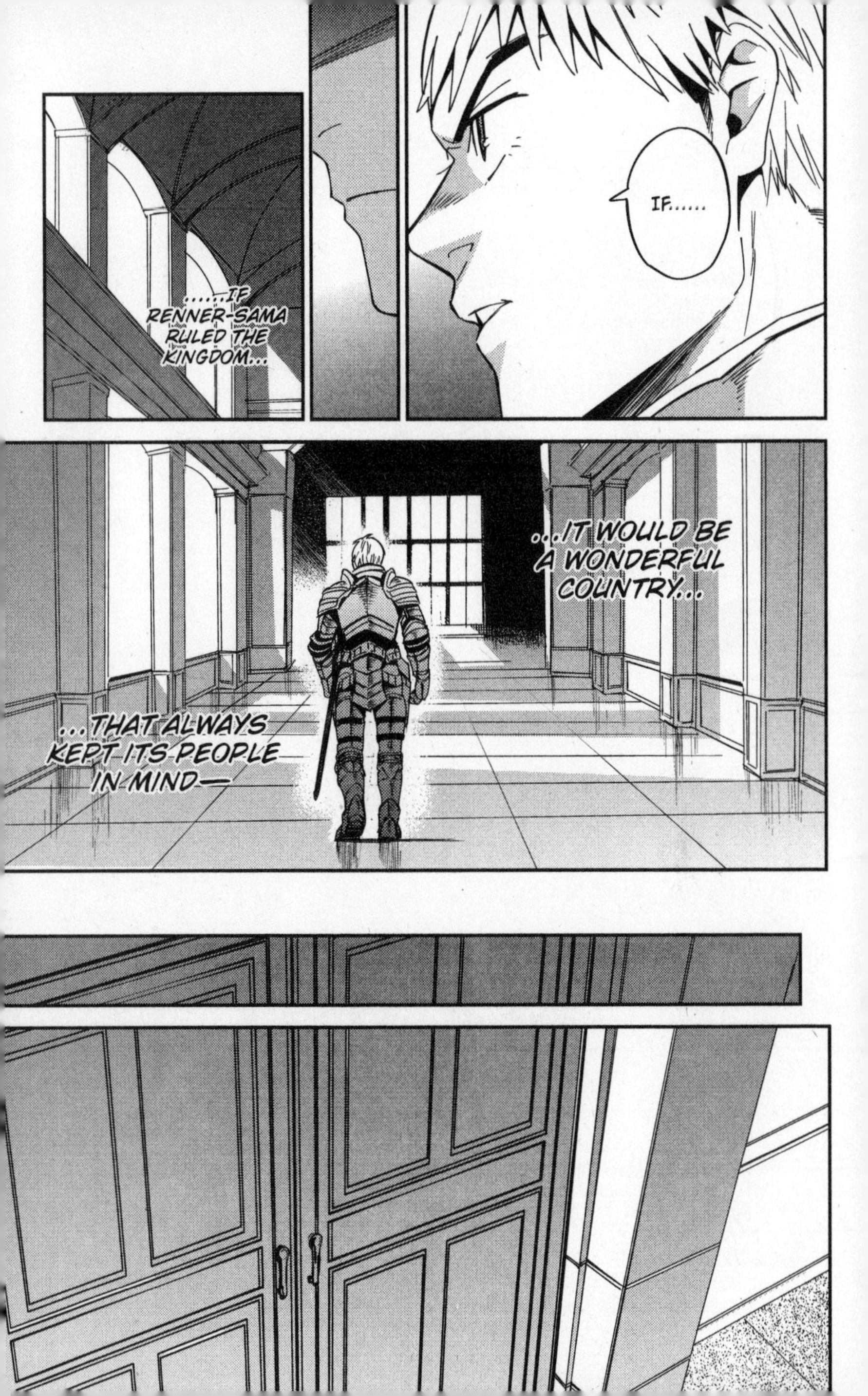
IF......
......IF RENNER-SAMA RULED THE KINGDOM...
...IT WOULD BE A WONDERFUL COUNTRY...
...THAT ALWAYS KEPT ITS PEOPLE IN MIND—

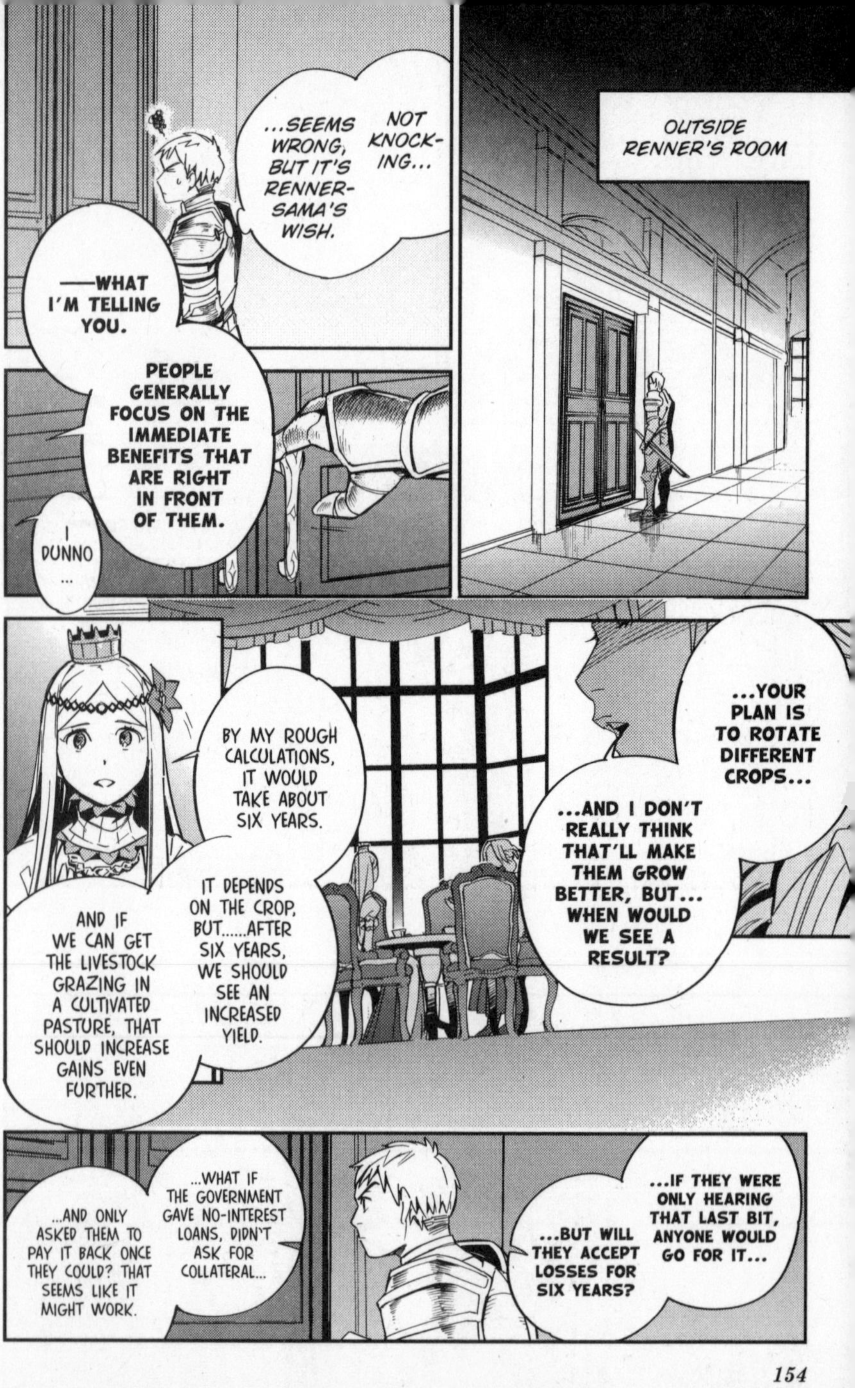
OUTSIDE RENNER'S ROOM
NOT KNOCKING...
...SEEMS WRONG, BUT IT'S RENNER-SAMA'S WISH.
——WHAT I'M TELLING YOU.
PEOPLE GENERALLY FOCUS ON THE IMMEDIATE BENEFITS THAT ARE RIGHT IN FRONT OF THEM.
I DUNNO...
...YOUR PLAN IS TO ROTATE DIFFERENT CROPS...
...AND I DON'T REALLY THINK THAT'LL MAKE THEM GROW BETTER, BUT... WHEN WOULD WE SEE A RESULT?
BY MY ROUGH CALCULATIONS, IT WOULD TAKE ABOUT SIX YEARS.
IT DEPENDS ON THE CROP, BUT......AFTER SIX YEARS, WE SHOULD SEE AN INCREASED YIELD.
AND IF WE CAN GET THE LIVESTOCK GRAZING IN A CULTIVATED PASTURE, THAT SHOULD INCREASE GAINS EVEN FURTHER.
...IF THEY WERE ONLY HEARING THAT LAST BIT, ANYONE WOULD GO FOR IT...
...BUT WILL THEY ACCEPT LOSSES FOR SIX YEARS?
...WHAT IF THE GOVERNMENT GAVE NO-INTEREST LOANS, DIDN'T ASK FOR COLLATERAL...
...AND ONLY ASKED THEM TO PAY IT BACK ONCE THEY COULD? THAT SEEMS LIKE IT MIGHT WORK.

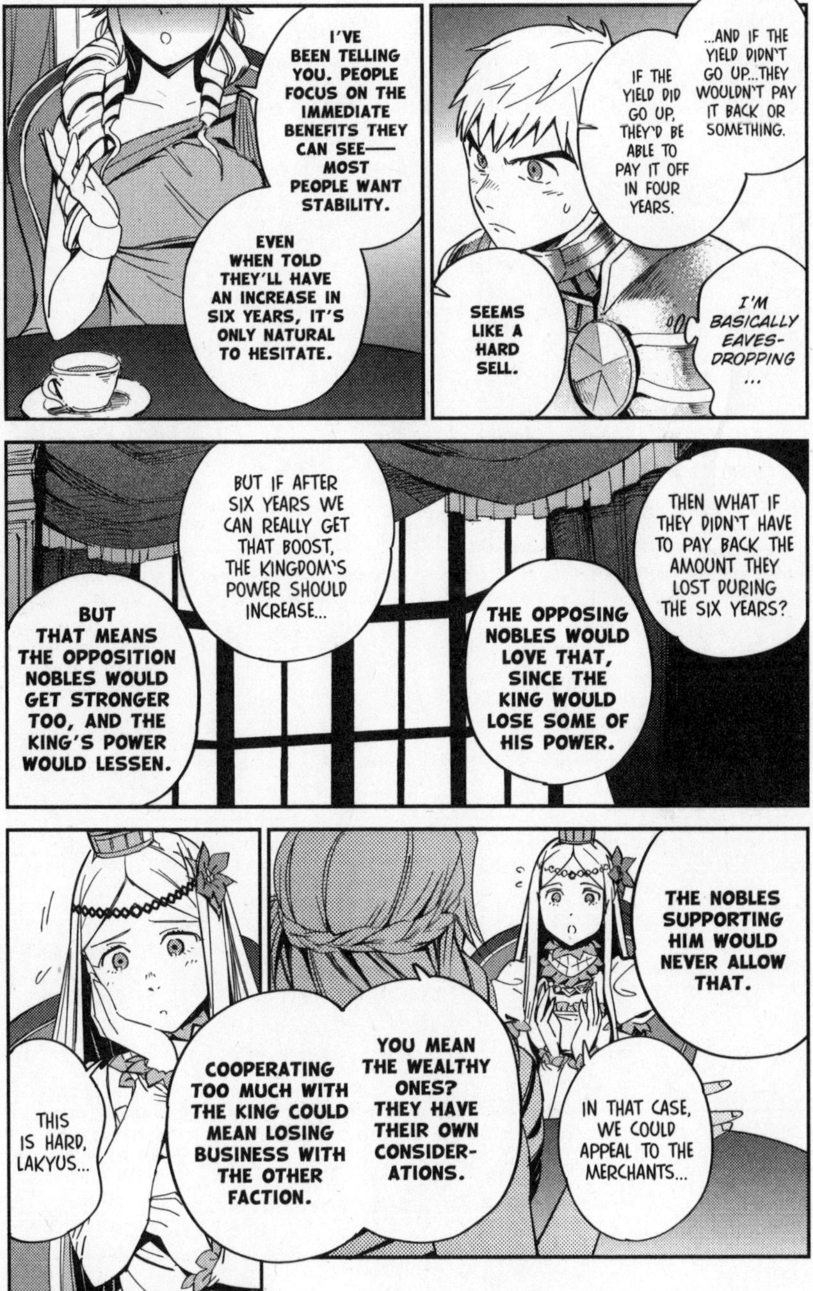
...AND IF THE YIELD DIDN'T GO UP...THEY WOULDN'T PAY IT BACK OR SOMETHING.
IF THE YIELD DID GO UP, THEY'D BE ABLE TO PAY IT OFF IN FOUR YEARS.
I'M BASICALLY EAVES-DROPPING...
SEEMS LIKE A HARD SELL.
I'VE BEEN TELLING YOU. PEOPLE FOCUS ON THE IMMEDIATE BENEFITS THEY CAN SEE—MOST PEOPLE WANT STABILITY.
EVEN WHEN TOLD THEY'LL HAVE AN INCREASE IN SIX YEARS, IT'S ONLY NATURAL TO HESITATE.
THEN WHAT IF THEY DIDN'T HAVE TO PAY BACK THE AMOUNT THEY LOST DURING THE SIX YEARS?
THE OPPOSING NOBLES WOULD LOVE THAT, SINCE THE KING WOULD LOSE SOME OF HIS POWER.
BUT IF AFTER SIX YEARS WE CAN REALLY GET THAT BOOST, THE KINGDOM'S POWER SHOULD INCREASE...
BUT THAT MEANS THE OPPOSITION NOBLES WOULD GET STRONGER TOO, AND THE KING'S POWER WOULD LESSEN.
THE NOBLES SUPPORTING HIM WOULD NEVER ALLOW THAT.
IN THAT CASE, WE COULD APPEAL TO THE MERCHANTS...
YOU MEAN THE WEALTHY ONES? THEY HAVE THEIR OWN CONSIDER-ATIONS.
COOPERATING TOO MUCH WITH THE KING COULD MEAN LOSING BUSINESS WITH THE OTHER FACTION.
THIS IS HARD, LAKYUS...

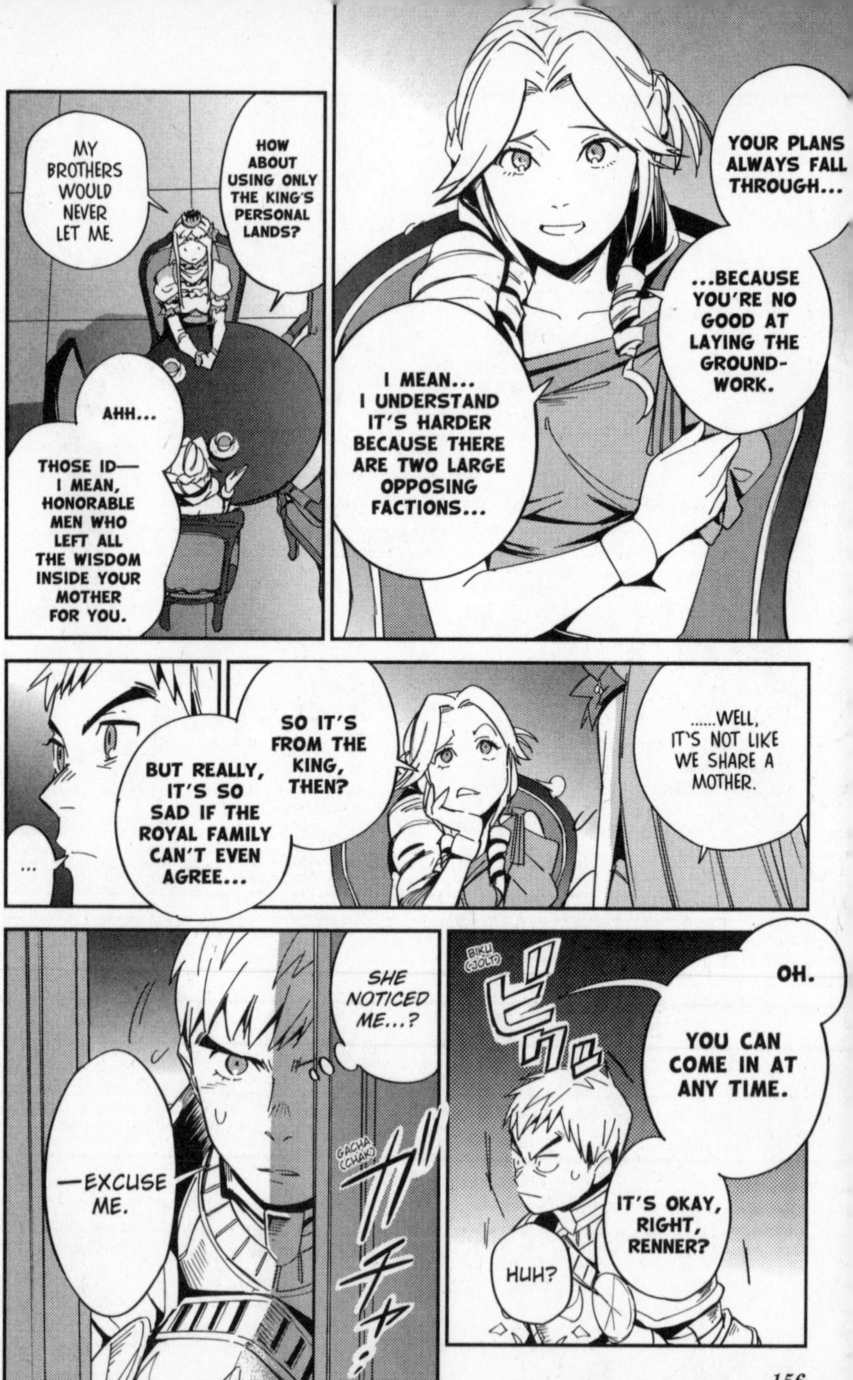
YOUR PLANS ALWAYS FALL THROUGH...
...BECAUSE YOU'RE NO GOOD AT LAYING THE GROUND-WORK.
I MEAN... I UNDERSTAND IT'S HARDER BECAUSE THERE ARE TWO LARGE OPPOSING FACTIONS...
HOW ABOUT USING ONLY THE KING'S PERSONAL LANDS?
MY BROTHERS WOULD NEVER LET ME.
AHH...
THOSE ID— I MEAN, HONORABLE MEN WHO LEFT ALL THE WISDOM INSIDE YOUR MOTHER FOR YOU.
......WELL, IT'S NOT LIKE WE SHARE A MOTHER.
SO IT'S FROM THE KING, THEN?
BUT REALLY, IT'S SO SAD IF THE ROYAL FAMILY CAN'T EVEN AGREE...
...
BIKU (JOLT)
OH.
YOU CAN COME IN AT ANY TIME.
IT'S OKAY, RIGHT, RENNER?
HUH?
SHE NOTICED ME...?
GACHA (CHAK)
—EXCUSE ME.

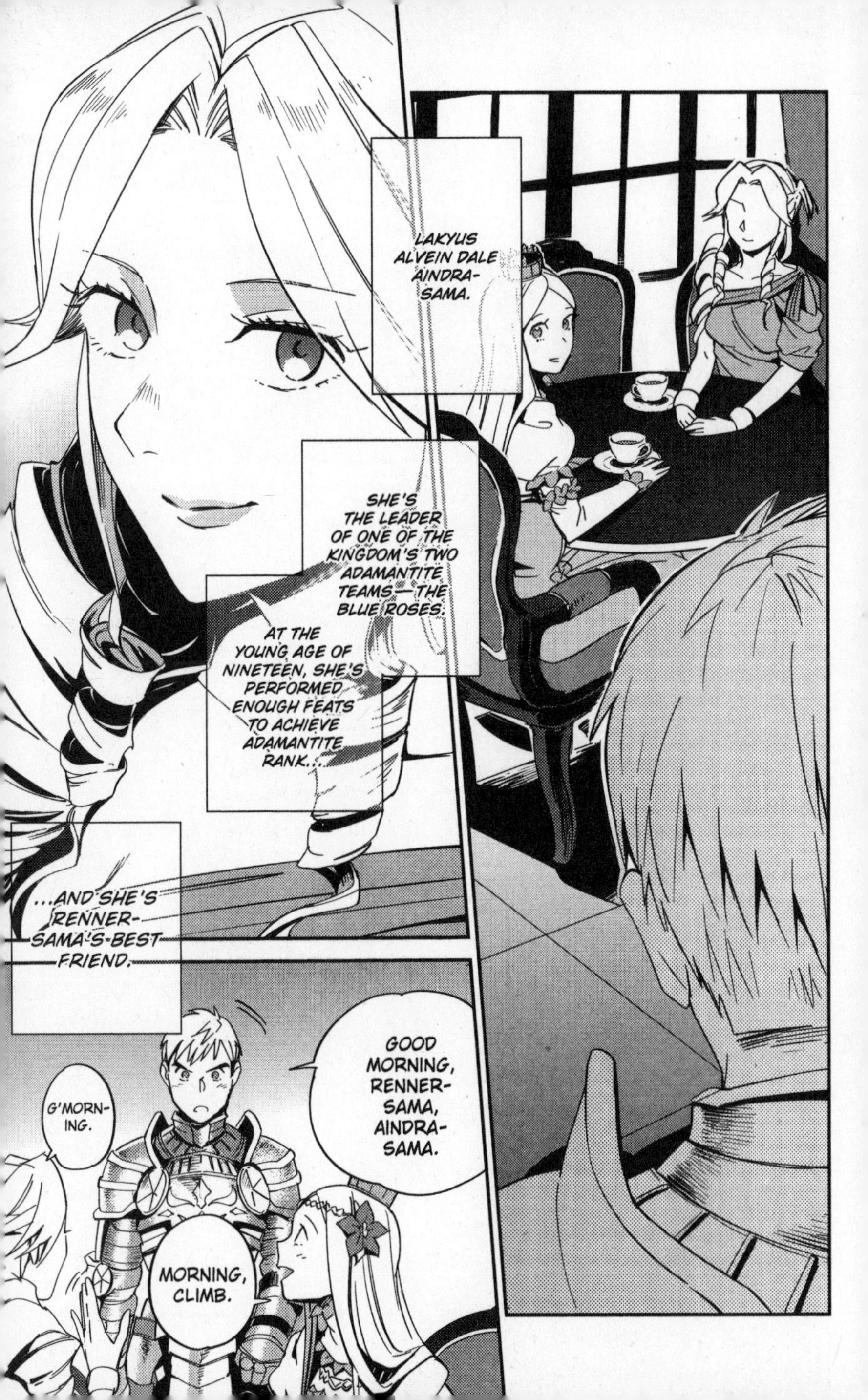
LAKYUS ALVEIN DALE AINDRA-SAMA.
SHE'S THE LEADER OF ONE OF THE KINGDOM'S TWO ADAMANTITE TEAMS—THE BLUE ROSES.
AT THE YOUNG AGE OF NINETEEN, SHE'S PERFORMED ENOUGH FEATS TO ACHIEVE ADAMANTITE RANK...
...AND SHE'S RENNER-SAMA'S BEST FRIEND.
GOOD MORNING, RENNER-SAMA, AINDRA-SAMA.
MORNING, CLIMB.
G'MORNING.

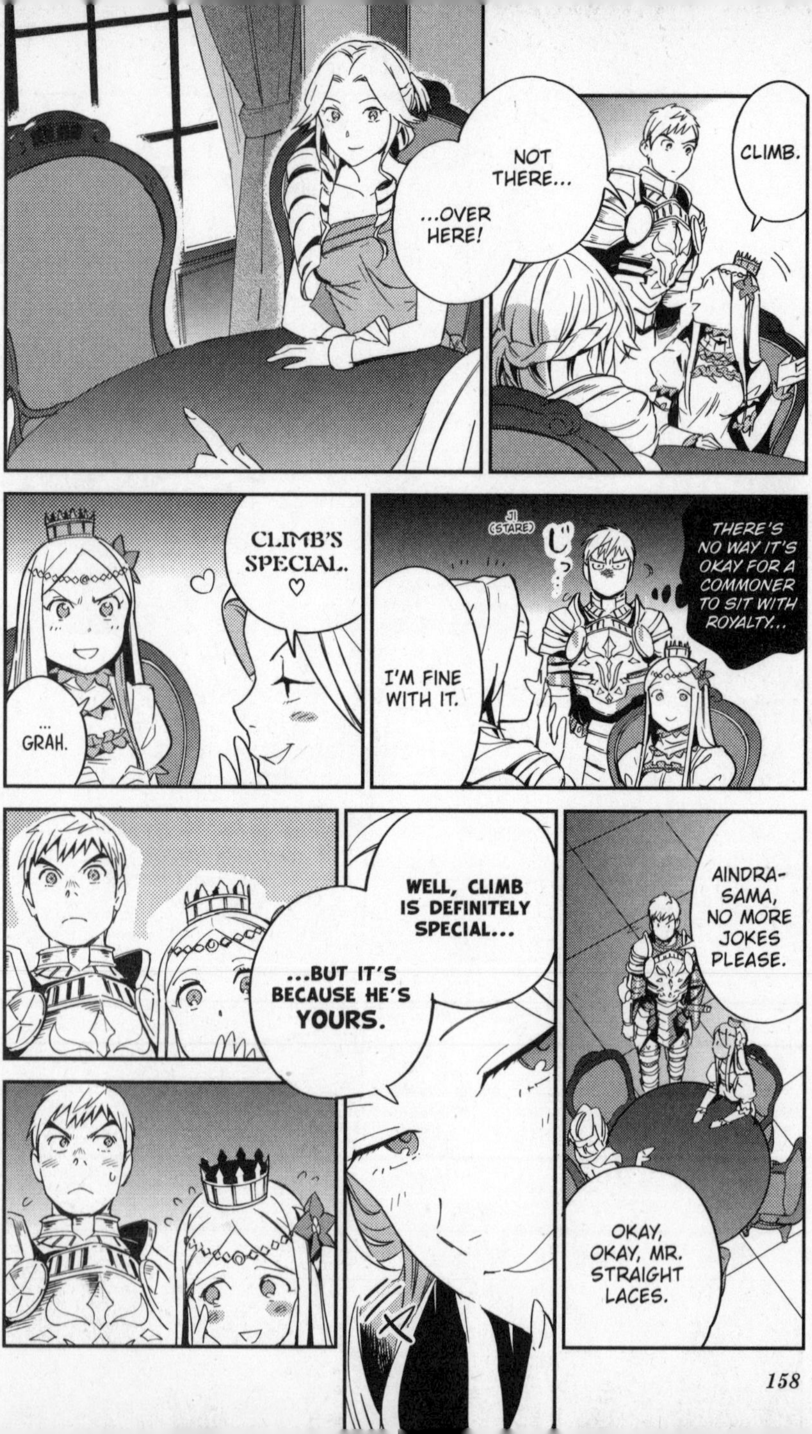
CLIMB.
NOT THERE...
...OVER HERE!
JI (STARE)
THERE'S NO WAY IT'S OKAY FOR A COMMONER TO SIT WITH ROYALTY...
I'M FINE WITH IT.
CLIMB'S SPECIAL. ♡
... GRAH.
AINDRA-SAMA, NO MORE JOKES PLEASE.
OKAY, OKAY, MR. STRAIGHT LACES.
WELL, CLIMB IS DEFINITELY SPECIAL...
...BUT IT'S BECAUSE HE'S YOURS.

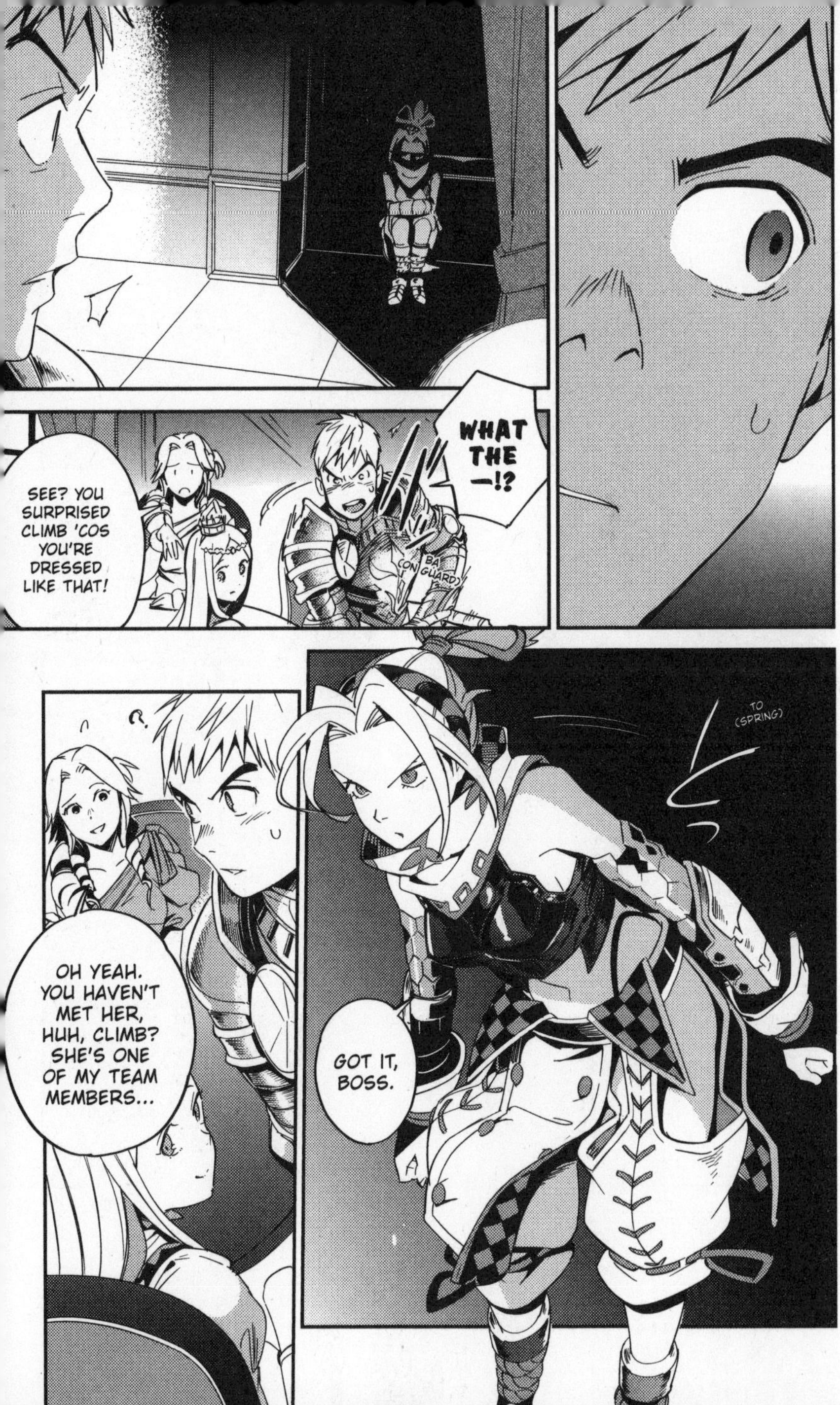
WHAT THE—!?
BA (ON GUARD)
SEE? YOU SURPRISED CLIMB 'COS YOU'RE DRESSED LIKE THAT!
TO (SPRING)
GOT IT, BOSS.
OH YEAH. YOU HAVEN'T MET HER, HUH, CLIMB? SHE'S ONE OF MY TEAM MEMBERS...

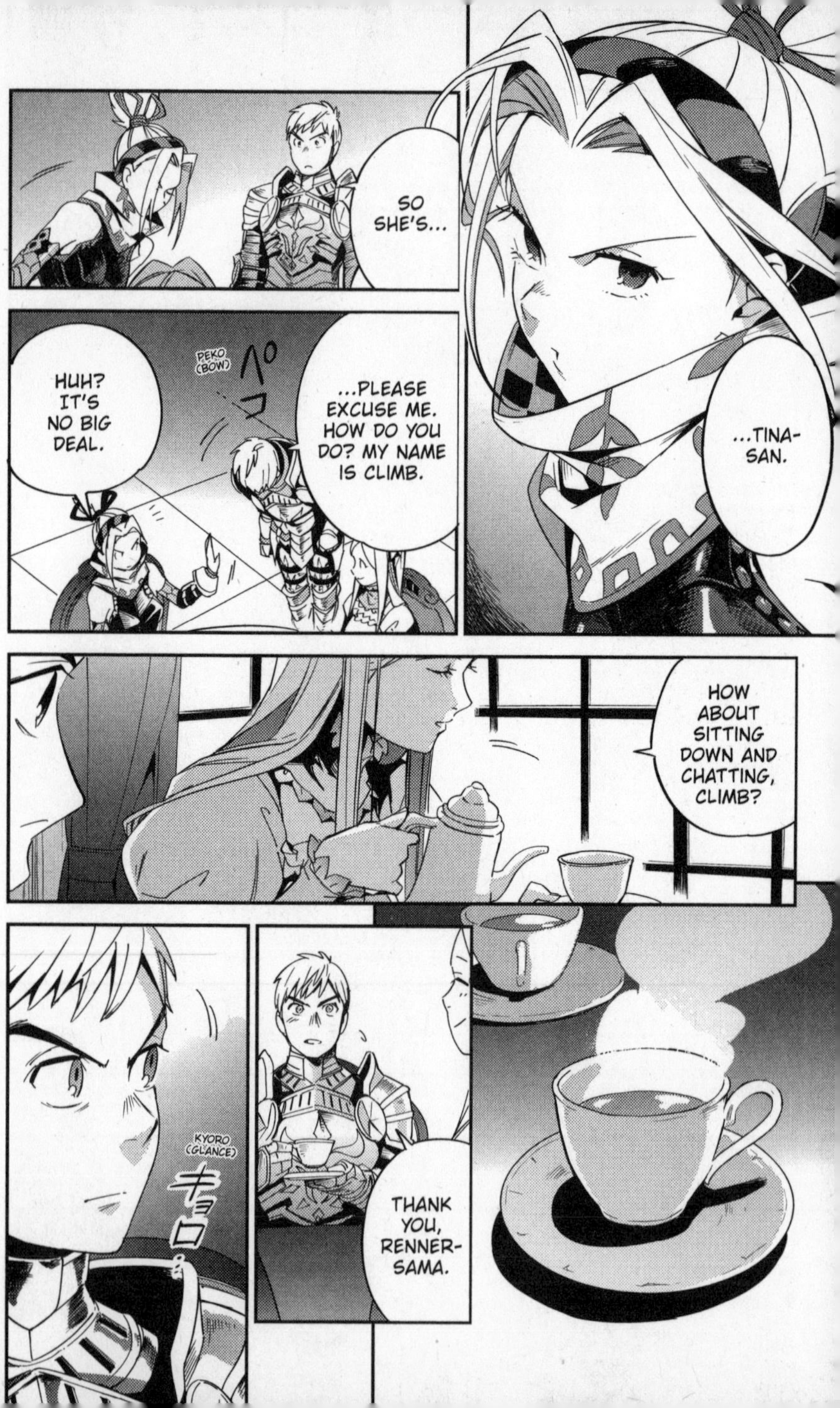
SO SHE'S...
...TINA-SAN.
PEKO (BOW)
...PLEASE EXCUSE ME. HOW DO YOU DO? MY NAME IS CLIMB.
HUH? IT'S NO BIG DEAL.
HOW ABOUT SITTING DOWN AND CHATTING, CLIMB?
THANK YOU, RENNER-SAMA.
KYORO (GLANCE)

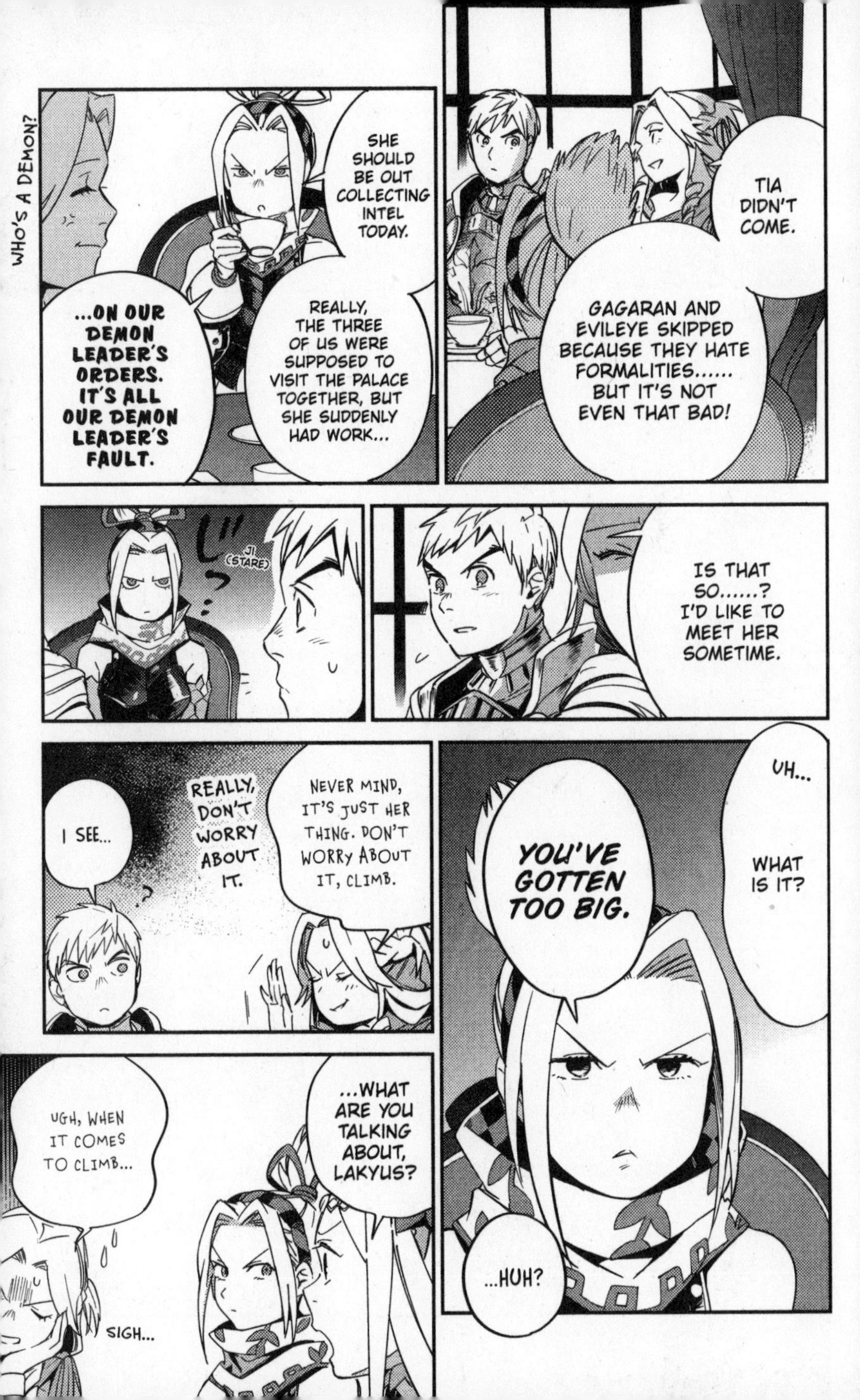
TIA DIDN'T COME.
GAGARAN AND EVILEYE SKIPPED BECAUSE THEY HATE FORMALITIES...... BUT IT'S NOT EVEN THAT BAD!
SHE SHOULD BE OUT COLLECTING INTEL TODAY.
REALLY, THE THREE OF US WERE SUPPOSED TO VISIT THE PALACE TOGETHER, BUT SHE SUDDENLY HAD WORK...
...ON OUR DEMON LEADER'S ORDERS. IT'S ALL OUR DEMON LEADER'S FAULT.
WHO'S A DEMON?
IS THAT SO......? I'D LIKE TO MEET HER SOMETIME.
JI (STARE)
UH...
WHAT IS IT?
YOU'VE GOTTEN TOO BIG.
...HUH?
NEVER MIND, IT'S JUST HER THING. DON'T WORRY ABOUT IT, CLIMB.
REALLY, DON'T WORRY ABOUT IT.
I SEE...
...WHAT ARE YOU TALKING ABOUT, LAKYUS?
UGH, WHEN IT COMES TO CLIMB...
SIGH...

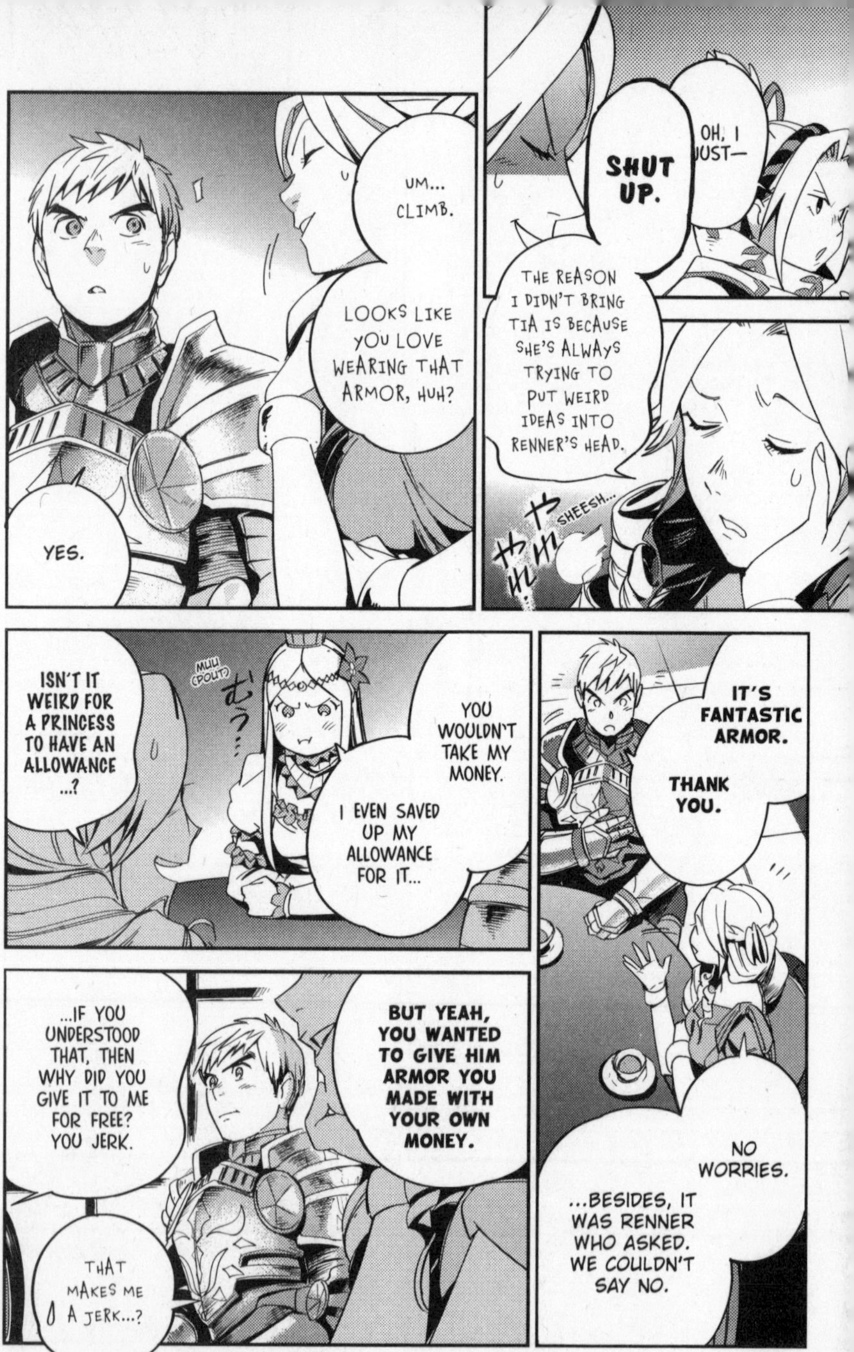
OH, I JUST—
SHUT UP.
THE REASON I DIDN'T BRING TIA IS BECAUSE SHE'S ALWAYS TRYING TO PUT WEIRD IDEAS INTO RENNER'S HEAD.
SHEESH...
UM... CLIMB.
LOOKS LIKE YOU LOVE WEARING THAT ARMOR, HUH?
YES.
IT'S FANTASTIC ARMOR.
THANK YOU.
NO WORRIES.
...BESIDES, IT WAS RENNER WHO ASKED. WE COULDN'T SAY NO.
YOU WOULDN'T TAKE MY MONEY.
I EVEN SAVED UP MY ALLOWANCE FOR IT...
MUU (POUT)
ISN'T IT WEIRD FOR A PRINCESS TO HAVE AN ALLOWANCE ...?
BUT YEAH, YOU WANTED TO GIVE HIM ARMOR YOU MADE WITH YOUR OWN MONEY.
...IF YOU UNDERSTOOD THAT, THEN WHY DID YOU GIVE IT TO ME FOR FREE? YOU JERK.
THAT MAKES ME A JERK...?

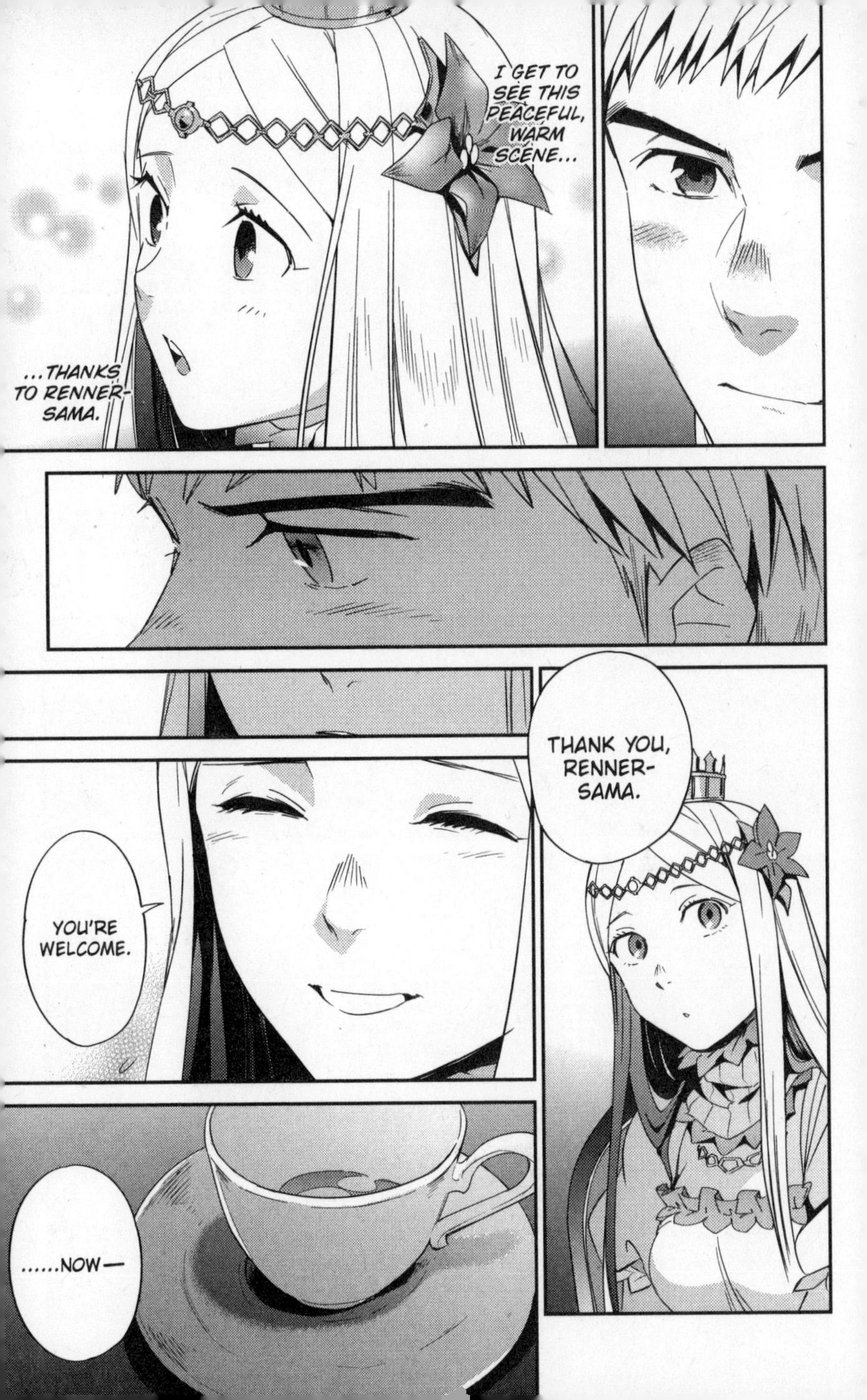
I GET TO SEE THIS PEACEFUL, WARM SCENE...
...THANKS TO RENNER-SAMA.
THANK YOU, RENNER-SAMA.
YOU'RE WELCOME.
......NOW—

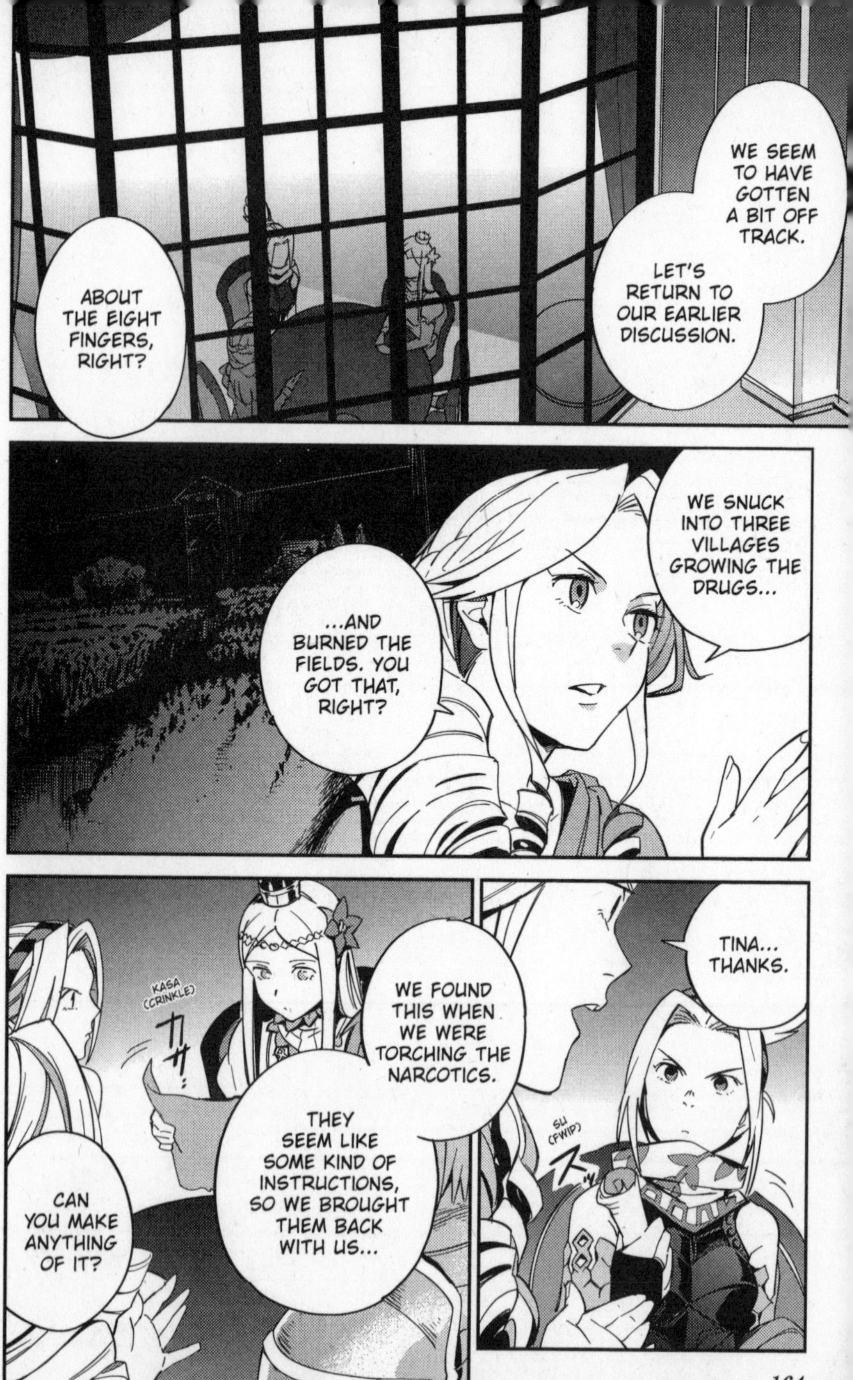
WE SEEM TO HAVE GOTTEN A BIT OFF TRACK.
LET'S RETURN TO OUR EARLIER DISCUSSION.
ABOUT THE EIGHT FINGERS, RIGHT?
WE SNUCK INTO THREE VILLAGES GROWING THE DRUGS...
...AND BURNED THE FIELDS. YOU GOT THAT, RIGHT?
TINA... THANKS.
SU (FWIP)
WE FOUND THIS WHEN WE WERE TORCHING THE NARCOTICS.
THEY SEEM LIKE SOME KIND OF INSTRUCTIONS, SO WE BROUGHT THEM BACK WITH US...
KASA (CRINKLE)
CAN YOU MAKE ANYTHING OF IT?

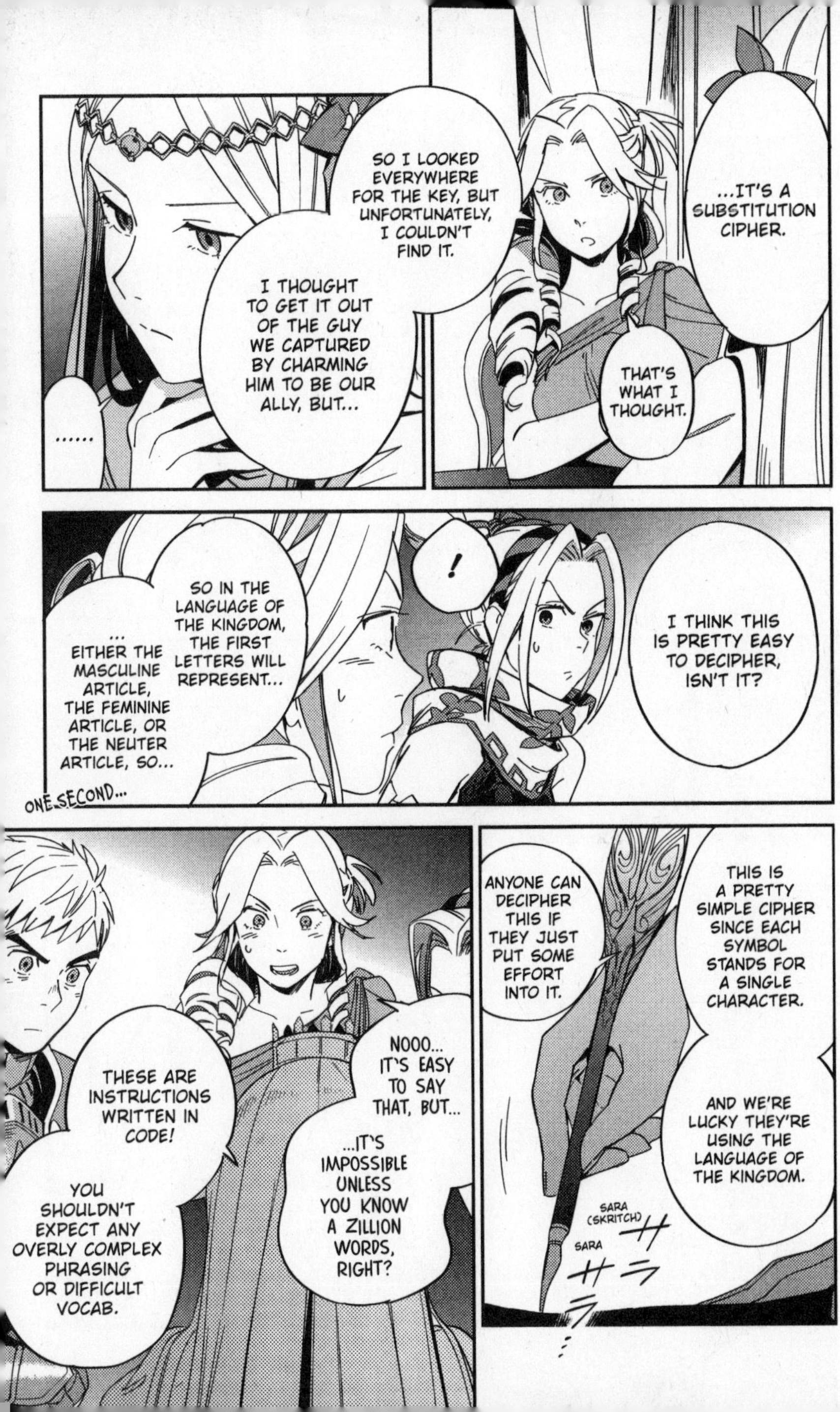
...IT'S A SUBSTITUTION CIPHER.
THAT'S WHAT I THOUGHT.
SO I LOOKED EVERYWHERE FOR THE KEY, BUT UNFORTUNATELY, I COULDN'T FIND IT.
I THOUGHT TO GET IT OUT OF THE GUY WE CAPTURED BY CHARMING HIM TO BE OUR ALLY, BUT...
......
I THINK THIS IS PRETTY EASY TO DECIPHER, ISN'T IT?
!
SO IN THE LANGUAGE OF THE KINGDOM, THE FIRST LETTERS WILL REPRESENT...
... EITHER THE MASCULINE ARTICLE, THE FEMININE ARTICLE, OR THE NEUTER ARTICLE, SO...
ONE SECOND...
THIS IS A PRETTY SIMPLE CIPHER SINCE EACH SYMBOL STANDS FOR A SINGLE CHARACTER.
ANYONE CAN DECIPHER THIS IF THEY JUST PUT SOME EFFORT INTO IT.
AND WE'RE LUCKY THEY'RE USING THE LANGUAGE OF THE KINGDOM.
SARA (SKRITCH)
SARA
NOOO... IT'S EASY TO SAY THAT, BUT...
...IT'S IMPOSSIBLE UNLESS YOU KNOW A ZILLION WORDS, RIGHT?
THESE ARE INSTRUCTIONS WRITTEN IN CODE!
YOU SHOULDN'T EXPECT ANY OVERLY COMPLEX PHRASING OR DIFFICULT VOCAB.

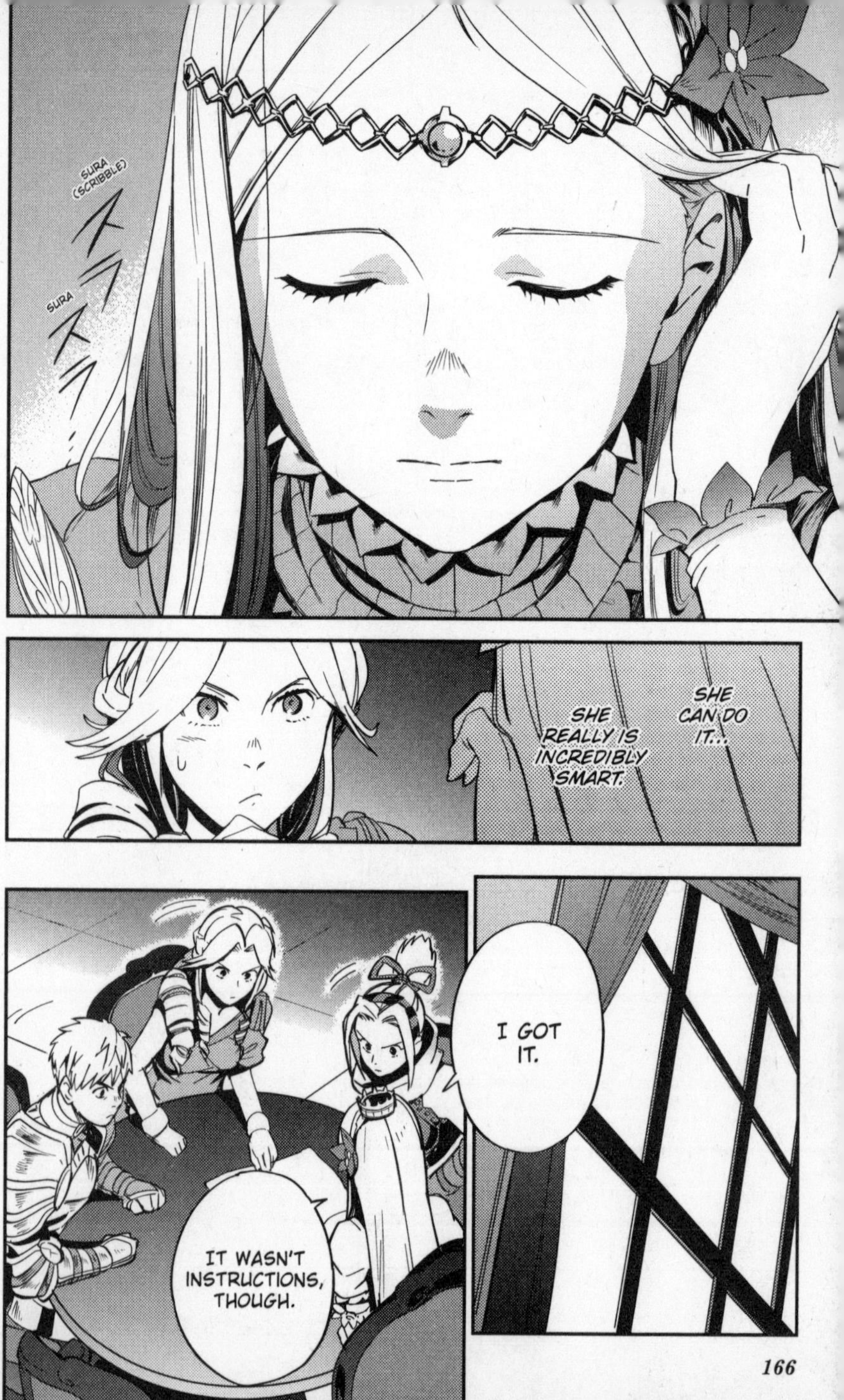
SURA (SCRIBBLE)
SURA
SHE CAN DO IT...
SHE REALLY IS INCREDIBLY SMART.
I GOT IT.
IT WASN'T INSTRUCTIONS, THOUGH.

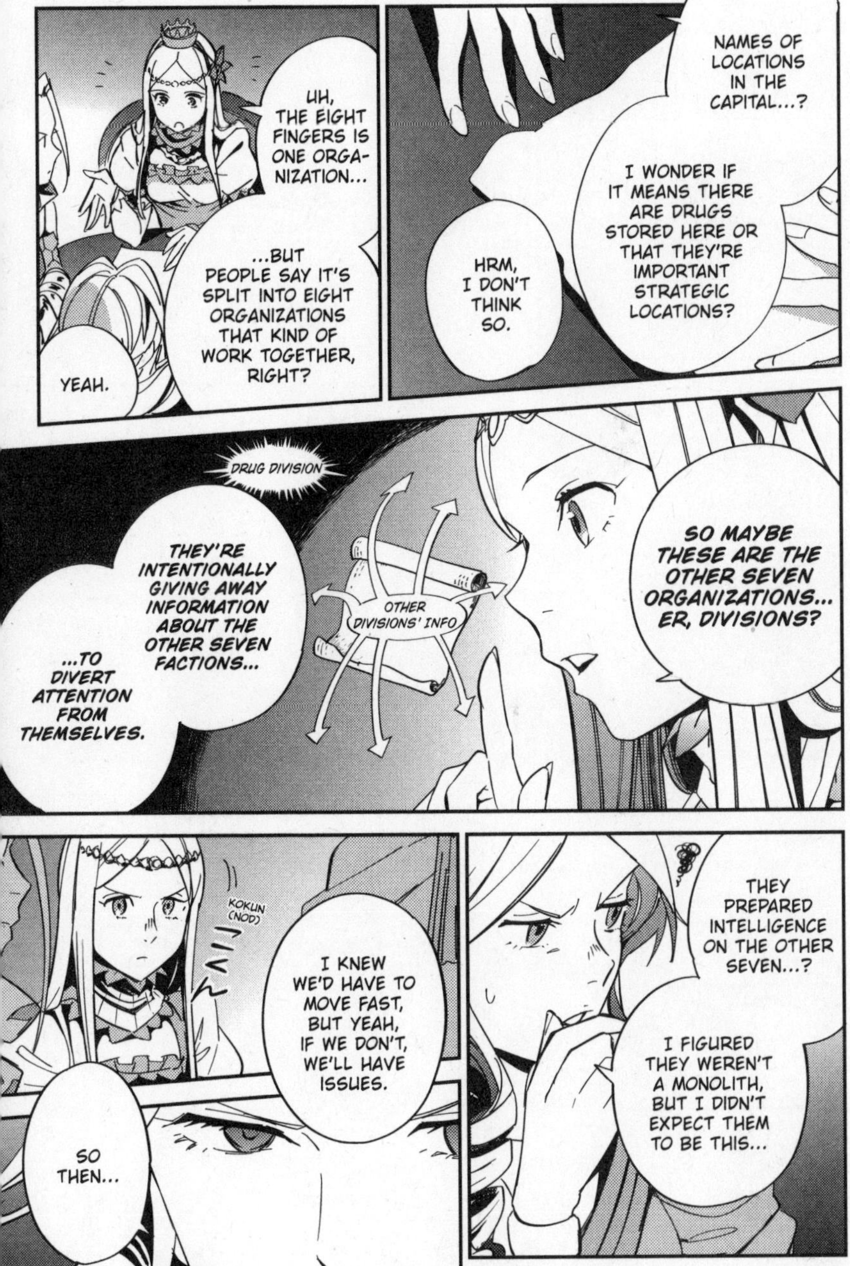
NAMES OF LOCATIONS IN THE CAPITAL...?
I WONDER IF IT MEANS THERE ARE DRUGS STORED HERE OR THAT THEY'RE IMPORTANT STRATEGIC LOCATIONS?
HRM, I DON'T THINK SO.
UH, THE EIGHT FINGERS IS ONE ORGA-NIZATION...
...BUT PEOPLE SAY IT'S SPLIT INTO EIGHT ORGANIZATIONS THAT KIND OF WORK TOGETHER, RIGHT?
YEAH.
SO MAYBE THESE ARE THE OTHER SEVEN ORGANIZATIONS... ER, DIVISIONS?
DRUG DIVISION
OTHER DIVISIONS' INFO
THEY'RE INTENTIONALLY GIVING AWAY INFORMATION ABOUT THE OTHER SEVEN FACTIONS...
...TO DIVERT ATTENTION FROM THEMSELVES.
THEY PREPARED INTELLIGENCE ON THE OTHER SEVEN...?
I FIGURED THEY WEREN'T A MONOLITH, BUT I DIDN'T EXPECT THEM TO BE THIS...
KOKUN (NOD)
I KNEW WE'D HAVE TO MOVE FAST, BUT YEAH, IF WE DON'T, WE'LL HAVE ISSUES.
SO THEN...

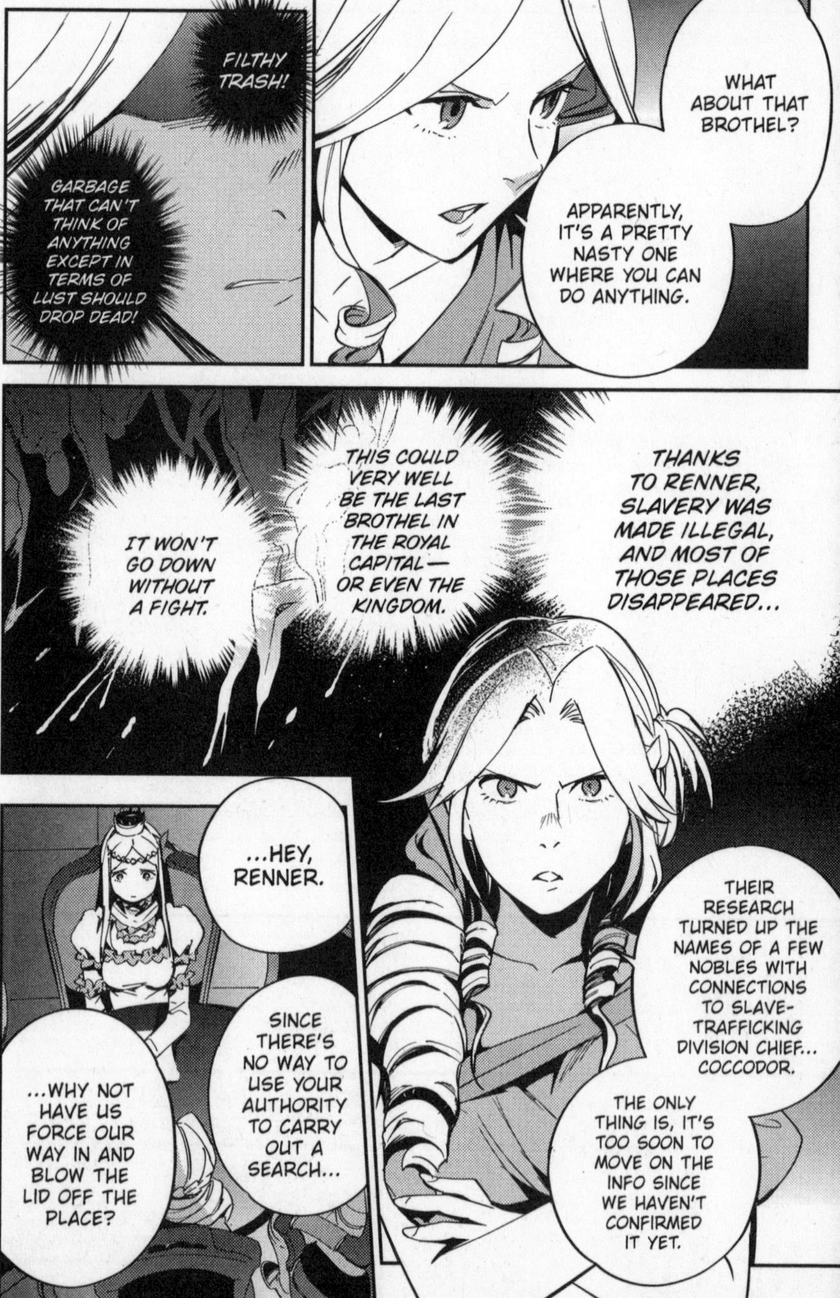
WHAT ABOUT THAT BROTHEL?
APPARENTLY, IT'S A PRETTY NASTY ONE WHERE YOU CAN DO ANYTHING.
FILTHY TRASH!
GARBAGE THAT CAN'T THINK OF ANYTHING EXCEPT IN TERMS OF LUST SHOULD DROP DEAD!
THANKS TO RENNER, SLAVERY WAS MADE ILLEGAL, AND MOST OF THOSE PLACES DISAPPEARED...
THIS COULD VERY WELL BE THE LAST BROTHEL IN THE ROYAL CAPITAL— OR EVEN THE KINGDOM.
IT WON'T GO DOWN WITHOUT A FIGHT.
THEIR RESEARCH TURNED UP THE NAMES OF A FEW NOBLES WITH CONNECTIONS TO SLAVE-TRAFFICKING DIVISION CHIEF... COCCODOR.
THE ONLY THING IS, IT'S TOO SOON TO MOVE ON THE INFO SINCE WE HAVEN'T CONFIRMED IT YET.
...HEY, RENNER.
SINCE THERE'S NO WAY TO USE YOUR AUTHORITY TO CARRY OUT A SEARCH...
...WHY NOT HAVE US FORCE OUR WAY IN AND BLOW THE LID OFF THE PLACE?

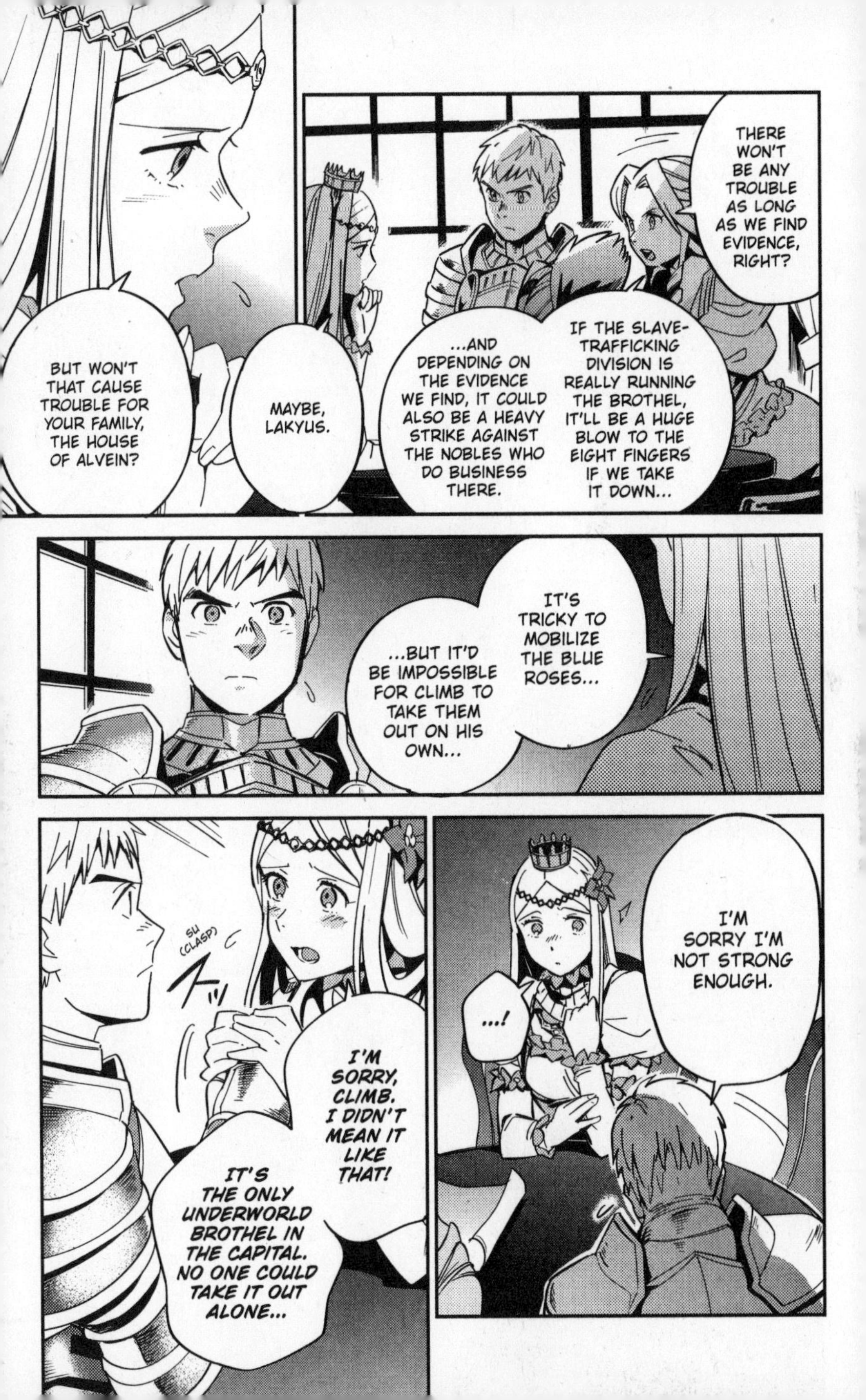
THERE WON'T BE ANY TROUBLE AS LONG AS WE FIND EVIDENCE, RIGHT?
IF THE SLAVE-TRAFFICKING DIVISION IS REALLY RUNNING THE BROTHEL, IT'LL BE A HUGE BLOW TO THE EIGHT FINGERS IF WE TAKE IT DOWN...
...AND DEPENDING ON THE EVIDENCE WE FIND, IT COULD ALSO BE A HEAVY STRIKE AGAINST THE NOBLES WHO DO BUSINESS THERE.
MAYBE, LAKYUS.
BUT WON'T THAT CAUSE TROUBLE FOR YOUR FAMILY, THE HOUSE OF ALVEIN?
IT'S TRICKY TO MOBILIZE THE BLUE ROSES...
...BUT IT'D BE IMPOSSIBLE FOR CLIMB TO TAKE THEM OUT ON HIS OWN...
I'M SORRY I'M NOT STRONG ENOUGH.
...!
SU (CLASP)
I'M SORRY, CLIMB. I DIDN'T MEAN IT LIKE THAT!
IT'S THE ONLY UNDERWORLD BROTHEL IN THE CAPITAL. NO ONE COULD TAKE IT OUT ALONE...

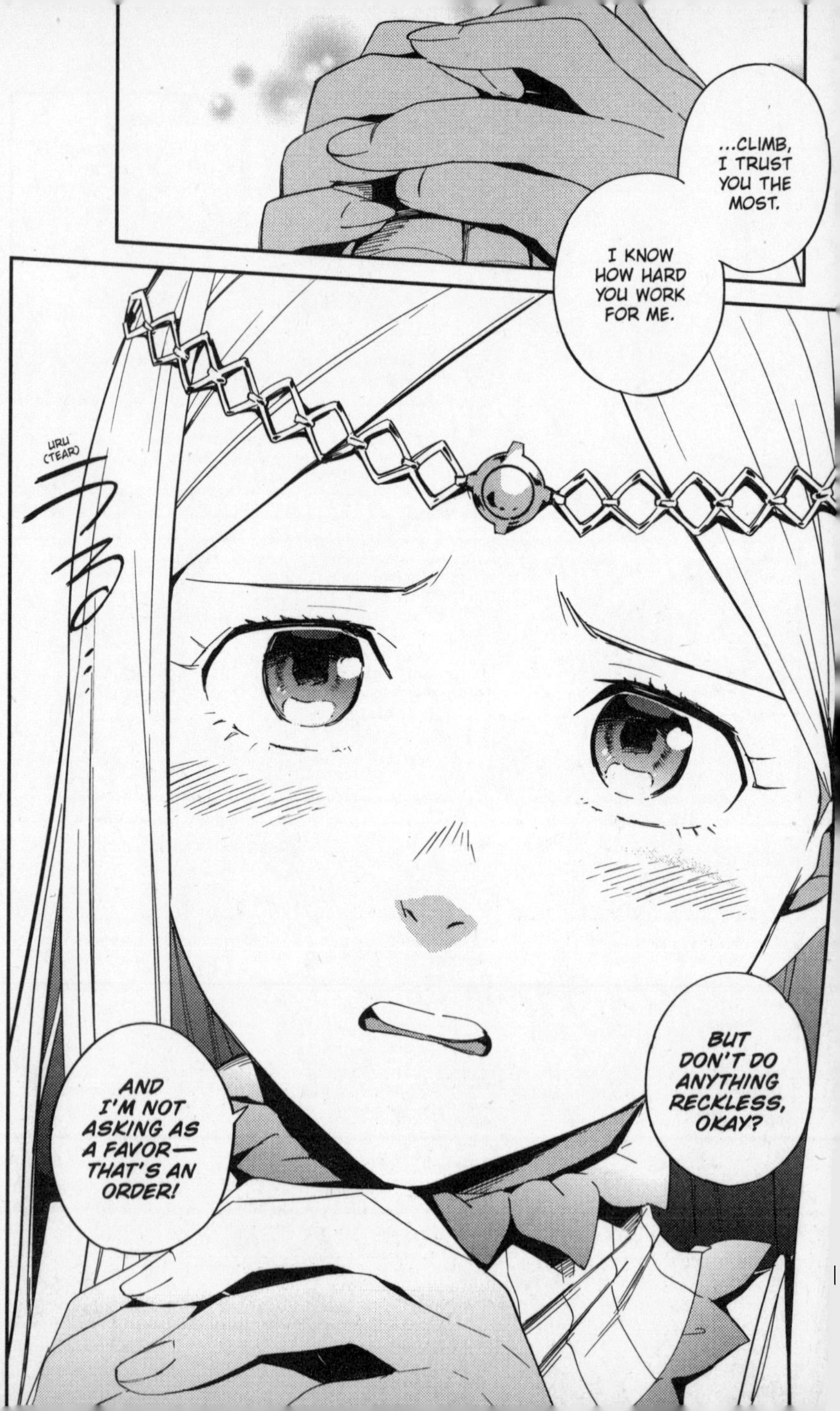
...CLIMB, I TRUST YOU THE MOST.
I KNOW HOW HARD YOU WORK FOR ME.
URU (TEAR)
BUT DON'T DO ANYTHING RECKLESS, OKAY?
AND I'M NOT ASKING AS A FAVOR—THAT'S AN ORDER!

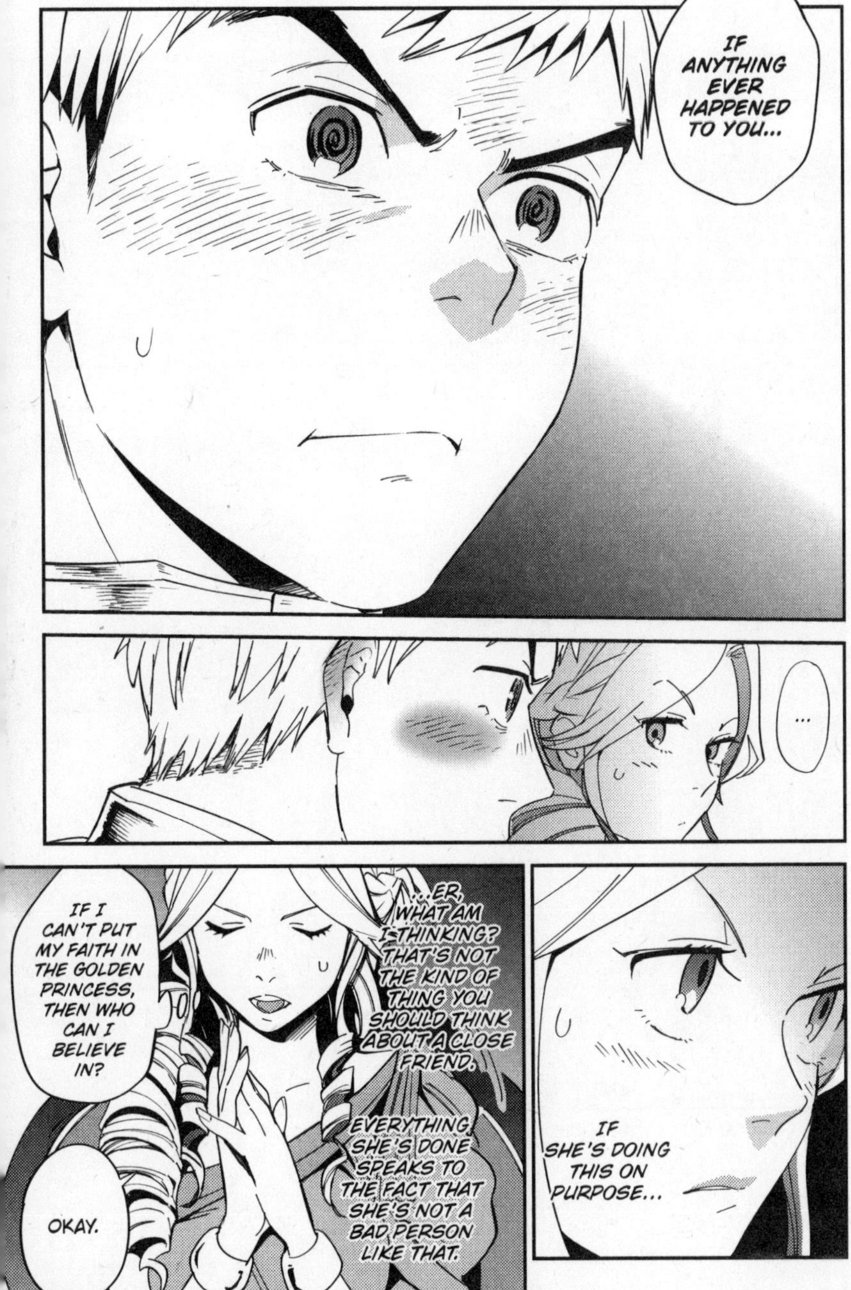
IF ANYTHING EVER HAPPENED TO YOU...
...
IF SHE'S DOING THIS ON PURPOSE...
...ER, WHAT AM I THINKING? THAT'S NOT THE KIND OF THING YOU SHOULD THINK ABOUT A CLOSE FRIEND.
EVERYTHING SHE'S DONE SPEAKS TO THE FACT THAT SHE'S NOT A BAD PERSON LIKE THAT.
IF I CAN'T PUT MY FAITH IN THE GOLDEN PRINCESS, THEN WHO CAN I BELIEVE IN?
OKAY.

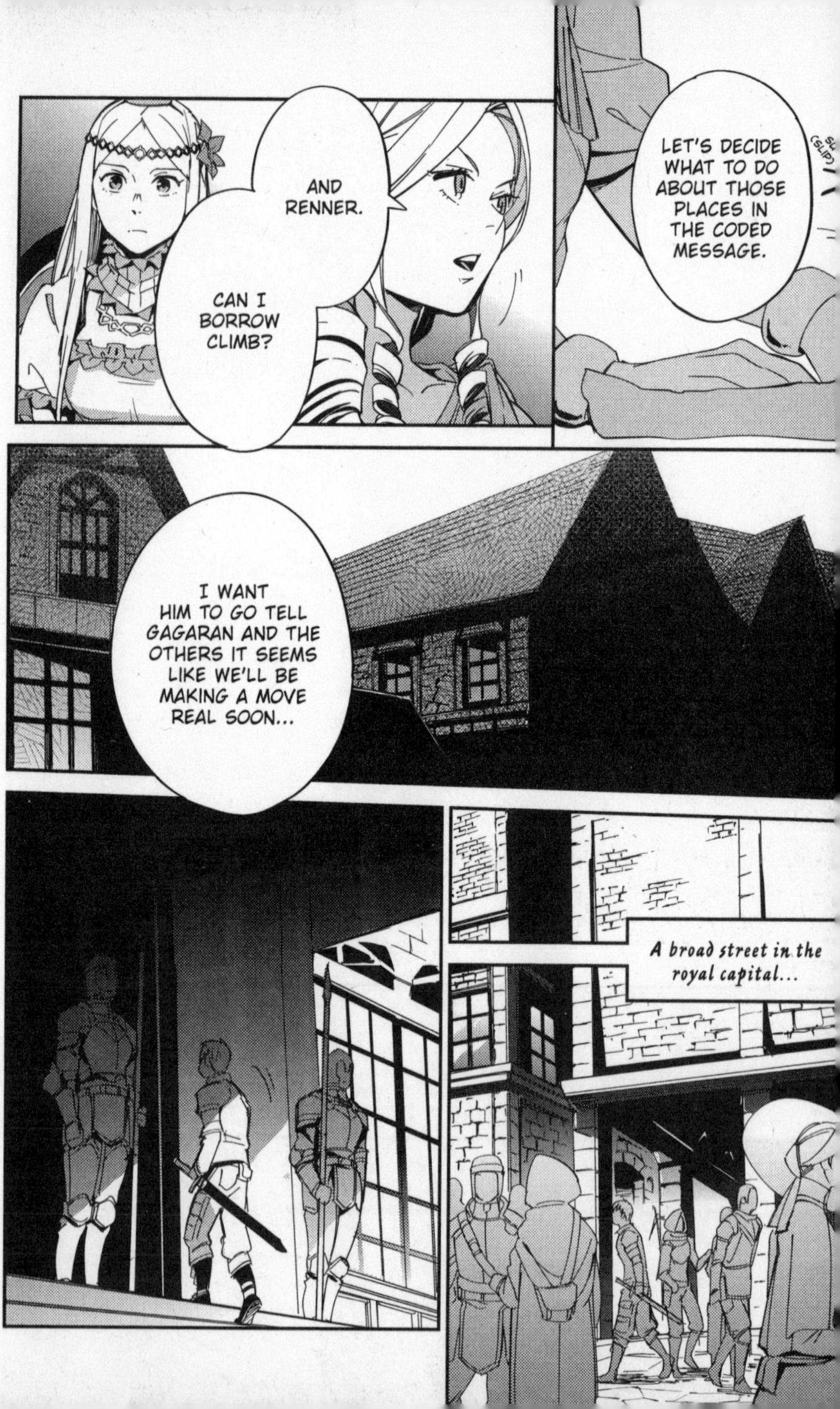
LET'S DECIDE WHAT TO DO ABOUT THOSE PLACES IN THE CODED MESSAGE.
(SLIP)
AND RENNER.
CAN I BORROW CLIMB?
I WANT HIM TO GO TELL GAGARAN AND THE OTHERS IT SEEMS LIKE WE'LL BE MAKING A MOVE REAL SOON...
A broad street in the royal capital...

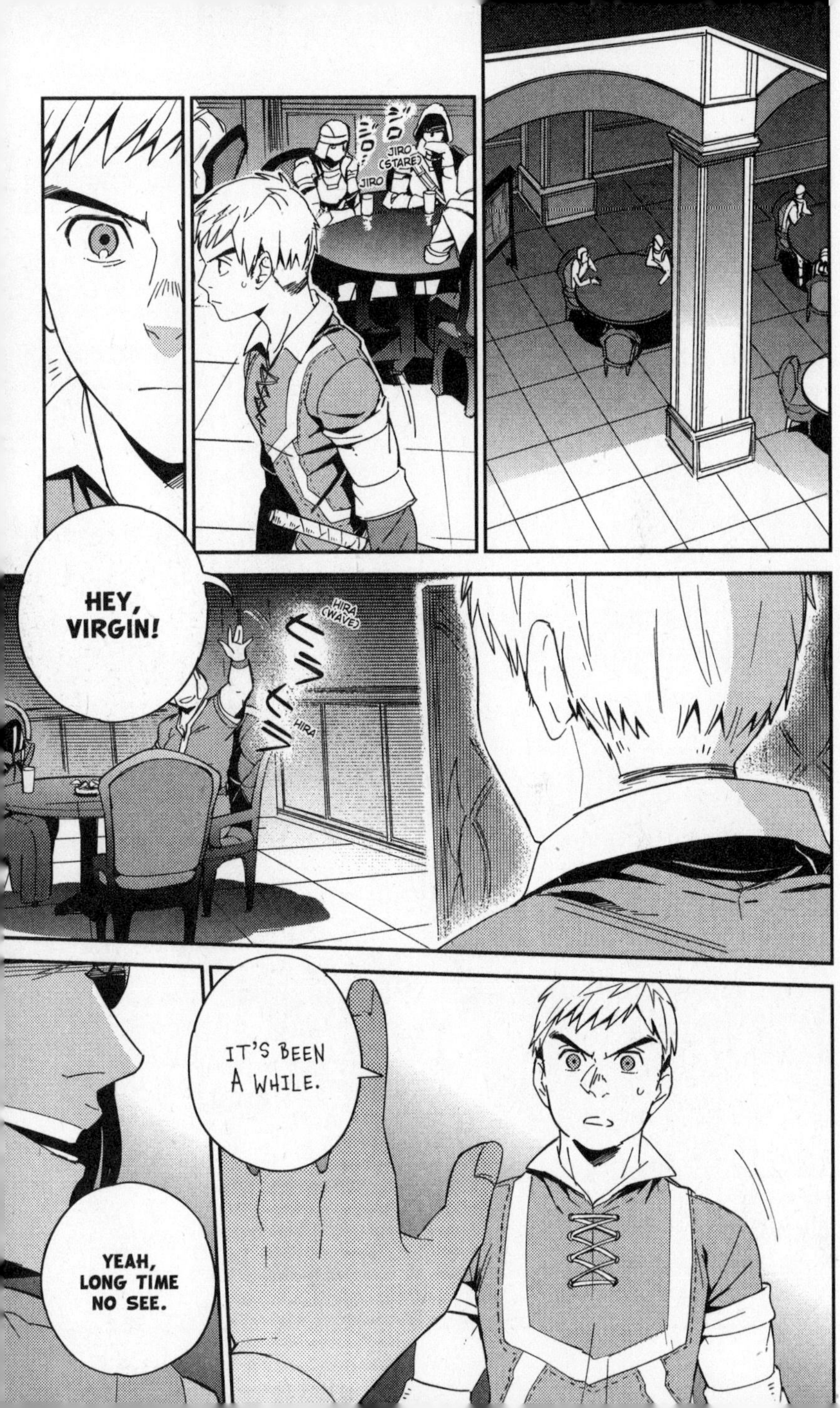
JIRO (STARE)
JIRO
HEY, VIRGIN!
HIRA (WAVE)
HIRA
IT'S BEEN A WHILE.
YEAH, LONG TIME NO SEE.

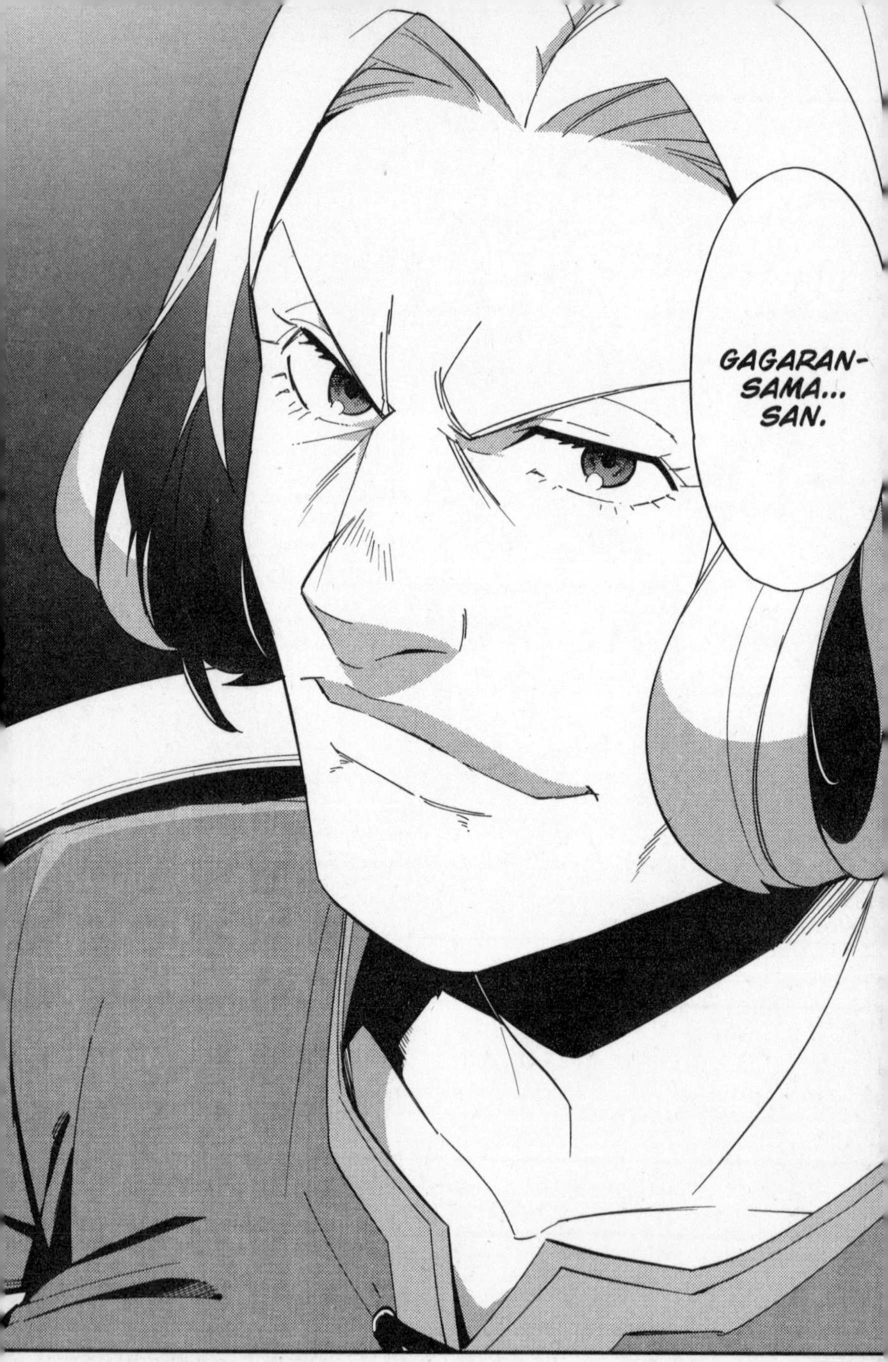
GAGARAN-SAMA... SAN.

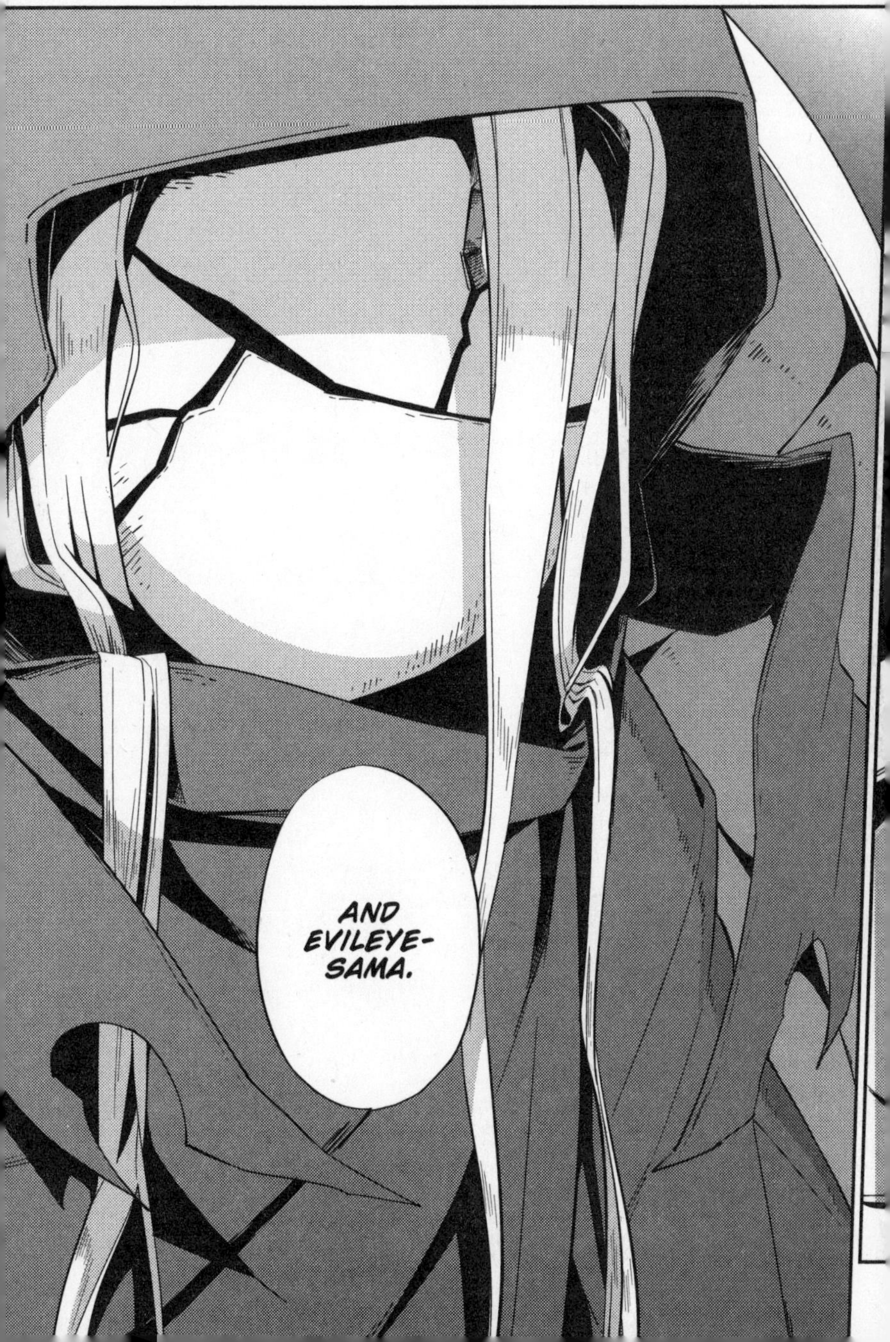
AND EVILEYE-SAMA.

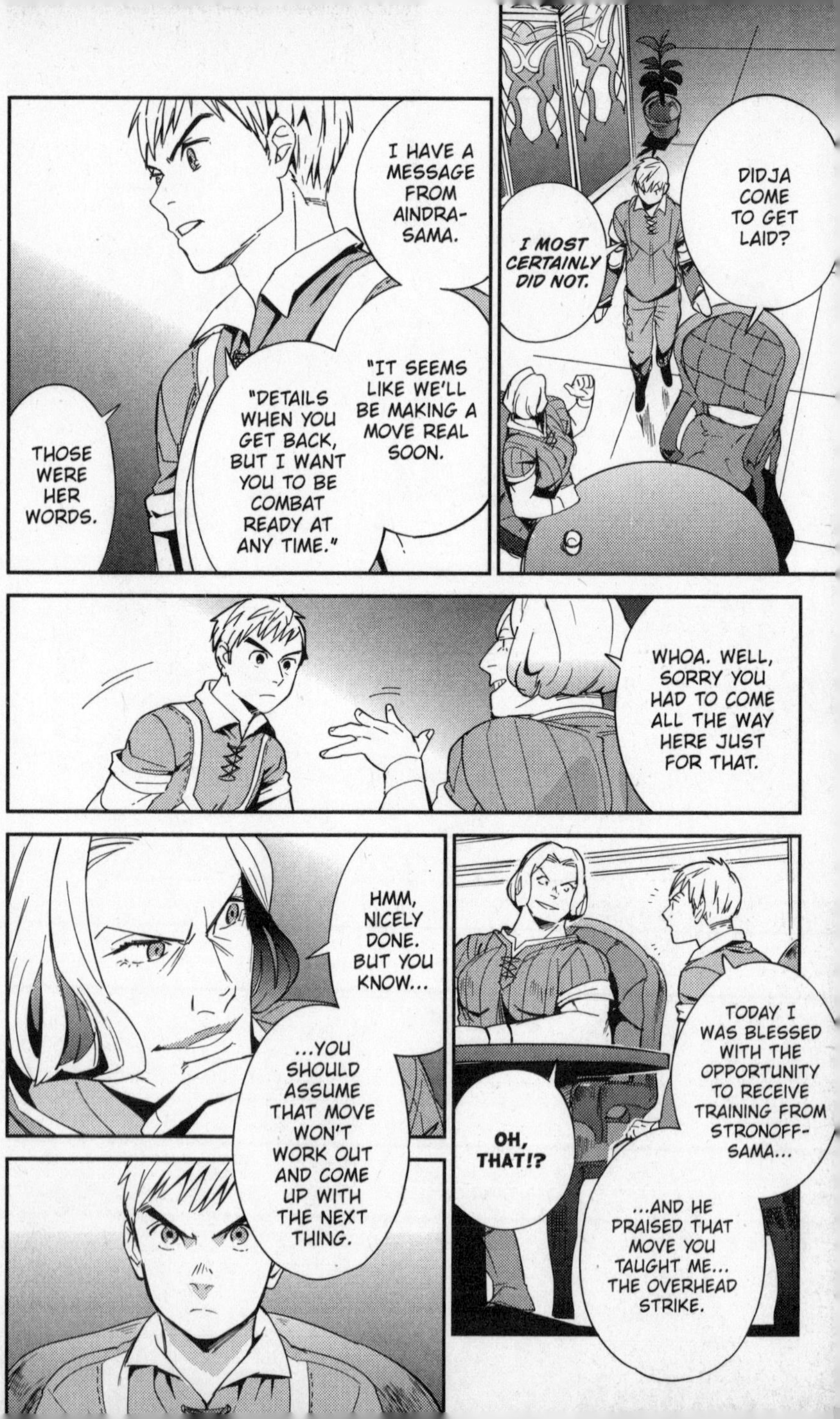
DIDJA COME TO GET LAID?
I MOST CERTAINLY DID NOT.
I HAVE A MESSAGE FROM AINDRA-SAMA.
"IT SEEMS LIKE WE'LL BE MAKING A MOVE REAL SOON.
"DETAILS WHEN YOU GET BACK, BUT I WANT YOU TO BE COMBAT READY AT ANY TIME."
THOSE WERE HER WORDS.
WHOA. WELL, SORRY YOU HAD TO COME ALL THE WAY HERE JUST FOR THAT.
TODAY I WAS BLESSED WITH THE OPPORTUNITY TO RECEIVE TRAINING FROM STRONOFF-SAMA...
...AND HE PRAISED THAT MOVE YOU TAUGHT ME... THE OVERHEAD STRIKE.
OH, THAT!?
HMM, NICELY DONE. BUT YOU KNOW...
...YOU SHOULD ASSUME THAT MOVE WON'T WORK OUT AND COME UP WITH THE NEXT THING.

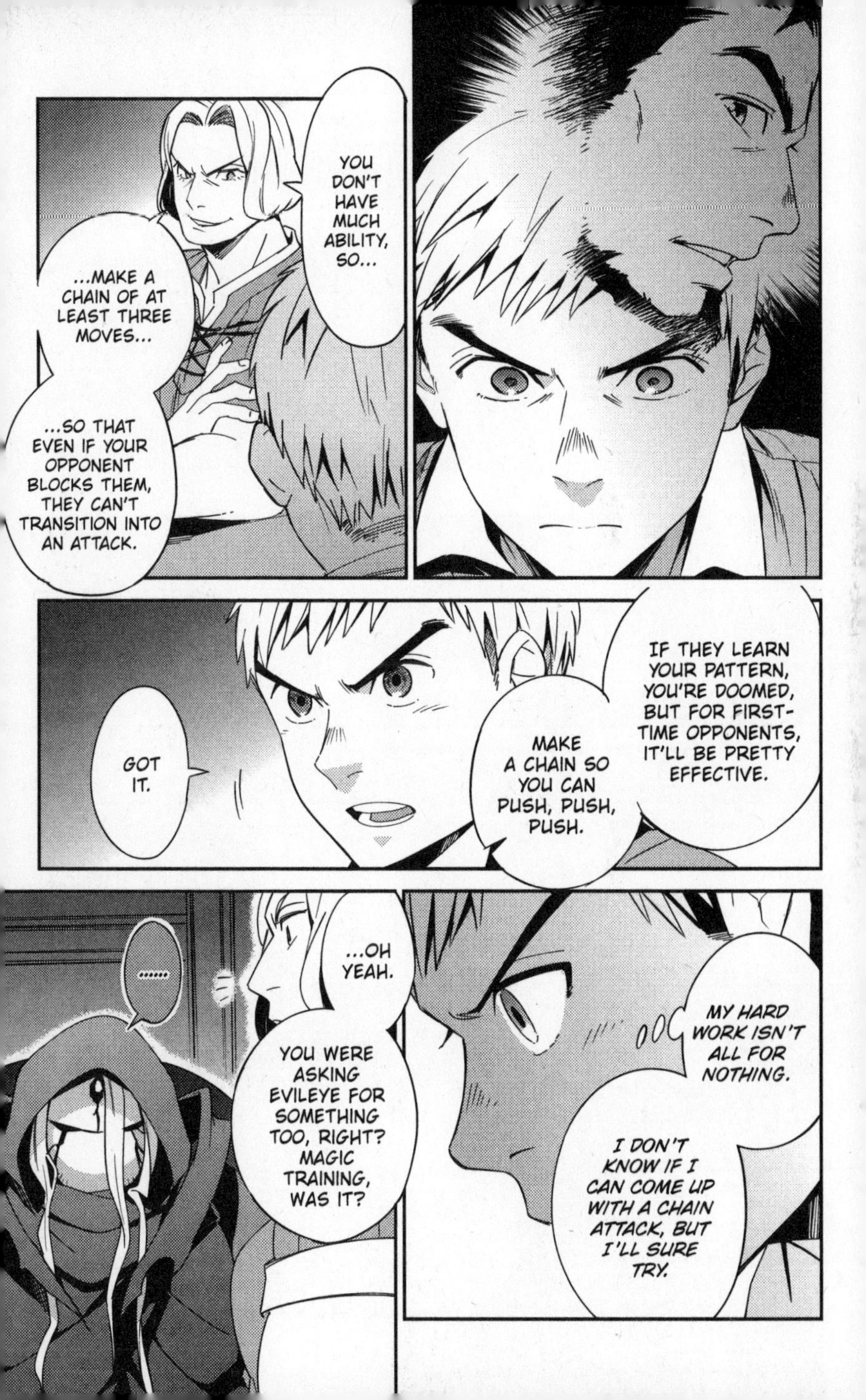
YOU DON'T HAVE MUCH ABILITY, SO...
...MAKE A CHAIN OF AT LEAST THREE MOVES...
...SO THAT EVEN IF YOUR OPPONENT BLOCKS THEM, THEY CAN'T TRANSITION INTO AN ATTACK.
IF THEY LEARN YOUR PATTERN, YOU'RE DOOMED, BUT FOR FIRST-TIME OPPONENTS, IT'LL BE PRETTY EFFECTIVE.
MAKE A CHAIN SO YOU CAN PUSH, PUSH, PUSH.
GOT IT.
MY HARD WORK ISN'T ALL FOR NOTHING.
I DON'T KNOW IF I CAN COME UP WITH A CHAIN ATTACK, BUT I'LL SURE TRY.
...OH YEAH.
YOU WERE ASKING EVILEYE FOR SOMETHING TOO, RIGHT? MAGIC TRAINING, WAS IT?
......

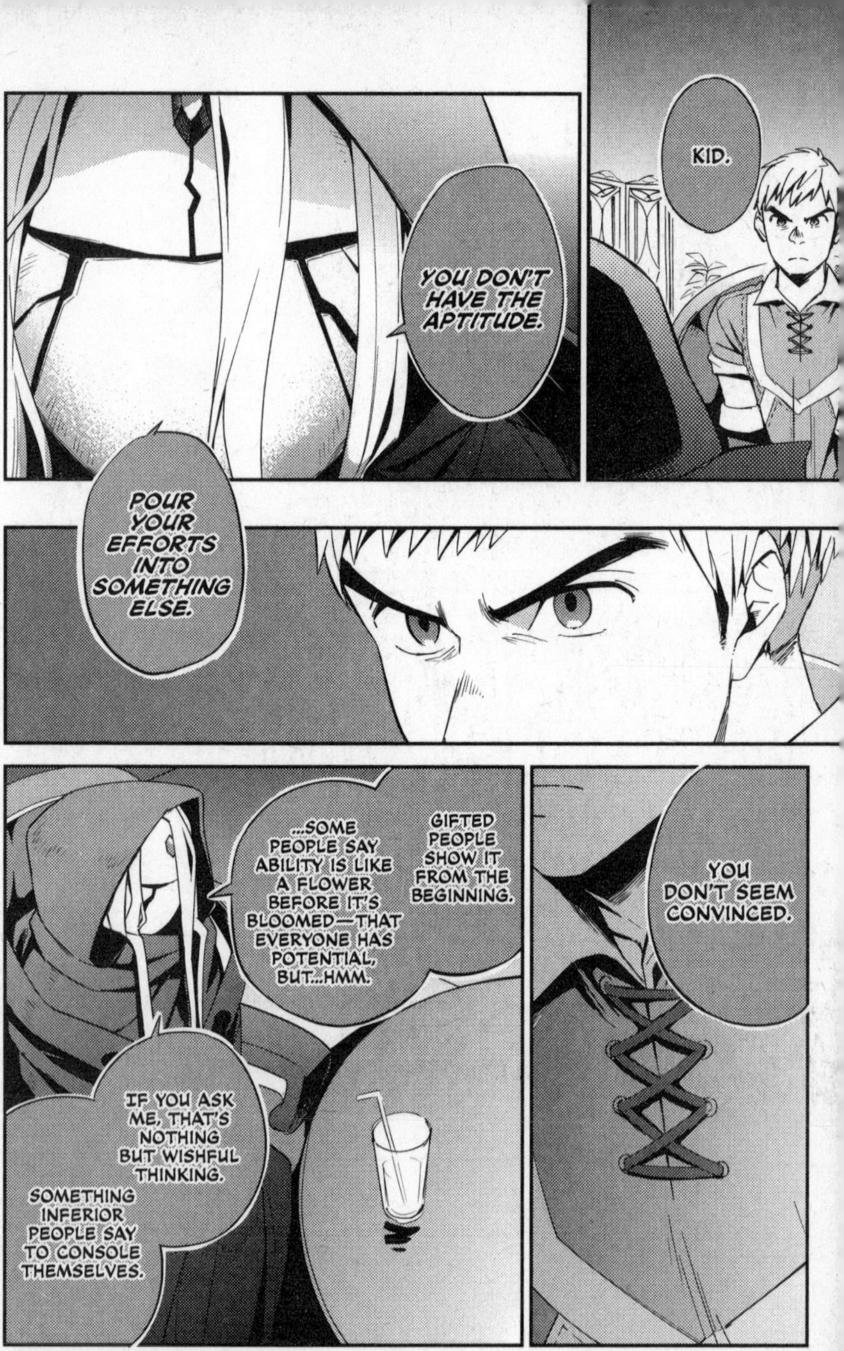
KID.
YOU DON'T HAVE THE APTITUDE.
POUR YOUR EFFORTS INTO SOMETHING ELSE.
YOU DON'T SEEM CONVINCED.
GIFTED PEOPLE SHOW IT FROM THE BEGINNING.
...SOME PEOPLE SAY ABILITY IS LIKE A FLOWER BEFORE IT'S BLOOMED—THAT EVERYONE HAS POTENTIAL, BUT...HMM.
IF YOU ASK ME, THAT'S NOTHING BUT WISHFUL THINKING.
SOMETHING INFERIOR PEOPLE SAY TO CONSOLE THEMSELVES.

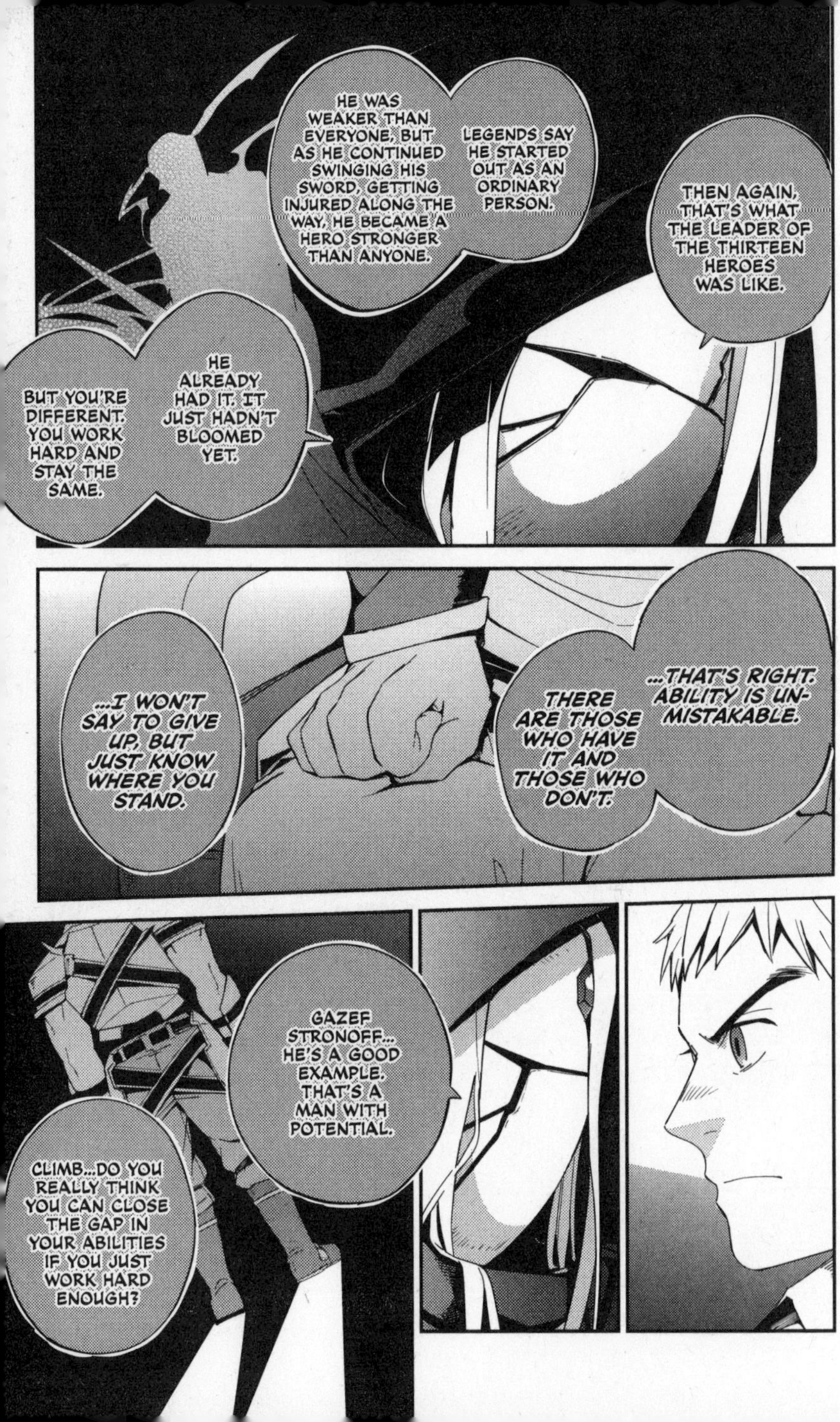
THEN AGAIN, THAT'S WHAT THE LEADER OF THE THIRTEEN HEROES WAS LIKE.
LEGENDS SAY HE STARTED OUT AS AN ORDINARY PERSON.
HE WAS WEAKER THAN EVERYONE, BUT AS HE CONTINUED SWINGING HIS SWORD, GETTING INJURED ALONG THE WAY, HE BECAME A HERO STRONGER THAN ANYONE.
HE ALREADY HAD IT. IT JUST HADN'T BLOOMED YET.
BUT YOU'RE DIFFERENT. YOU WORK HARD AND STAY THE SAME.
...THAT'S RIGHT. ABILITY IS UN-MISTAKABLE.
THERE ARE THOSE WHO HAVE IT AND THOSE WHO DON'T.
...I WON'T SAY TO GIVE UP, BUT JUST KNOW WHERE YOU STAND.
GAZEF STRONOFF... HE'S A GOOD EXAMPLE. THAT'S A MAN WITH POTENTIAL.
CLIMB...DO YOU REALLY THINK YOU CAN CLOSE THE GAP IN YOUR ABILITIES IF YOU JUST WORK HARD ENOUGH?

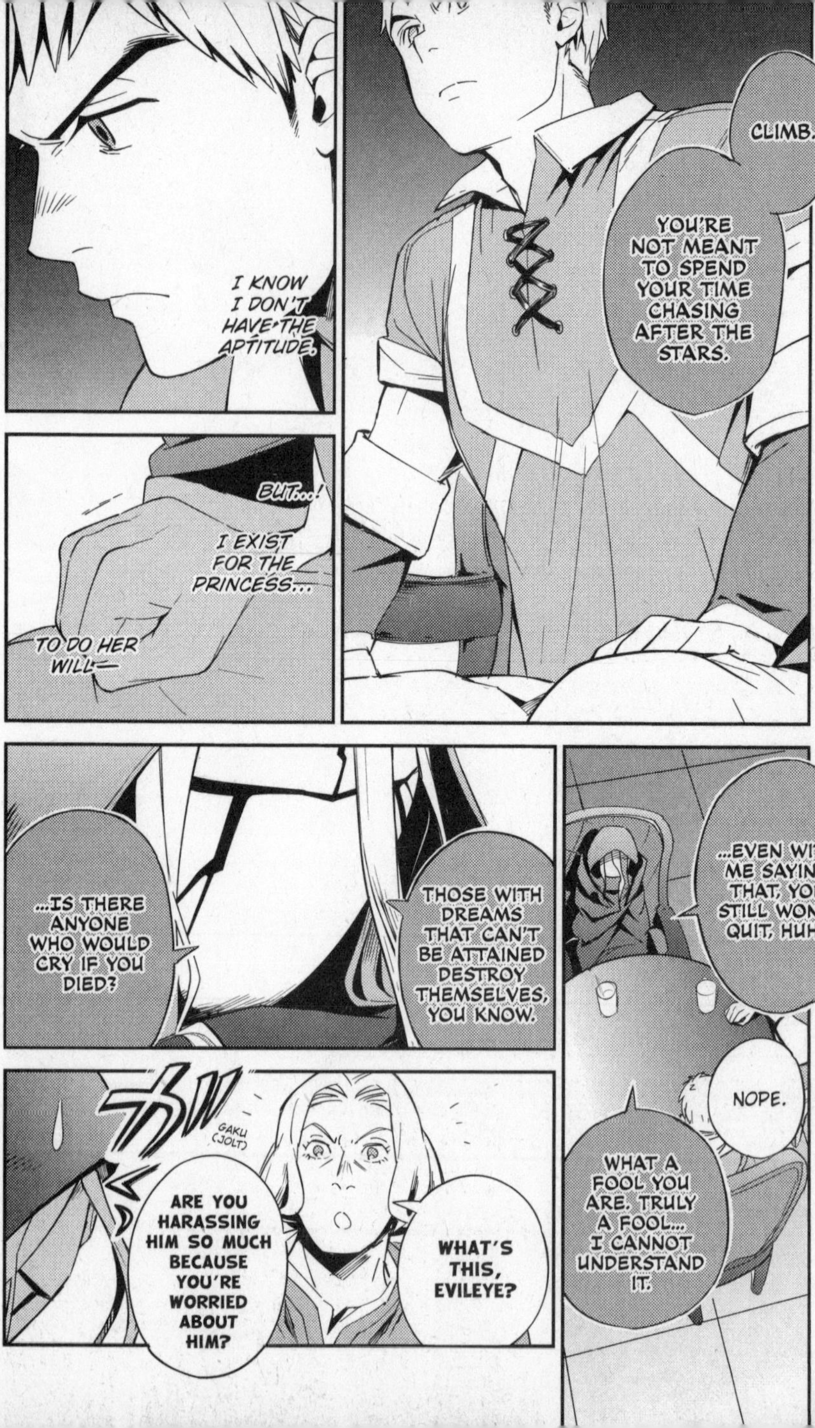
CLIMB.
YOU'RE NOT MEANT TO SPEND YOUR TIME CHASING AFTER THE STARS.
I KNOW I DON'T HAVE THE APTITUDE.
BUT...!
I EXIST FOR THE PRINCESS...
TO DO HER WILL—
...EVEN WITH ME SAYING THAT, YOU STILL WON'T QUIT, HUH?
NOPE.
WHAT A FOOL YOU ARE. TRULY A FOOL... I CANNOT UNDERSTAND IT.
THOSE WITH DREAMS THAT CAN'T BE ATTAINED DESTROY THEMSELVES, YOU KNOW.
...IS THERE ANYONE WHO WOULD CRY IF YOU DIED?
WHAT'S THIS, EVILEYE?
ARE YOU HARASSING HIM SO MUCH BECAUSE YOU'RE WORRIED ABOUT HIM?
GAKU (JOLT)

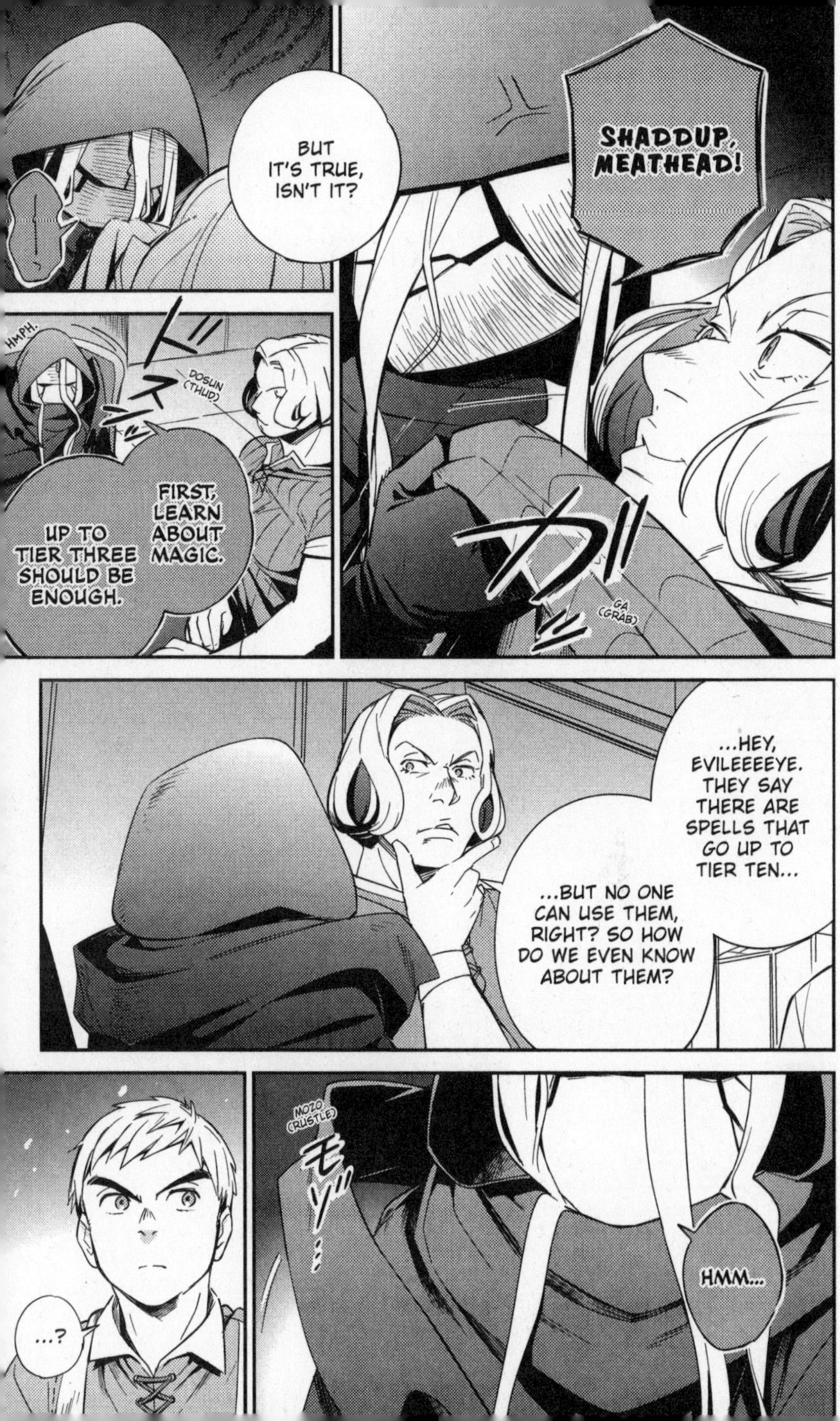
SHADDUP, MEATHEAD!
GA (GRAB)
BUT IT'S TRUE, ISN'T IT?
HMPH.
DOSUN (THUD)
FIRST, LEARN ABOUT MAGIC.
UP TO TIER THREE SHOULD BE ENOUGH.
...HEY, EVILEEEEYE. THEY SAY THERE ARE SPELLS THAT GO UP TO TIER TEN...
...BUT NO ONE CAN USE THEM, RIGHT? SO HOW DO WE EVEN KNOW ABOUT THEM?
MOZO (RUSTLE)
HMM...
...?

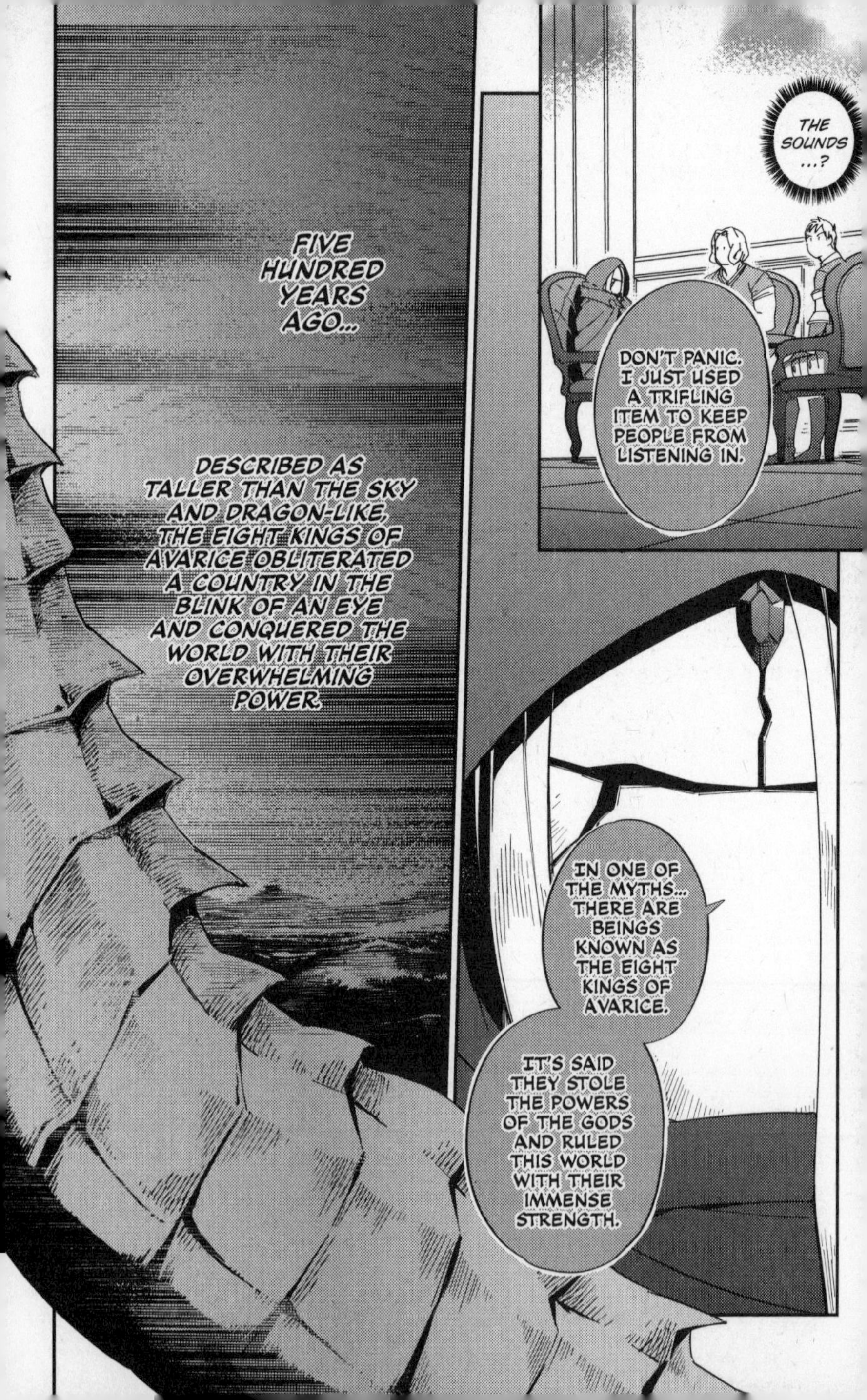
THE SOUNDS ...?
DON'T PANIC. I JUST USED A TRIFLING ITEM TO KEEP PEOPLE FROM LISTENING IN.
IN ONE OF THE MYTHS... THERE ARE BEINGS KNOWN AS THE EIGHT KINGS OF AVARICE.
IT'S SAID THEY STOLE THE POWERS OF THE GODS AND RULED THIS WORLD WITH THEIR IMMENSE STRENGTH.
FIVE HUNDRED YEARS AGO...
DESCRIBED AS TALLER THAN THE SKY AND DRAGON-LIKE, THE EIGHT KINGS OF AVARICE OBLITERATED A COUNTRY IN THE BLINK OF AN EYE AND CONQUERED THE WORLD WITH THEIR OVERWHELMING POWER.

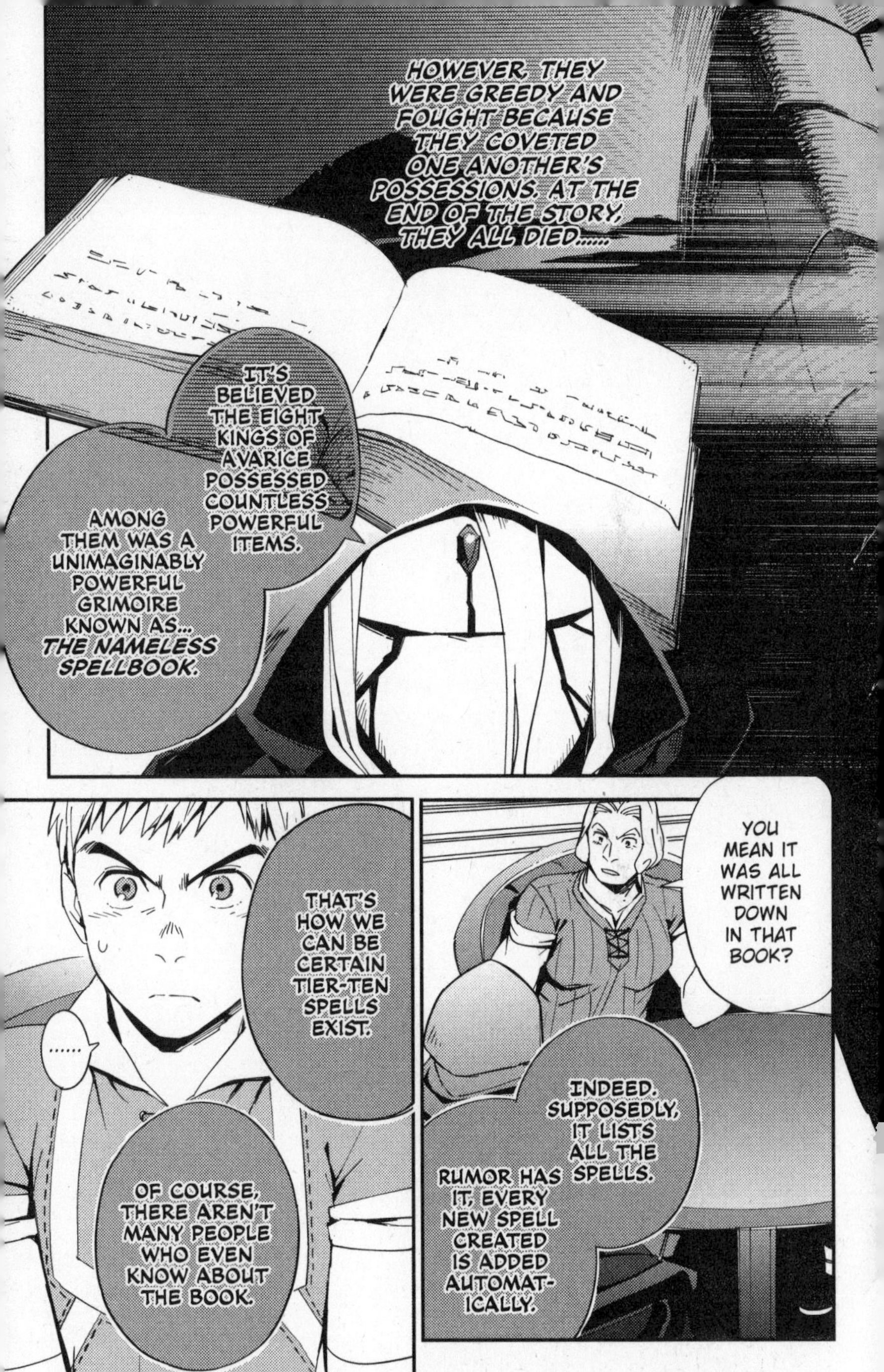
HOWEVER, THEY WERE GREEDY AND FOUGHT BECAUSE THEY COVETED ONE ANOTHER'S POSSESSIONS. AT THE END OF THE STORY, THEY ALL DIED......
IT'S BELIEVED THE EIGHT KINGS OF AVARICE POSSESSED COUNTLESS POWERFUL ITEMS.
AMONG THEM WAS A UNIMAGINABLY POWERFUL GRIMOIRE KNOWN AS... *THE NAMELESS SPELLBOOK.*
YOU MEAN IT WAS ALL WRITTEN DOWN IN THAT BOOK?
INDEED. SUPPOSEDLY, IT LISTS ALL THE SPELLS.
RUMOR HAS IT, EVERY NEW SPELL CREATED IS ADDED AUTOMAT-ICALLY.
THAT'S HOW WE CAN BE CERTAIN TIER-TEN SPELLS EXIST.
......
OF COURSE, THERE AREN'T MANY PEOPLE WHO EVEN KNOW ABOUT THE BOOK.

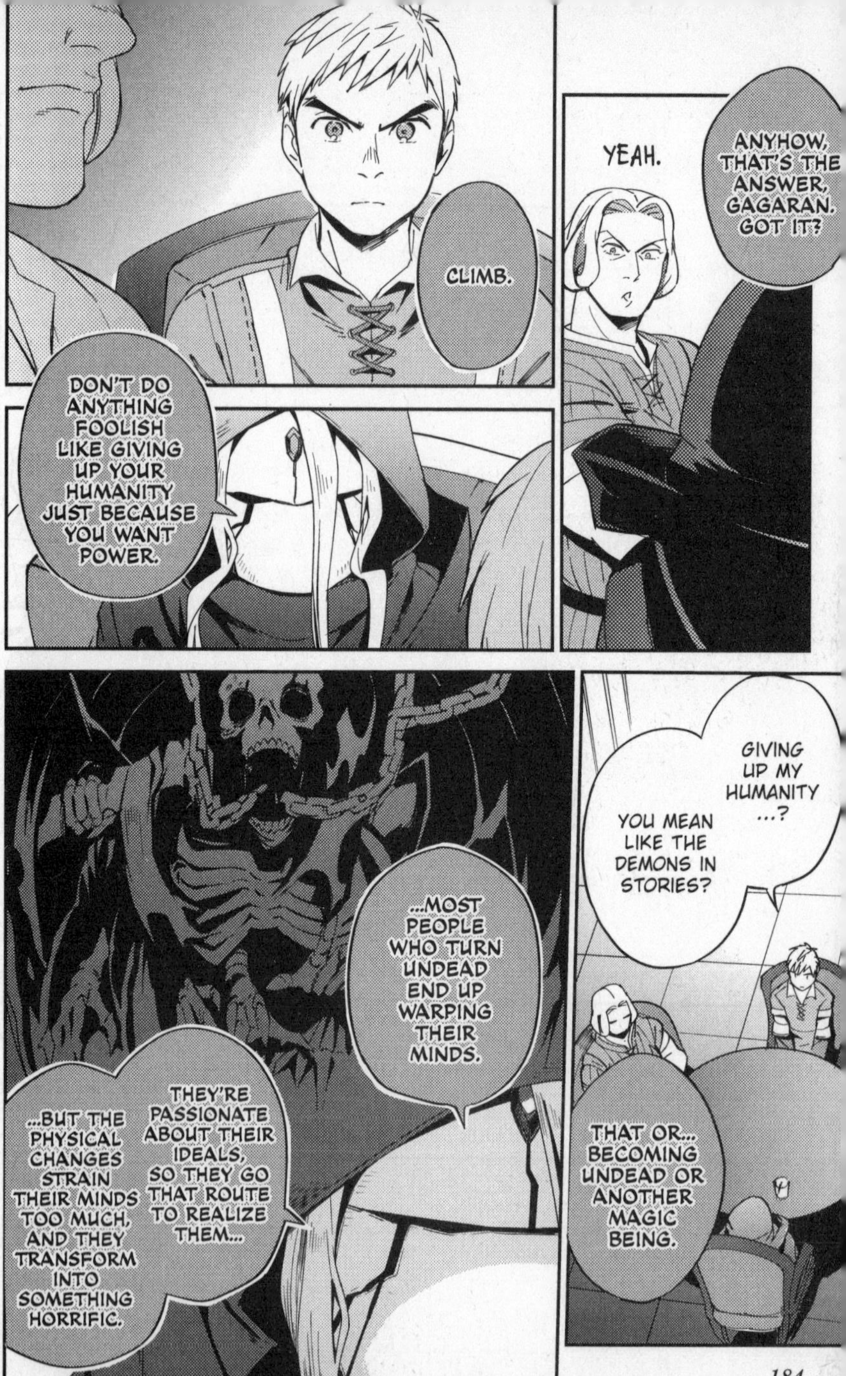
ANYHOW, THAT'S THE ANSWER, GAGARAN. GOT IT?
YEAH.
CLIMB.
DON'T DO ANYTHING FOOLISH LIKE GIVING UP YOUR HUMANITY JUST BECAUSE YOU WANT POWER.
GIVING UP MY HUMANITY ...?
YOU MEAN LIKE THE DEMONS IN STORIES?
THAT OR... BECOMING UNDEAD OR ANOTHER MAGIC BEING.
...MOST PEOPLE WHO TURN UNDEAD END UP WARPING THEIR MINDS.
THEY'RE PASSIONATE ABOUT THEIR IDEALS, SO THEY GO THAT ROUTE TO REALIZE THEM...
...BUT THE PHYSICAL CHANGES STRAIN THEIR MINDS TOO MUCH, AND THEY TRANSFORM INTO SOMETHING HORRIFIC.

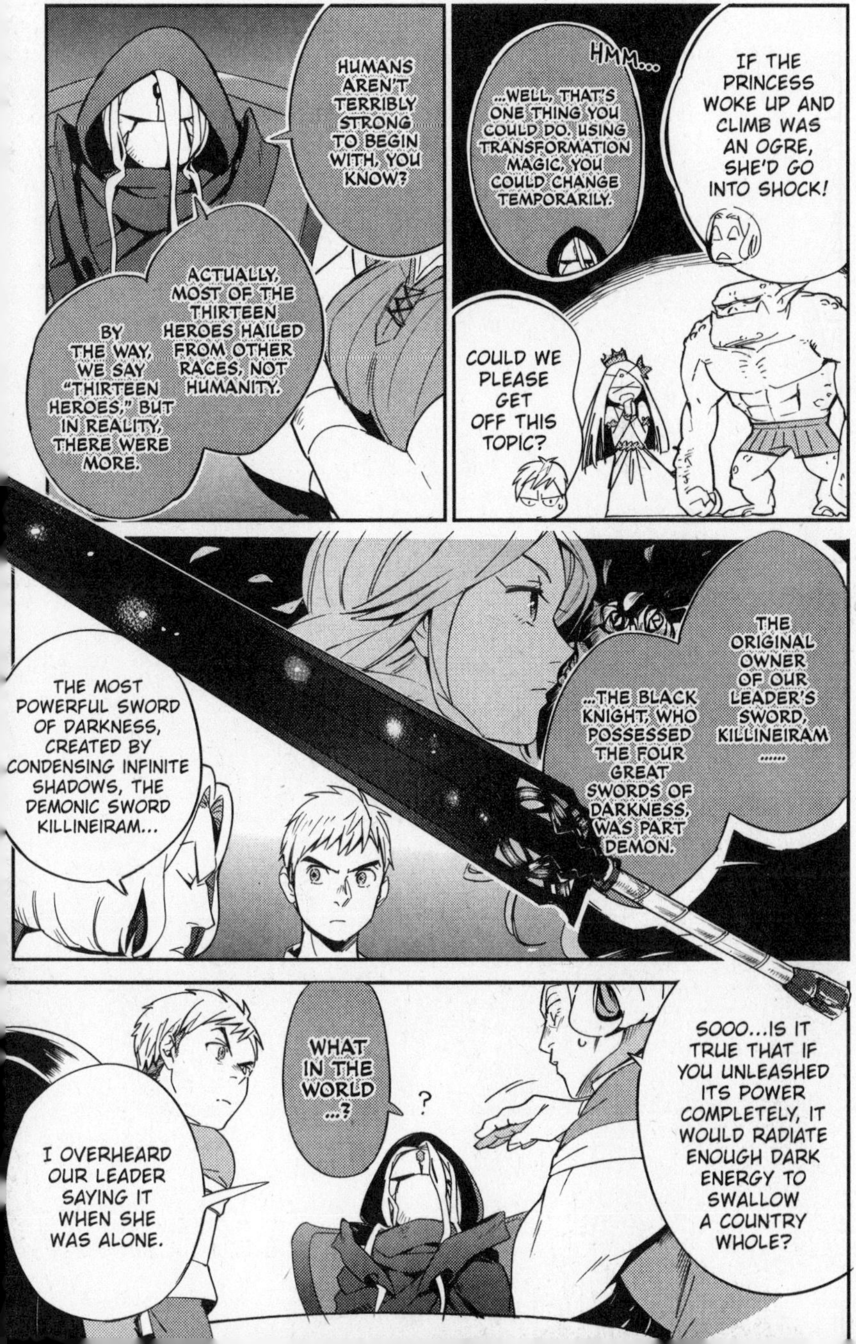
HMM...
...WELL, THAT'S ONE THING YOU COULD DO. USING TRANSFORMATION MAGIC, YOU COULD CHANGE TEMPORARILY.
IF THE PRINCESS WOKE UP AND CLIMB WAS AN OGRE, SHE'D GO INTO SHOCK!
COULD WE PLEASE GET OFF THIS TOPIC?
HUMANS AREN'T TERRIBLY STRONG TO BEGIN WITH, YOU KNOW?
ACTUALLY, MOST OF THE THIRTEEN HEROES HAILED FROM OTHER RACES, NOT HUMANITY.
BY THE WAY, WE SAY "THIRTEEN HEROES," BUT IN REALITY, THERE WERE MORE.
THE ORIGINAL OWNER OF OUR LEADER'S SWORD, KILLINEIRAM......
...THE BLACK KNIGHT, WHO POSSESSED THE FOUR GREAT SWORDS OF DARKNESS, WAS PART DEMON.
THE MOST POWERFUL SWORD OF DARKNESS, CREATED BY CONDENSING INFINITE SHADOWS, THE DEMONIC SWORD KILLINEIRAM...
SOOO...IS IT TRUE THAT IF YOU UNLEASHED ITS POWER COMPLETELY, IT WOULD RADIATE ENOUGH DARK ENERGY TO SWALLOW A COUNTRY WHOLE?
?
WHAT IN THE WORLD...?
I OVERHEARD OUR LEADER SAYING IT WHEN SHE WAS ALONE.

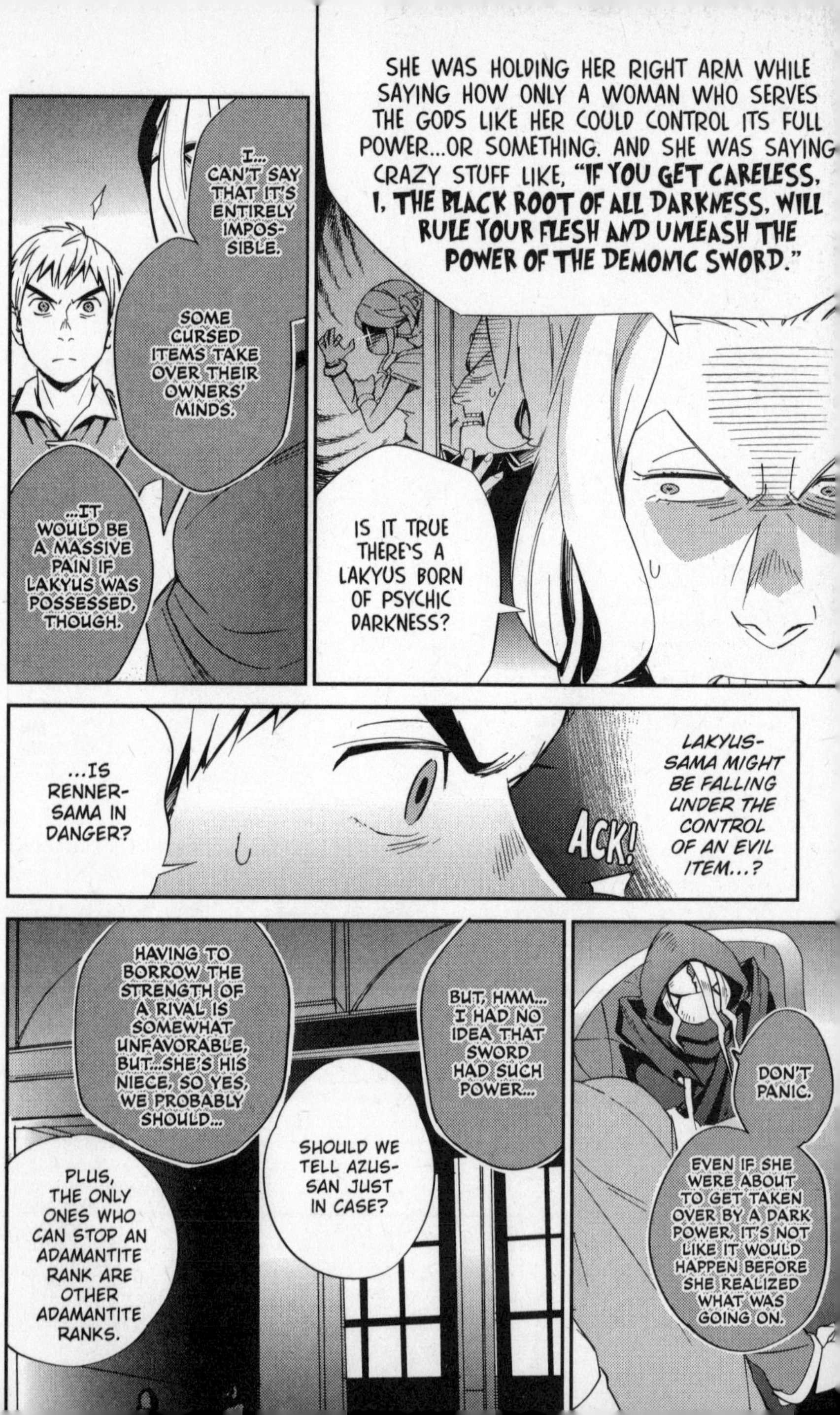
SHE WAS HOLDING HER RIGHT ARM WHILE SAYING HOW ONLY A WOMAN WHO SERVES THE GODS LIKE HER COULD CONTROL ITS FULL POWER...OR SOMETHING. AND SHE WAS SAYING CRAZY STUFF LIKE, "IF YOU GET CARELESS, I, THE BLACK ROOT OF ALL DARKNESS, WILL RULE YOUR FLESH AND UNLEASH THE POWER OF THE DEMONIC SWORD."
IS IT TRUE THERE'S A LAKYUS BORN OF PSYCHIC DARKNESS?
I... CAN'T SAY THAT IT'S ENTIRELY IMPOSSIBLE.
SOME CURSED ITEMS TAKE OVER THEIR OWNERS' MINDS.
...IT WOULD BE A MASSIVE PAIN IF LAKYUS WAS POSSESSED, THOUGH.
LAKYUS-SAMA MIGHT BE FALLING UNDER THE CONTROL OF AN EVIL ITEM...?
ACK!
...IS RENNER-SAMA IN DANGER?
DON'T PANIC.
EVEN IF SHE WERE ABOUT TO GET TAKEN OVER BY A DARK POWER, IT'S NOT LIKE IT WOULD HAPPEN BEFORE SHE REALIZED WHAT WAS GOING ON.
BUT, HMM... I HAD NO IDEA THAT SWORD HAD SUCH POWER...
SHOULD WE TELL AZUS-SAN JUST IN CASE?
HAVING TO BORROW THE STRENGTH OF A RIVAL IS SOMEWHAT UNFAVORABLE, BUT...SHE'S HIS NIECE, SO YES, WE PROBABLY SHOULD...
PLUS, THE ONLY ONES WHO CAN STOP AN ADAMANTITE RANK ARE OTHER ADAMANTITE RANKS.

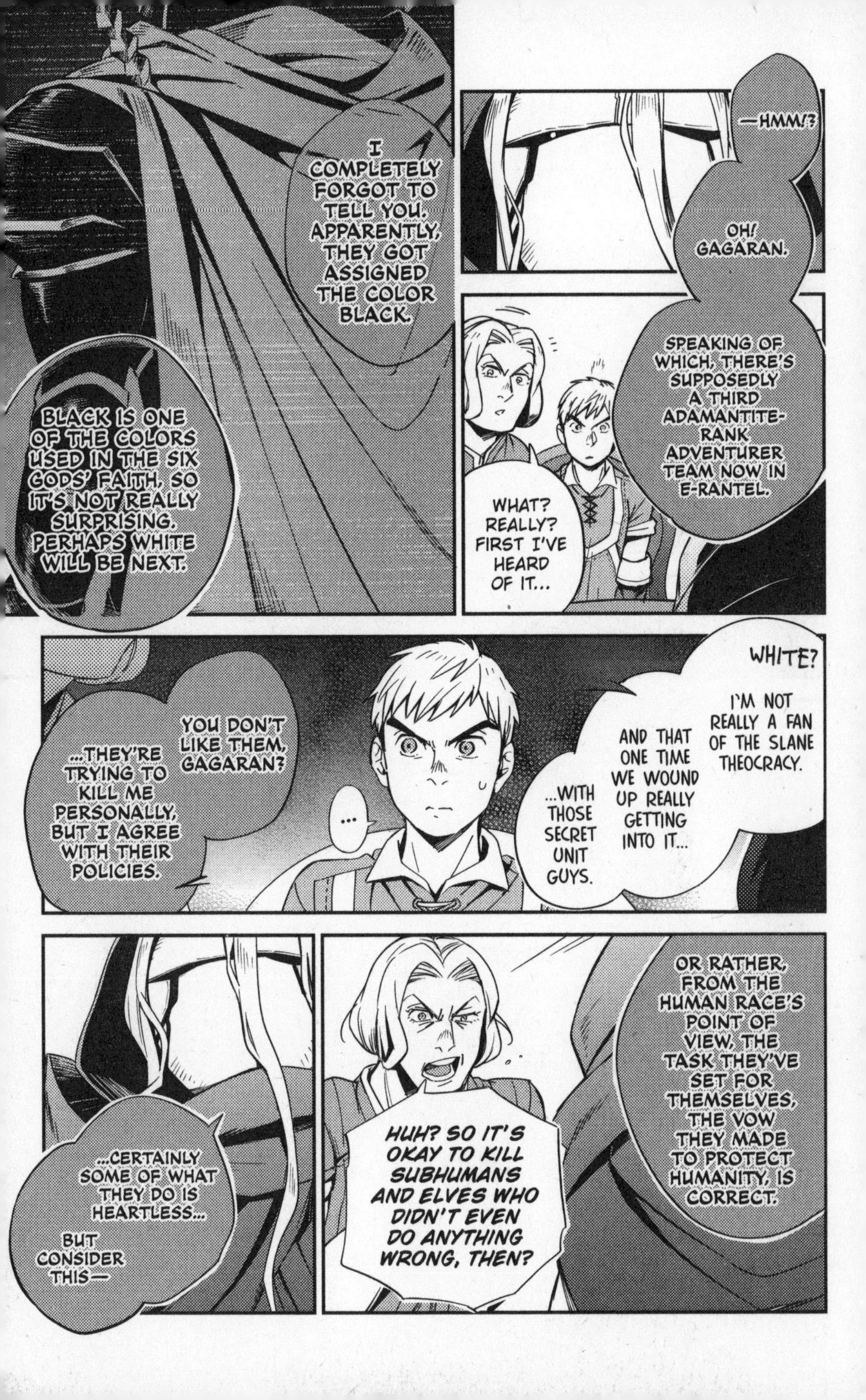
—HMM!?
OH! GAGARAN.
SPEAKING OF WHICH, THERE'S SUPPOSEDLY A THIRD ADAMANTITE-RANK ADVENTURER TEAM NOW IN E-RANTEL.
WHAT? REALLY? FIRST I'VE HEARD OF IT...
I COMPLETELY FORGOT TO TELL YOU. APPARENTLY, THEY GOT ASSIGNED THE COLOR BLACK.
BLACK IS ONE OF THE COLORS USED IN THE SIX GODS' FAITH, SO IT'S NOT REALLY SURPRISING. PERHAPS WHITE WILL BE NEXT.
WHITE?
I'M NOT REALLY A FAN OF THE SLANE THEOCRACY.
AND THAT ONE TIME WE WOUND UP REALLY GETTING INTO IT...
...WITH THOSE SECRET UNIT GUYS.
...
YOU DON'T LIKE THEM, GAGARAN?
...THEY'RE TRYING TO KILL ME PERSONALLY, BUT I AGREE WITH THEIR POLICIES.
OR RATHER, FROM THE HUMAN RACE'S POINT OF VIEW, THE TASK THEY'VE SET FOR THEMSELVES, THE VOW THEY MADE TO PROTECT HUMANITY, IS CORRECT.
HUH? SO IT'S OKAY TO KILL SUBHUMANS AND ELVES WHO DIDN'T EVEN DO ANYTHING WRONG, THEN?
...CERTAINLY SOME OF WHAT THEY DO IS HEARTLESS...
BUT CONSIDER THIS—

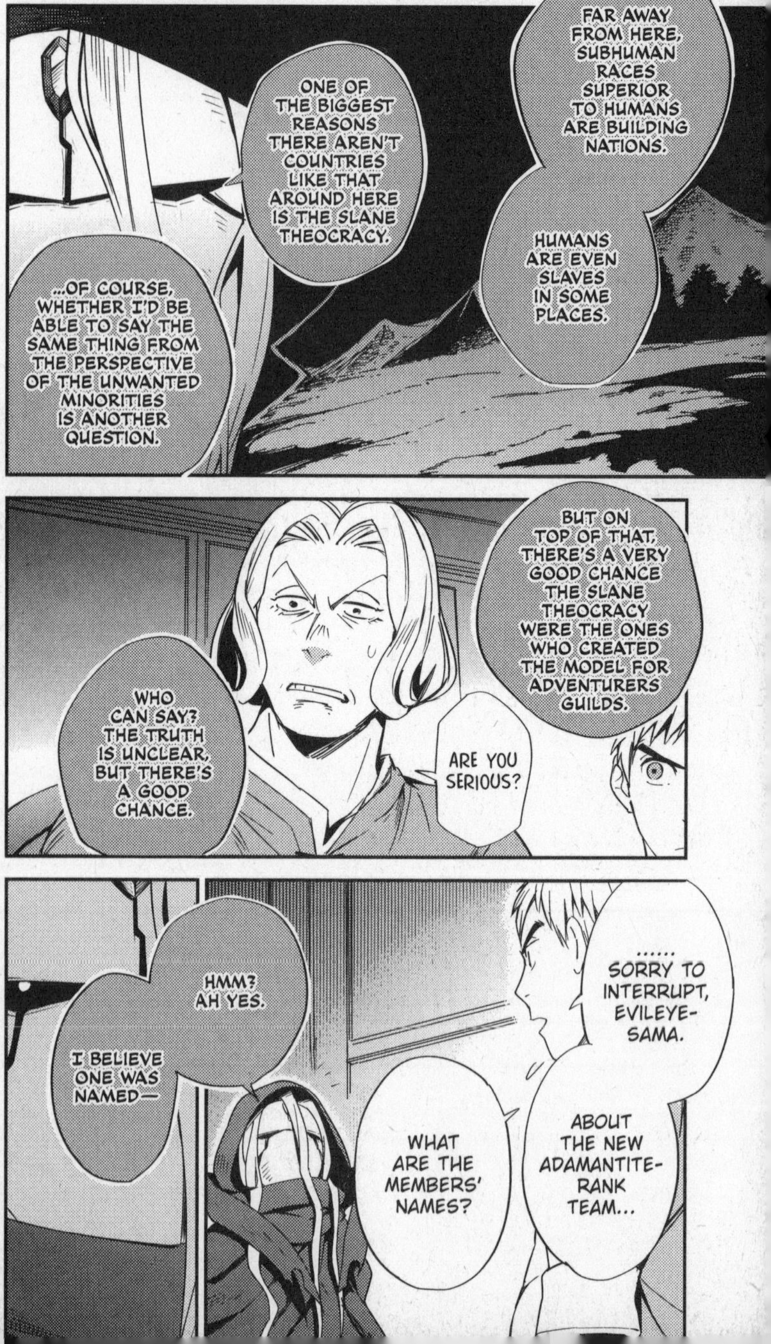
FAR AWAY FROM HERE, SUBHUMAN RACES SUPERIOR TO HUMANS ARE BUILDING NATIONS.
HUMANS ARE EVEN SLAVES IN SOME PLACES.
ONE OF THE BIGGEST REASONS THERE AREN'T COUNTRIES LIKE THAT AROUND HERE IS THE SLANE THEOCRACY.
...OF COURSE, WHETHER I'D BE ABLE TO SAY THE SAME THING FROM THE PERSPECTIVE OF THE UNWANTED MINORITIES IS ANOTHER QUESTION.
BUT ON TOP OF THAT, THERE'S A VERY GOOD CHANCE THE SLANE THEOCRACY WERE THE ONES WHO CREATED THE MODEL FOR ADVENTURERS GUILDS.
ARE YOU SERIOUS?
WHO CAN SAY? THE TRUTH IS UNCLEAR, BUT THERE'S A GOOD CHANCE.
...... SORRY TO INTERRUPT, EVILEYE-SAMA.
ABOUT THE NEW ADAMANTITE-RANK TEAM...
WHAT ARE THE MEMBERS' NAMES?
HMM? AH YES.
I BELIEVE ONE WAS NAMED—

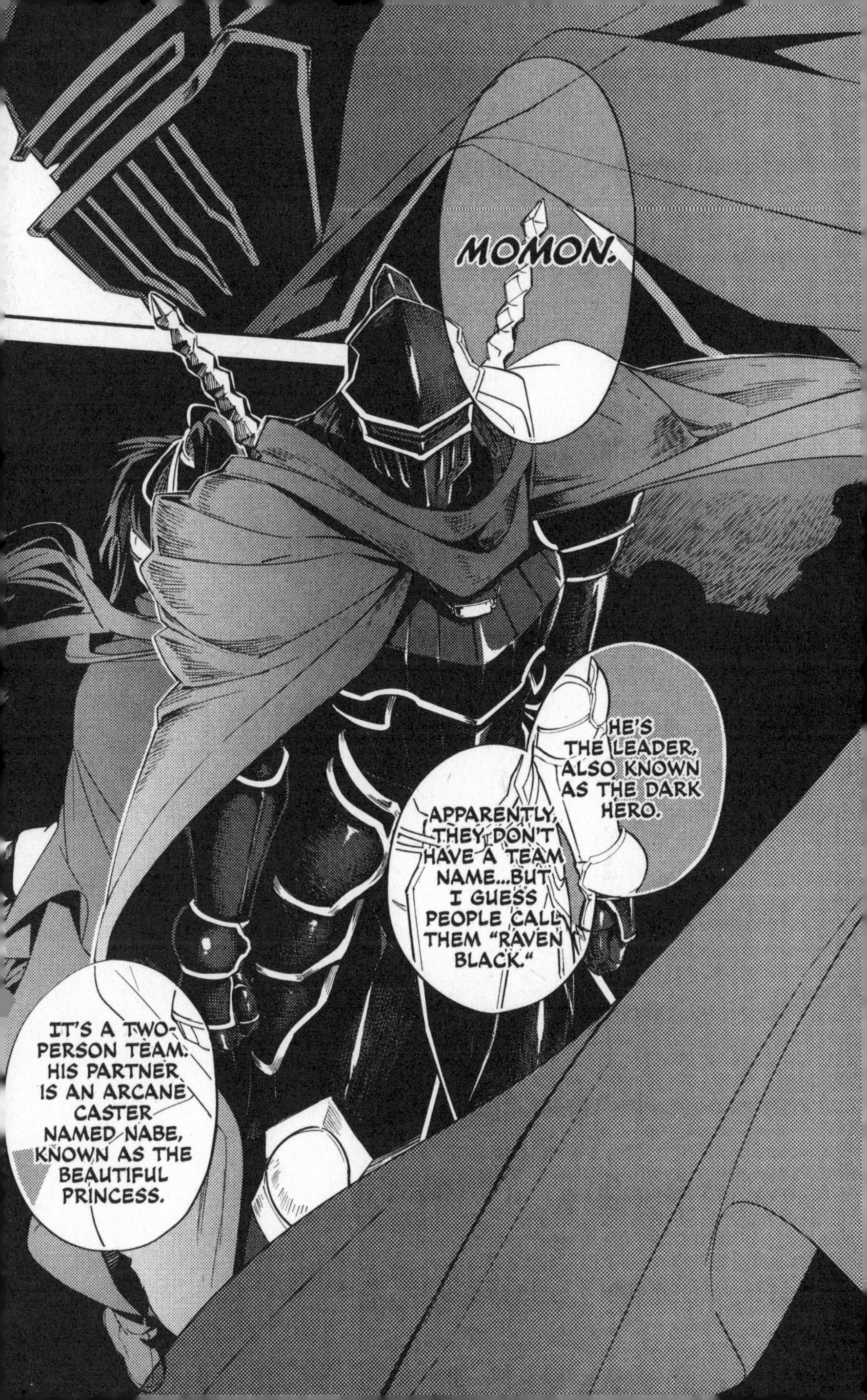
MOMON.
HE'S THE LEADER, ALSO KNOWN AS THE DARK HERO.
APPARENTLY, THEY DON'T HAVE A TEAM NAME...BUT I GUESS PEOPLE CALL THEM "RAVEN BLACK."
IT'S A TWO-PERSON TEAM. HIS PARTNER IS AN ARCANE CASTER NAMED NABE, KNOWN AS THE BEAUTIFUL PRINCESS.

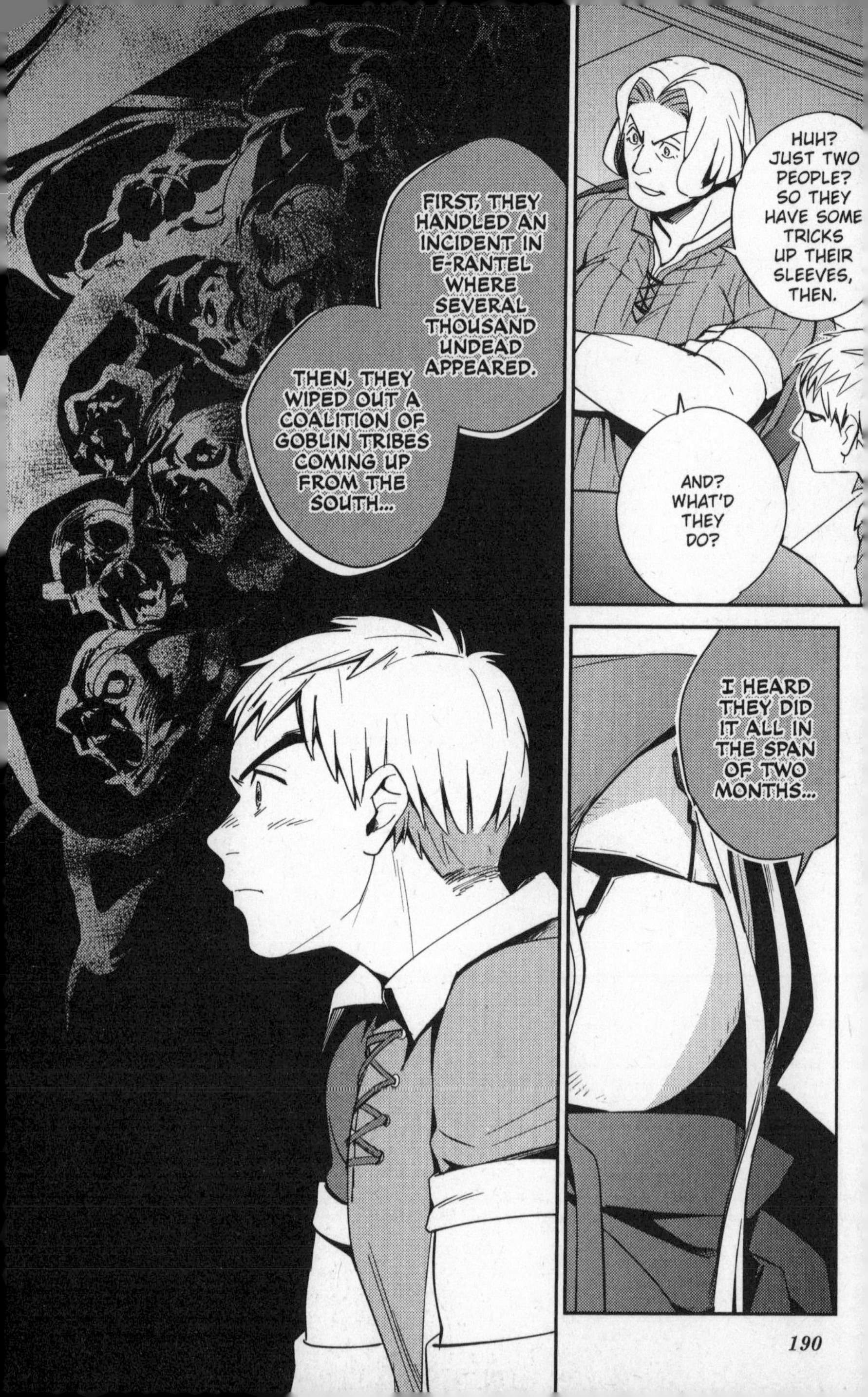
HUH? JUST TWO PEOPLE? SO THEY HAVE SOME TRICKS UP THEIR SLEEVES, THEN.
AND? WHAT'D THEY DO?
I HEARD THEY DID IT ALL IN THE SPAN OF TWO MONTHS...
FIRST, THEY HANDLED AN INCIDENT IN E-RANTEL WHERE SEVERAL THOUSAND UNDEAD APPEARED.
THEN, THEY WIPED OUT A COALITION OF GOBLIN TRIBES COMING UP FROM THE SOUTH...

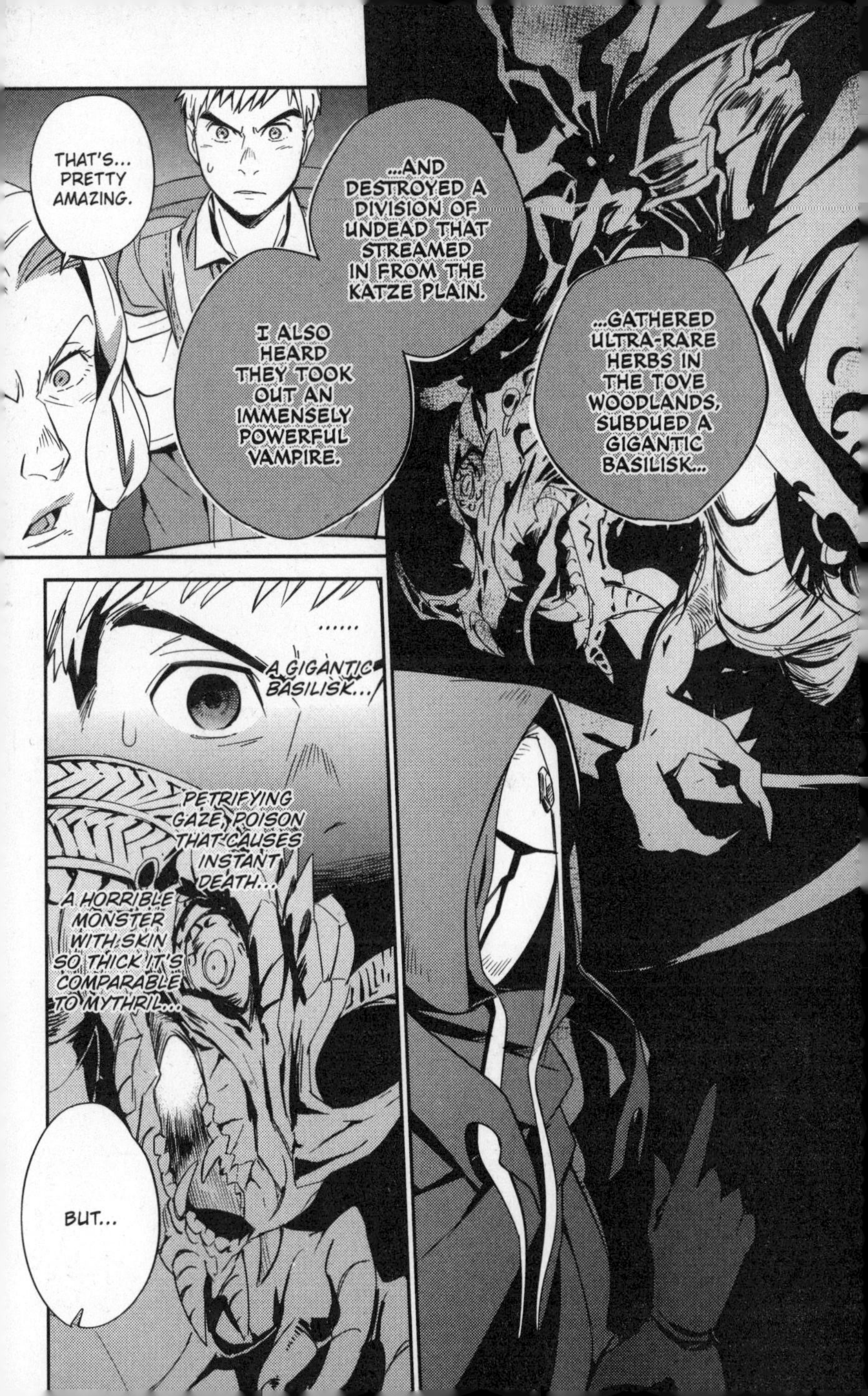
...GATHERED ULTRA-RARE HERBS IN THE TOVE WOODLANDS, SUBDUED A GIGANTIC BASILISK...
...AND DESTROYED A DIVISION OF UNDEAD THAT STREAMED IN FROM THE KATZE PLAIN.
I ALSO HEARD THEY TOOK OUT AN IMMENSELY POWERFUL VAMPIRE.
THAT'S... PRETTY AMAZING.
......
A GIGANTIC BASILISK...
PETRIFYING GAZE, POISON THAT CAUSES INSTANT DEATH...
A HORRIBLE MONSTER WITH SKIN SO THICK IT'S COMPARABLE TO MYTHRIL...
BUT...

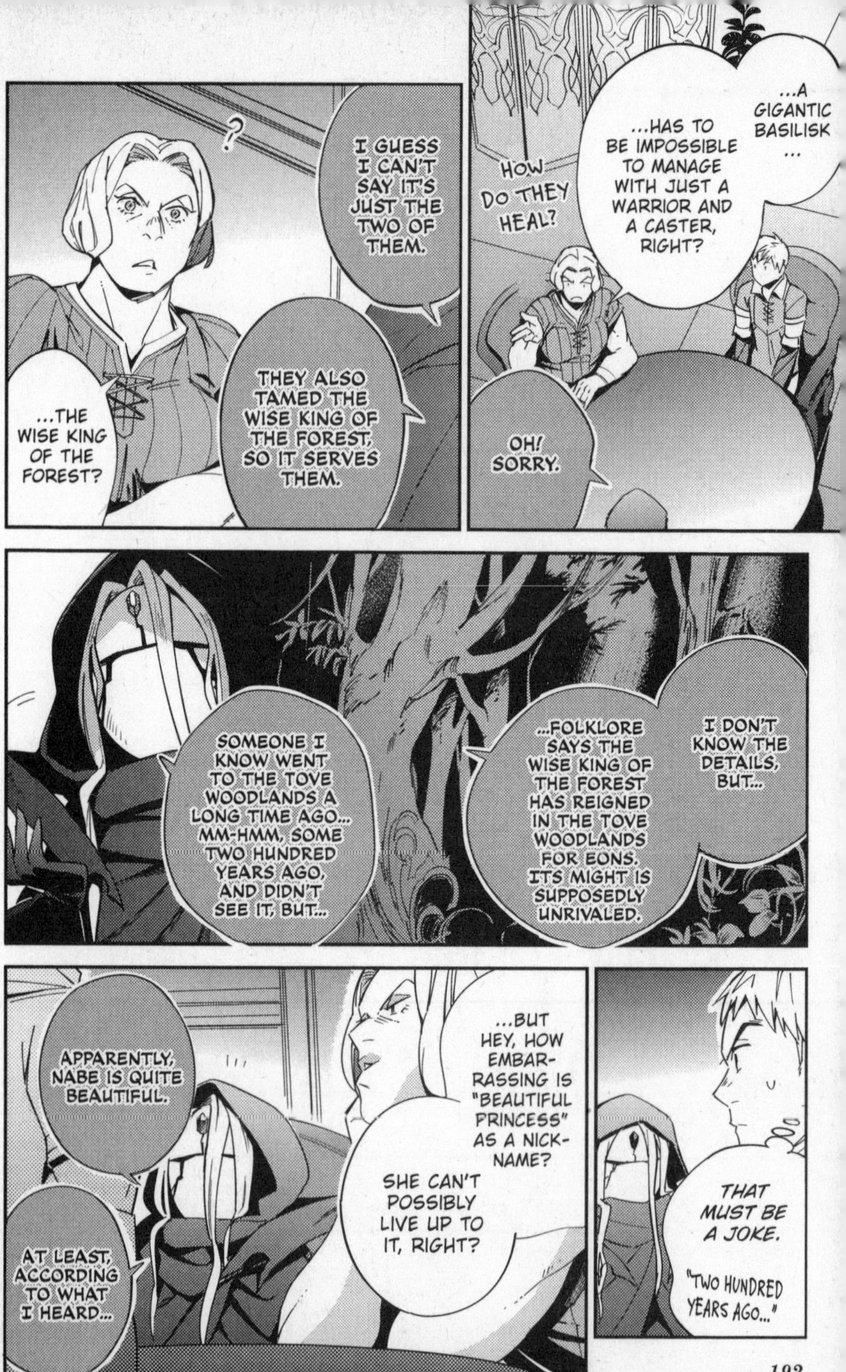
...A GIGANTIC BASILISK...
...HAS TO BE IMPOSSIBLE TO MANAGE WITH JUST A WARRIOR AND A CASTER, RIGHT?
HOW DO THEY HEAL?
OH! SORRY.
?
I GUESS I CAN'T SAY IT'S JUST THE TWO OF THEM.
THEY ALSO TAMED THE WISE KING OF THE FOREST, SO IT SERVES THEM.
...THE WISE KING OF THE FOREST?
I DON'T KNOW THE DETAILS, BUT...
...FOLKLORE SAYS THE WISE KING OF THE FOREST HAS REIGNED IN THE TOVE WOODLANDS FOR EONS. ITS MIGHT IS SUPPOSEDLY UNRIVALED.
SOMEONE I KNOW WENT TO THE TOVE WOODLANDS A LONG TIME AGO... MM-HMM, SOME TWO HUNDRED YEARS AGO, AND DIDN'T SEE IT, BUT...
THAT MUST BE A JOKE.
"TWO HUNDRED YEARS AGO..."
...BUT HEY, HOW EMBAR-RASSING IS "BEAUTIFUL PRINCESS" AS A NICK-NAME?
SHE CAN'T POSSIBLY LIVE UP TO IT, RIGHT?
APPARENTLY, NABE IS QUITE BEAUTIFUL.
AT LEAST, ACCORDING TO WHAT I HEARD...

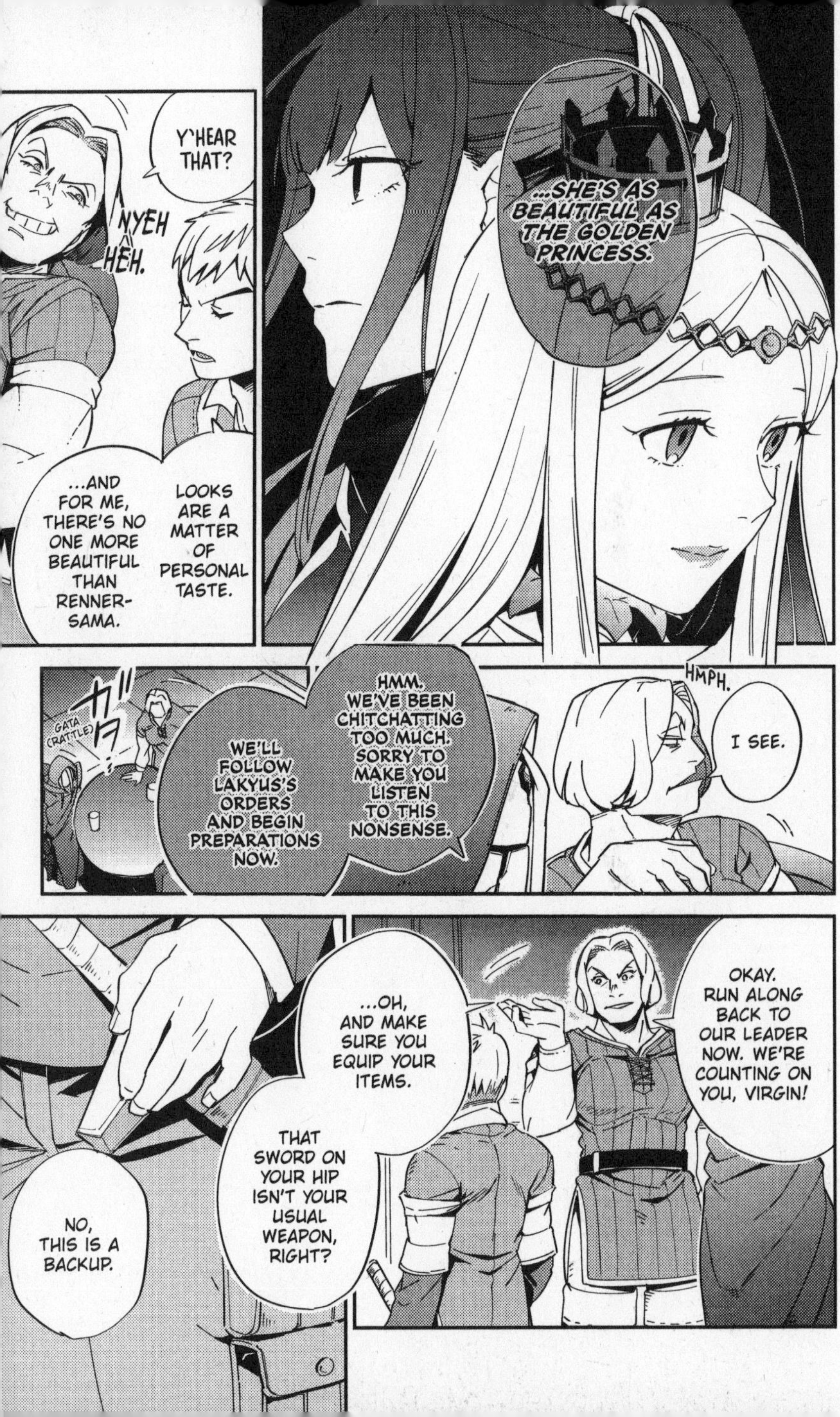
...SHE'S AS BEAUTIFUL AS THE GOLDEN PRINCESS.
Y'HEAR THAT?
NYEH HEH.
LOOKS ARE A MATTER OF PERSONAL TASTE.
...AND FOR ME, THERE'S NO ONE MORE BEAUTIFUL THAN RENNER-SAMA.
HMPH.
I SEE.
HMM. WE'VE BEEN CHITCHATTING TOO MUCH. SORRY TO MAKE YOU LISTEN TO THIS NONSENSE.
WE'LL FOLLOW LAKYUS'S ORDERS AND BEGIN PREPARATIONS NOW.
GATA (RATTLE)
OKAY. RUN ALONG BACK TO OUR LEADER NOW. WE'RE COUNTING ON YOU, VIRGIN!
...OH, AND MAKE SURE YOU EQUIP YOUR ITEMS.
THAT SWORD ON YOUR HIP ISN'T YOUR USUAL WEAPON, RIGHT?
NO, THIS IS A BACKUP.

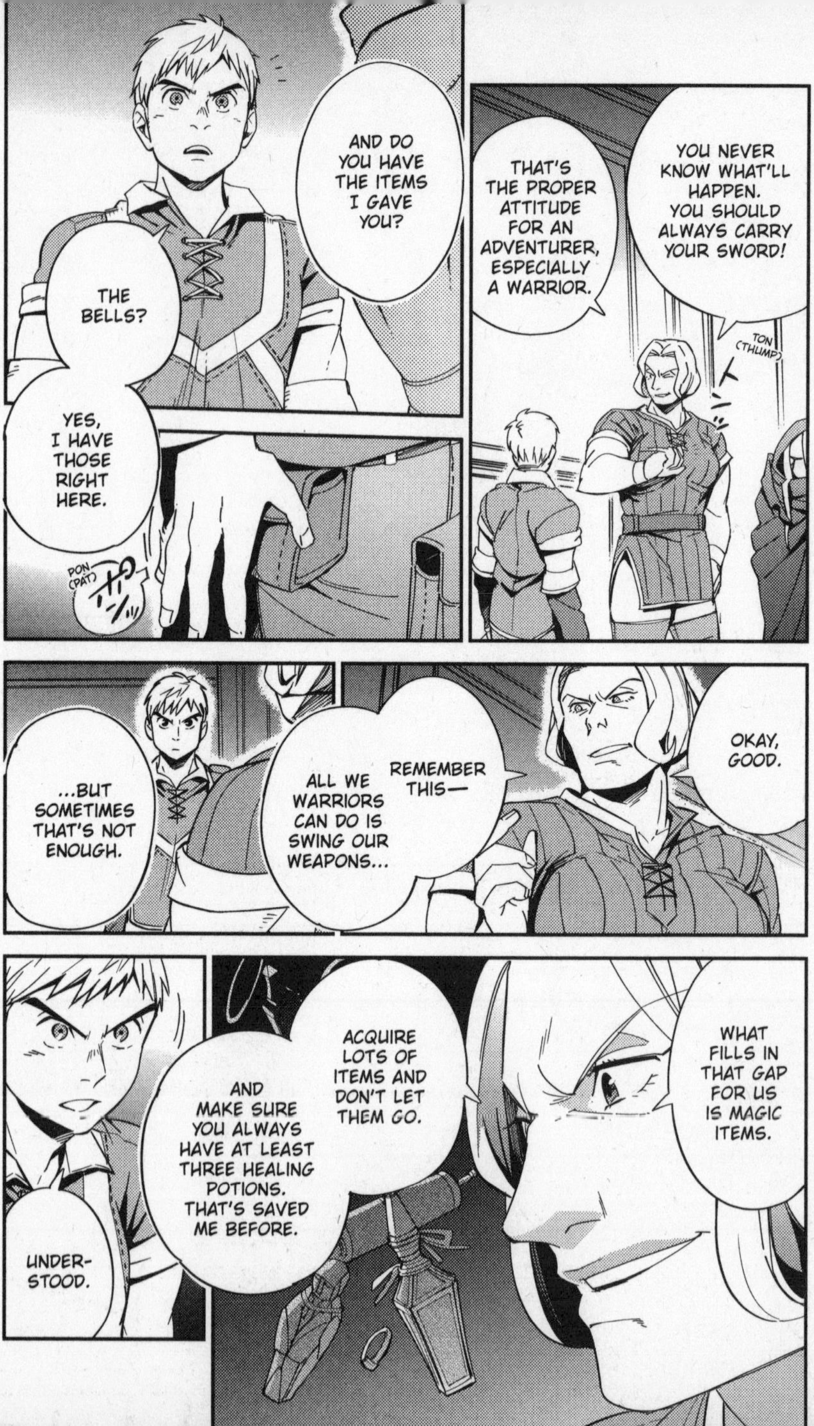
YOU NEVER KNOW WHAT'LL HAPPEN. YOU SHOULD ALWAYS CARRY YOUR SWORD!
THAT'S THE PROPER ATTITUDE FOR AN ADVENTURER, ESPECIALLY A WARRIOR.
TON (THUMP)
AND DO YOU HAVE THE ITEMS I GAVE YOU?
THE BELLS?
YES, I HAVE THOSE RIGHT HERE.
PON (PAT)
OKAY, GOOD.
REMEMBER THIS—
ALL WE WARRIORS CAN DO IS SWING OUR WEAPONS...
...BUT SOMETIMES THAT'S NOT ENOUGH.
WHAT FILLS IN THAT GAP FOR US IS MAGIC ITEMS.
ACQUIRE LOTS OF ITEMS AND DON'T LET THEM GO.
AND MAKE SURE YOU ALWAYS HAVE AT LEAST THREE HEALING POTIONS. THAT'S SAVED ME BEFORE.
UNDER-STOOD.

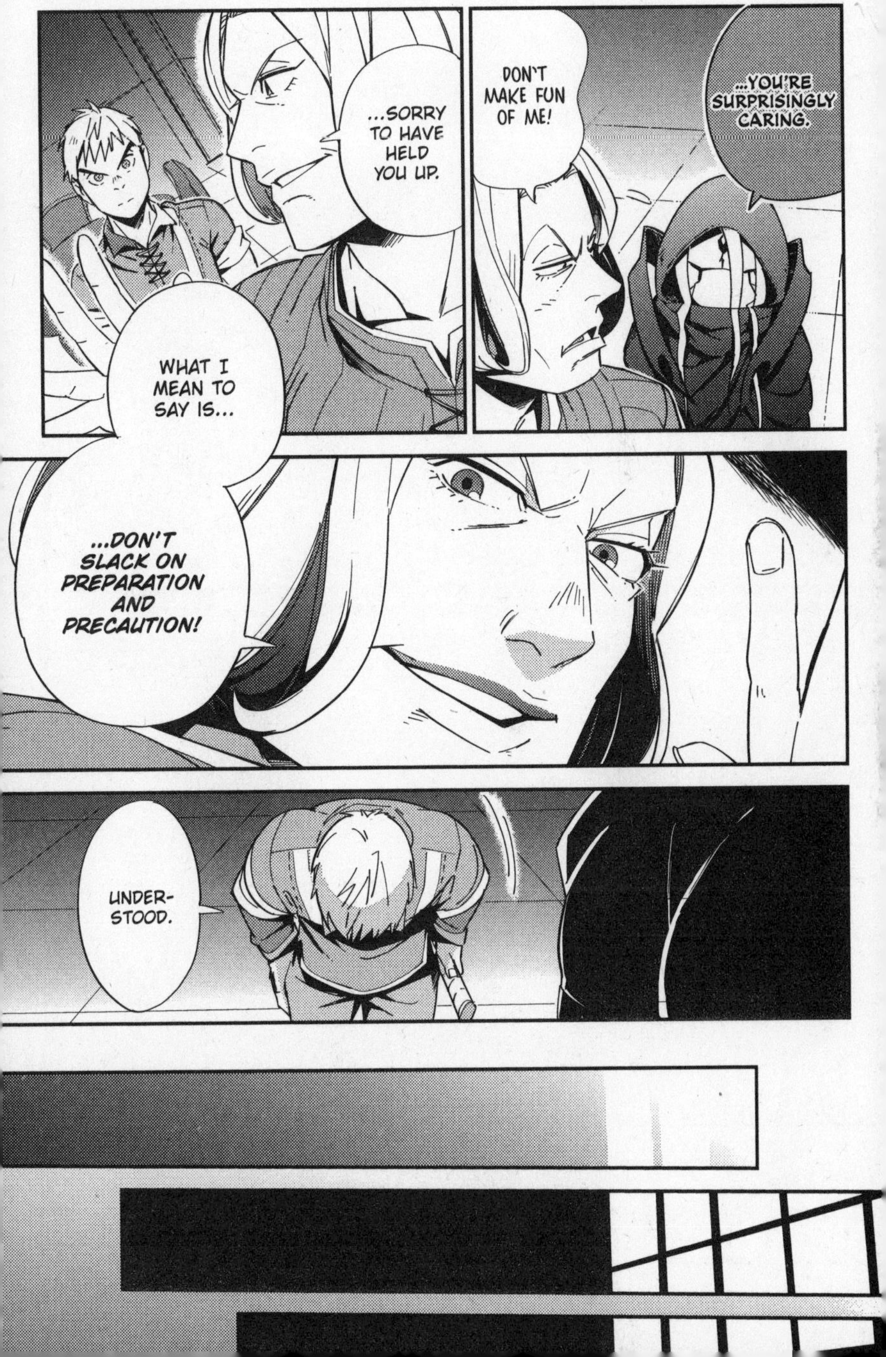
...YOU'RE SURPRISINGLY CARING.
DON'T MAKE FUN OF ME!
...SORRY TO HAVE HELD YOU UP.
WHAT I MEAN TO SAY IS...
...DON'T SLACK ON PREPARATION AND PRECAUTION!
UNDER-STOOD.

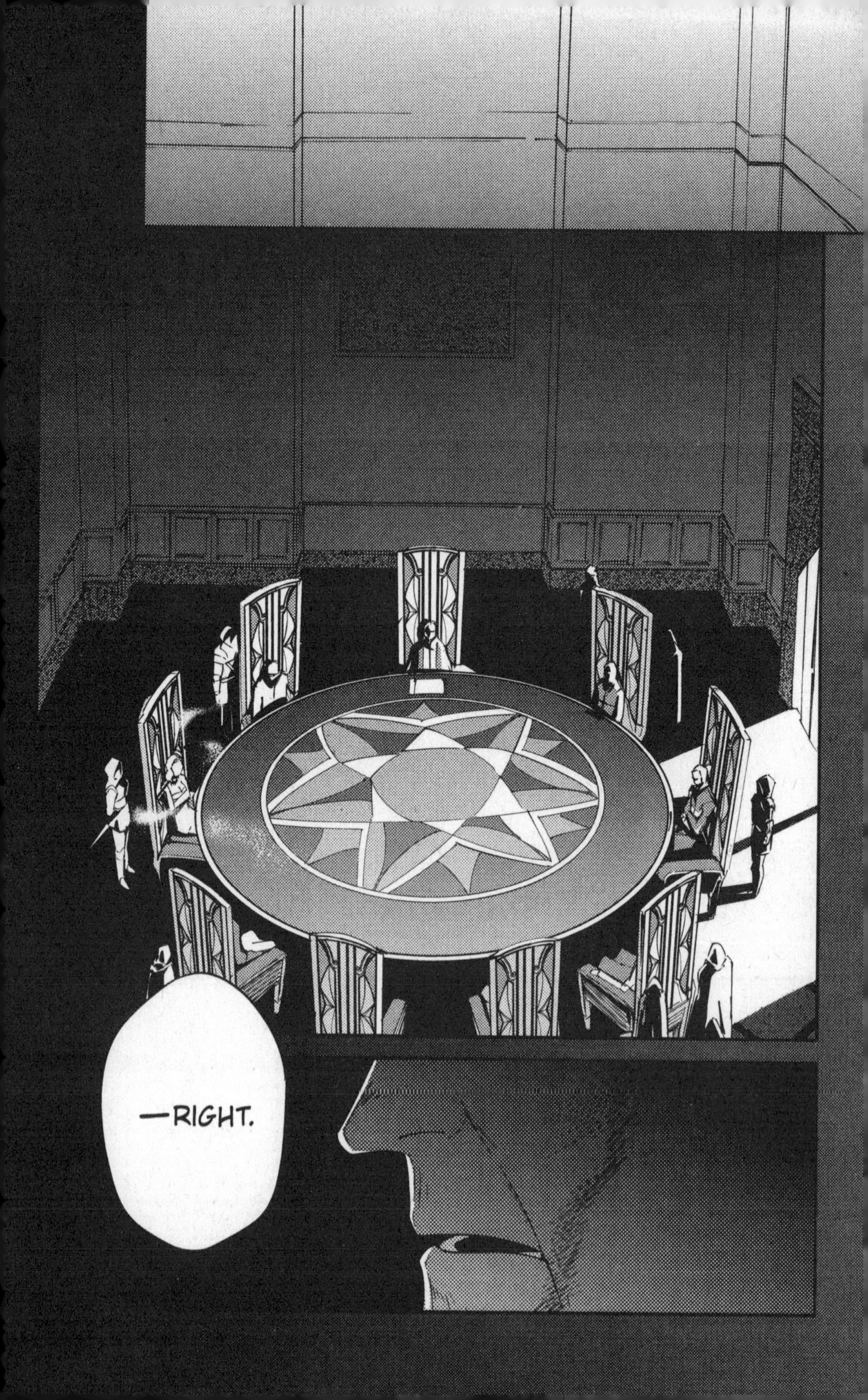
—RIGHT.

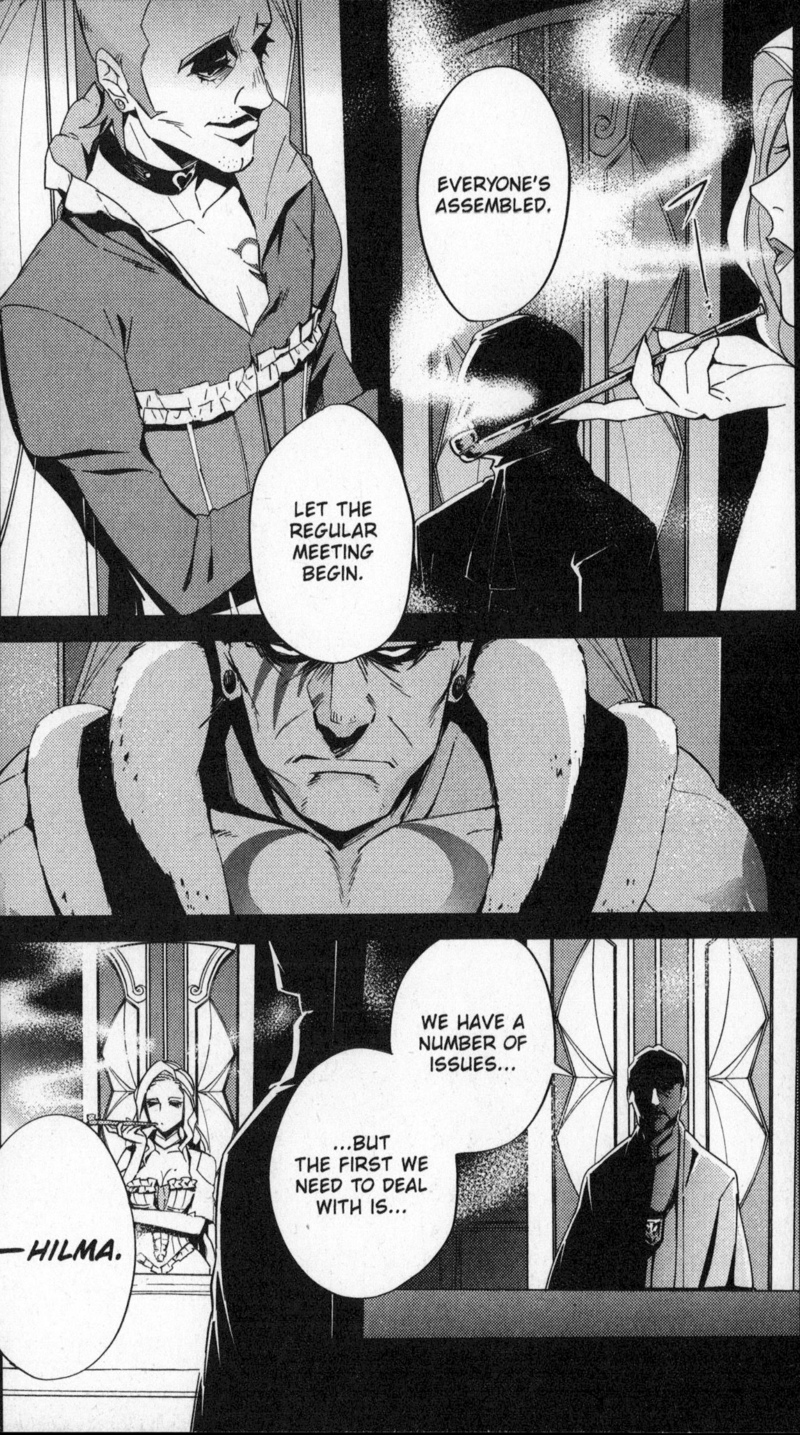
EVERYONE'S ASSEMBLED.
LET THE REGULAR MEETING BEGIN.
WE HAVE A NUMBER OF ISSUES...
...BUT THE FIRST WE NEED TO DEAL WITH IS...
—HILMA.

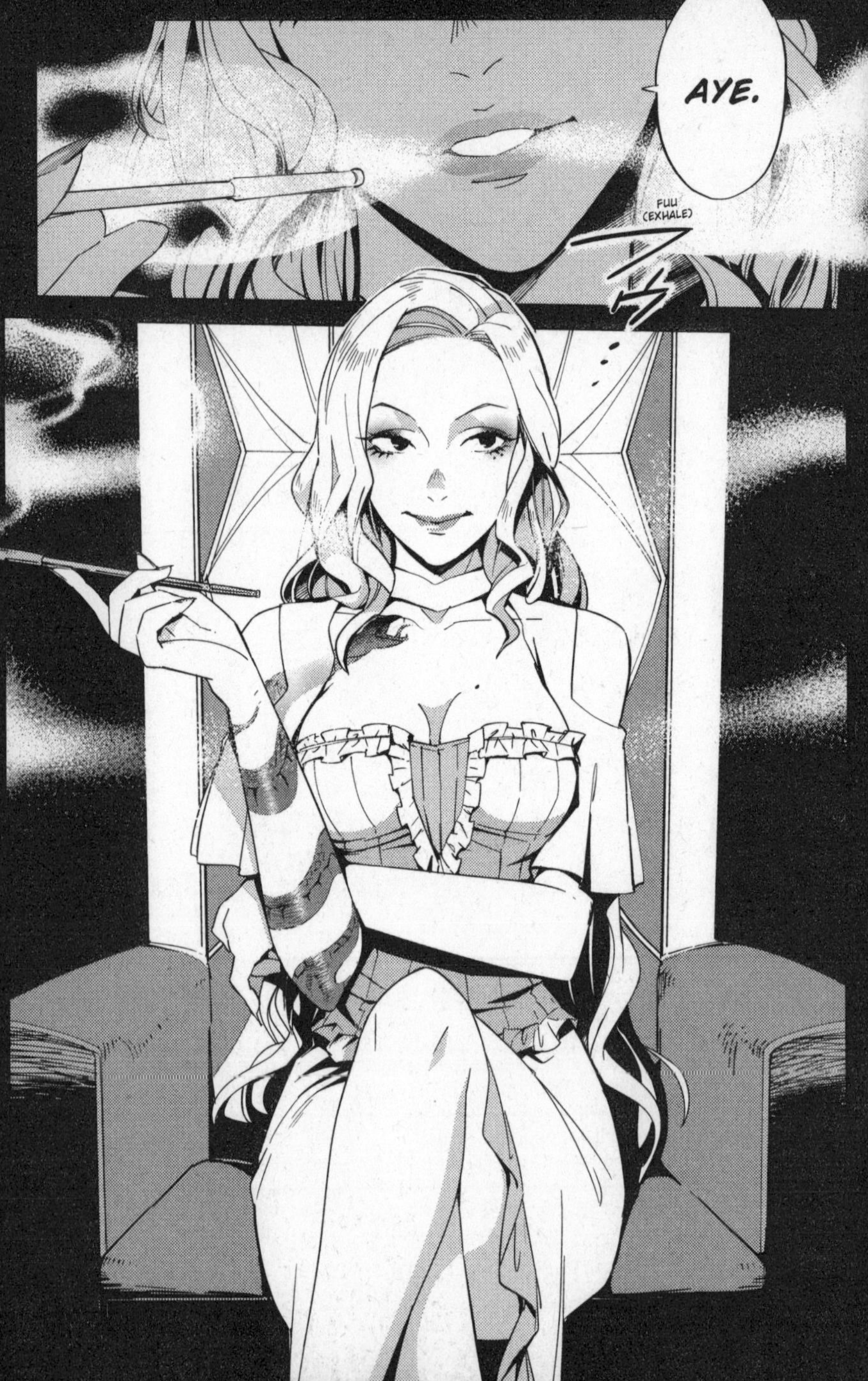
AYE.
FUU (EXHALE)

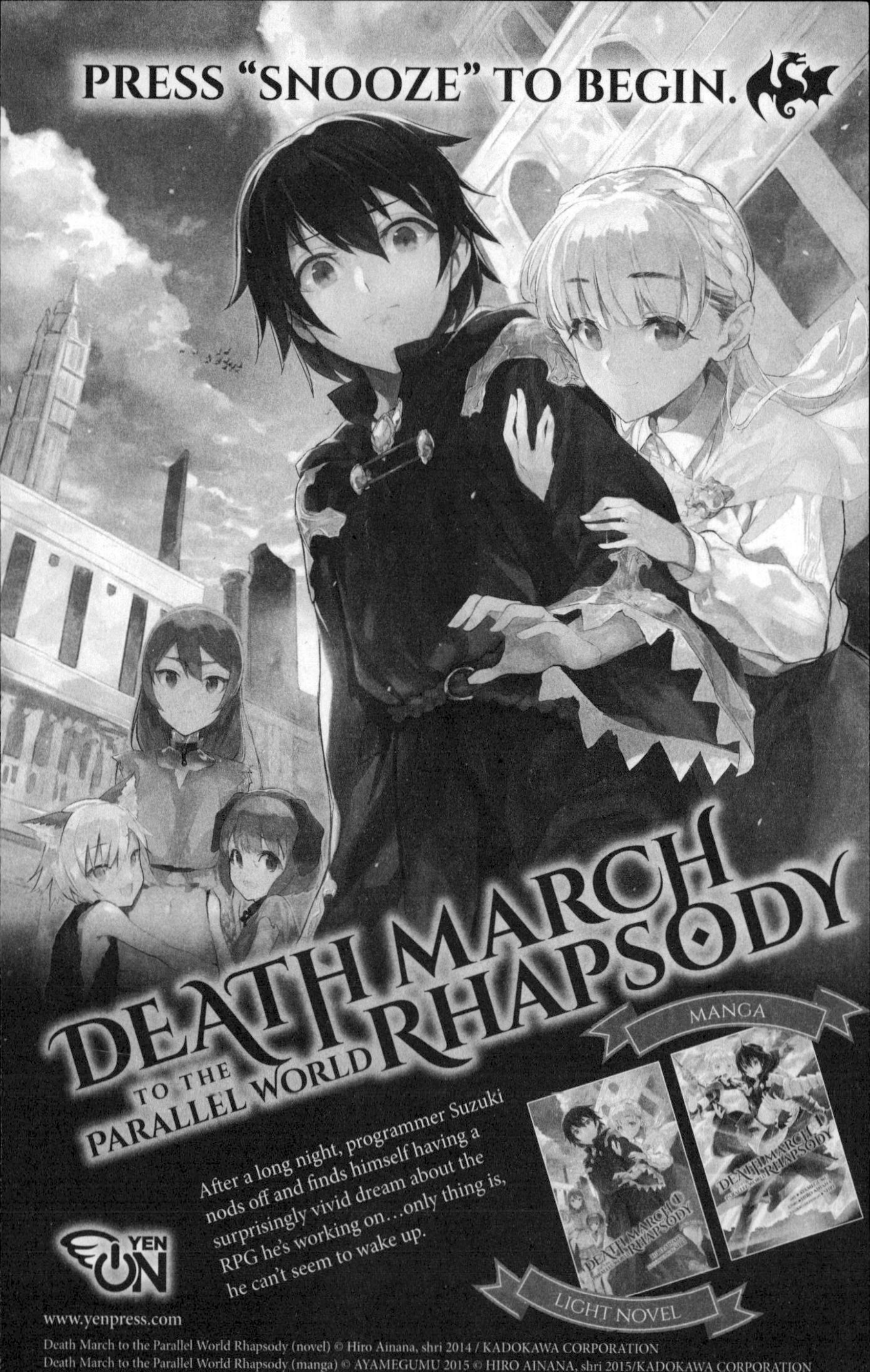
PRESS "SNOOZE" TO BEGIN.
DEATH MARCH TO THE PARALLEL WORLD RHAPSODY
After a long night, programmer Suzuki nods off and finds himself having a surprisingly vivid dream about the RPG he's working on…only thing is, he can't seem to wake up.
MANGA
LIGHT NOVEL
YEN ON
www.yenpress.com

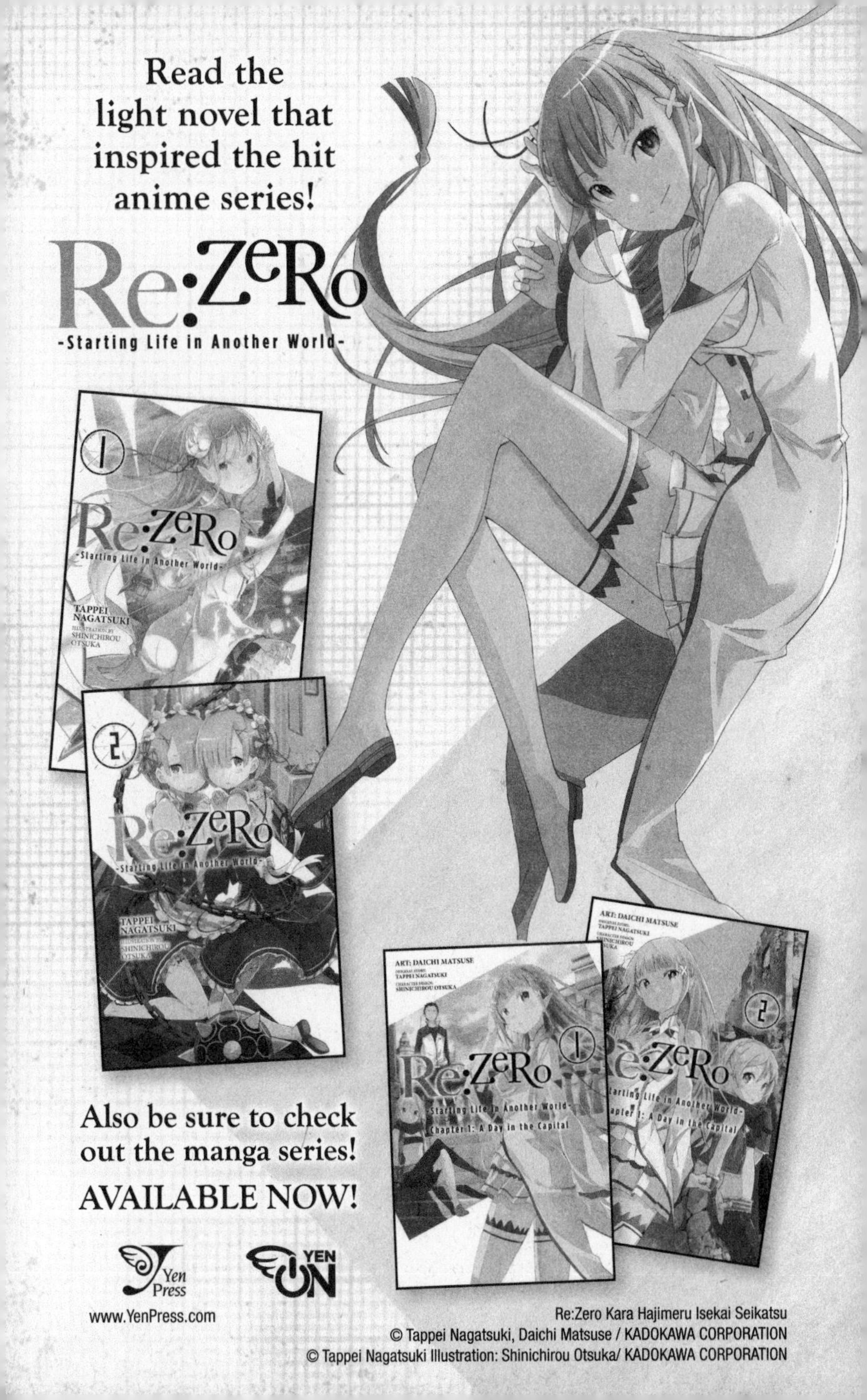
Read the light novel that inspired the hit anime series!
Re:ZeRo
-Starting Life in Another World-
Also be sure to check out the manga series!
AVAILABLE NOW!
Yen Press
YEN ON
www.YenPress.com
Re:Zero Kara Hajimeru Isekai Seikatsu
© Tappei Nagatsuki, Daichi Matsuse / KADOKAWA CORPORATION
© Tappei Nagatsuki Illustration: Shinichirou Otsuka/ KADOKAWA CORPORATION

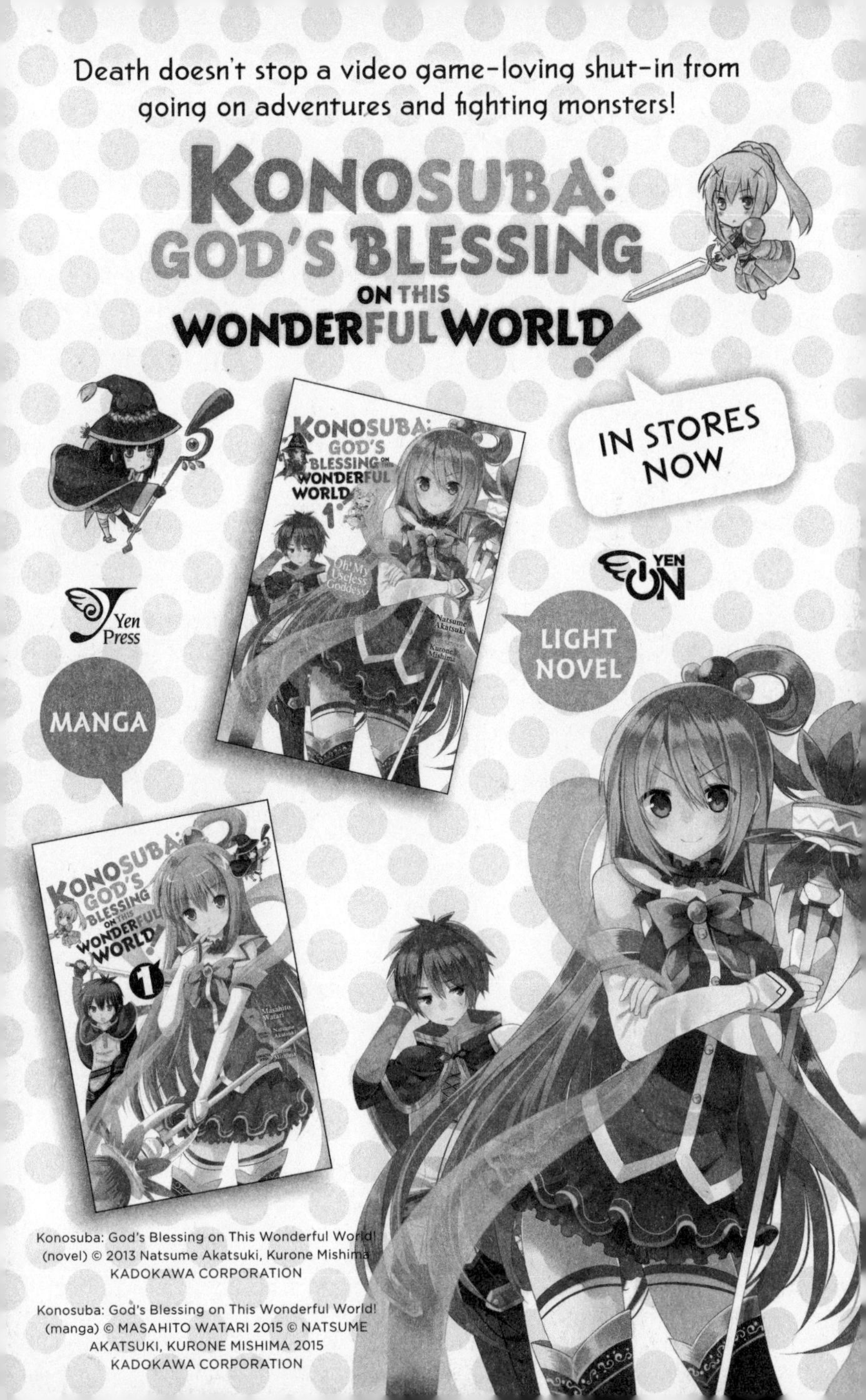
Death doesn't stop a video game-loving shut-in from going on adventures and fighting monsters!
KONOSUBA: GOD'S BLESSING ON THIS WONDERFUL WORLD!
KONOSUBA: GOD'S BLESSING ON THIS WONDERFUL WORLD 1
Oh! My Useless Goddess!
Natsume Akatsuki
Kurone Mishima
IN STORES NOW
YEN ON
LIGHT NOVEL
Yen Press
MANGA
KONOSUBA: GOD'S BLESSING ON THIS WONDERFUL WORLD! 1
Masahito Watari
Konosuba: God's Blessing on This Wonderful World! (novel) © 2013 Natsume Akatsuki, Kurone Mishima KADOKAWA CORPORATION
Konosuba: God's Blessing on This Wonderful World! (manga) © MASAHITO WATARI 2015 © NATSUME AKATSUKI, KURONE MISHIMA 2015 KADOKAWA CORPORATION

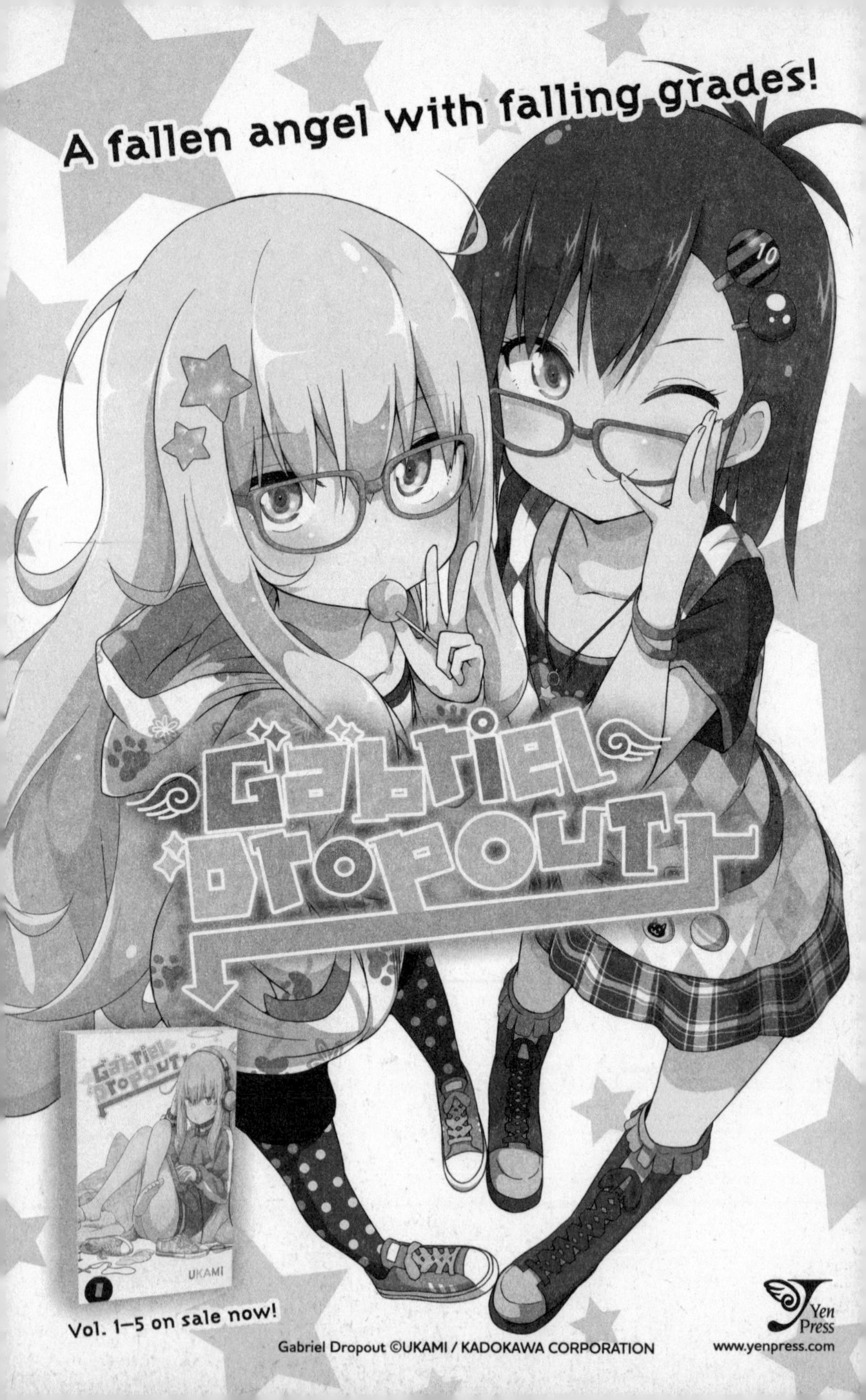

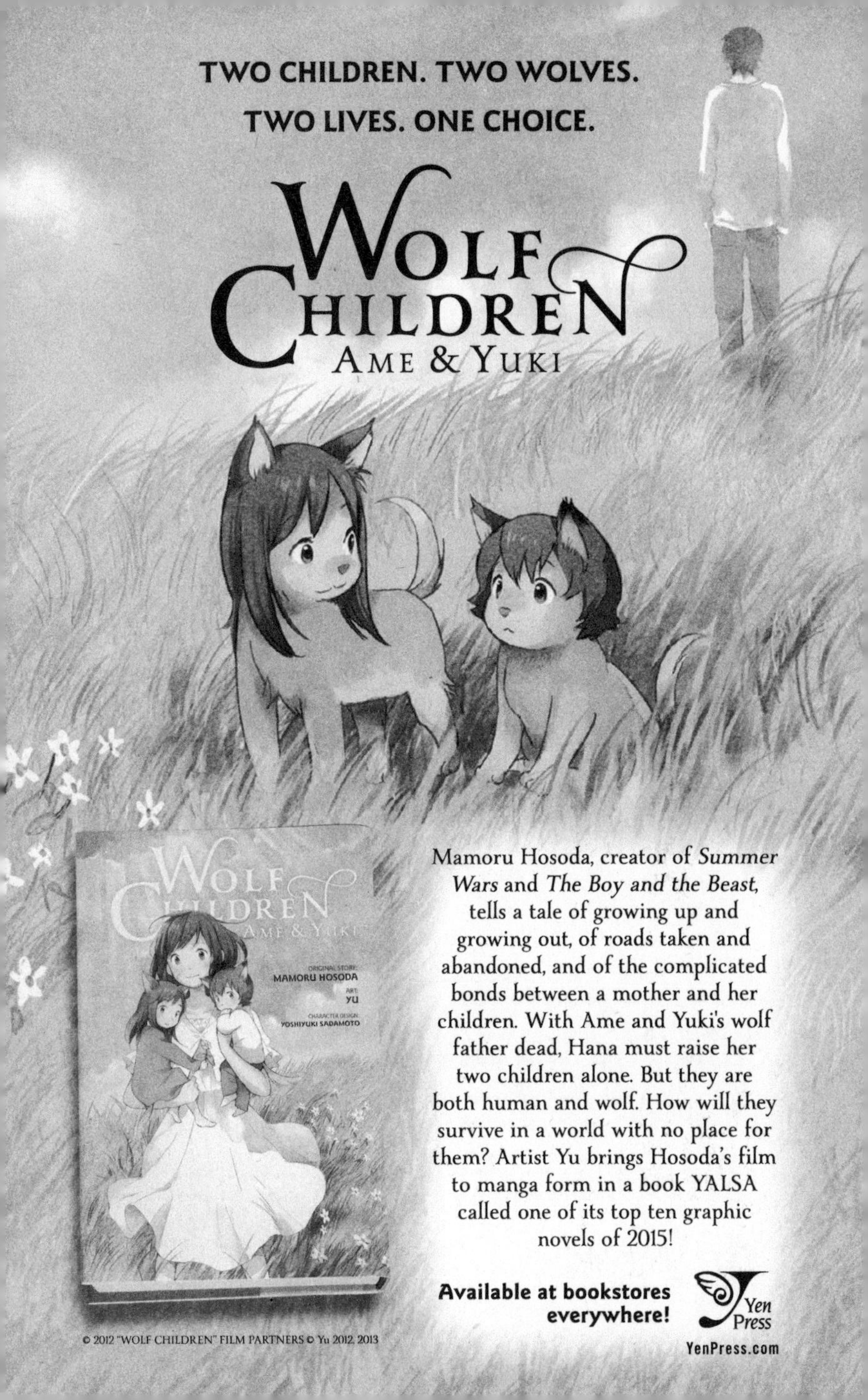
TWO CHILDREN. TWO WOLVES.
TWO LIVES. ONE CHOICE.
WOLF CHILDREN
AME & YUKI
WOLF CHILDREN
AME & YUKI
ORIGINAL STORY:
MAMORU HOSODA
ART:
YU
CHARACTER DESIGN:
YOSHIYUKI SADAMOTO
Mamoru Hosoda, creator of Summer Wars and The Boy and the Beast, tells a tale of growing up and growing out, of roads taken and abandoned, and of the complicated bonds between a mother and her children. With Ame and Yuki's wolf father dead, Hana must raise her two children alone. But they are both human and wolf. How will they survive in a world with no place for them? Artist Yu brings Hosoda's film to manga form in a book YALSA called one of its top ten graphic novels of 2015!
Available at bookstores everywhere!
Yen Press
YenPress.com
© 2012 "WOLF CHILDREN" FILM PARTNERS © Yu 2012, 2013

OVERLORD ❽

Art: Hugin Miyama
Original Story: Kugane Maruyama
Character Design: so-bin
Scenario: Satoshi Oshio

Translation: Emily Balistrieri   •   **Lettering: Brndn Blakeslee**

OVERLORD Volume 8
© Hugin MIYAMA 2017
© Satoshi OSHIO 2017
© 2012 Kugane Maruyama
First published in Japan in 2017 by KADOKAWA CORPORATION, Tokyo
English translation rights arranged with KADOKAWA CORPORATION, Tokyo
through Tuttle-Mori Agency, Inc.

English translation © 2018 by Yen Press, LLC

Yen Press
1290 Avenue of the Americas
New York, NY 10104

Visit us at yenpress.com
facebook.com/yenpress
twitter.com/yenpress
yenpress.tumblr.com
instagram.com/yenpress

First Yen Press Edition: November 2018

Yen Press is an imprint of Yen Press, LLC.
The Yen Press name and logo are trademarks of Yen Press, LLC.

Library of Congress Control Number: 2016932688

ISBNs: 978-1-9753-2813-9 (paperback)
         978-1-9753-8280-3 (ebook)

10 9 8 7 6 5 4 3 2 1

WOR

Printed in the United States of America